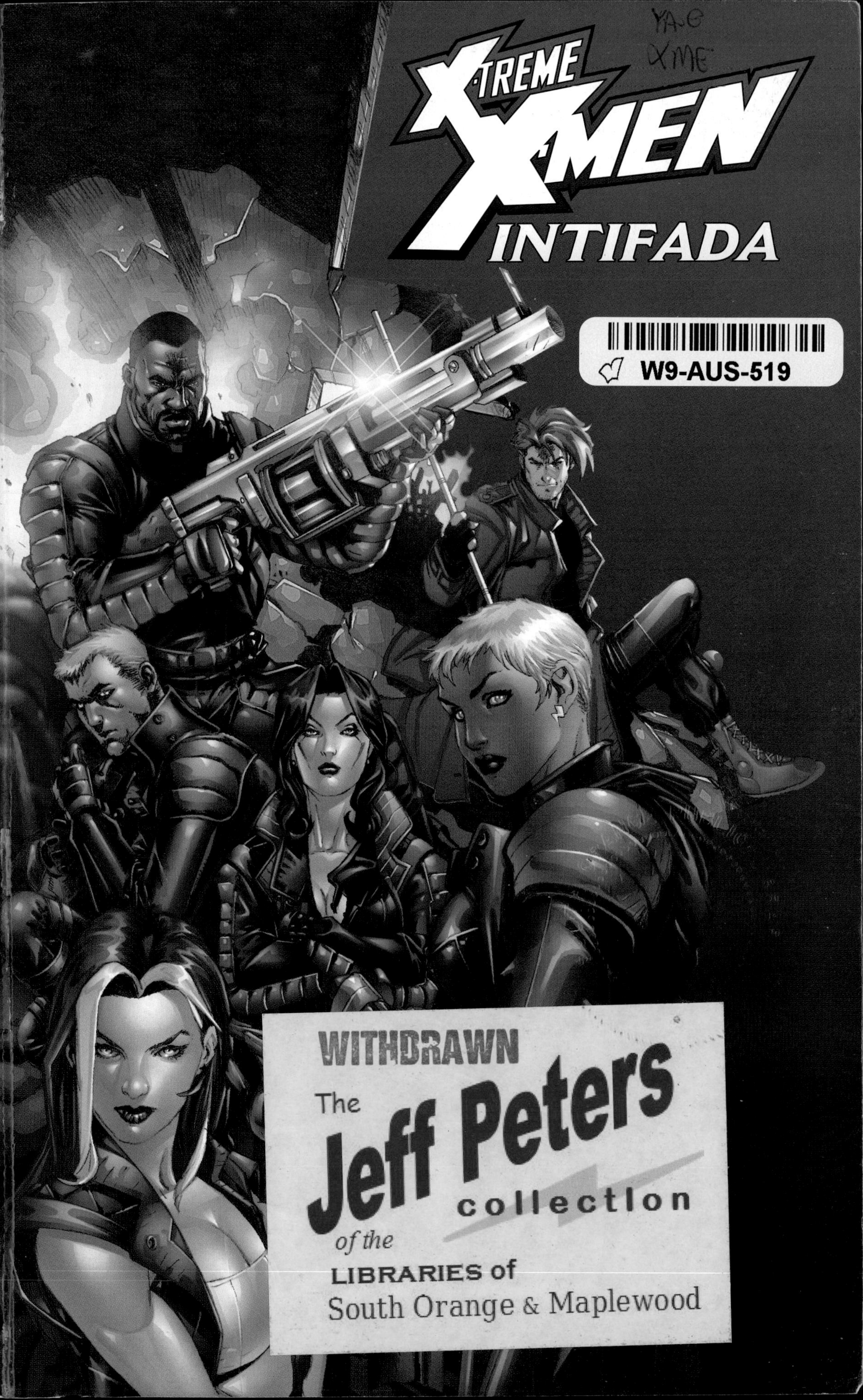
X-TREME X-MEN
INTIFADA

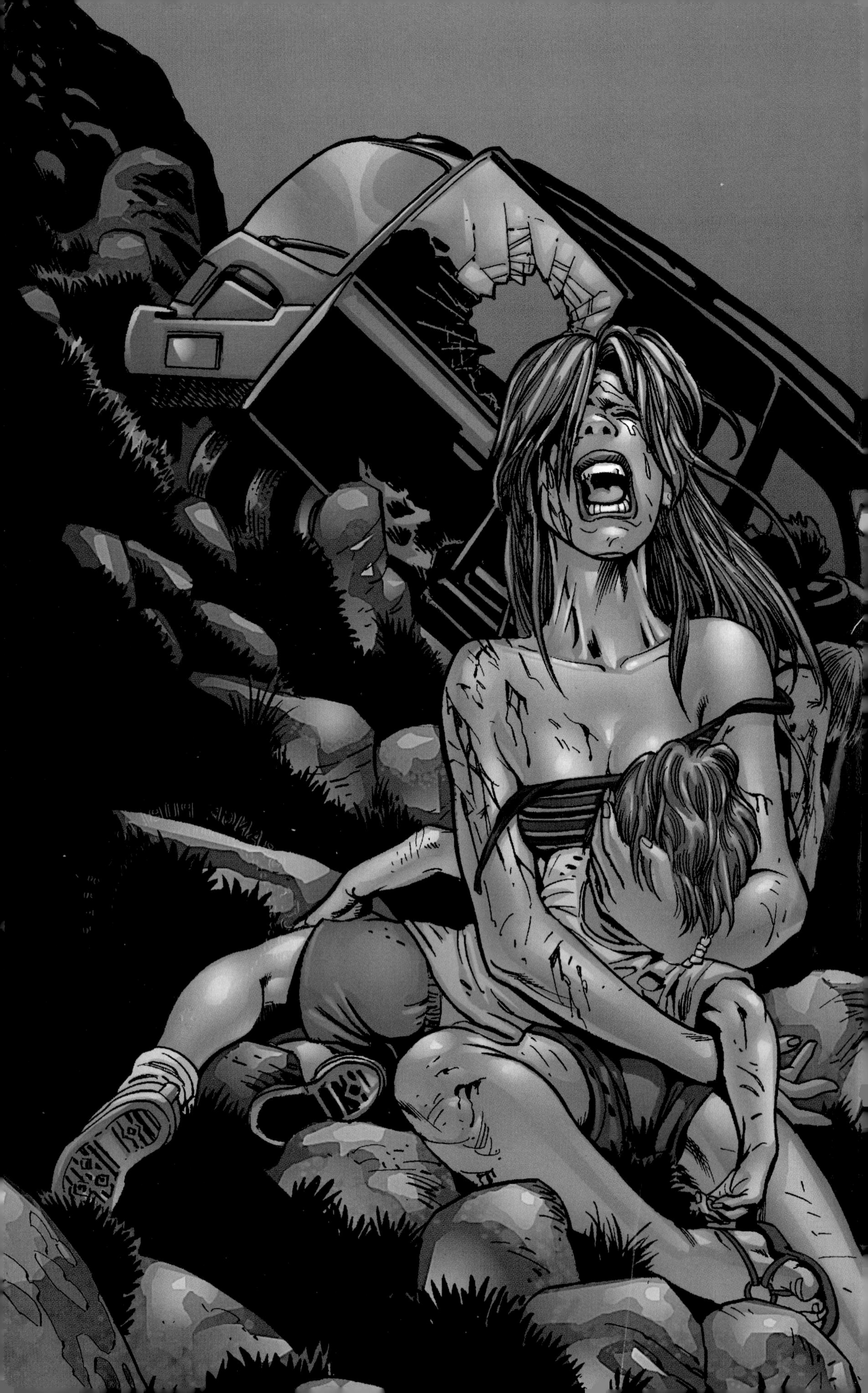

X-TREME X-MEN
INTIFADA

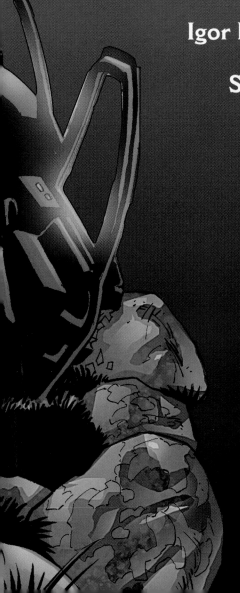

Writer
Chris Claremont

Pencils
Igor Kordey and **Salvador Larroca**

Inks
Scott Hanna and **Greg Adams**

Colors
Liquid! Graphics

Letters
Virtual Calligraphy's Randy Gentile
and **Rus Wooton** with **Tom Orzechowski**

Cover Art
Salvador Larroca

Assistant Editors
Annie Thornton and **Stephanie Moore**

Editors
Mike Raicht and **Mike Marts**

Collections Editor
Jeff Youngquist

Assistant Editor
Jennifer Grünwald

Book Designer
Meghan Kerns

Editor in Chief
Joe Quesada

Publisher
Dan Buckley

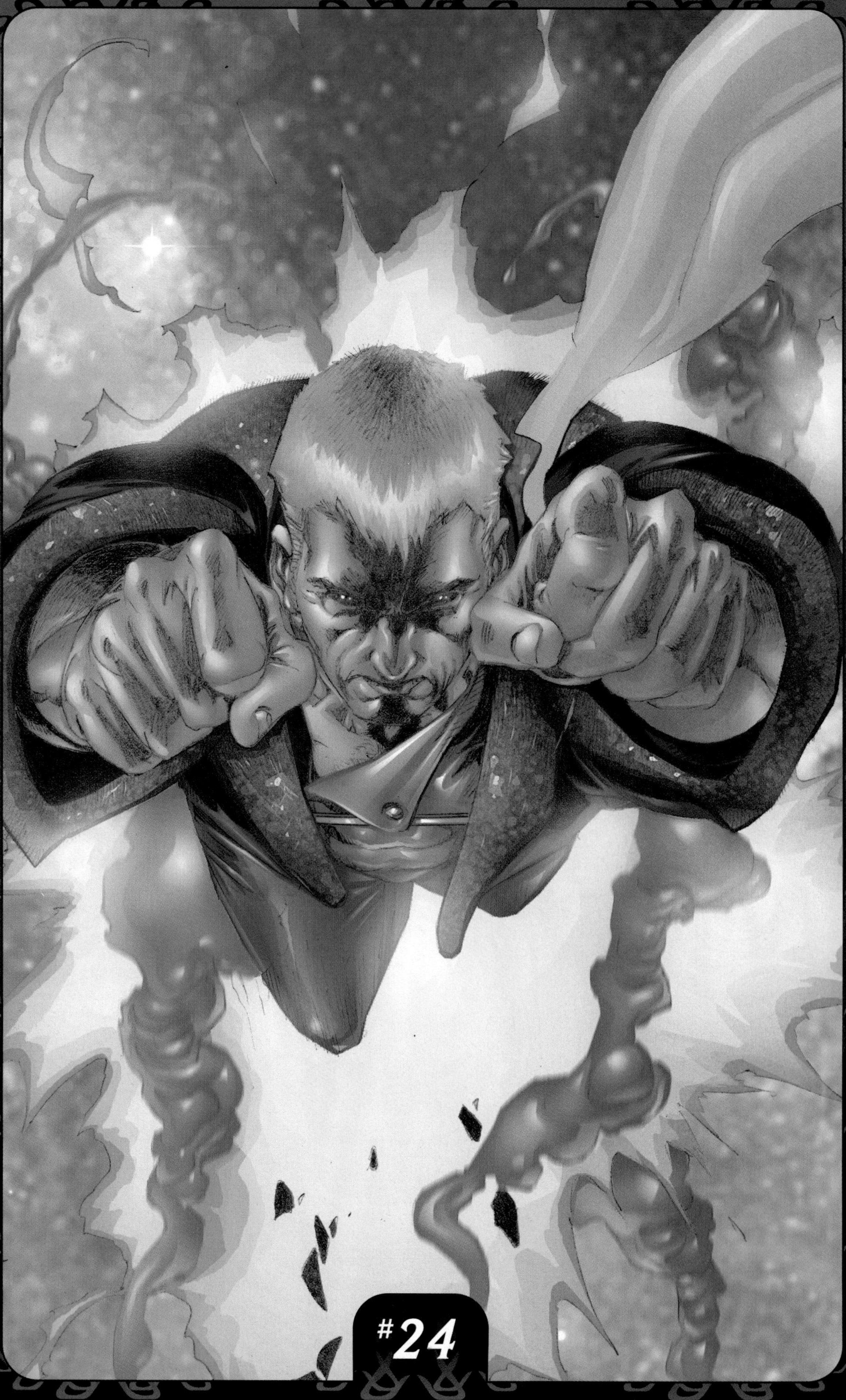
#24

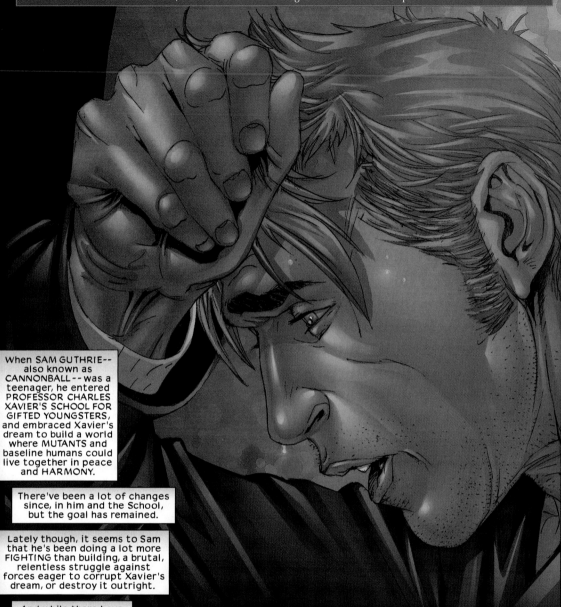

The world has changed. The mutant children of Humanity have come out of the closet, determined to claim their rightful place in a world that still looks on them with fear and even hatred. Standing alone to preserve the peace is a team of outcast heroes whose lives and purpose are defined by a simple and fundamental truth: whatever our genes, we are all ultimately *human*. And if there is to be a future, we must *all* learn to live together. X-treme times require **X-treme X-Men.**

When SAM GUTHRIE-- also known as CANNONBALL--was a teenager, he entered PROFESSOR CHARLES XAVIER'S SCHOOL FOR GIFTED YOUNGSTERS, and embraced Xavier's dream to build a world where MUTANTS and baseline humans could live together in peace and HARMONY.

There've been a lot of changes since, in him and the School, but the goal has remained.

Lately though, it seems to Sam that he's been doing a lot more FIGHTING than building, a brutal, relentless struggle against forces eager to corrupt Xavier's dream, or destroy it outright.

And while there have been VICTORIES along the way, there have also been CASUALTIES.

And they have taken their TOLL.

STORM
Ororo Munroe
Weather Manipulator;
Leader of X-treme X-Men

CHARLES XAVIER
Telepath;
Xavier Institute
Headmaster

LILA CHENEY
Inter-stellar Teleporter;
Inter-stellar Thief,
Inter-stellar Rock Star

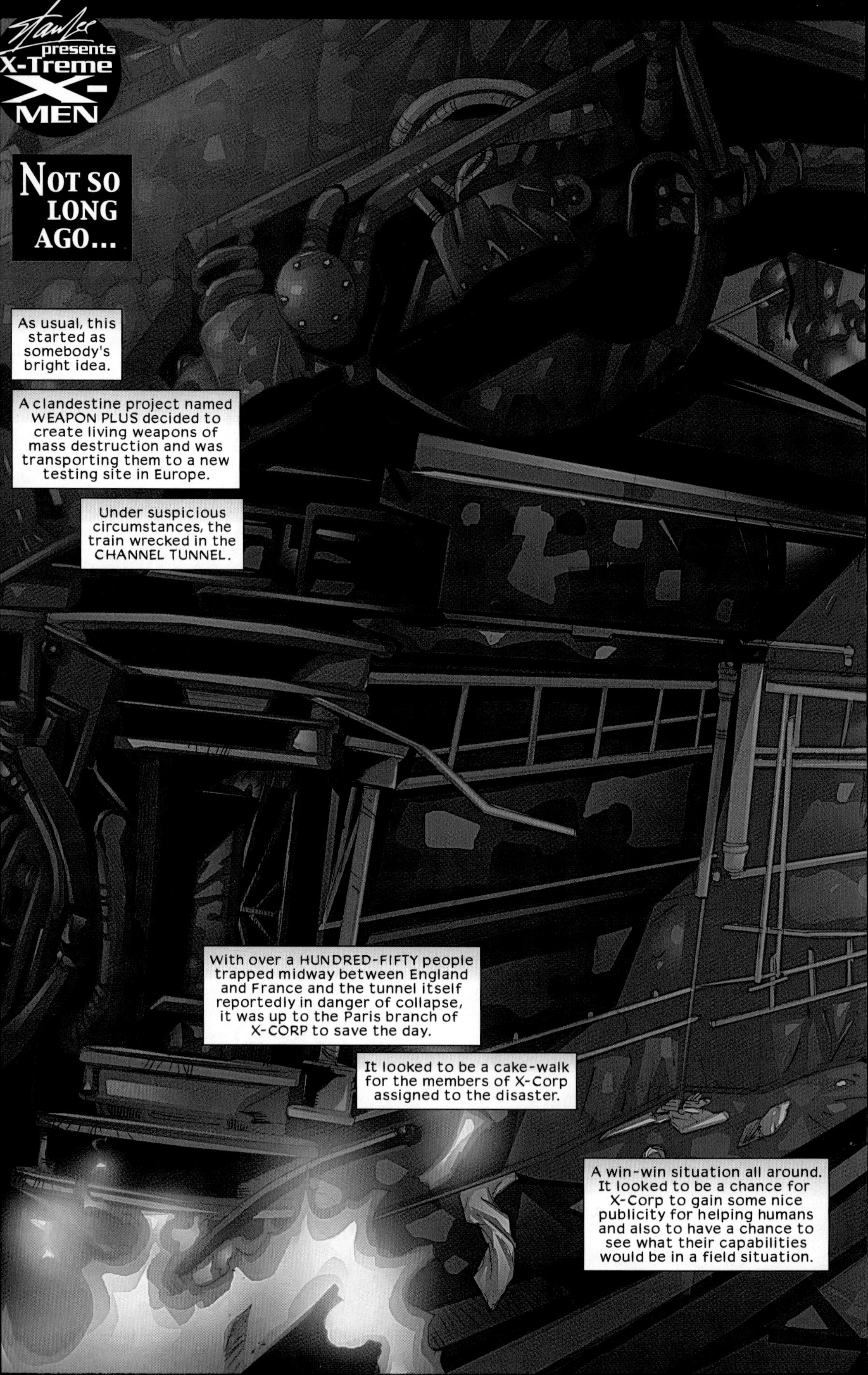
Stan Lee presents X-Treme X-Men
NOT SO LONG AGO...
As usual, this started as somebody's bright idea.
A clandestine project named WEAPON PLUS decided to create living weapons of mass destruction and was transporting them to a new testing site in Europe.
Under suspicious circumstances, the train wrecked in the CHANNEL TUNNEL.
With over a HUNDRED-FIFTY people trapped midway between England and France and the tunnel itself reportedly in danger of collapse, it was up to the Paris branch of X-CORP to save the day.
It looked to be a cake-walk for the members of X-Corp assigned to the disaster.
A win-win situation all around. It looked to be a chance for X-Corp to gain some nice publicity for helping humans and also to have a chance to see what their capabilities would be in a field situation.

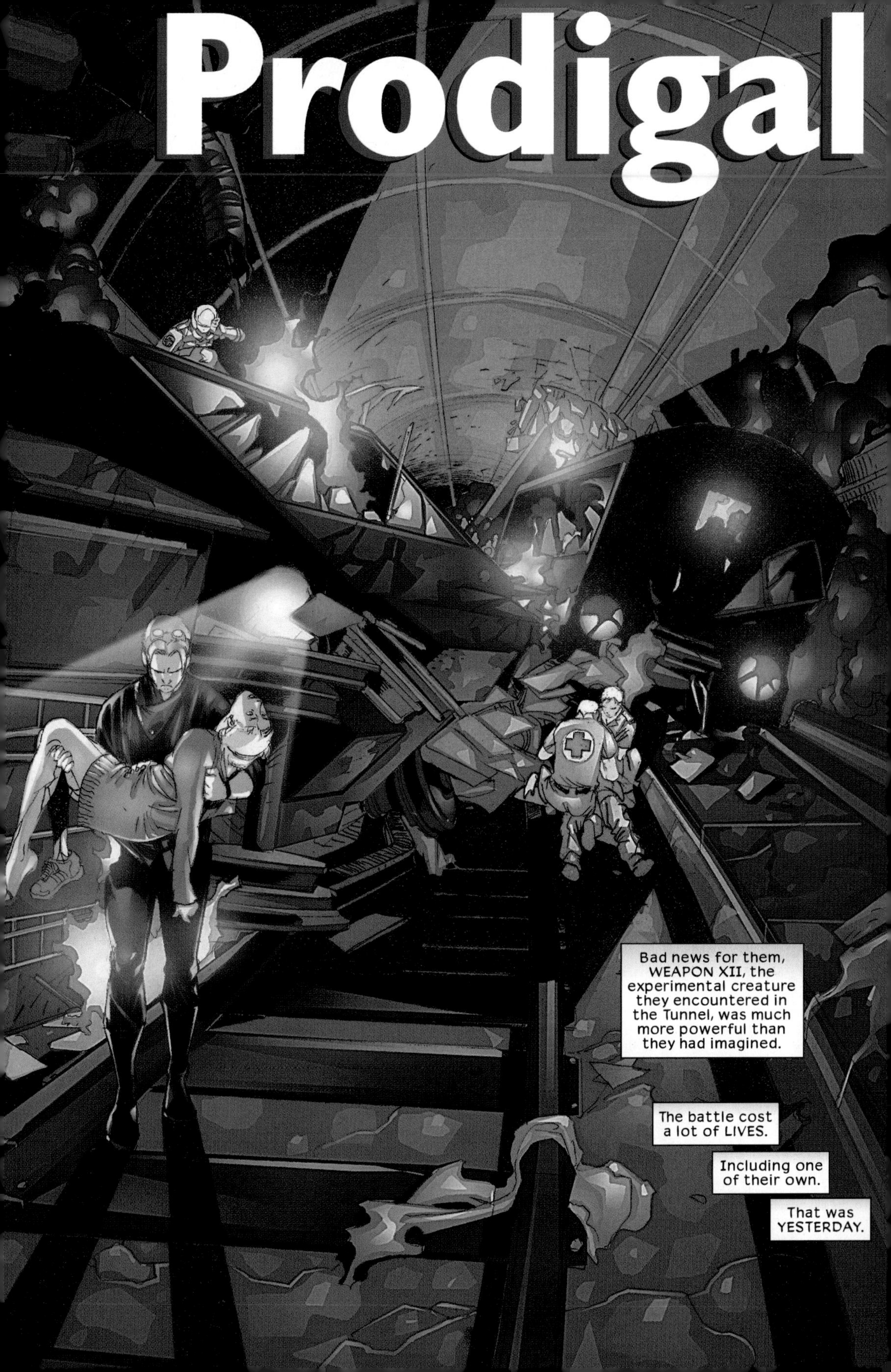
Prodigal
Bad news for them, WEAPON XII, the experimental creature they encountered in the Tunnel, was much more powerful than they had imagined.
The battle cost a lot of LIVES.
Including one of their own.
That was YESTERDAY.

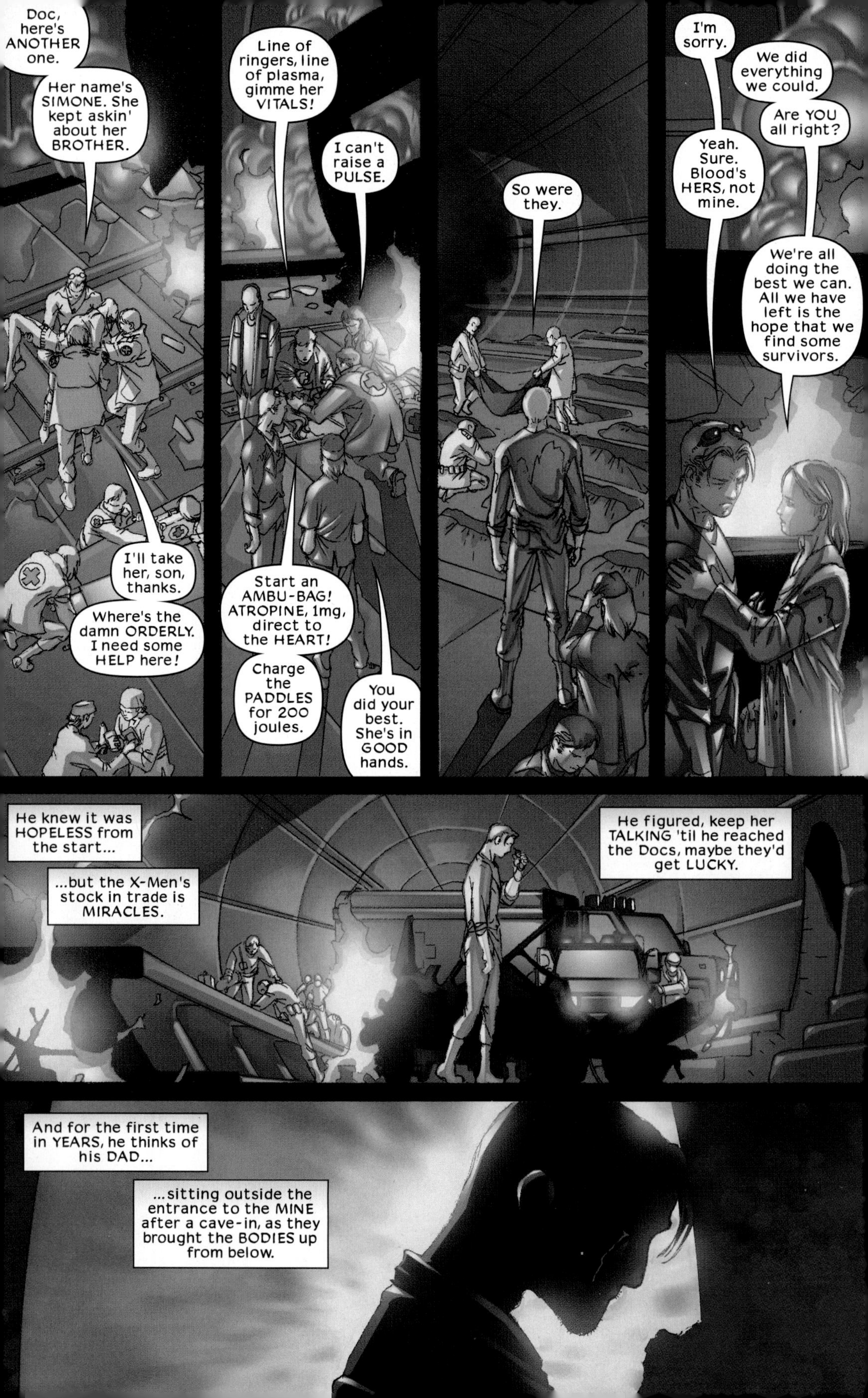
Doc, here's ANOTHER one.
Her name's SIMONE. She kept askin' about her BROTHER.
I'll take her, son, thanks.
Where's the damn ORDERLY. I need some HELP here!
Line of ringers, line of plasma, gimme her VITALS!
I can't raise a PULSE.
Start an AMBU-BAG! ATROPINE, 1mg, direct to the HEART!
Charge the PADDLES for 200 joules.
You did your best. She's in GOOD hands.
So were they.
I'm sorry.
We did everything we could.
Are YOU all right?
Yeah. Sure. Blood's HERS, not mine.
We're all doing the best we can. All we have left is the hope that we find some survivors.
He knew it was HOPELESS from the start...
...but the X-Men's stock in trade is MIRACLES.
He figured, keep her TALKING 'til he reached the Docs, maybe they'd get LUCKY.
And for the first time in YEARS, he thinks of his DAD...
...sitting outside the entrance to the MINE after a cave-in, as they brought the BODIES up from below.

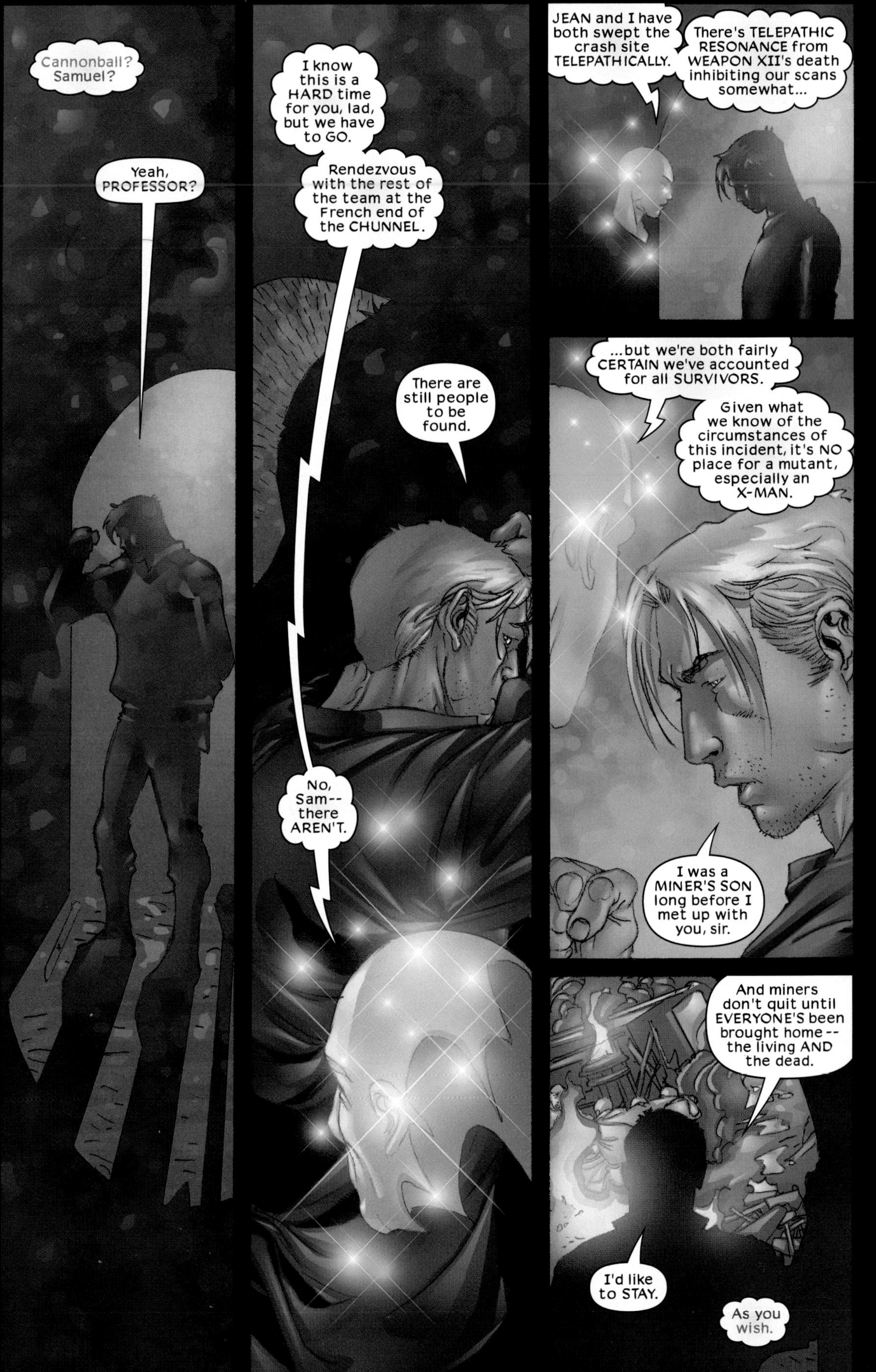
Cannonball? Samuel?
Yeah, PROFESSOR?
I know this is a HARD time for you, lad, but we have to GO.
Rendezvous with the rest of the team at the French end of the CHUNNEL.
There are still people to be found.
No, Sam-- there AREN'T.
JEAN and I have both swept the crash site TELEPATHICALLY.
There's TELEPATHIC RESONANCE from WEAPON XII's death inhibiting our scans somewhat...
...but we're both fairly CERTAIN we've accounted for all SURVIVORS.
Given what we know of the circumstances of this incident, it's NO place for a mutant, especially an X-MAN.
I was a MINER'S SON long before I met up with you, sir.
And miners don't quit until EVERYONE'S been brought home -- the living AND the dead.
I'd like to STAY.
As you wish.

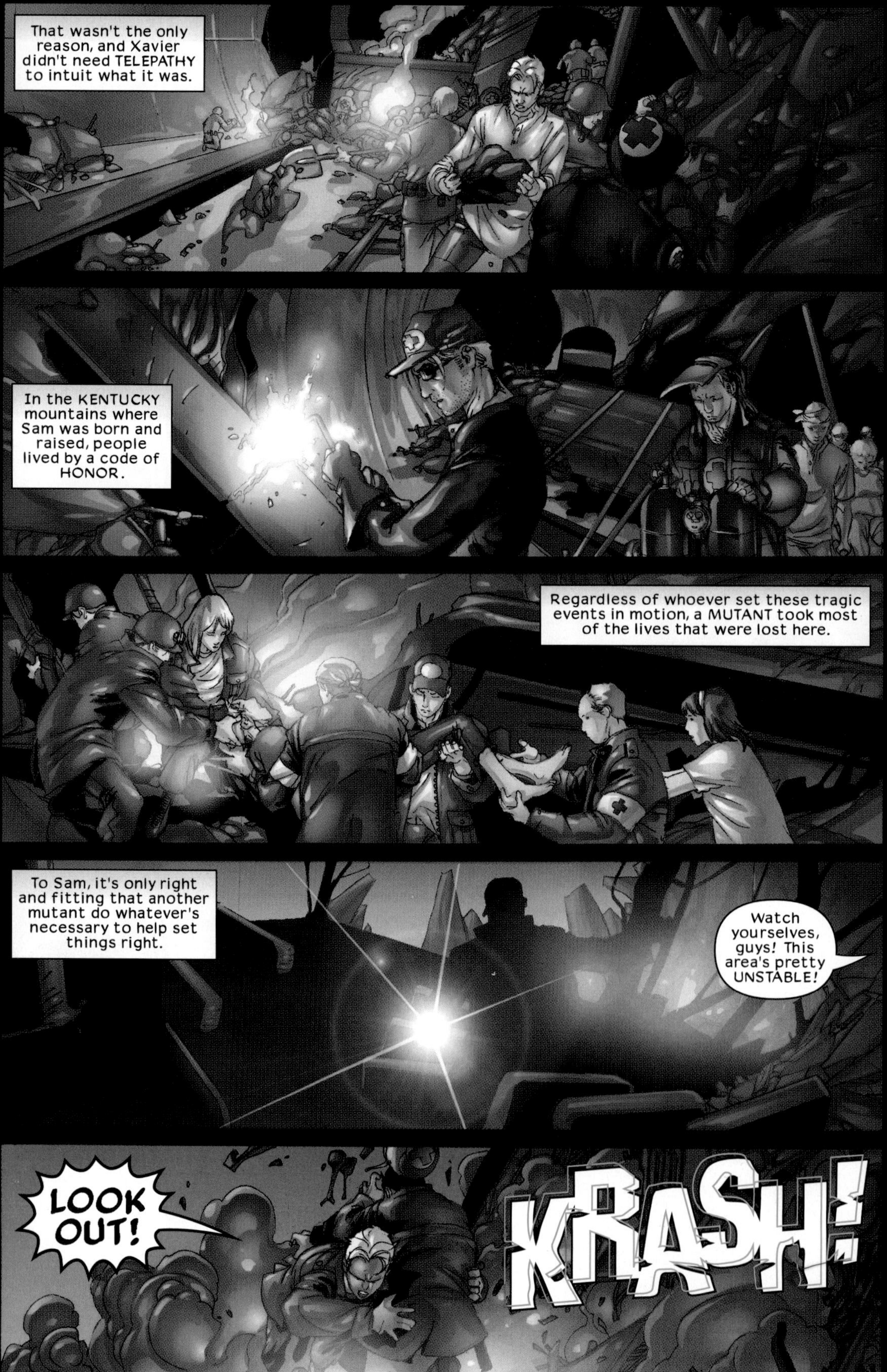
That wasn't the only reason, and Xavier didn't need TELEPATHY to intuit what it was.
In the KENTUCKY mountains where Sam was born and raised, people lived by a code of HONOR.
Regardless of whoever set these tragic events in motion, a MUTANT took most of the lives that were lost here.
To Sam, it's only right and fitting that another mutant do whatever's necessary to help set things right.
Watch yourselves, guys! This area's pretty UNSTABLE!
LOOK OUT!
KRASH!

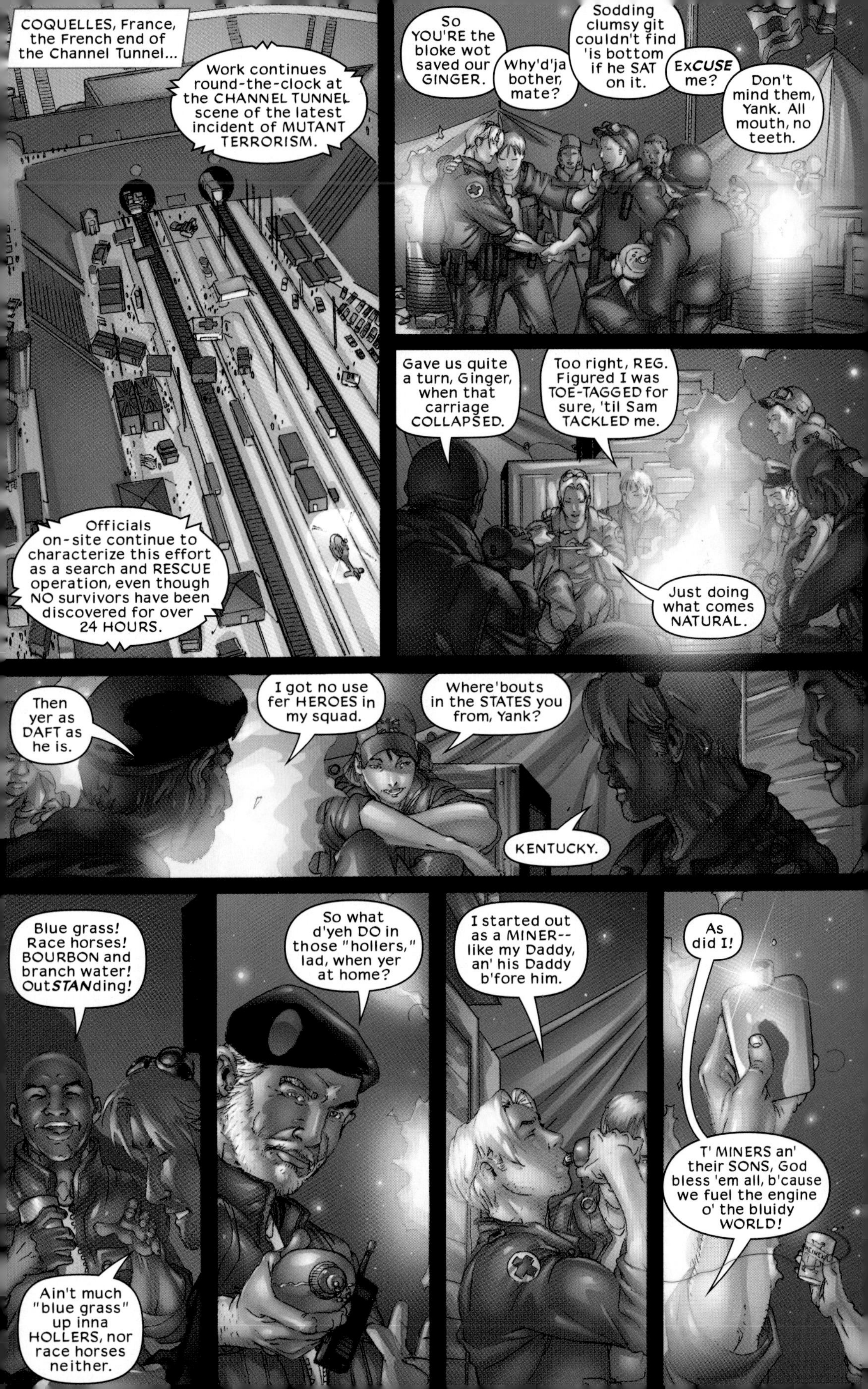
COQUELLES, France, the French end of the Channel Tunnel...
Work continues round-the-clock at the CHANNEL TUNNEL scene of the latest incident of MUTANT TERRORISM.
Officials on-site continue to characterize this effort as a search and RESCUE operation, even though NO survivors have been discovered for over 24 HOURS.
So YOU'RE the bloke wot saved our GINGER.
Why'd'ja bother, mate?
Sodding clumsy git couldn't find 'is bottom if he SAT on it.
ExCUSE me?
Don't mind them, Yank. All mouth, no teeth.
Gave us quite a turn, Ginger, when that carriage COLLAPSED.
Too right, REG. Figured I was TOE-TAGGED for sure, 'til Sam TACKLED me.
Just doing what comes NATURAL.
Then yer as DAFT as he is.
I got no use fer HEROES in my squad.
Where'bouts in the STATES you from, Yank?
KENTUCKY.
Blue grass! Race horses! BOURBON and branch water! OutSTANding!
Ain't much "blue grass" up inna HOLLERS, nor race horses neither.
So what d'yeh DO in those "hollers," lad, when yer at home?
I started out as a MINER-- like my Daddy, an' his Daddy b'fore him.
As did I!
T' MINERS an' their SONS, God bless 'em all, b'cause we fuel the engine o' the bluidy WORLD!

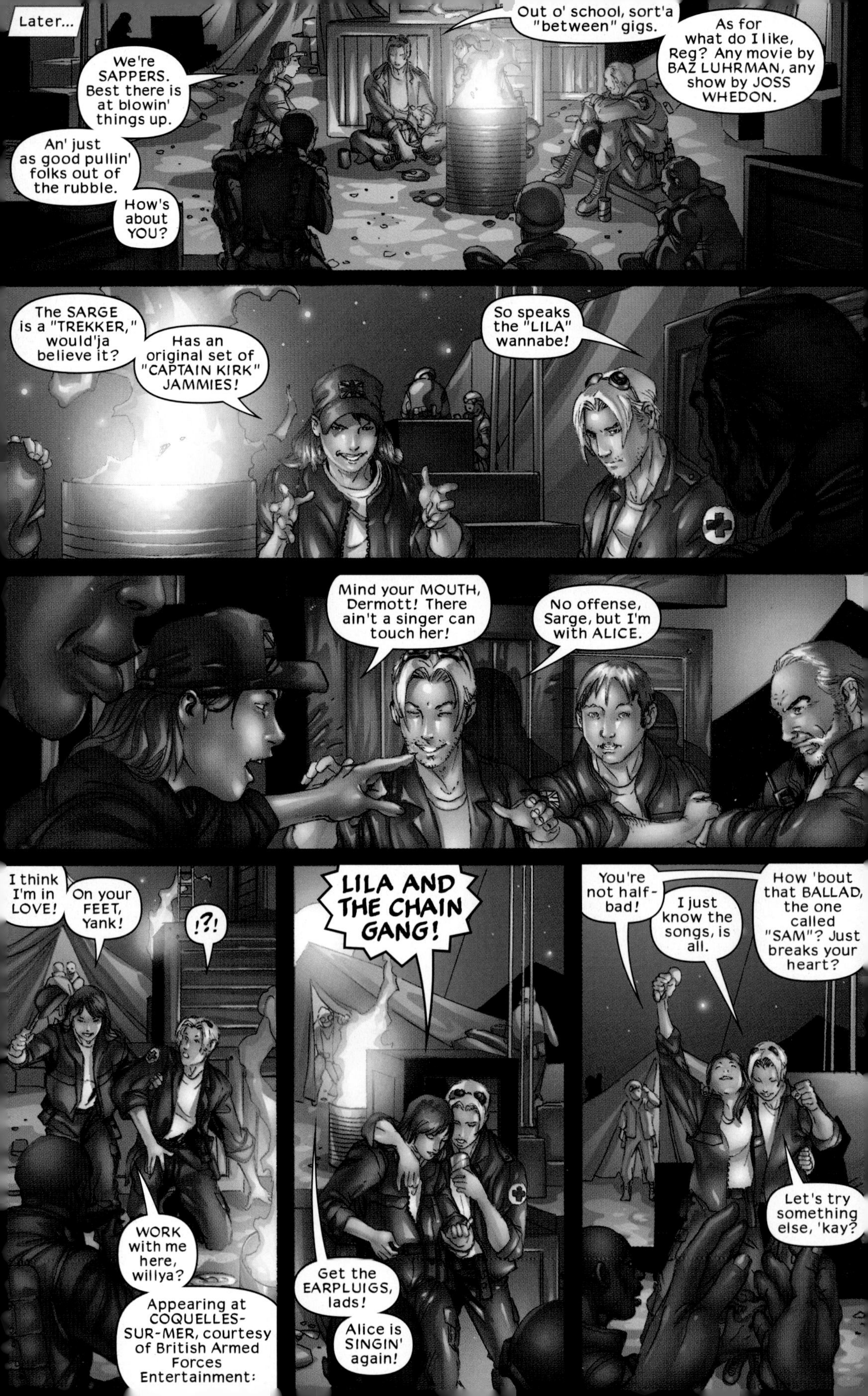

Later...
We're SAPPERS. Best there is at blowin' things up.
An' just as good pullin' folks out of the rubble.
How's about YOU?
Out o' school, sort'a "between" gigs.
As for what do I like, Reg? Any movie by BAZ LUHRMAN, any show by JOSS WHEDON.
The SARGE is a "TREKKER," would'ja believe it?
Has an original set of "CAPTAIN KIRK" JAMMIES!
So speaks the "LILA" wannabe!
Mind your MOUTH, Dermott! There ain't a singer can touch her!
No offense, Sarge, but I'm with ALICE.
I think I'm in LOVE!
On your FEET, Yank!
!?!
WORK with me here, willya?
Appearing at COQUELLES-SUR-MER, courtesy of British Armed Forces Entertainment:
LILA AND THE CHAIN GANG!
Get the EARPLUIGS, lads!
Alice is SINGIN' again!
You're not half-bad!
I just know the songs, is all.
How 'bout that BALLAD, the one called "SAM"? Just breaks your heart?
Let's try something else, 'kay?

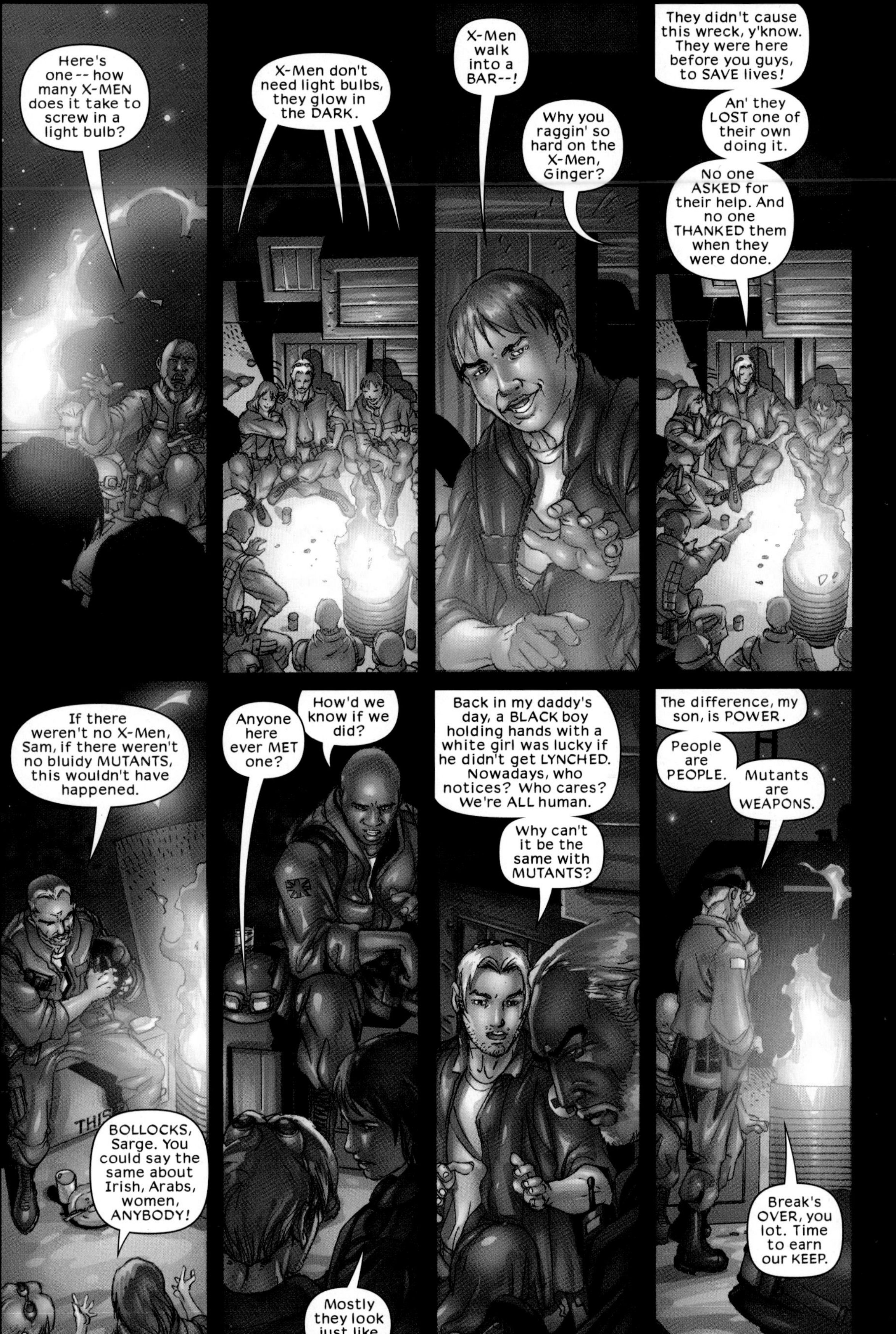

Here's one -- how many X-MEN does it take to screw in a light bulb?
X-Men don't need light bulbs, they glow in the DARK.
X-Men walk into a BAR--!
Why you raggin' so hard on the X-Men, Ginger?
They didn't cause this wreck, y'know. They were here before you guys, to SAVE lives!
An' they LOST one of their own doing it.
No one ASKED for their help. And no one THANKED them when they were done.
If there weren't no X-Men, Sam, if there weren't no bluidy MUTANTS, this wouldn't have happened.
BOLLOCKS, Sarge. You could say the same about Irish, Arabs, women, ANYBODY!
Anyone here ever MET one?
How'd we know if we did?
Mostly they look just like US.
Back in my daddy's day, a BLACK boy holding hands with a white girl was lucky if he didn't get LYNCHED. Nowadays, who notices? Who cares? We're ALL human.
Why can't it be the same with MUTANTS?
The difference, my son, is POWER.
People are PEOPLE.
Mutants are WEAPONS.
Break's OVER, you lot. Time to earn our KEEP.

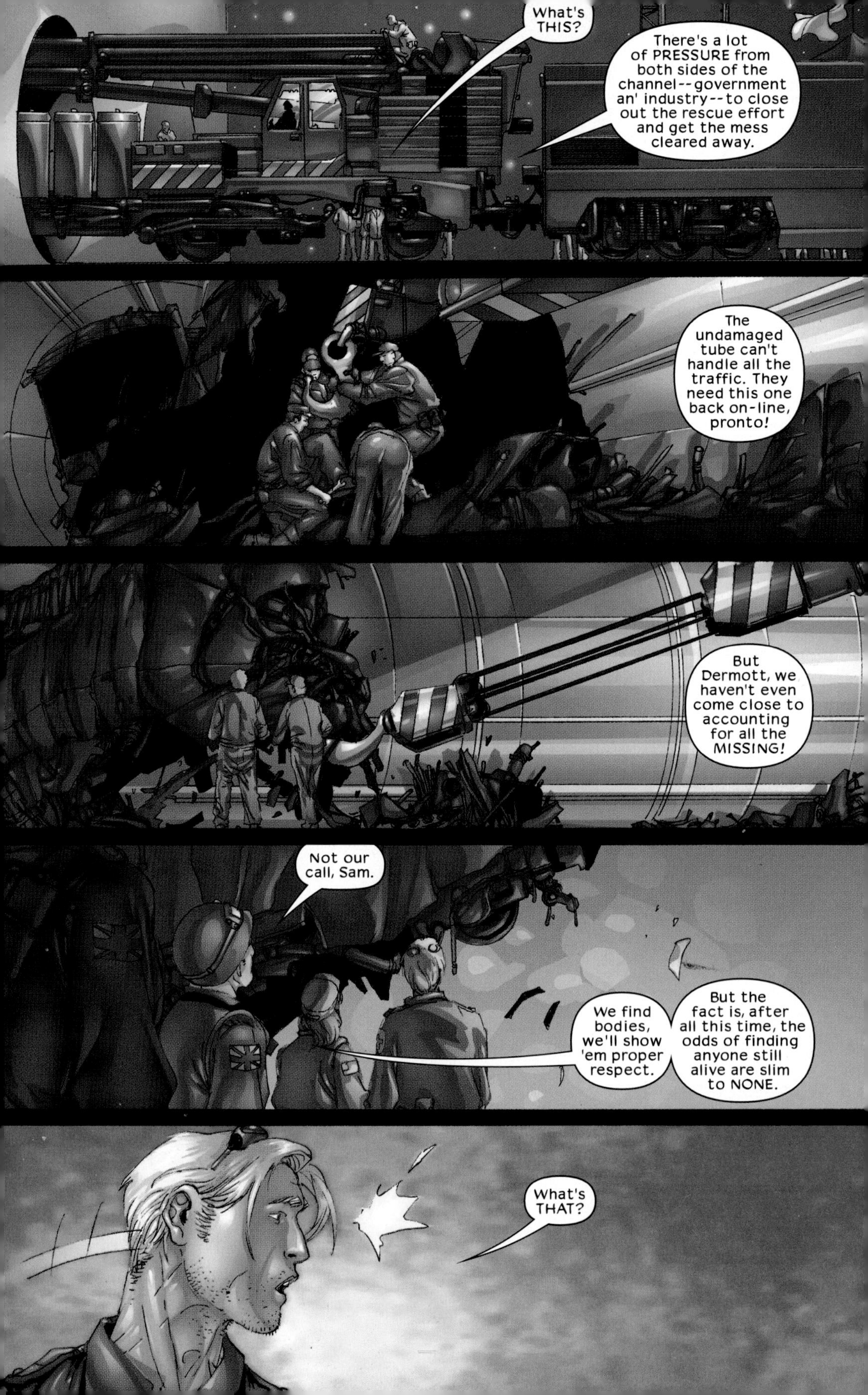
What's THIS?
There's a lot of PRESSURE from both sides of the channel--government an' industry--to close out the rescue effort and get the mess cleared away.
The undamaged tube can't handle all the traffic. They need this one back on-line, pronto!
But Dermott, we haven't even come close to accounting for all the MISSING!
Not our call, Sam.
We find bodies, we'll show 'em proper respect.
But the fact is, after all this time, the odds of finding anyone still alive are slim to NONE.
What's THAT?

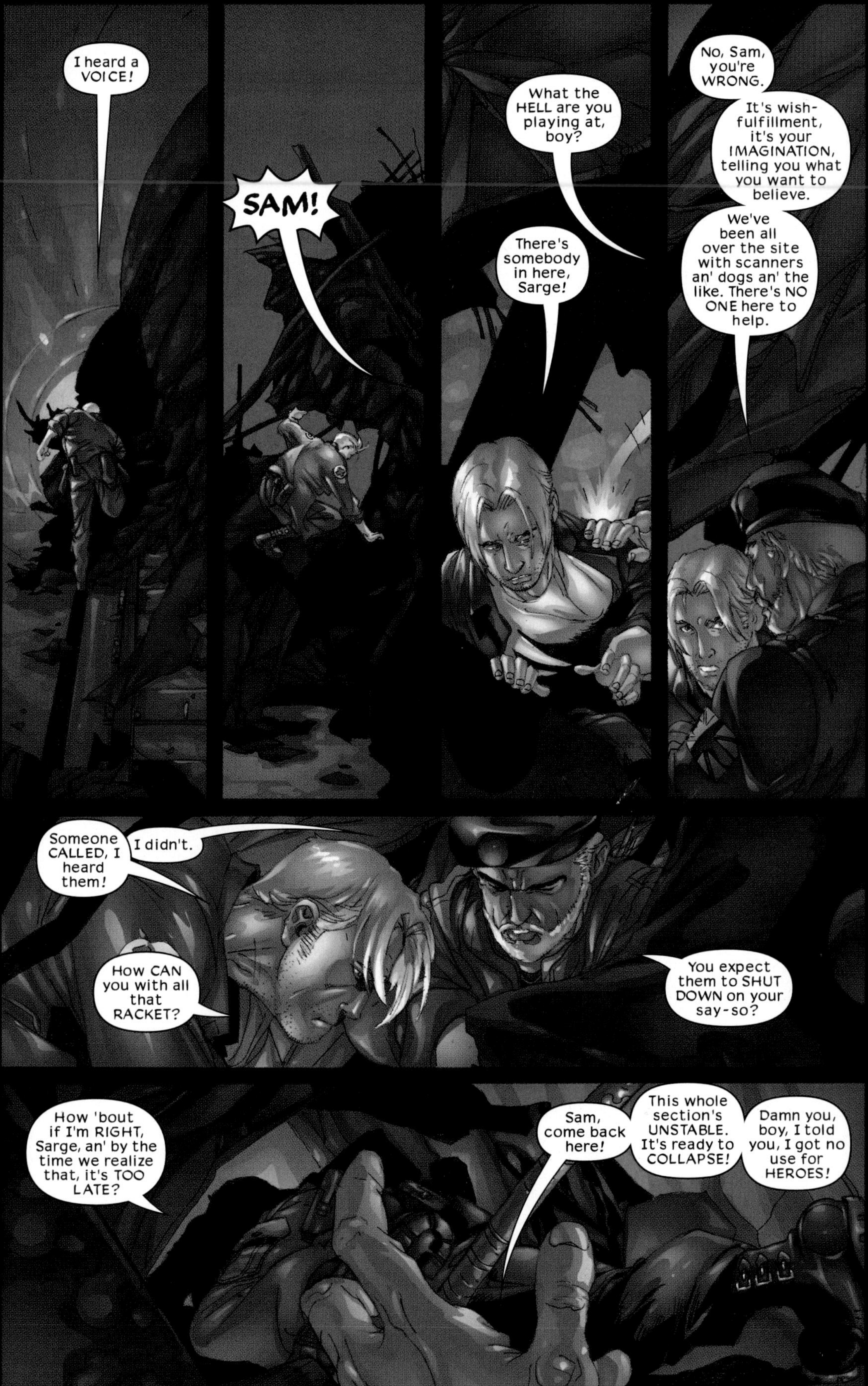
I heard a VOICE!
SAM!
What the HELL are you playing at, boy?
There's somebody in here, Sarge!
No, Sam, you're WRONG.
It's wish-fulfillment, it's your IMAGINATION, telling you what you want to believe.
We've been all over the site with scanners an' dogs an' the like. There's NO ONE here to help.
Someone CALLED, I heard them!
I didn't.
How CAN you with all that RACKET?
You expect them to SHUT DOWN on your say-so?
How 'bout if I'm RIGHT, Sarge, an' by the time we realize that, it's TOO LATE?
Sam, come back here!
This whole section's UNSTABLE. It's ready to COLLAPSE!
Damn you, boy, I told you, I got no use for HEROES!

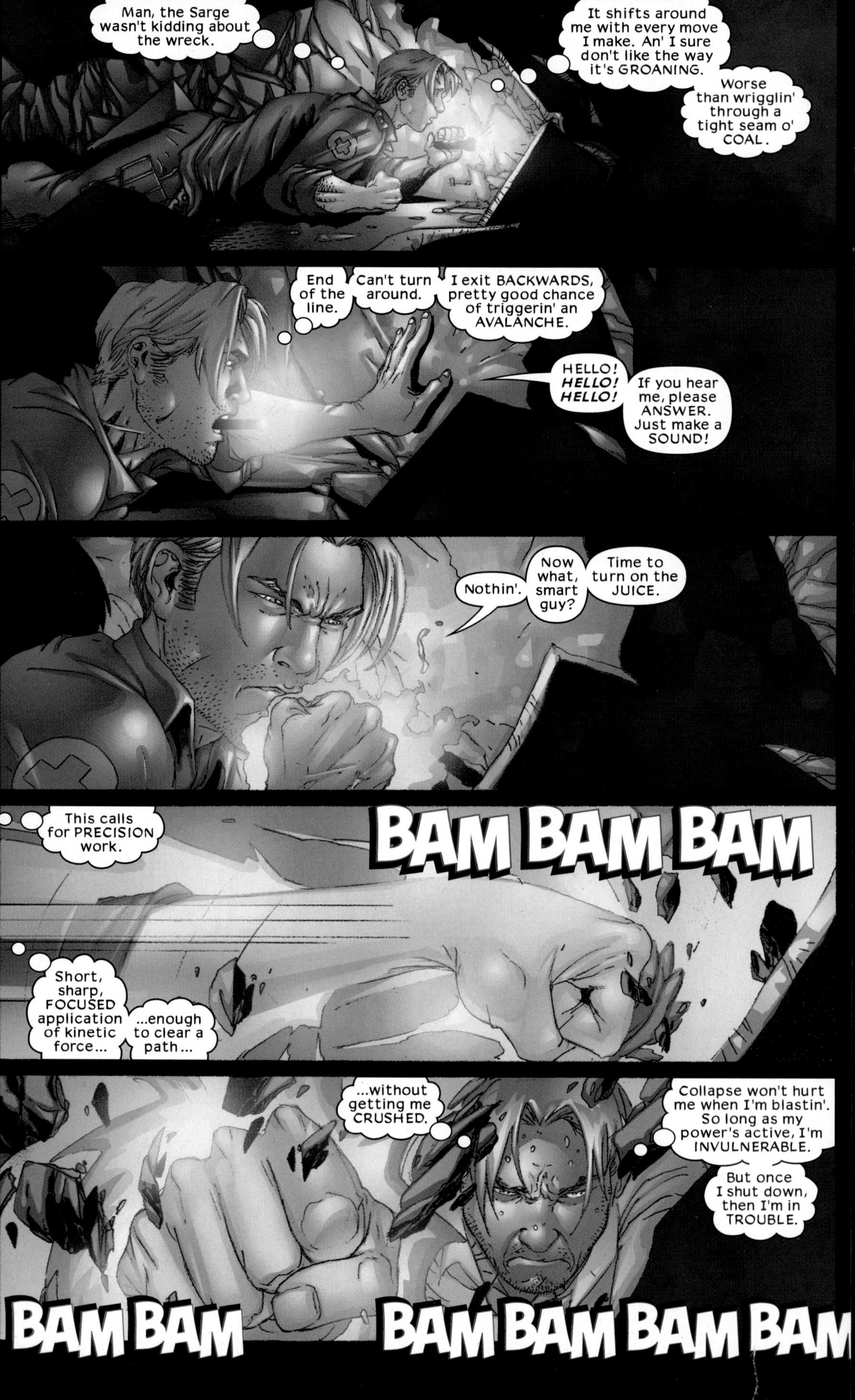

Man, the Sarge wasn't kidding about the wreck.
It shifts around me with every move I make. An' I sure don't like the way it's GROANING.
Worse than wrigglin' through a tight seam o' COAL.
End of the line.
Can't turn around.
I exit BACKWARDS, pretty good chance of triggerin' an AVALANCHE.
HELLO! *HELLO! HELLO!*
If you hear me, please ANSWER. Just make a SOUND!
Nothin'.
Now what, smart guy?
Time to turn on the JUICE.
This calls for PRECISION work.
BAM BAM BAM
Short, sharp, FOCUSED application of kinetic force...
...enough to clear a path...
...without getting me CRUSHED.
Collapse won't hurt me when I'm blastin'. So long as my power's active, I'm INVULNERABLE.
But once I shut down, then I'm in TROUBLE.
BAM BAM
BAM BAM BAM BAM

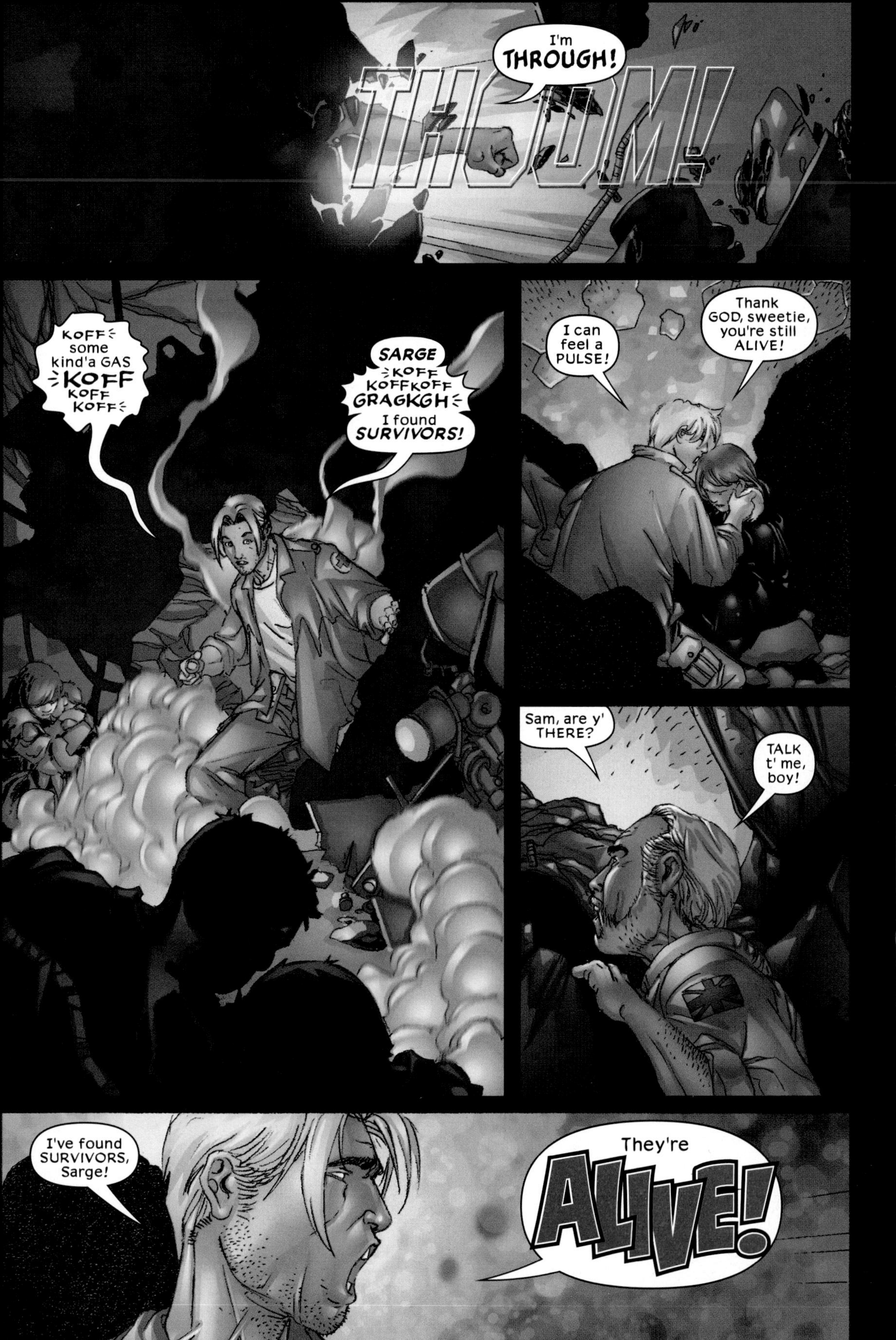
THOOM!
I'm THROUGH!
KOFF some kind'a GAS KOFF KOFF KOFF
SARGE KOFF KOFFKOFF GRAGKGH I found SURVIVORS!
I can feel a PULSE!
Thank GOD, sweetie, you're still ALIVE!
Sam, are y' THERE?
TALK t' me, boy!
I've found SURVIVORS, Sarge!
They're ALIVE!

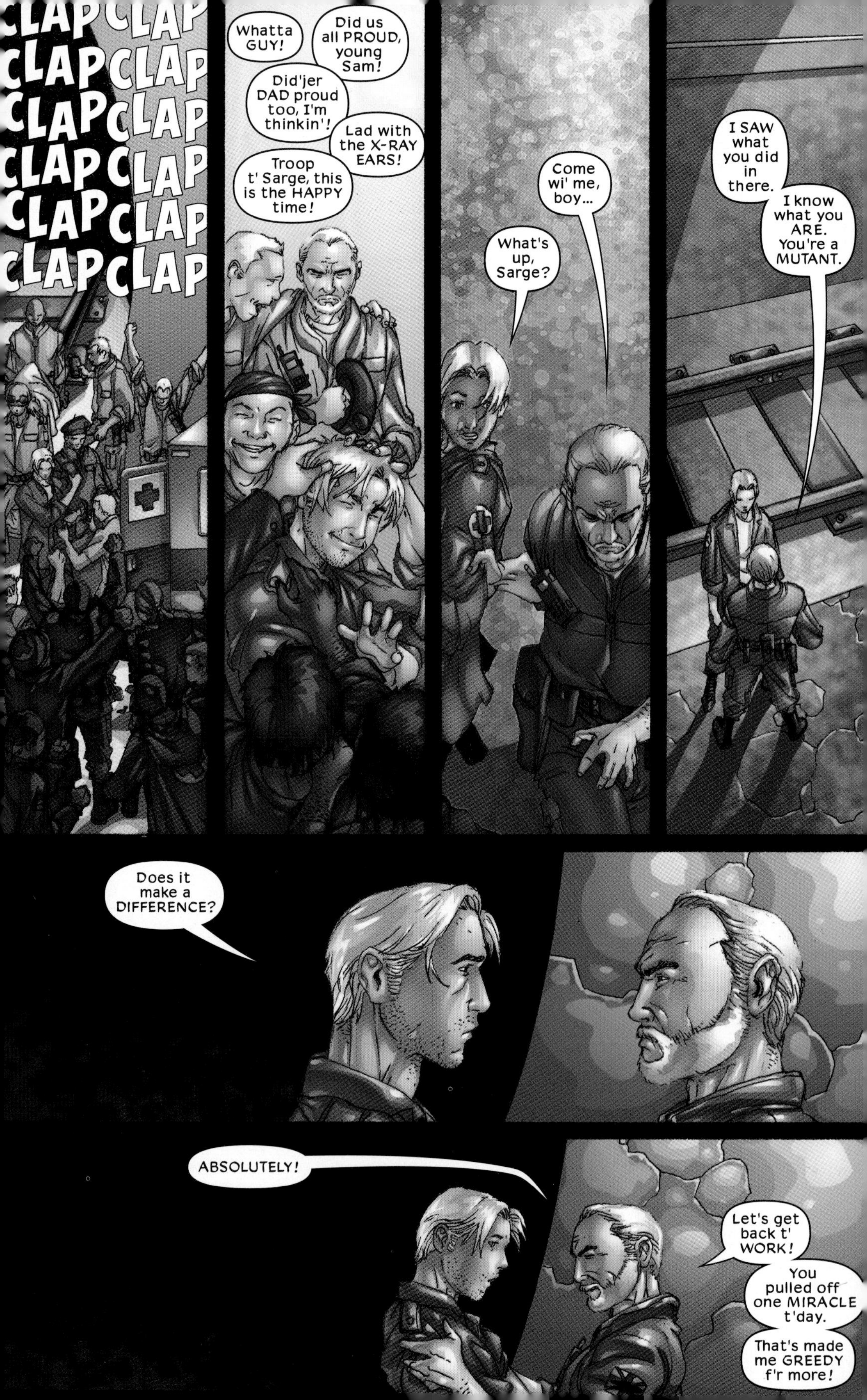
CLAP CLAP
CLAP CLAP
CLAP CLAP
CLAP CLAP
CLAP CLAP
CLAP CLAP
Whatta GUY!
Did us all PROUD, young Sam!
Did'jer DAD proud too, I'm thinkin'!
Lad with the X-RAY EARS!
Troop t' Sarge, this is the HAPPY time!
Come wi' me, boy...
What's up, Sarge?
I SAW what you did in there.
I know what you ARE. You're a MUTANT.
Does it make a DIFFERENCE?
ABSOLUTELY!
Let's get back t' WORK!
You pulled off one MIRACLE t'day.
That's made me GREEDY f'r more!

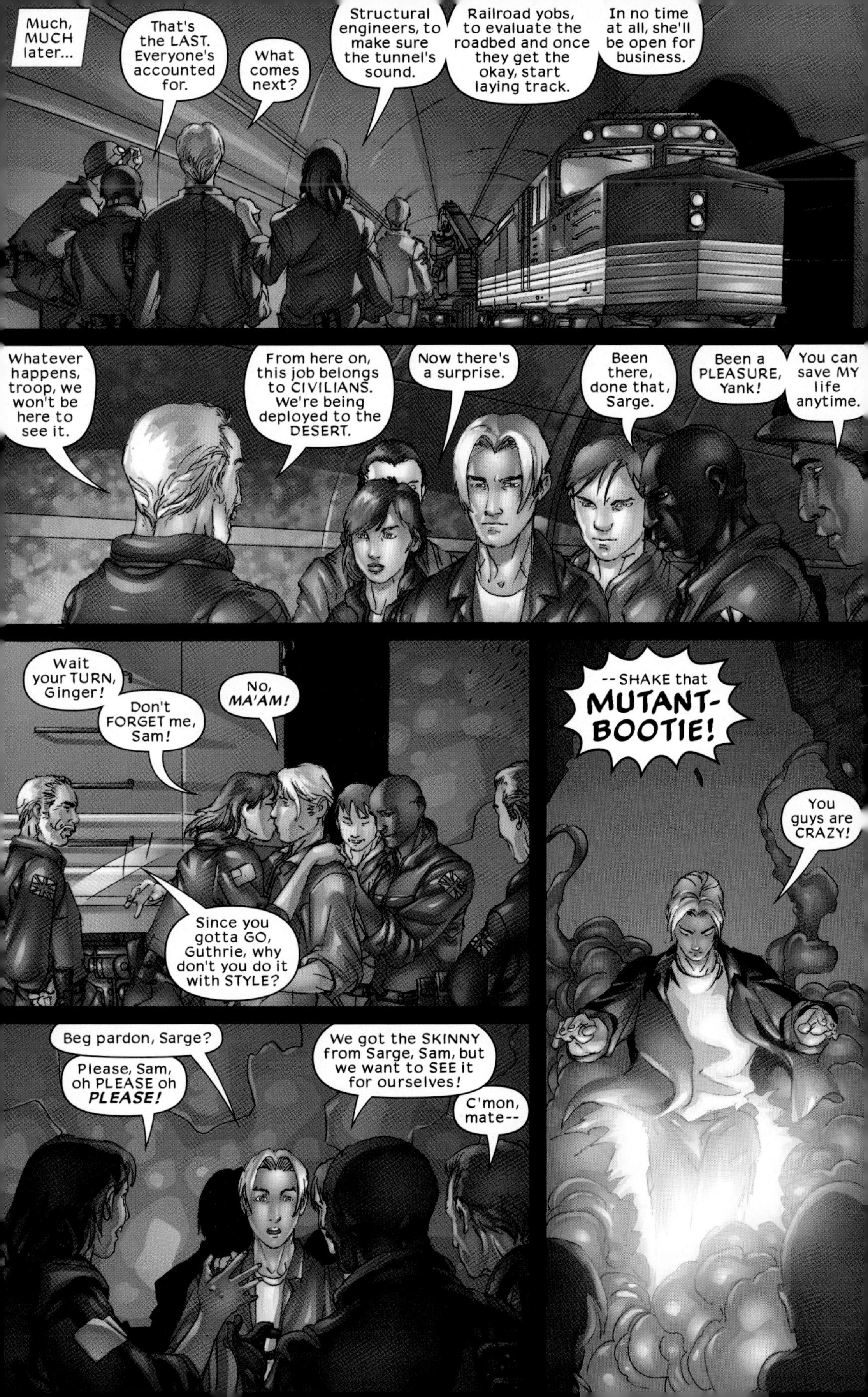
Much, MUCH later...
That's the LAST. Everyone's accounted for.
What comes next?
Structural engineers, to make sure the tunnel's sound.
Railroad yobs, to evaluate the roadbed and once they get the okay, start laying track.
In no time at all, she'll be open for business.
Whatever happens, troop, we won't be here to see it.
From here on, this job belongs to CIVILIANS. We're being deployed to the DESERT.
Now there's a surprise.
Been there, done that, Sarge.
Been a PLEASURE, Yank!
You can save MY life anytime.
Wait your TURN, Ginger!
Don't FORGET me, Sam!
No, MA'AM!
Since you gotta GO, Guthrie, why don't you do it with STYLE?
Beg pardon, Sarge?
Please, Sam, oh PLEASE oh PLEASE!
We got the SKINNY from Sarge, Sam, but we want to SEE it for ourselves!
C'mon, mate--
--SHAKE that MUTANT-BOOTIE!
You guys are CRAZY!

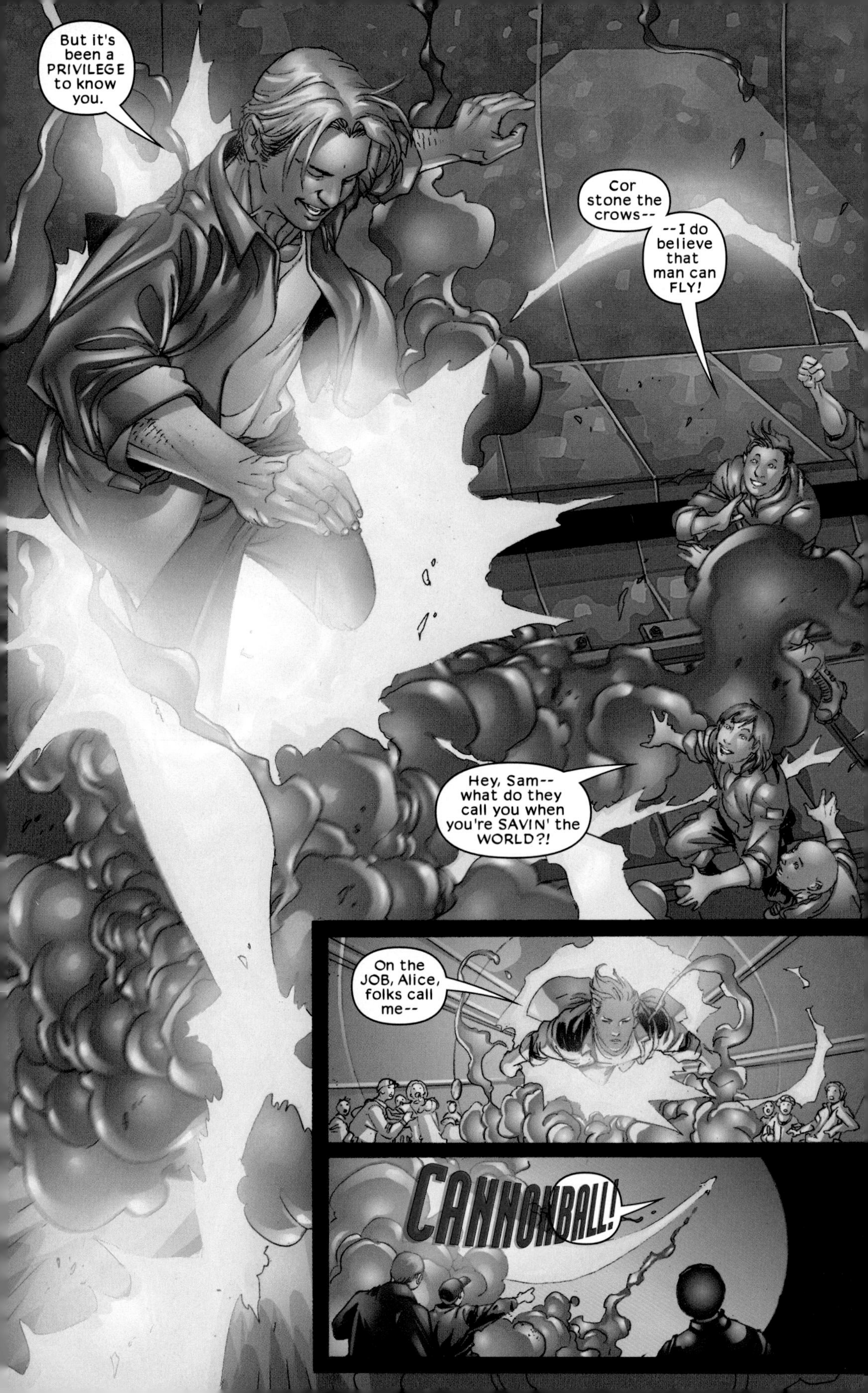
But it's been a PRIVILEGE to know you.
Cor stone the crows--
--I do believe that man can FLY!
Hey, Sam--what do they call you when you're SAVIN' the WORLD?!
On the JOB, Alice, folks call me--
CANNONBALL!

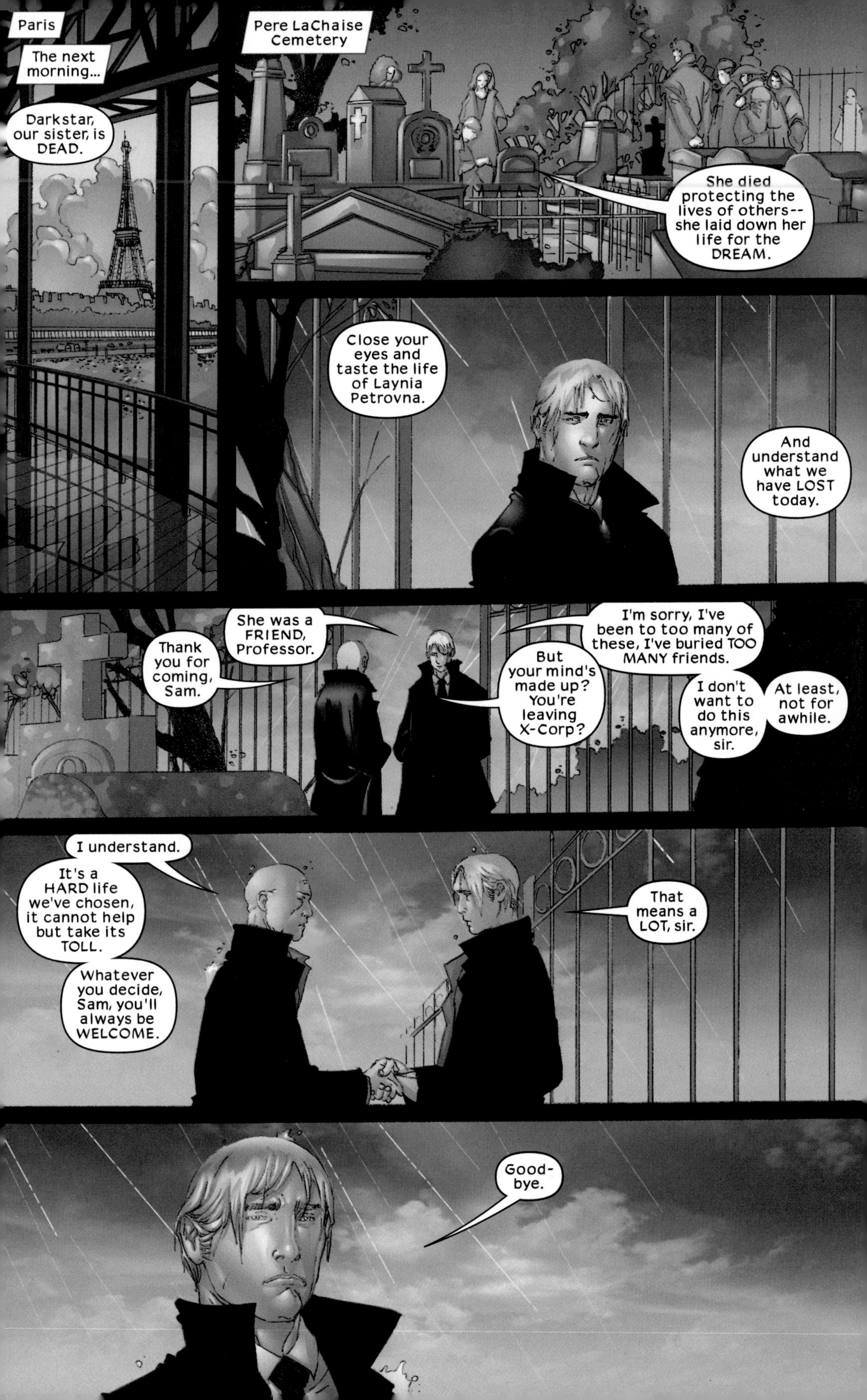
Paris
The next morning...
Darkstar, our sister, is DEAD.
Pere LaChaise Cemetery
She died protecting the lives of others-- she laid down her life for the DREAM.
Close your eyes and taste the life of Laynia Petrovna.
And understand what we have LOST today.
Thank you for coming, Sam.
She was a FRIEND, Professor.
But your mind's made up? You're leaving X-Corp?
I'm sorry, I've been to too many of these, I've buried TOO MANY friends.
I don't want to do this anymore, sir.
At least, not for awhile.
I understand.
It's a HARD life we've chosen, it cannot help but take its TOLL.
Whatever you decide, Sam, you'll always be WELCOME.
That means a LOT, sir.
Good-bye.

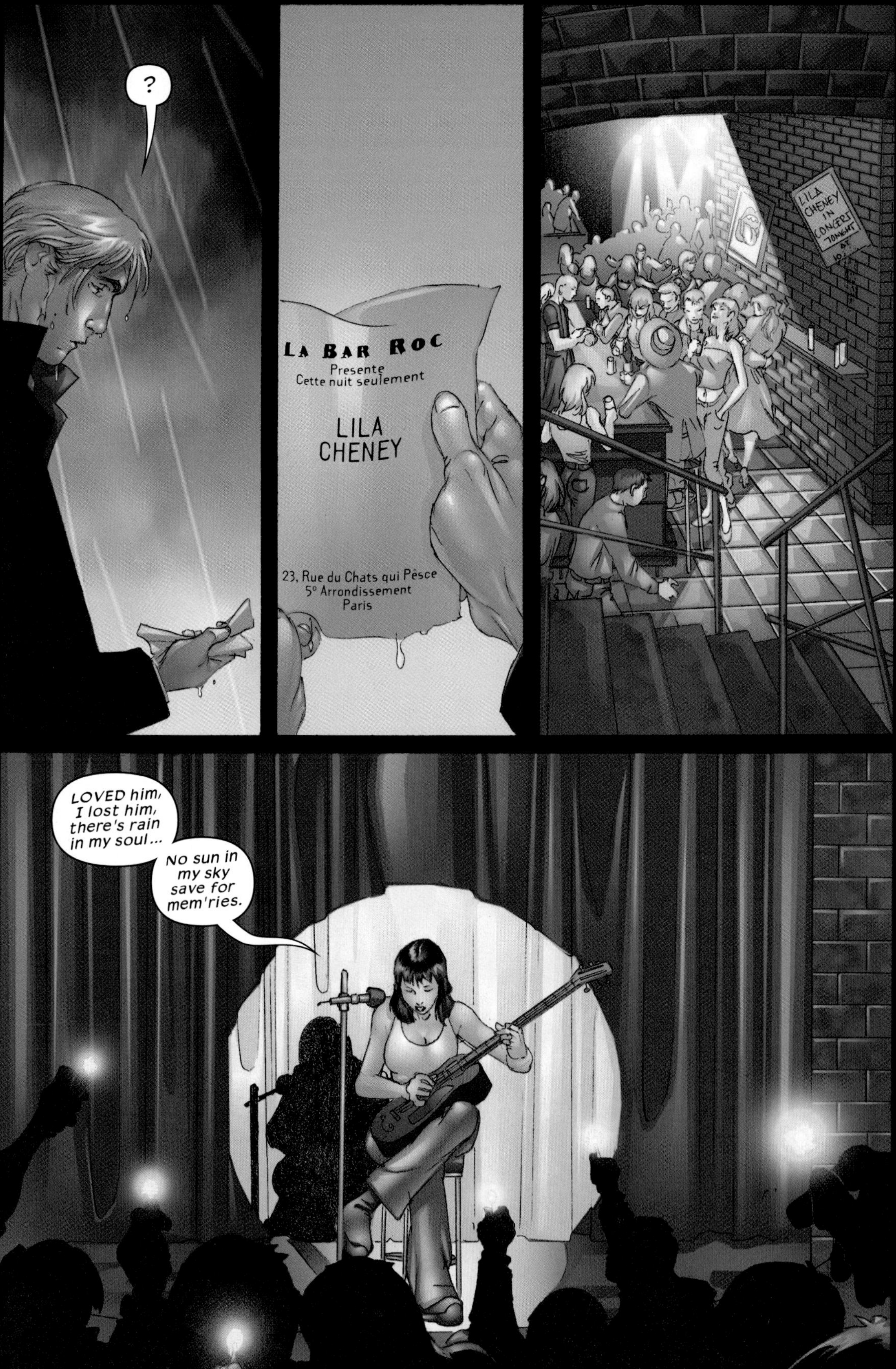
?
LA BAR ROC
Presente
Cette nuit seulement
LILA
CHENEY
23, Rue du Chats qui Pêsce
5° Arrondissement
Paris
LILA CHENEY IN CONCERT TONIGHT
LOVED him, I lost him, there's rain in my soul...
No sun in my sky save for mem'ries.

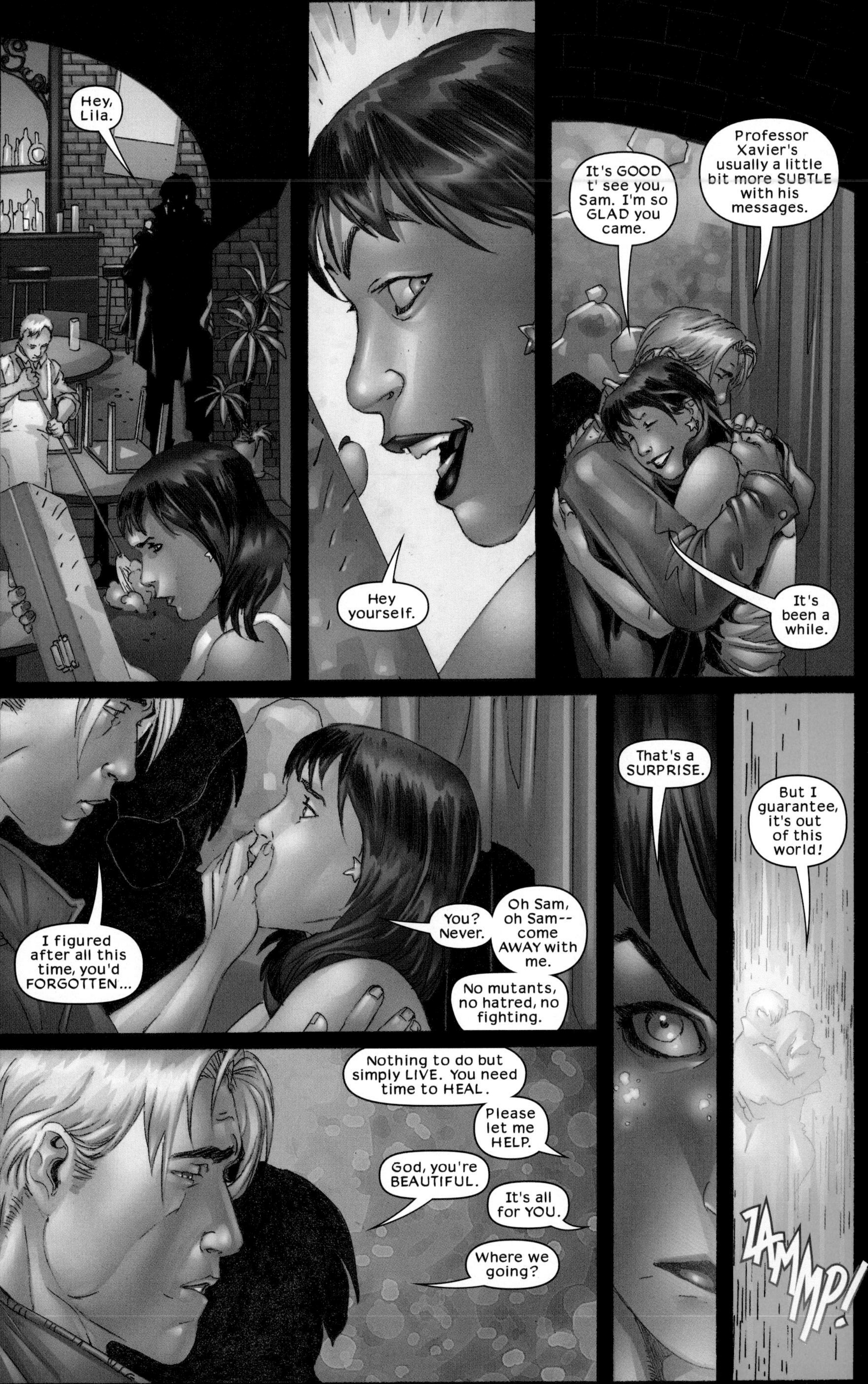
Hey, Lila.
Hey yourself.
It's GOOD t' see you, Sam. I'm so GLAD you came.
Professor Xavier's usually a little bit more SUBTLE with his messages.
It's been a while.
I figured after all this time, you'd FORGOTTEN...
You? Never.
Oh Sam, oh Sam-- come AWAY with me.
No mutants, no hatred, no fighting.
That's a SURPRISE.
But I guarantee, it's out of this world!
Nothing to do but simply LIVE. You need time to HEAL.
Please let me HELP.
God, you're BEAUTIFUL.
It's all for YOU.
Where we going?
ZAMMMP!

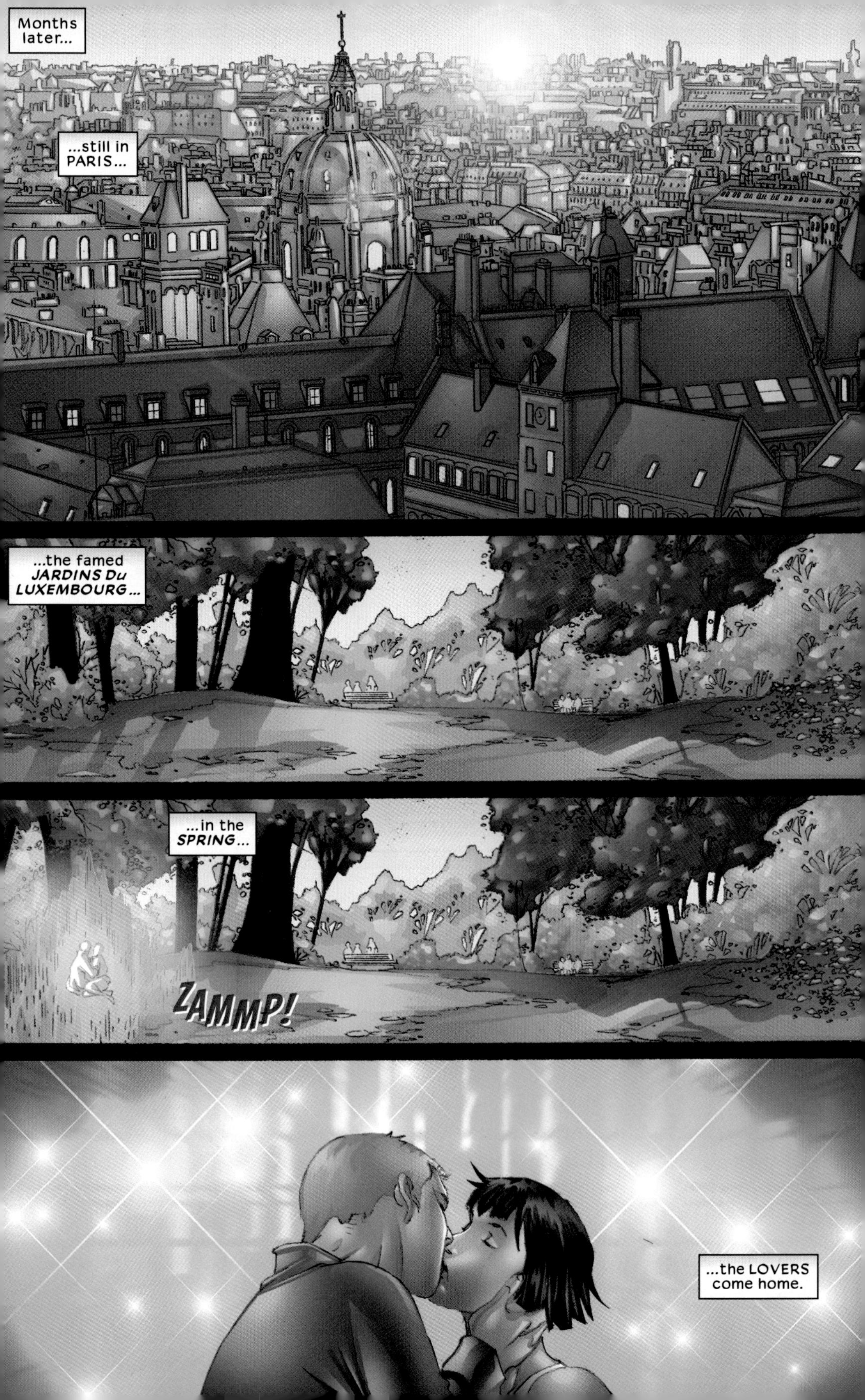
Months later...
...still in PARIS...
...the famed JARDINS Du LUXEMBOURG...
...in the SPRING...
ZAMMP!
...the LOVERS come home.

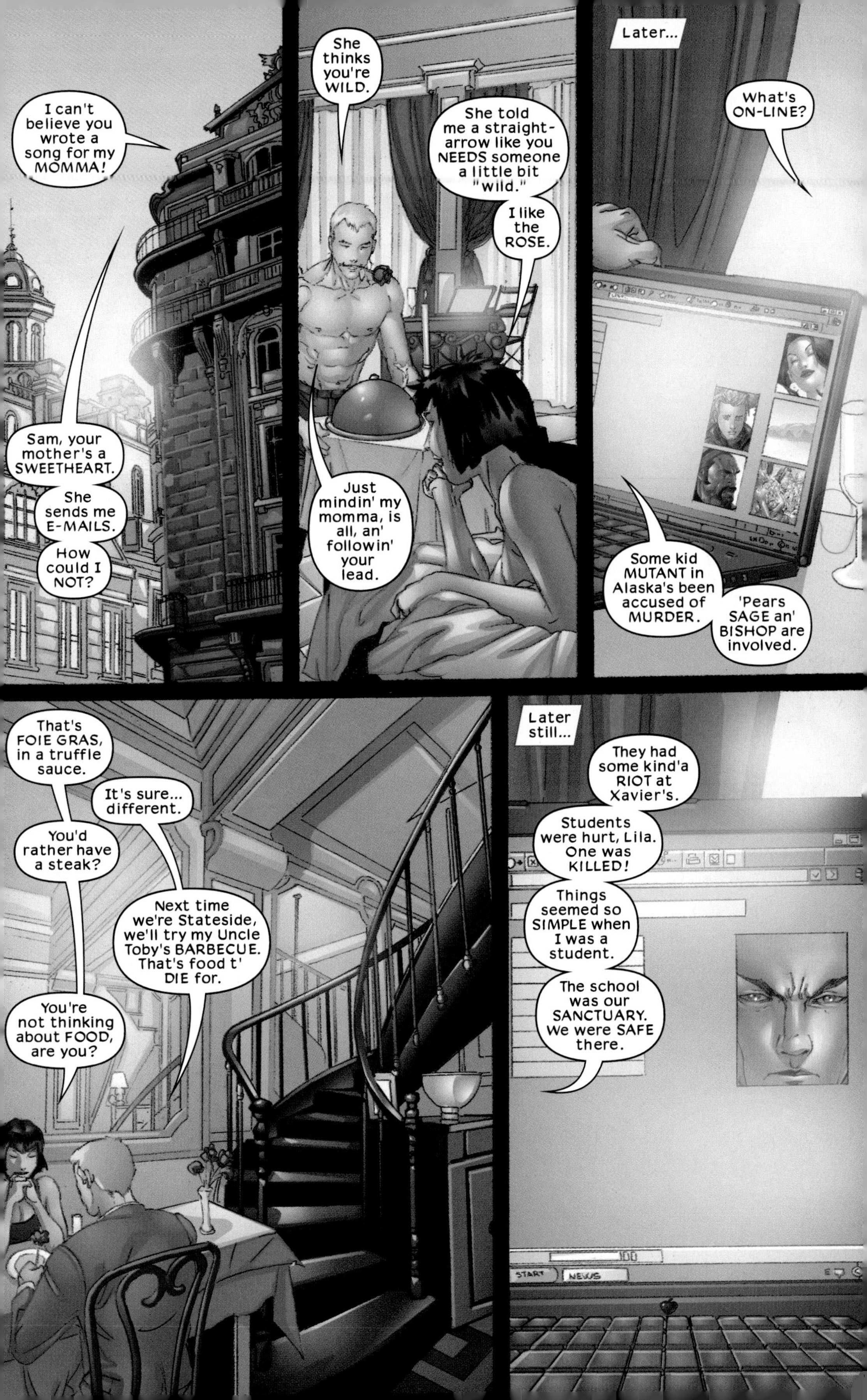
I can't believe you wrote a song for my MOMMA!
Sam, your mother's a SWEETHEART.
She sends me E-MAILS.
How could I NOT?
She thinks you're WILD.
She told me a straight-arrow like you NEEDS someone a little bit "wild."
I like the ROSE.
Just mindin' my momma, is all, an' followin' your lead.
Later...
What's ON-LINE?
Some kid MUTANT in Alaska's been accused of MURDER.
'Pears SAGE an' BISHOP are involved.
That's FOIE GRAS, in a truffle sauce.
It's sure... different.
You'd rather have a steak?
Next time we're Stateside, we'll try my Uncle Toby's BARBECUE. That's food t' DIE for.
You're not thinking about FOOD, are you?
Later still...
They had some kind'a RIOT at Xavier's.
Students were hurt, Lila. One was KILLED!
Things seemed so SIMPLE when I was a student.
The school was our SANCTUARY. We were SAFE there.
START
NEWS

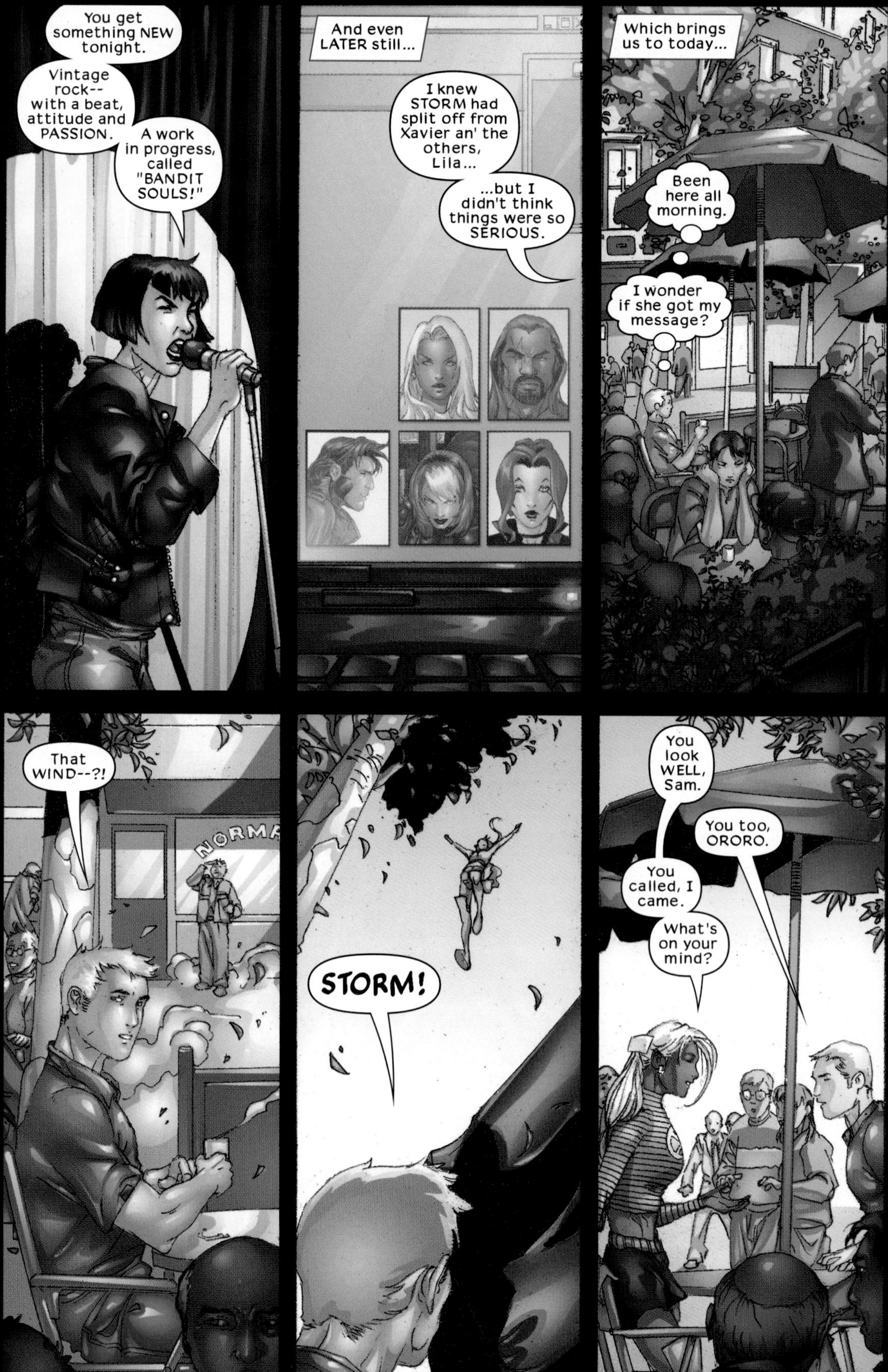
You get something NEW tonight.
Vintage rock--with a beat, attitude and PASSION.
A work in progress, called "BANDIT SOULS!"
And even LATER still...
I knew STORM had split off from Xavier an' the others, Lila...
...but I didn't think things were so SERIOUS.
Which brings us to today...
Been here all morning.
I wonder if she got my message?
That WIND--?!
STORM!
You look WELL, Sam.
You too, ORORO.
You called, I came.
What's on your mind?

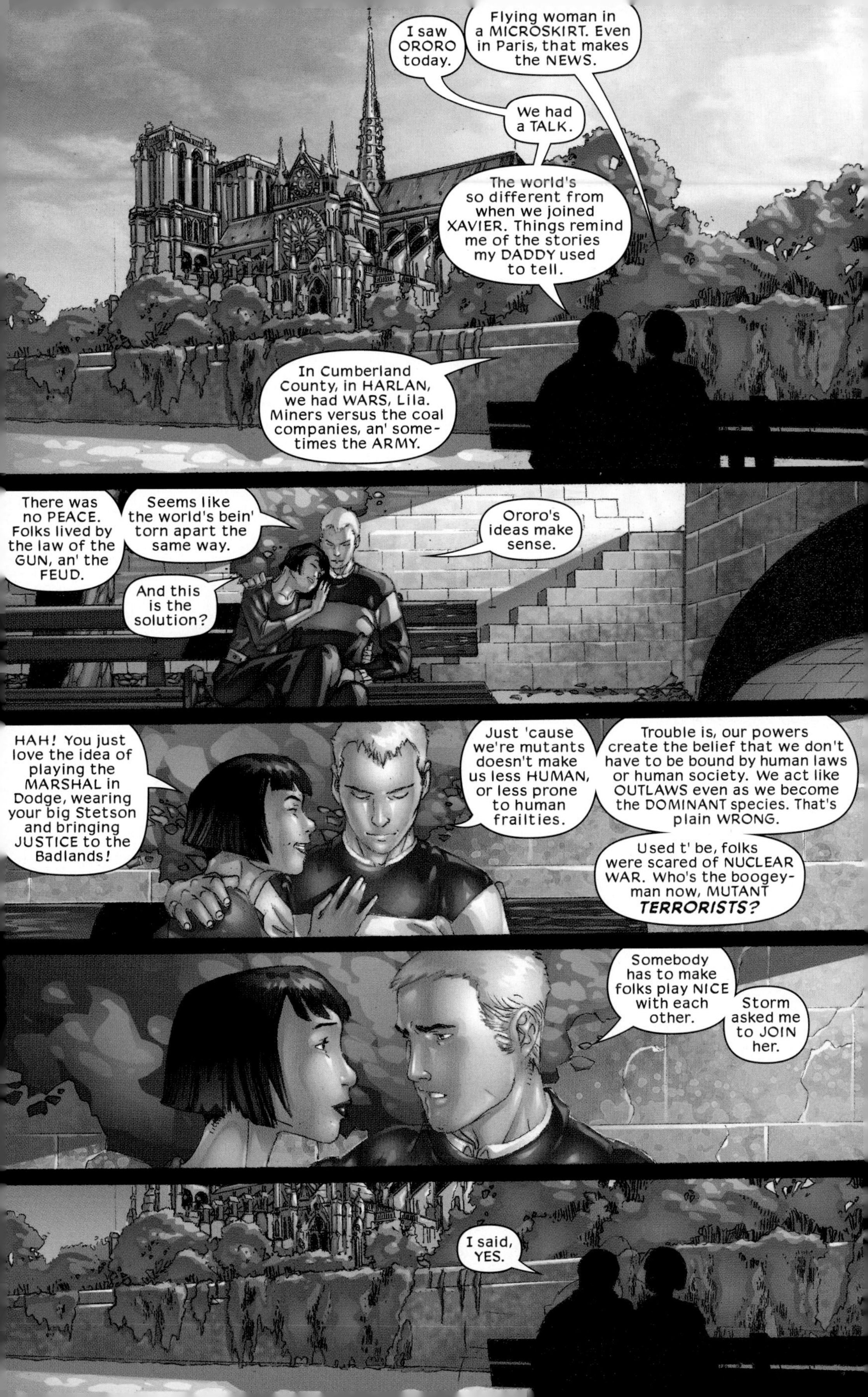
I saw ORORO today.
Flying woman in a MICROSKIRT. Even in Paris, that makes the NEWS.
We had a TALK.
The world's so different from when we joined XAVIER. Things remind me of the stories my DADDY used to tell.
In Cumberland County, in HARLAN, we had WARS, Lila. Miners versus the coal companies, an' sometimes the ARMY.
There was no PEACE. Folks lived by the law of the GUN, an' the FEUD.
Seems like the world's bein' torn apart the same way.
And this is the solution?
Ororo's ideas make sense.
HAH! You just love the idea of playing the MARSHAL in Dodge, wearing your big Stetson and bringing JUSTICE to the Badlands!
Just 'cause we're mutants doesn't make us less HUMAN, or less prone to human frailties.
Trouble is, our powers create the belief that we don't have to be bound by human laws or human society. We act like OUTLAWS even as we become the DOMINANT species. That's plain WRONG.
Used t' be, folks were scared of NUCLEAR WAR. Who's the boogeyman now, MUTANT TERRORISTS?
Somebody has to make folks play NICE with each other.
Storm asked me to JOIN her.
I said, YES.

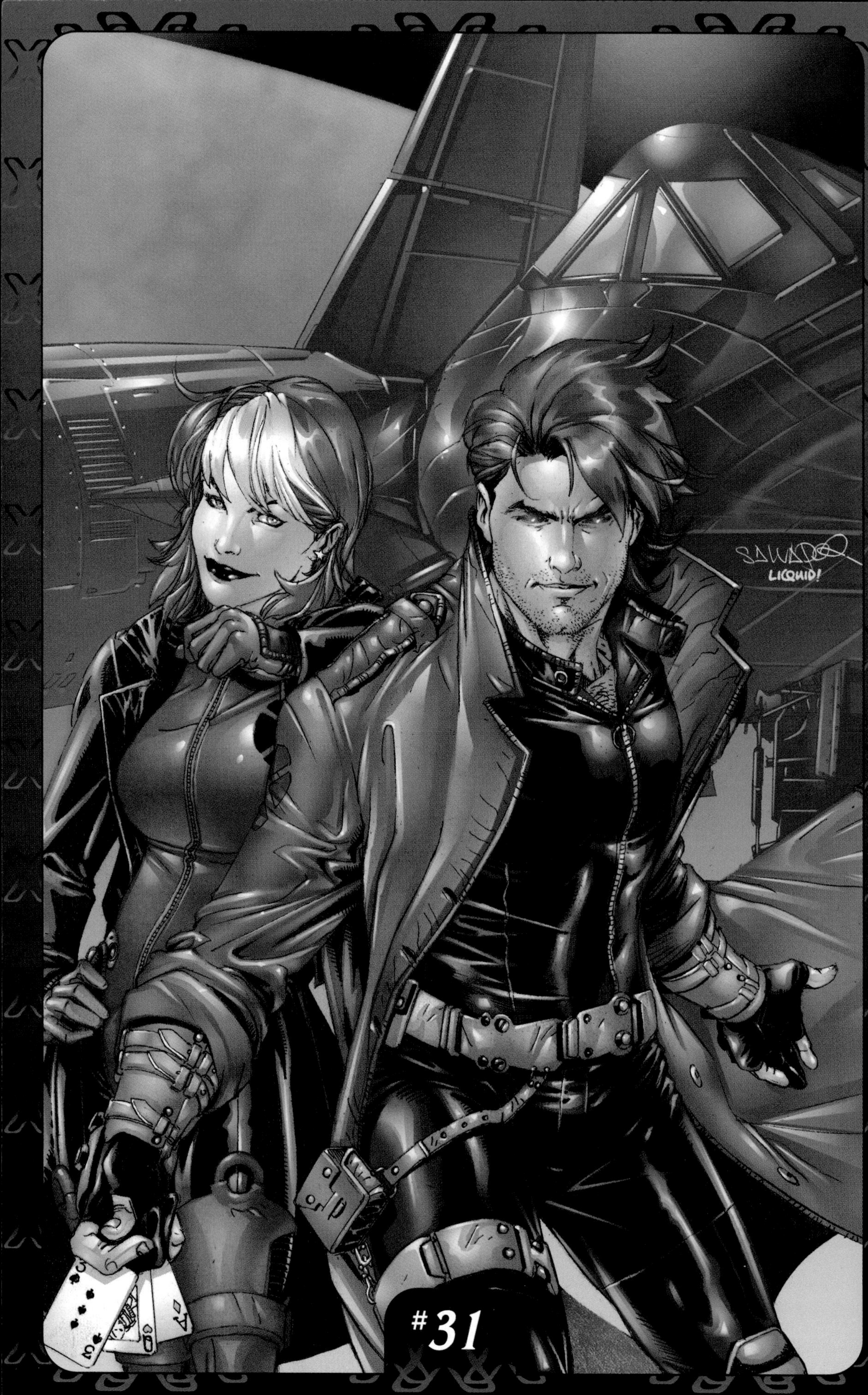
LIQUID!
#31

GAMBIT
(Remy LeBeau)
Explosive
Kinesis

ROGUE
Ability to Absorb
Powers and Psyches

BISHOP
Energy Caster

SAGE
Living Computer,
Cyberpath

CANNONBALL
(Sam Guthrie)
Flight and
Invulnerability

LILA CHENEY
Inter-stellar teleporter,
inter-stellar thief,
inter-stellar rock star.
Sam's sweetie!

STORM
(Ororo Munroe)
Weather
Manipulator;
Leader of
X-Treme X-Men

Months ago, aiding in the *X-Treme* team's successful defense of the world from an invading army, *Rogue* and *Gambit* were grievously *wounded*.

Despite a speedy initial recovery, both heroes have apparently *lost* their mutant powers.

As a result, Rogue has taken a *leave of absence* from the team, so that she and Gambit can spend some quality time together, without the constant pressures and responsibilities of their roles as *X-Men*...

...and discover, just like *normal* folks, what that means for their lives and their *relationship*.

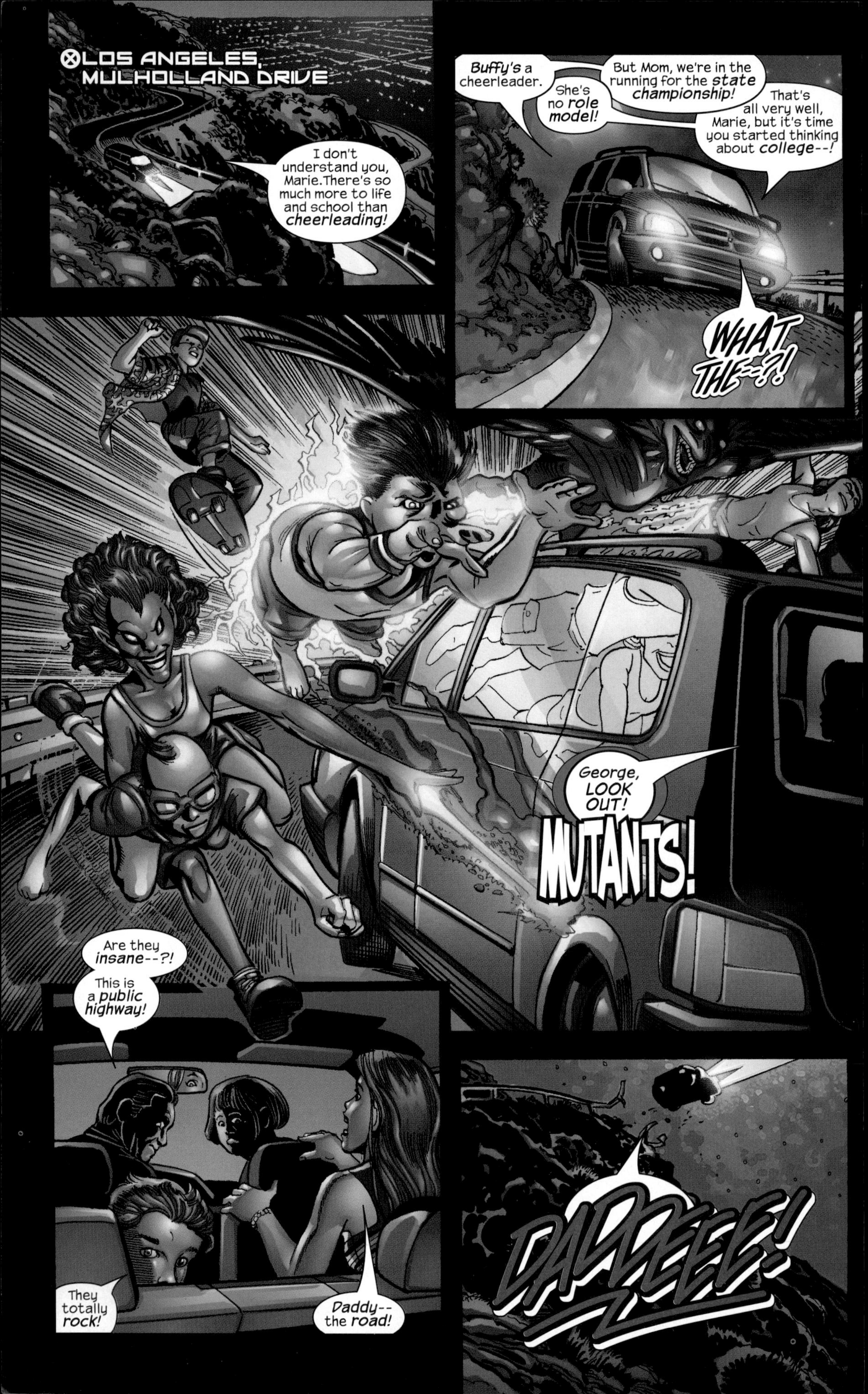
LOS ANGELES, MULHOLLAND DRIVE
I don't understand you, Marie. There's so much more to life and school than cheerleading!
Buffy's a cheerleader.
She's no role model!
But Mom, we're in the running for the state championship!
That's all very well, Marie, but it's time you started thinking about college--!
WHAT THE--?!
George, LOOK OUT!
MUTANTS!
Are they insane--?!
This is a public highway!
They totally rock!
Daddy-- the road!
DADDEEE!

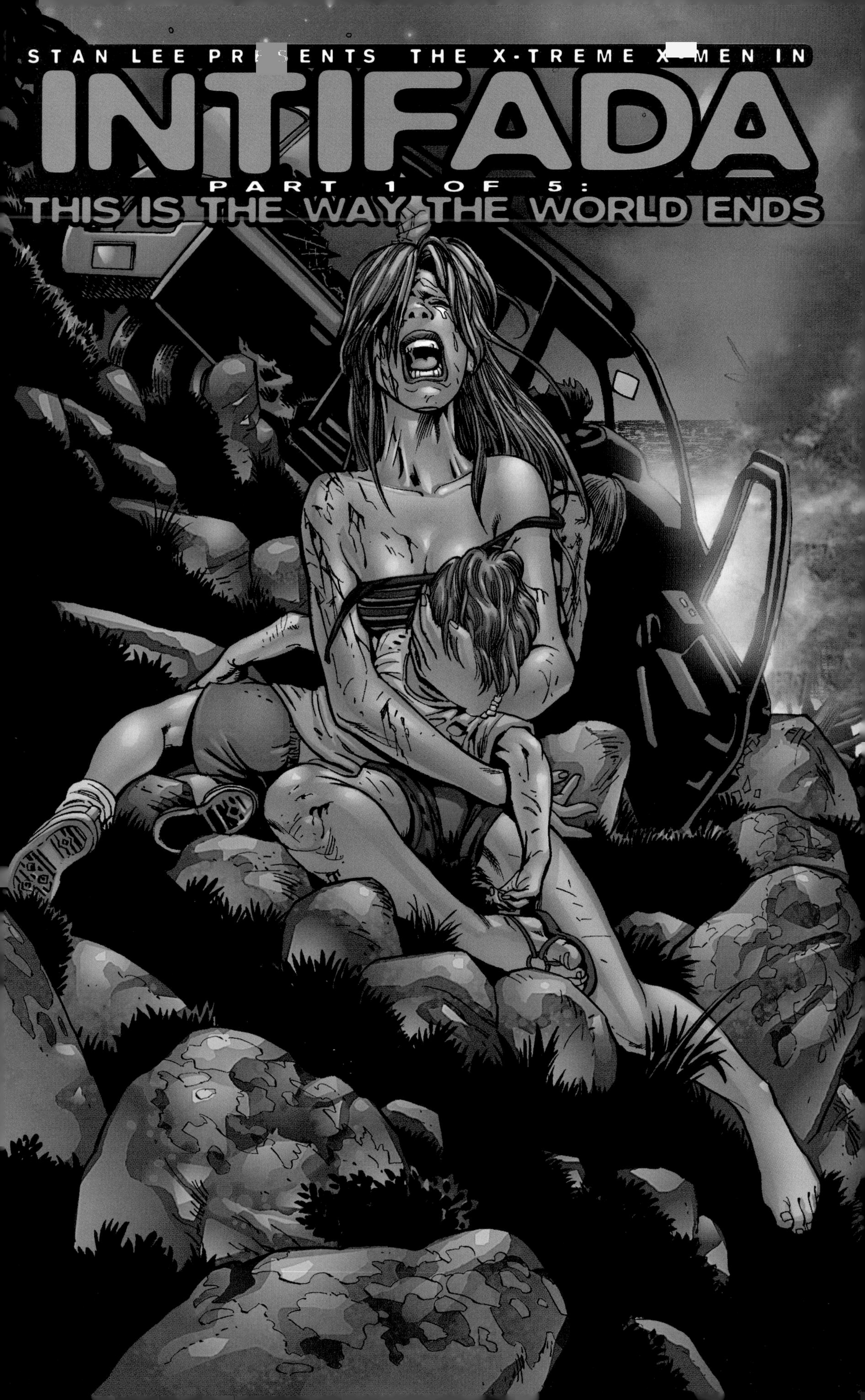
STAN LEE PRESENTS THE X-TREME X-MEN IN
INTIFADA
PART 1 OF 5:
THIS IS THE WAY THE WORLD ENDS

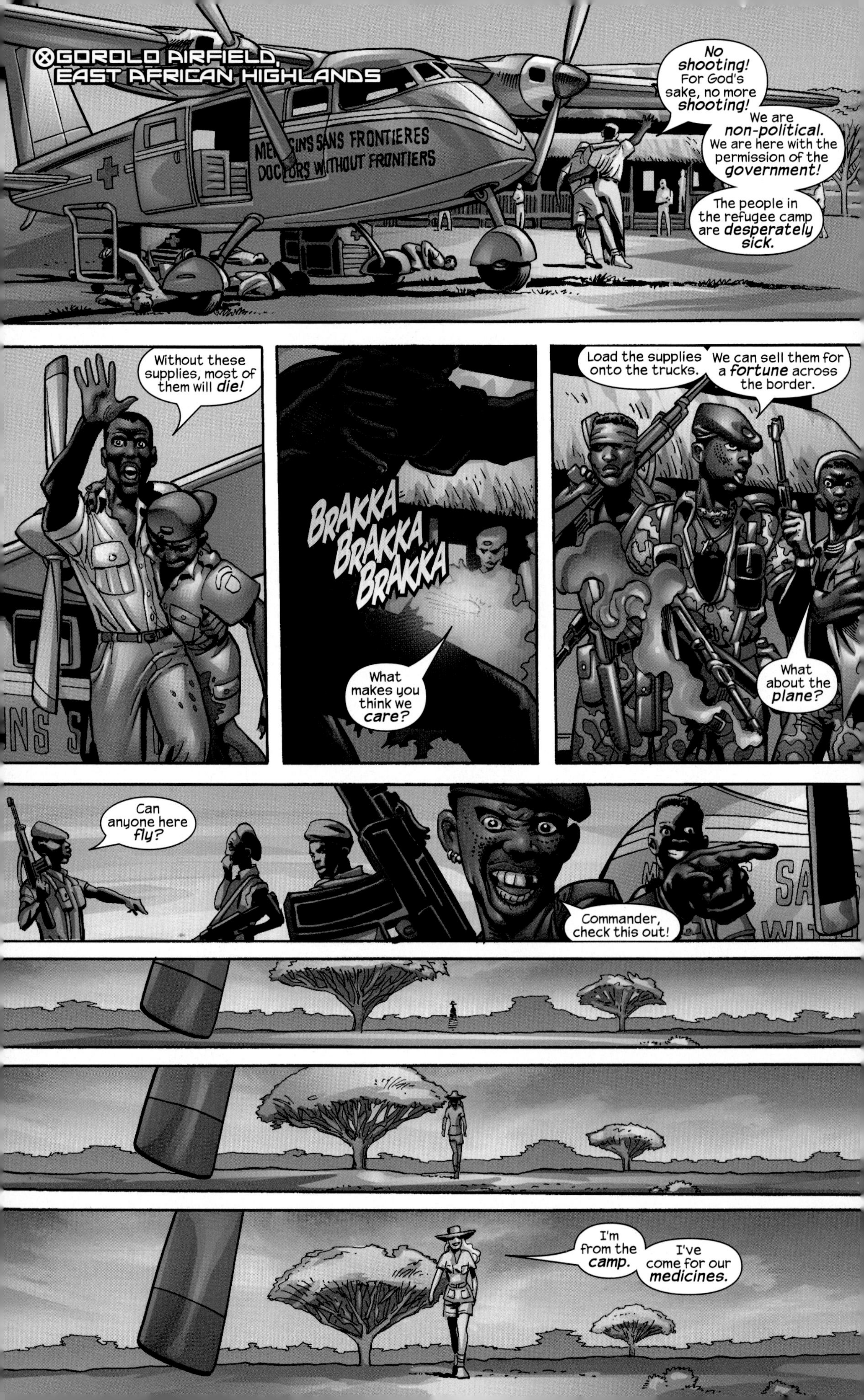
GOROLO AIRFIELD, EAST AFRICAN HIGHLANDS
MEDECINS SANS FRONTIERES
DOCTORS WITHOUT FRONTIERS
No shooting! For God's sake, no more shooting!
We are non-political. We are here with the permission of the government!
The people in the refugee camp are desperately sick.
Without these supplies, most of them will die!
BRAKKA BRAKKA BRAKKA
What makes you think we care?
Load the supplies onto the trucks.
We can sell them for a fortune across the border.
What about the plane?
Can anyone here fly?
Commander, check this out!
I'm from the camp.
I've come for our medicines.

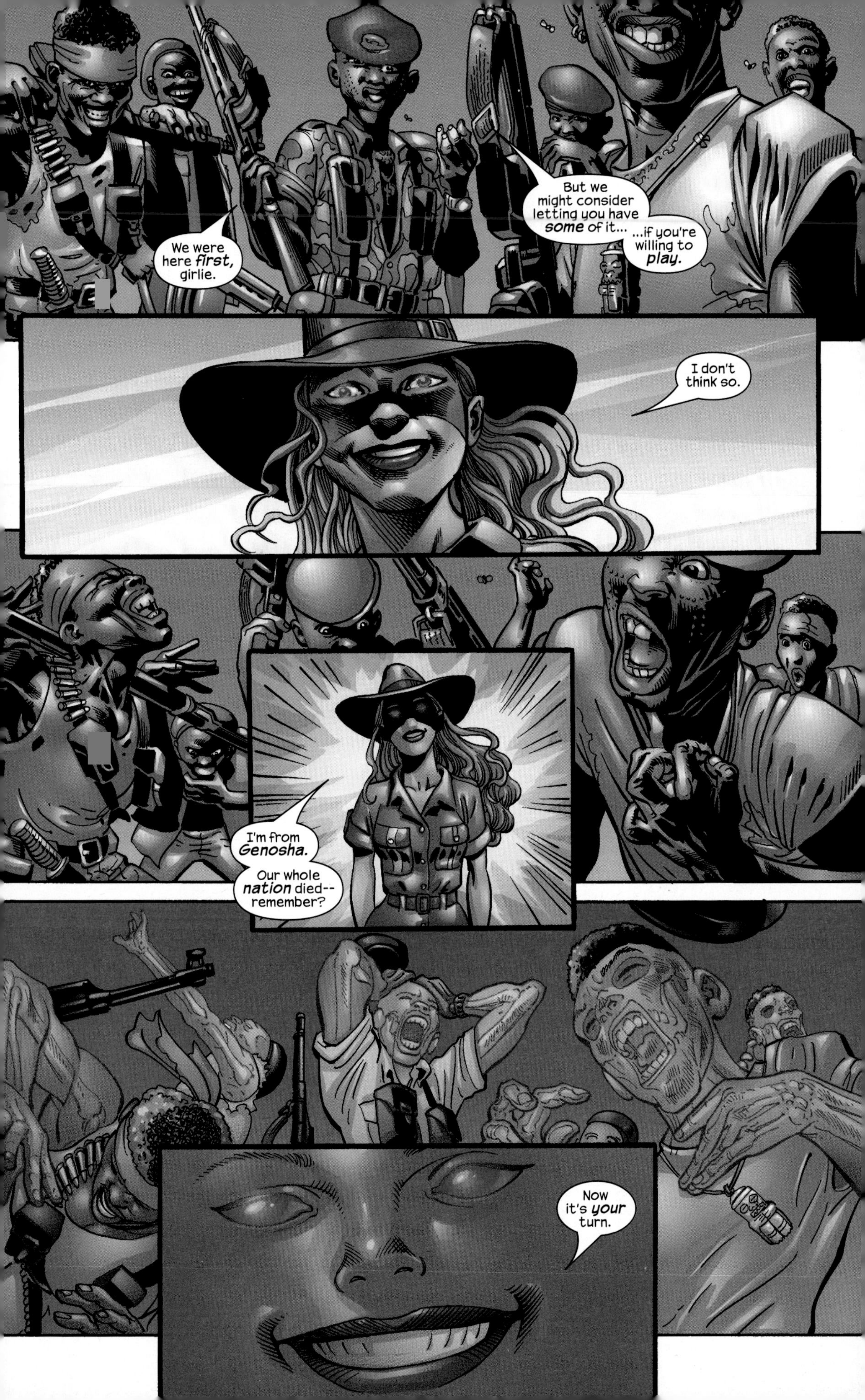
We were here *first,* girlie.
But we might consider letting you have *some* of it...
...if you're willing to *play.*
I don't think so.
I'm from *Genosha.*
Our whole *nation* died--remember?
Now it's *your* turn.

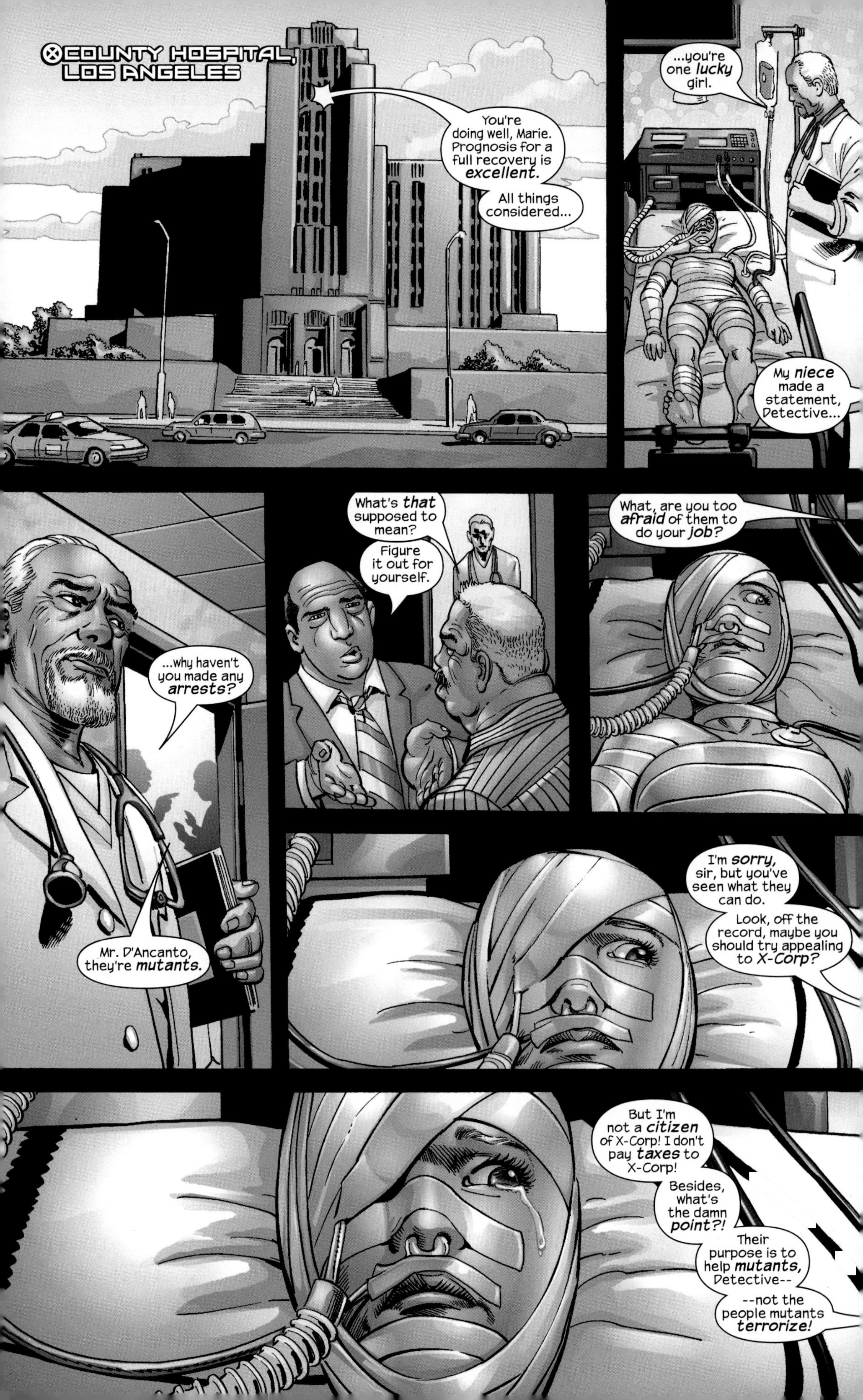
COUNTY HOSPITAL, LOS ANGELES
You're doing well, Marie. Prognosis for a full recovery is excellent.
All things considered...
...you're one lucky girl.
My niece made a statement, Detective...
...why haven't you made any arrests?
Mr. D'Ancanto, they're mutants.
What's that supposed to mean?
Figure it out for yourself.
What, are you too afraid of them to do your job?
I'm sorry, sir, but you've seen what they can do.
Look, off the record, maybe you should try appealing to X-Corp?
But I'm not a citizen of X-Corp! I don't pay taxes to X-Corp!
Besides, what's the damn point?!
Their purpose is to help mutants, Detective--
--not the people mutants terrorize!

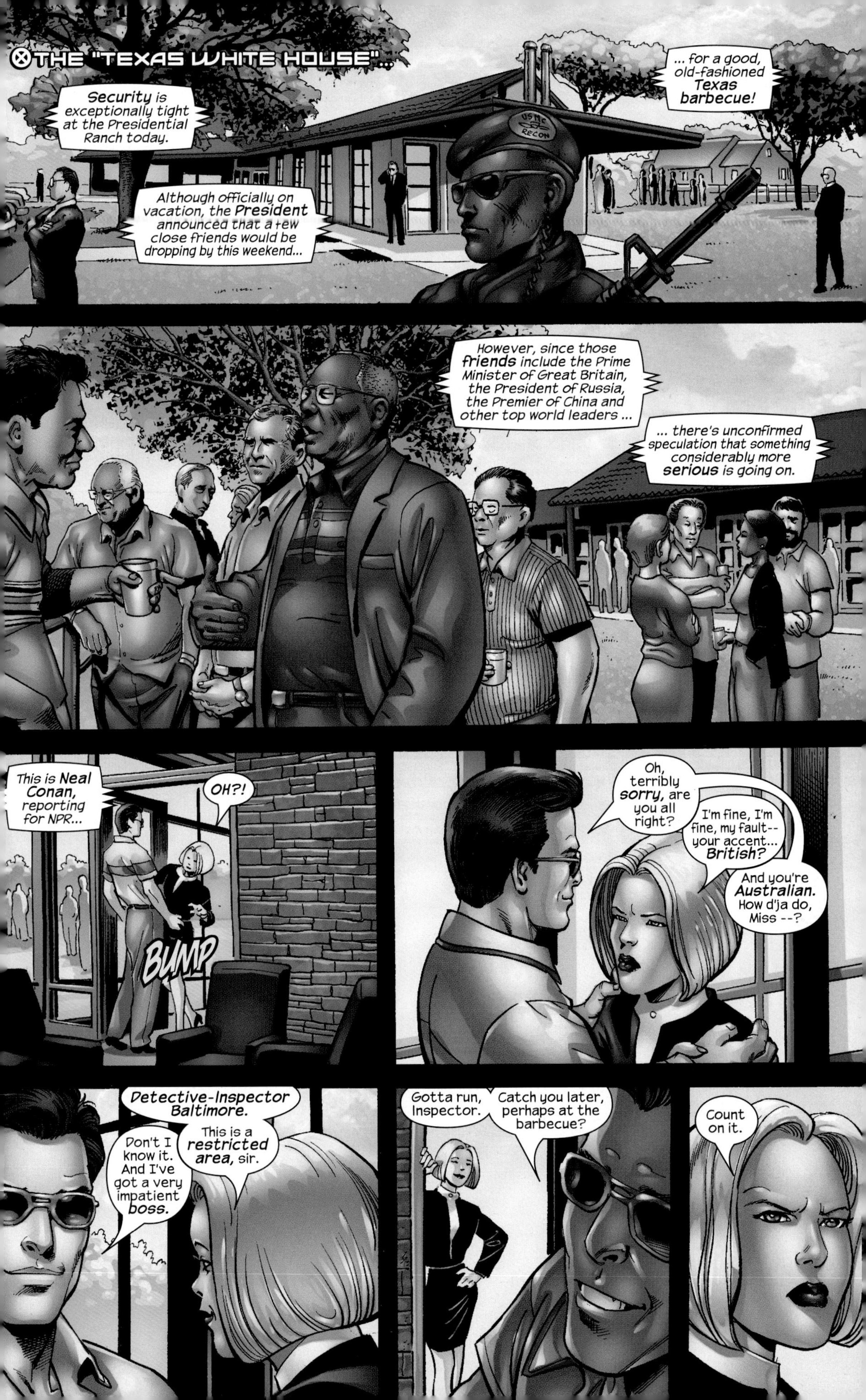

THE "TEXAS WHITE HOUSE"...
Security is exceptionally tight at the Presidential Ranch today.
Although officially on vacation, the President announced that a few close friends would be dropping by this weekend...
... for a good, old-fashioned Texas barbecue!
However, since those friends include the Prime Minister of Great Britain, the President of Russia, the Premier of China and other top world leaders ...
... there's unconfirmed speculation that something considerably more serious is going on.
This is Neal Conan, reporting for NPR...
OH?!
BUMP
Oh, terribly sorry, are you all right?
I'm fine, I'm fine, my fault-- your accent... British?
And you're Australian. How d'ja do, Miss --?
Detective-Inspector Baltimore.
This is a restricted area, sir.
Don't I know it. And I've got a very impatient boss.
Gotta run, Inspector.
Catch you later, perhaps at the barbecue?
Count on it.

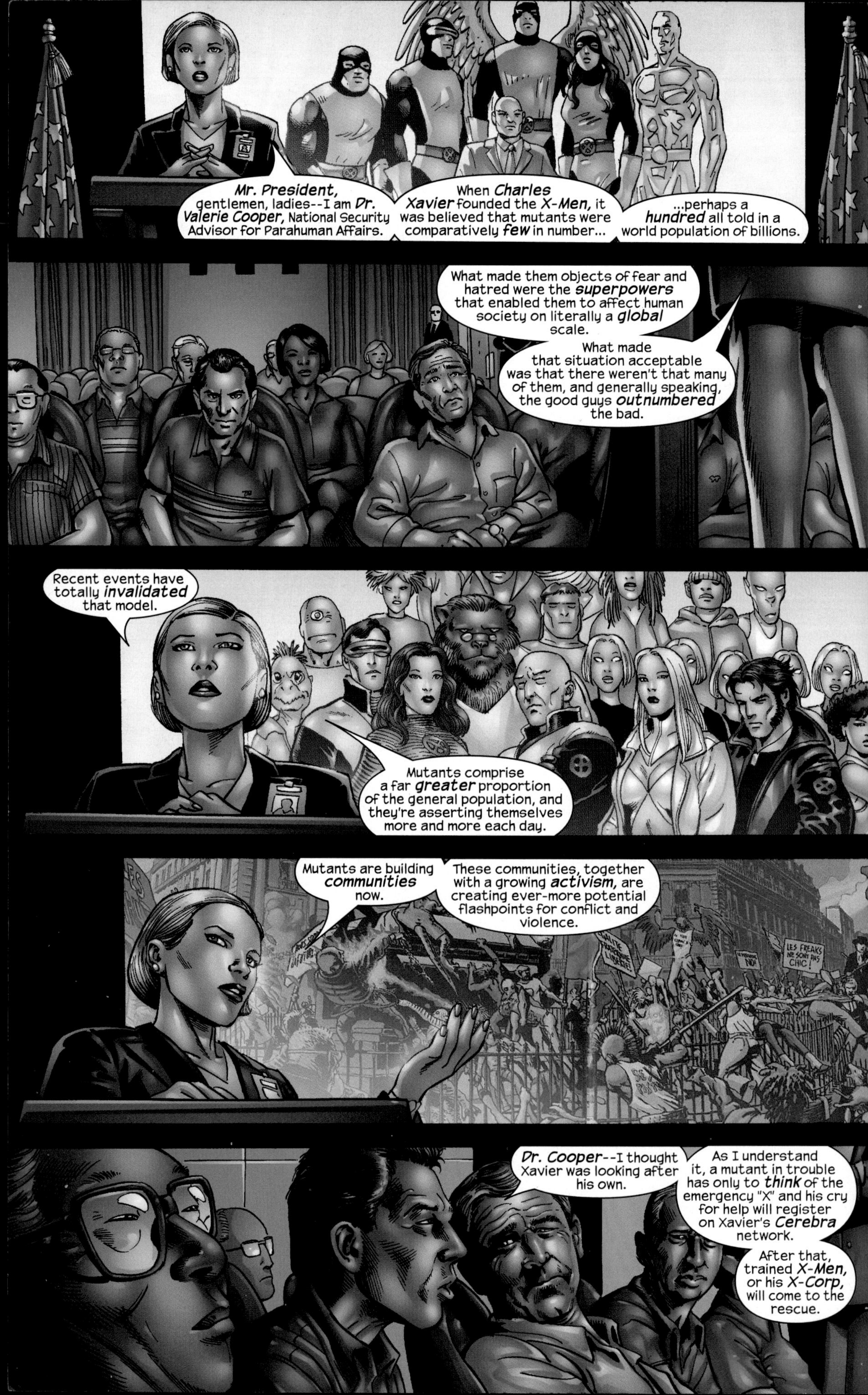
Mr. President, gentlemen, ladies--I am Dr. Valerie Cooper, National Security Advisor for Parahuman Affairs.
When Charles Xavier founded the X-Men, it was believed that mutants were comparatively few in number...
...perhaps a hundred all told in a world population of billions.
What made them objects of fear and hatred were the superpowers that enabled them to affect human society on literally a global scale.
What made that situation acceptable was that there weren't that many of them, and generally speaking, the good guys outnumbered the bad.
Recent events have totally invalidated that model.
Mutants comprise a far greater proportion of the general population, and they're asserting themselves more and more each day.
Mutants are building communities now.
These communities, together with a growing activism, are creating ever-more potential flashpoints for conflict and violence.
LES FREAKS NE SONT PAS CHIC!
Dr. Cooper--I thought Xavier was looking after his own.
As I understand it, a mutant in trouble has only to think of the emergency "X" and his cry for help will register on Xavier's Cerebra network.
After that, trained X-Men, or his X-Corp, will come to the rescue.

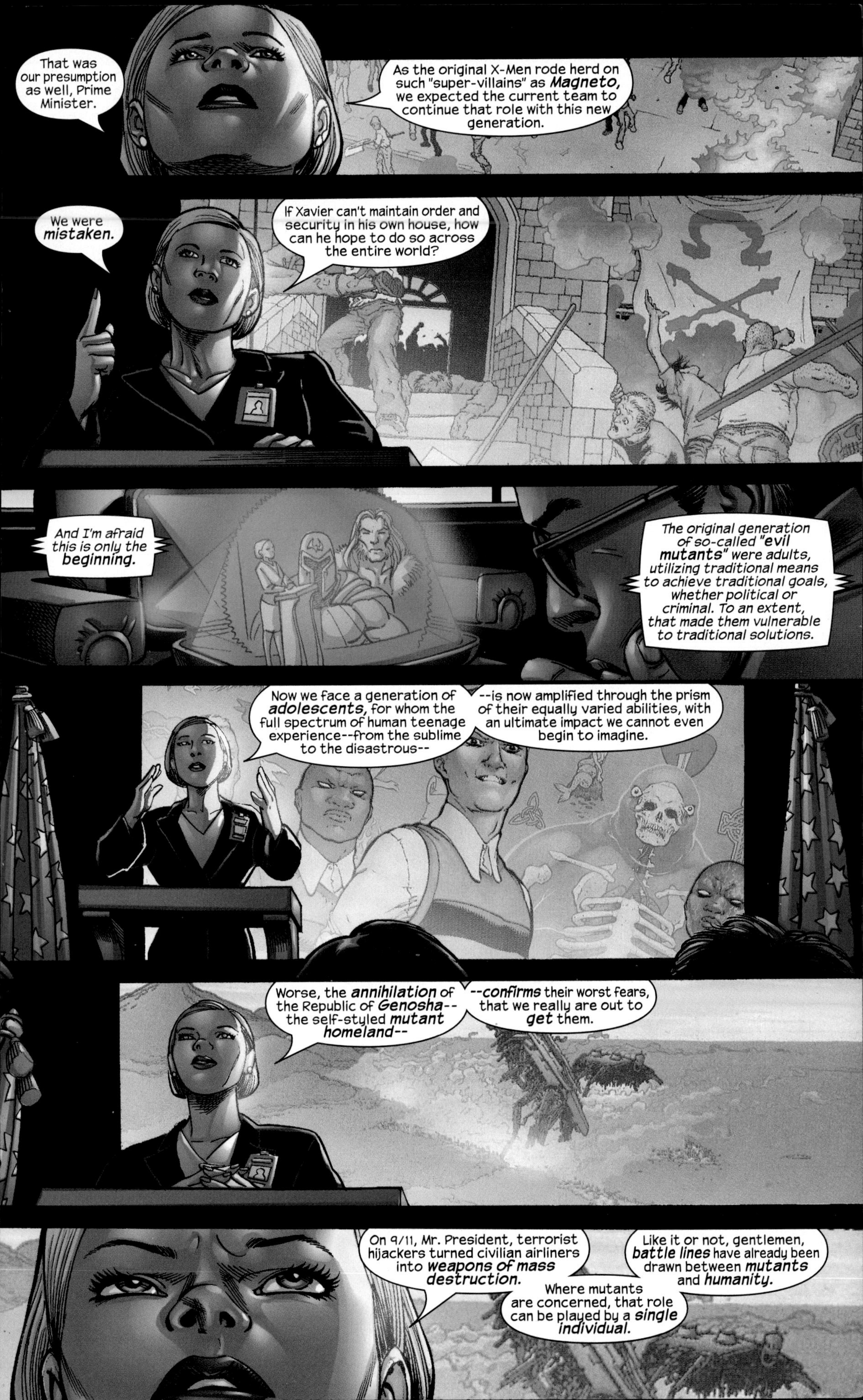

That was our presumption as well, Prime Minister.
As the original X-Men rode herd on such "super-villains" as *Magneto,* we expected the current team to continue that role with this new generation.
We were *mistaken.*
If Xavier can't maintain order and security in his own house, how can he hope to do so across the entire world?
And I'm afraid this is only the *beginning.*
The original generation of so-called *"evil mutants"* were adults, utilizing traditional means to achieve traditional goals, whether political or criminal. To an extent, that made them vulnerable to traditional solutions.
Now we face a generation of *adolescents,* for whom the full spectrum of human teenage experience--from the sublime to the disastrous--
--is now amplified through the prism of their equally varied abilities, with an ultimate impact we cannot even begin to imagine.
Worse, the *annihilation* of the Republic of *Genosha*--the self-styled *mutant homeland*--
--*confirms* their worst fears, that we really are out to *get* them.
On 9/11, Mr. President, terrorist hijackers turned civilian airliners into *weapons of mass destruction.*
Where mutants are concerned, that role can be played by a *single individual.*
Like it or not, gentlemen, *battle lines* have already been drawn between *mutants* and *humanity.*

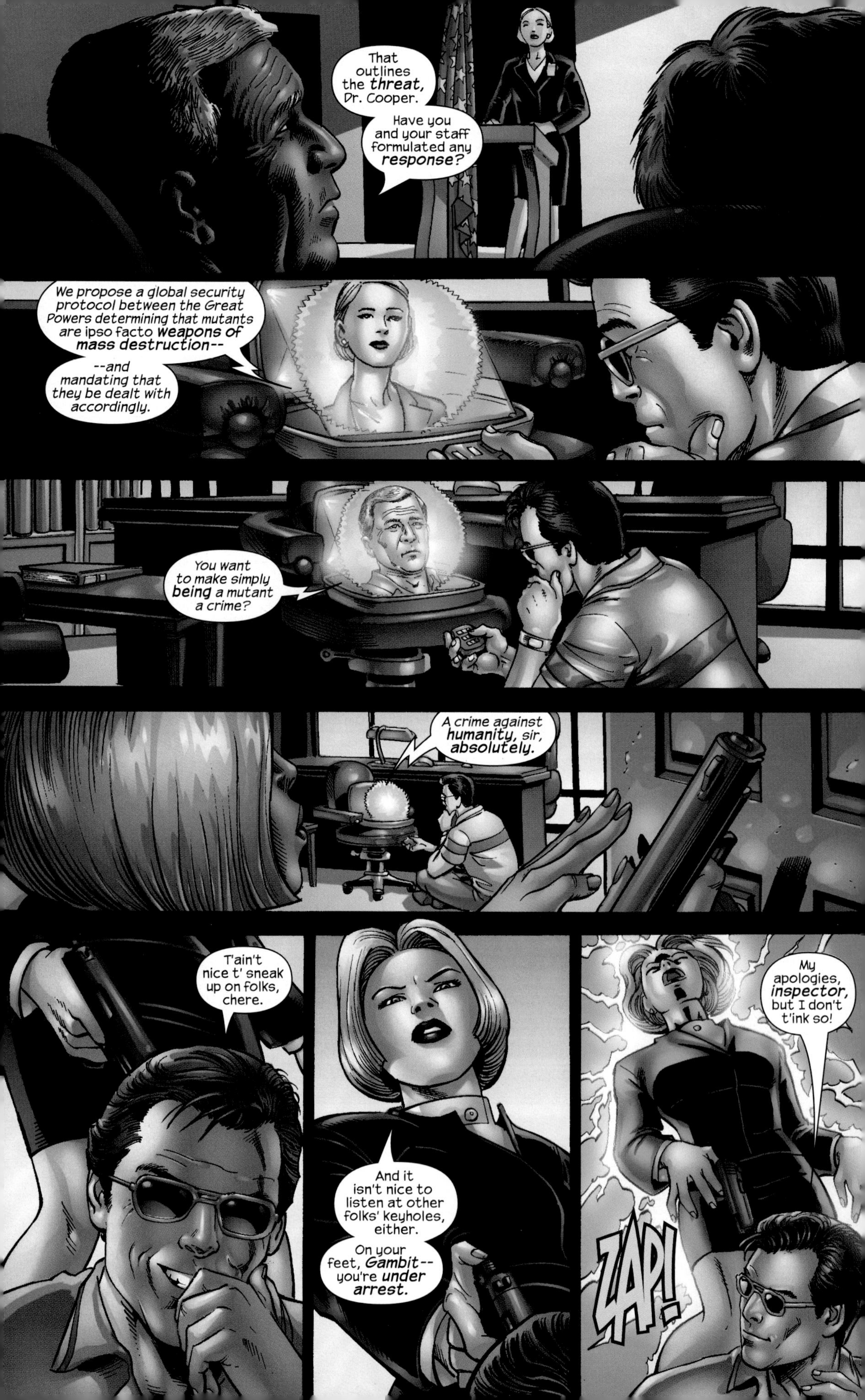
That outlines the threat, Dr. Cooper.
Have you and your staff formulated any response?
We propose a global security protocol between the Great Powers determining that mutants are ipso facto weapons of mass destruction--
--and mandating that they be dealt with accordingly.
You want to make simply being a mutant a crime?
A crime against humanity, sir, absolutely.
T'ain't nice t' sneak up on folks, chere.
And it isn't nice to listen at other folks' keyholes, either.
On your feet, Gambit-- you're under arrest.
My apologies, inspector, but I don't t'ink so!
ZAP!

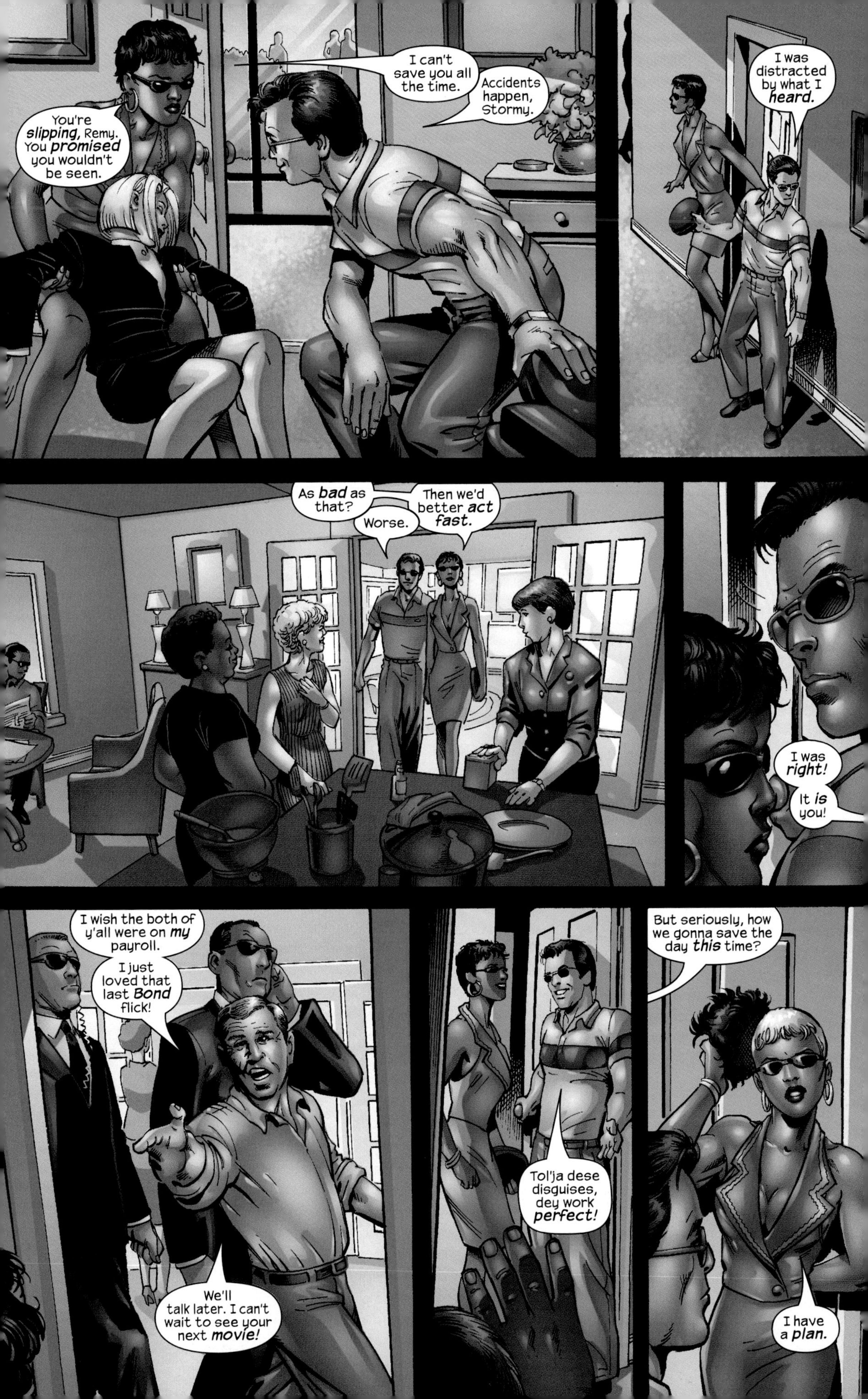

You're slipping, Remy. You promised you wouldn't be seen.
I can't save you all the time.
Accidents happen, Stormy.
I was distracted by what I heard.
As bad as that?
Worse.
Then we'd better act fast.
I was right!
It is you!
I wish the both of y'all were on my payroll.
I just loved that last Bond flick!
We'll talk later. I can't wait to see your next movie!
Tol'ja dese disguises, dey work perfect!
But seriously, how we gonna save the day this time?
I have a plan.

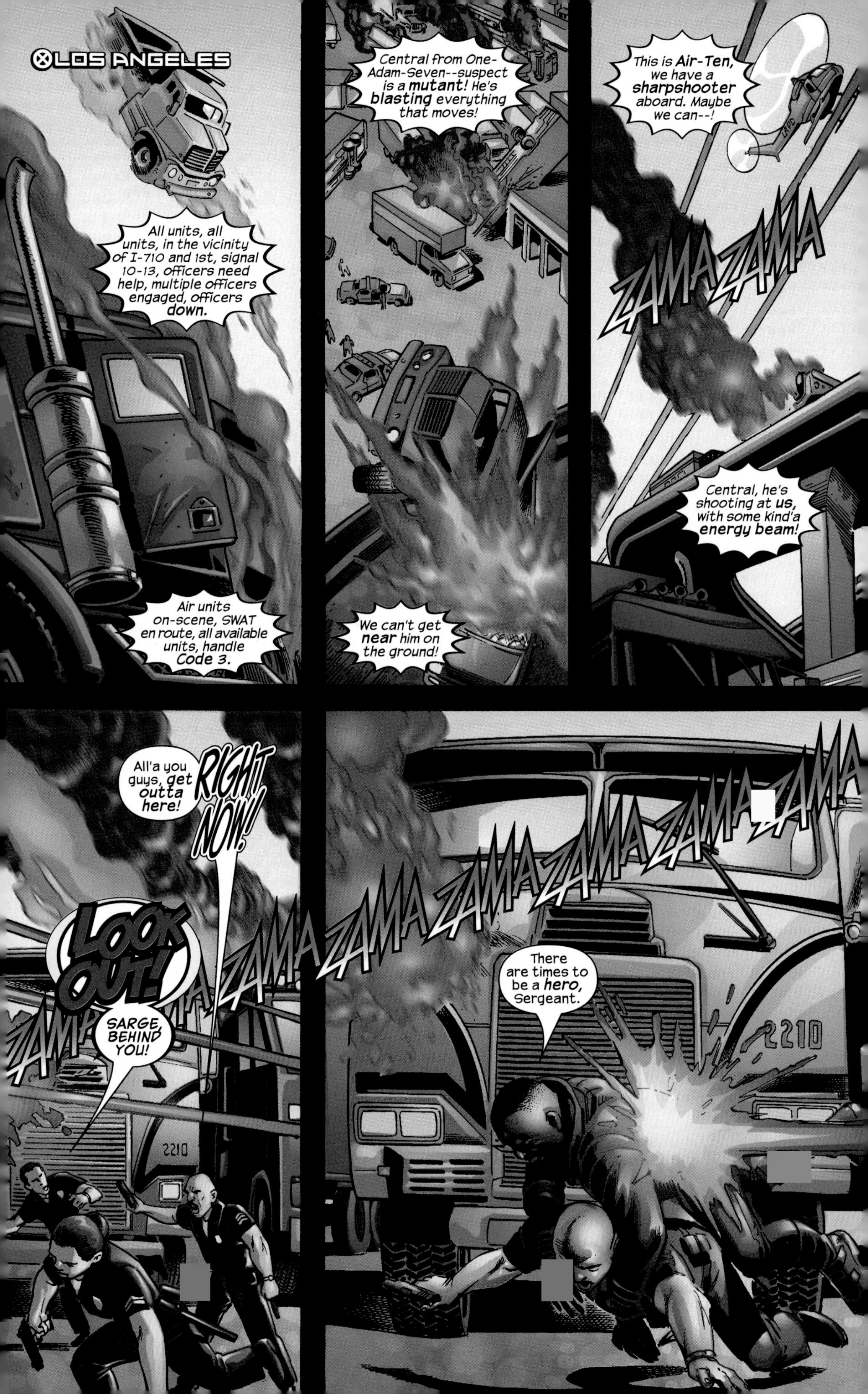

LOS ANGELES
All units, all units, in the vicinity of I-710 and 1st, signal 10-13, officers need help, multiple officers engaged, officers down.
Air units on-scene, SWAT en route, all available units, handle Code 3.
Central from One-Adam-Seven--suspect is a mutant! He's blasting everything that moves!
We can't get near him on the ground!
This is Air-Ten, we have a sharpshooter aboard. Maybe we can--!
ZAMAZAMA
Central, he's shooting at us, with some kind'a energy beam!
All'a you guys, get outta here!
RIGHT NOW!
LOOK OUT!
SARGE, BEHIND YOU!
ZAMAZAMAZAMAZAMAZAMAZAMAZAMAZAMA
2210
There are times to be a hero, Sergeant.
2210

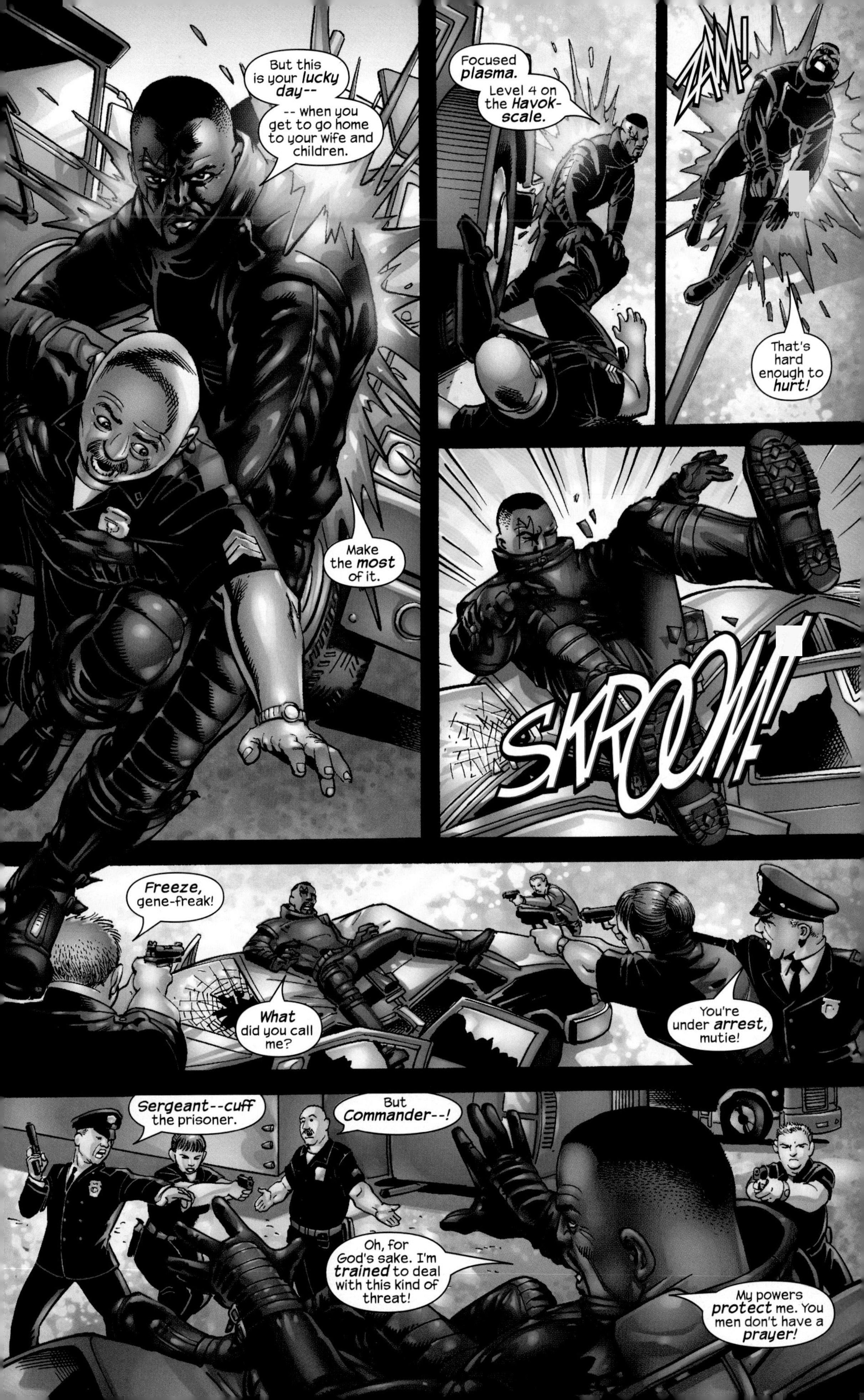
But this is your lucky day--
-- when you get to go home to your wife and children.
Make the most of it.
Focused plasma.
Level 4 on the Havok-scale.
ZAM!
That's hard enough to hurt!
SKROOM!
Freeze, gene-freak!
What did you call me?
You're under arrest, mutie!
Sergeant--cuff the prisoner.
But Commander--!
Oh, for God's sake. I'm trained to deal with this kind of threat!
My powers protect me. You men don't have a prayer!

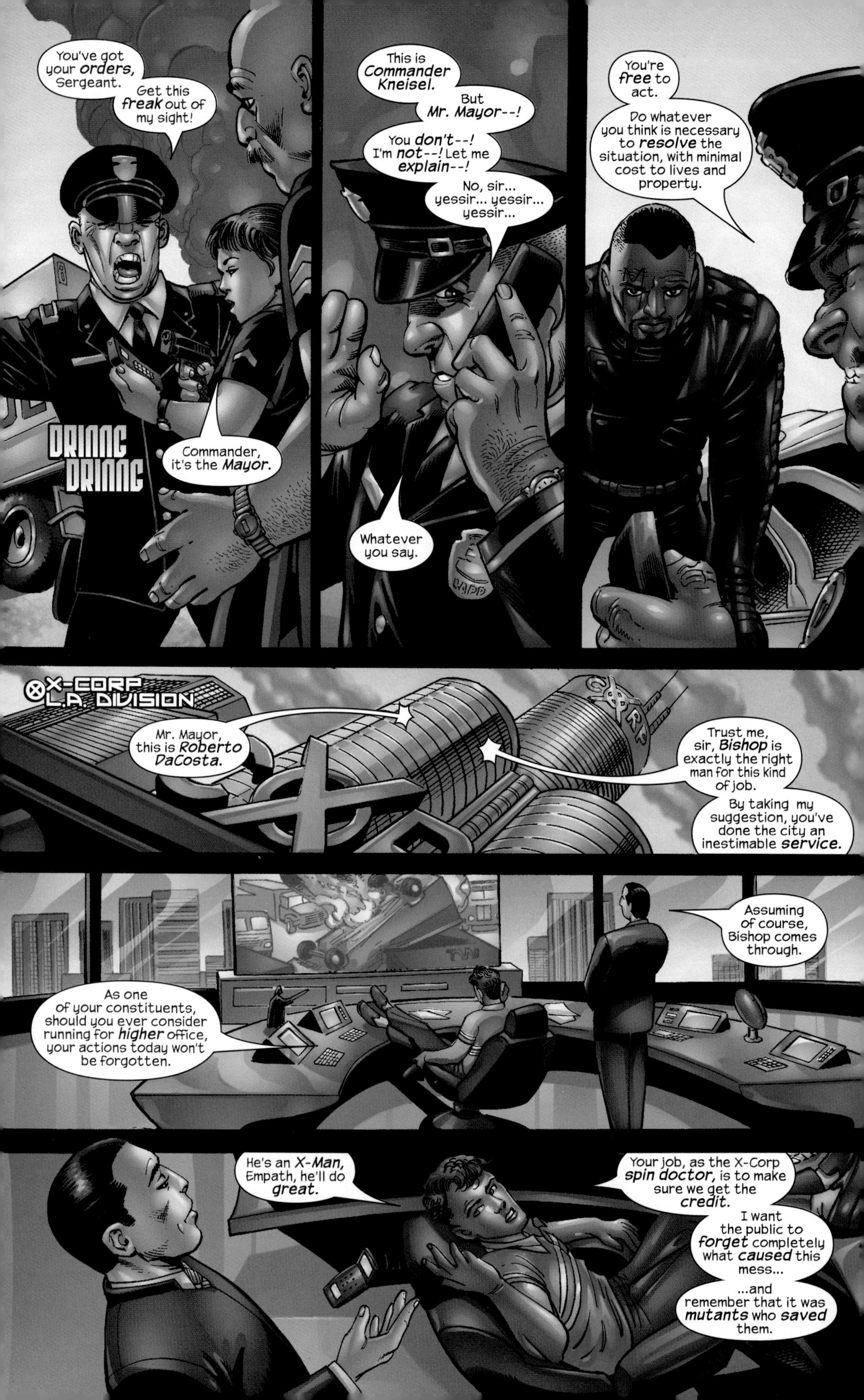
You've got your orders, Sergeant.
Get this freak out of my sight!
DRINNG DRINNG
Commander, it's the Mayor.
This is Commander Kneisel.
But Mr. Mayor--!
You don't--! I'm not--! Let me explain--!
No, sir... yessir... yessir... yessir...
Whatever you say.
You're free to act.
Do whatever you think is necessary to resolve the situation, with minimal cost to lives and property.
X-CORP L.A. DIVISION
Mr. Mayor, this is Roberto DaCosta.
Trust me, sir, Bishop is exactly the right man for this kind of job.
By taking my suggestion, you've done the city an inestimable service.
As one of your constituents, should you ever consider running for higher office, your actions today won't be forgotten.
Assuming of course, Bishop comes through.
He's an X-Man, Empath, he'll do great.
Your job, as the X-Corp spin doctor, is to make sure we get the credit.
I want the public to forget completely what caused this mess...
...and remember that it was mutants who saved them.

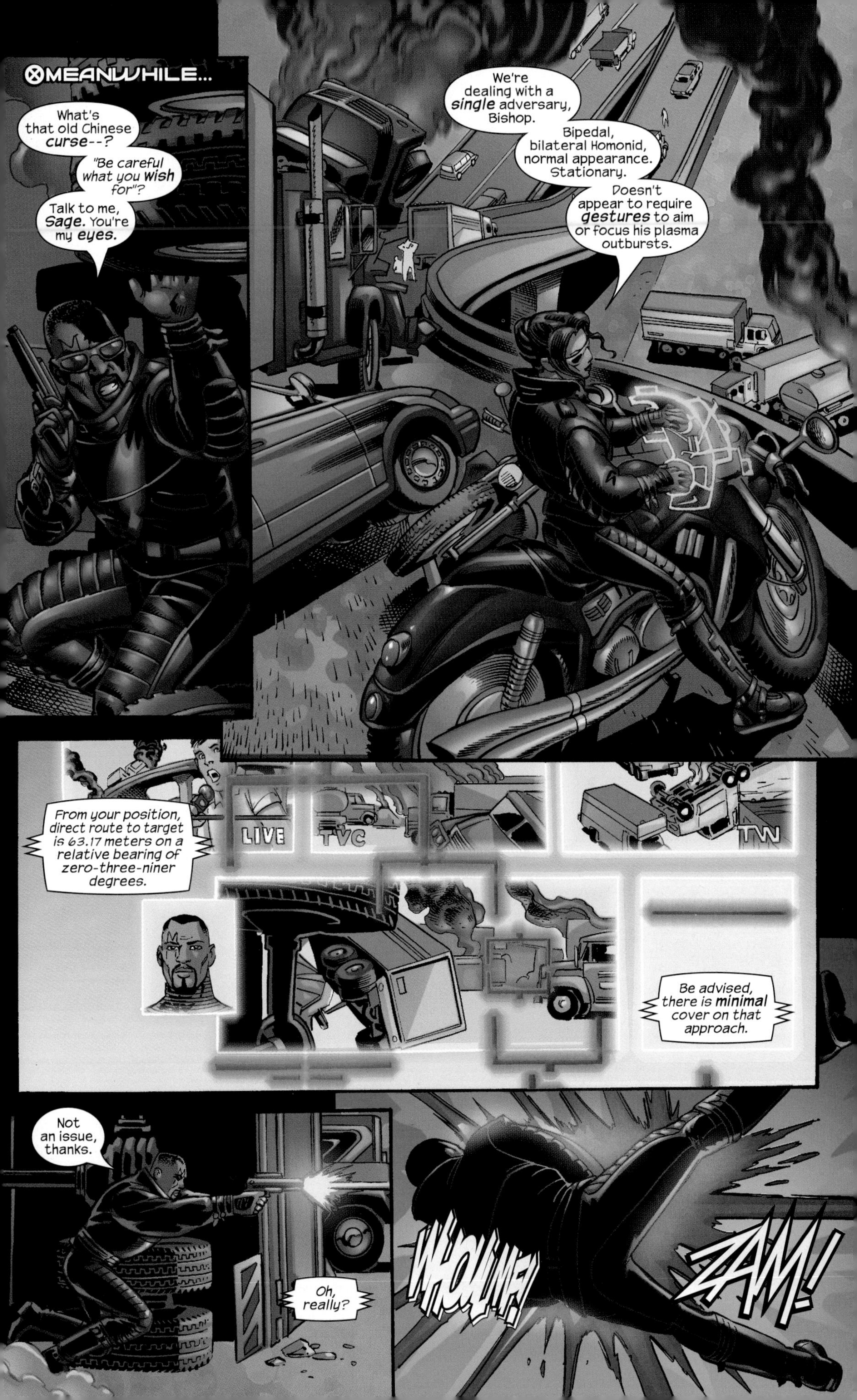
MEANWHILE...
What's that old Chinese curse--?
"Be careful what you wish for"?
Talk to me, Sage. You're my eyes.
We're dealing with a single adversary, Bishop.
Bipedal, bilateral Homonid, normal appearance. Stationary.
Doesn't appear to require gestures to aim or focus his plasma outbursts.
LIVE
TVC
TW
From your position, direct route to target is 63.17 meters on a relative bearing of zero-three-niner degrees.
Be advised, there is minimal cover on that approach.
Not an issue, thanks.
Oh, really?
WHOOMF!
ZAM!

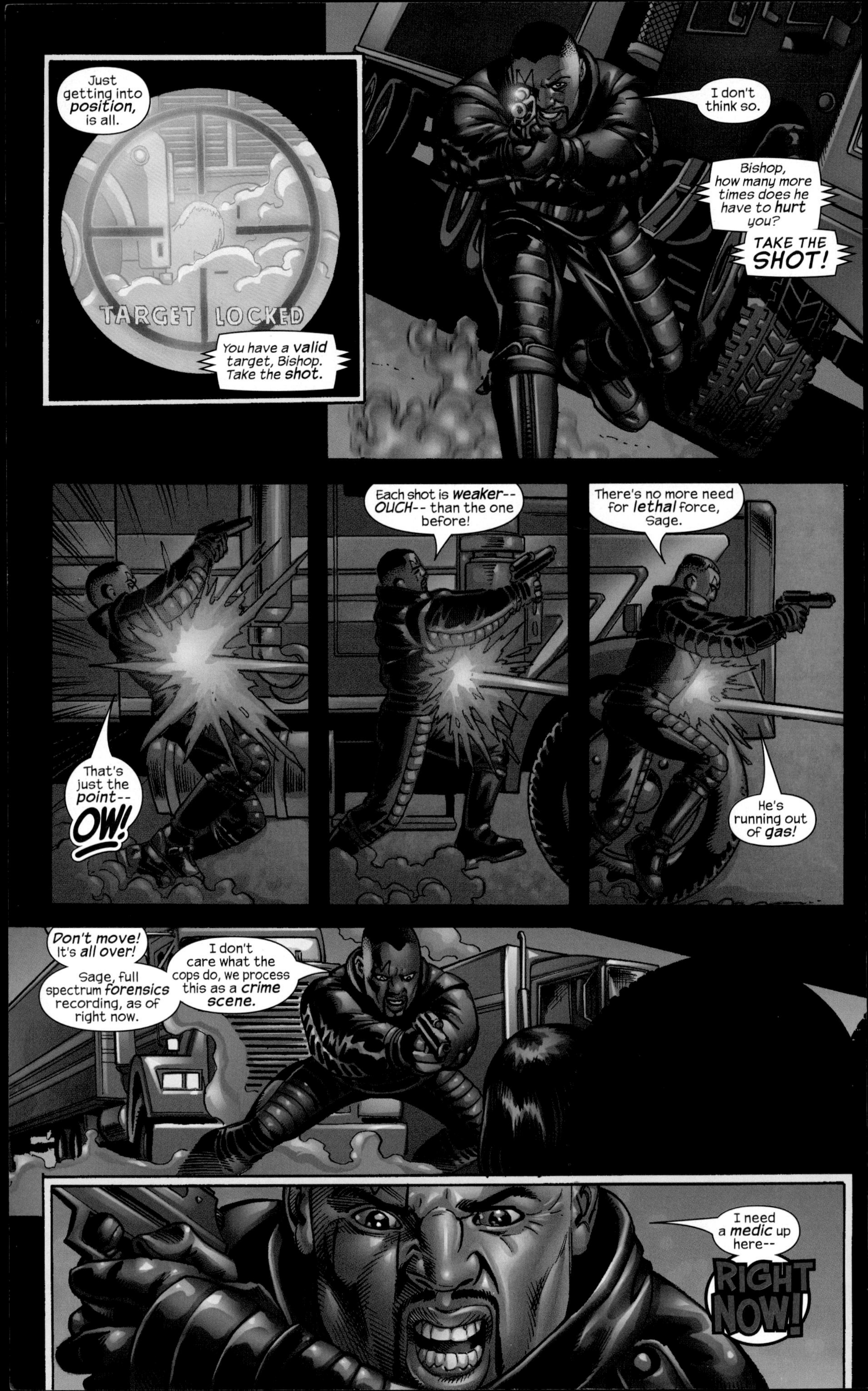

Just getting into position, is all.
TARGET LOCKED
You have a valid target, Bishop. Take the shot.
I don't think so.
Bishop, how many more times does he have to hurt you?
TAKE THE SHOT!
That's just the point--
OW!
Each shot is weaker-- OUCH-- than the one before!
There's no more need for lethal force, Sage.
He's running out of gas!
Don't move! It's all over!
Sage, full spectrum forensics recording, as of right now.
I don't care what the cops do, we process this as a crime scene.
I need a medic up here--
RIGHT NOW!

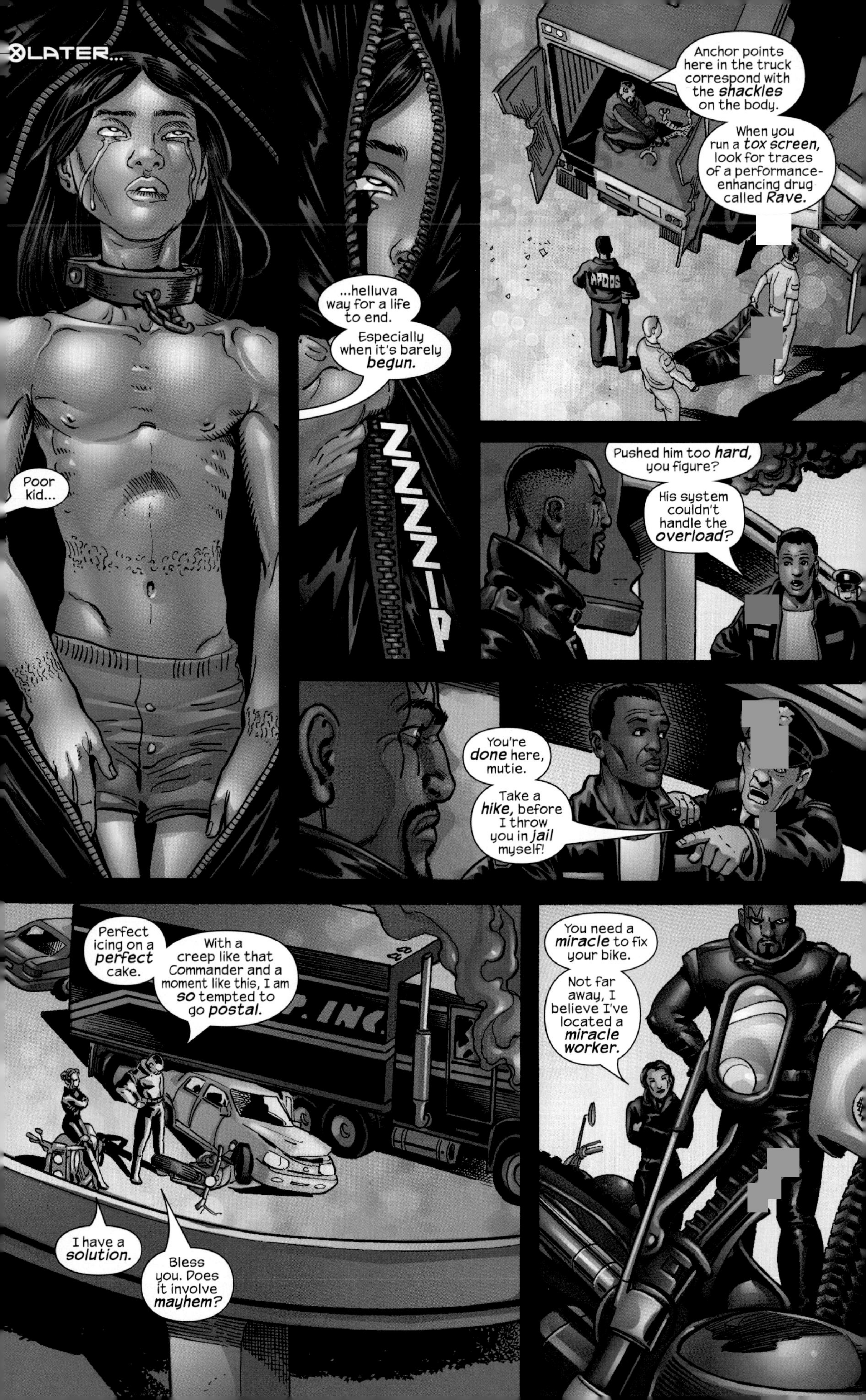
LATER...
Poor kid...
...helluva way for a life to end.
Especially when it's barely begun.
ZZZZIP
Anchor points here in the truck correspond with the shackles on the body.
When you run a tox screen, look for traces of a performance-enhancing drug called Rave.
Pushed him too hard, you figure?
His system couldn't handle the overload?
You're done here, mutie.
Take a hike, before I throw you in jail myself!
Perfect icing on a perfect cake.
With a creep like that Commander and a moment like this, I am so tempted to go postal.
I have a solution.
Bless you. Does it involve mayhem?
You need a miracle to fix your bike.
Not far away, I believe I've located a miracle worker.

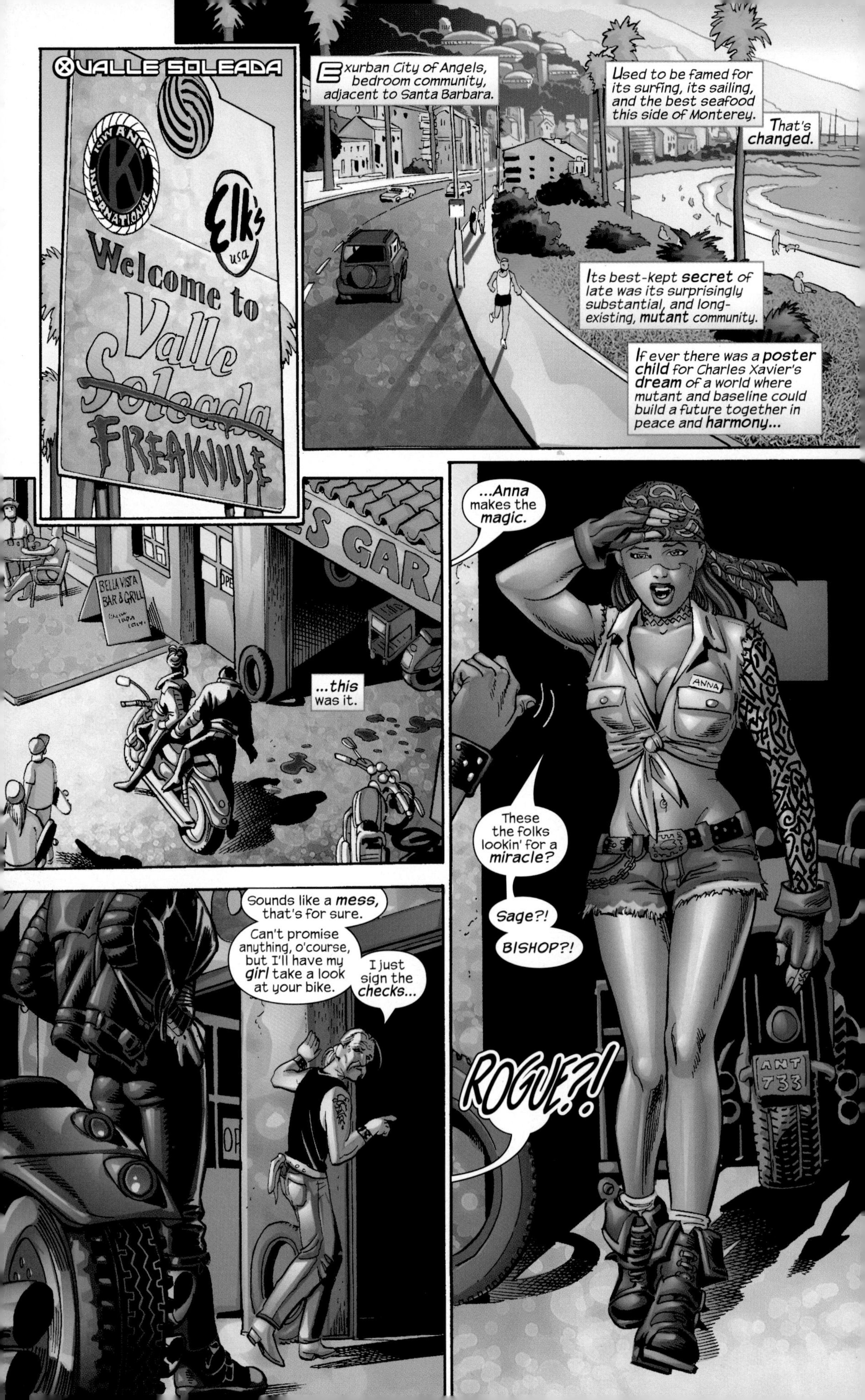
VALLE SOLEADA
KIWANIS INTERNATIONAL
Elk's usa
Welcome to Valle Soleada
FREAKVILLE
Exurban City of Angels, bedroom community, adjacent to Santa Barbara.
Used to be famed for its surfing, its sailing, and the best seafood this side of Monterey.
That's changed.
Its best-kept secret of late was its surprisingly substantial, and long-existing, mutant community.
If ever there was a poster child for Charles Xavier's dream of a world where mutant and baseline could build a future together in peace and harmony...
BELLA VISTA BAR & GRILL
...this was it.
Sounds like a mess, that's for sure.
Can't promise anything, o'course, but I'll have my girl take a look at your bike.
I just sign the checks...
...Anna makes the magic.
ANNA
These the folks lookin' for a miracle?
Sage?!
BISHOP?!
ROGUE?!
ANT 733

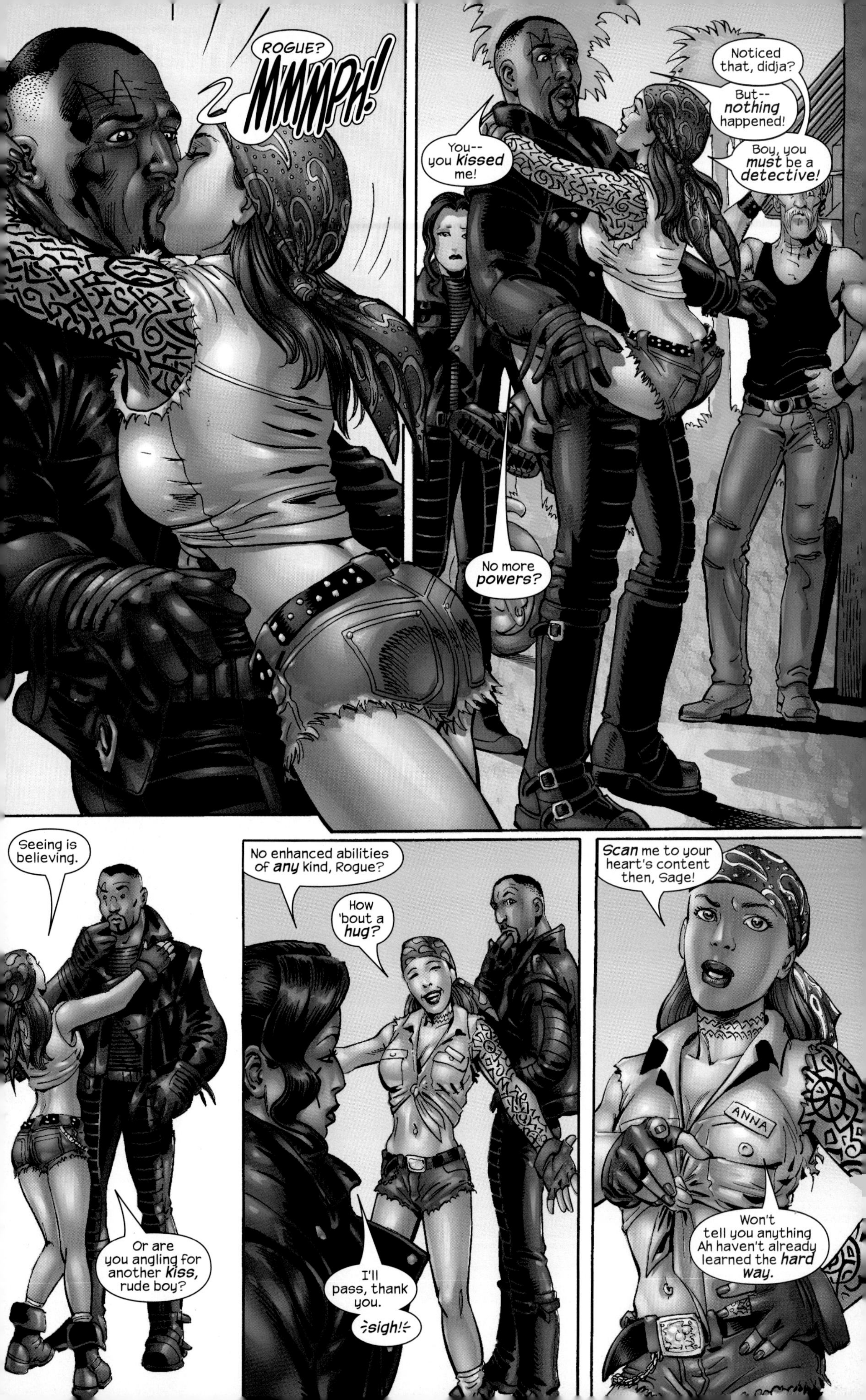
ROGUE?
MMMPH!
You--
you kissed
me!
Noticed
that, didja?
But--
nothing
happened!
Boy, you
must be a
detective!
No more
powers?
Seeing is
believing.
Or are
you angling for
another kiss,
rude boy?
No enhanced abilities
of any kind, Rogue?
How
'bout a
hug?
I'll
pass, thank
you.
sigh!
Scan me to your
heart's content
then, Sage!
ANNA
Won't
tell you anything
Ah haven't already
learned the hard
way.

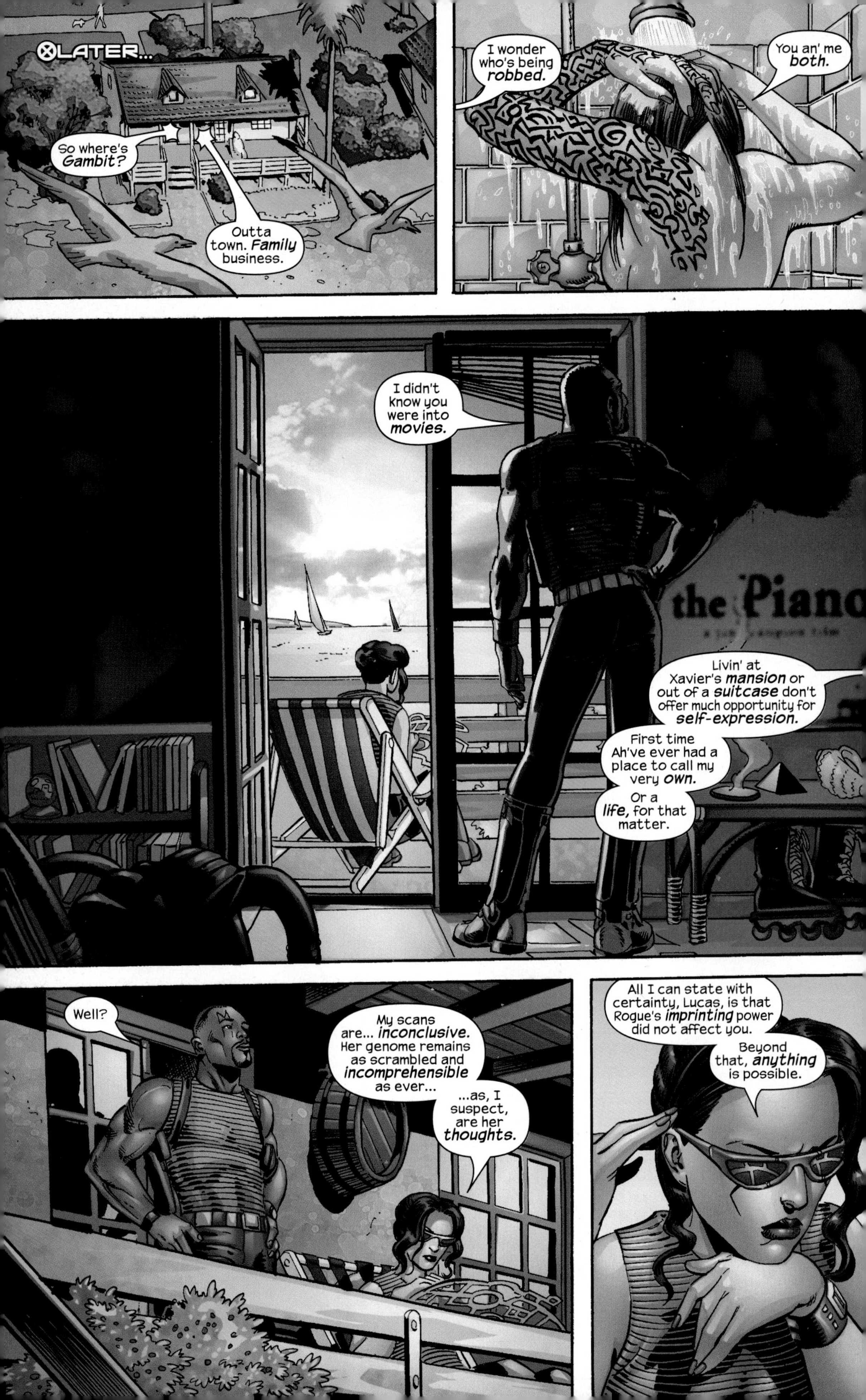
LATER...
So where's Gambit?
Outta town. Family business.
I wonder who's being robbed.
You an' me both.
I didn't know you were into movies.
the Piano
Livin' at Xavier's mansion or out of a suitcase don't offer much opportunity for self-expression.
First time Ah've ever had a place to call my very own.
Or a life, for that matter.
Well?
My scans are... inconclusive. Her genome remains as scrambled and incomprehensible as ever...
...as, I suspect, are her thoughts.
All I can state with certainty, Lucas, is that Rogue's imprinting power did not affect you.
Beyond that, anything is possible.

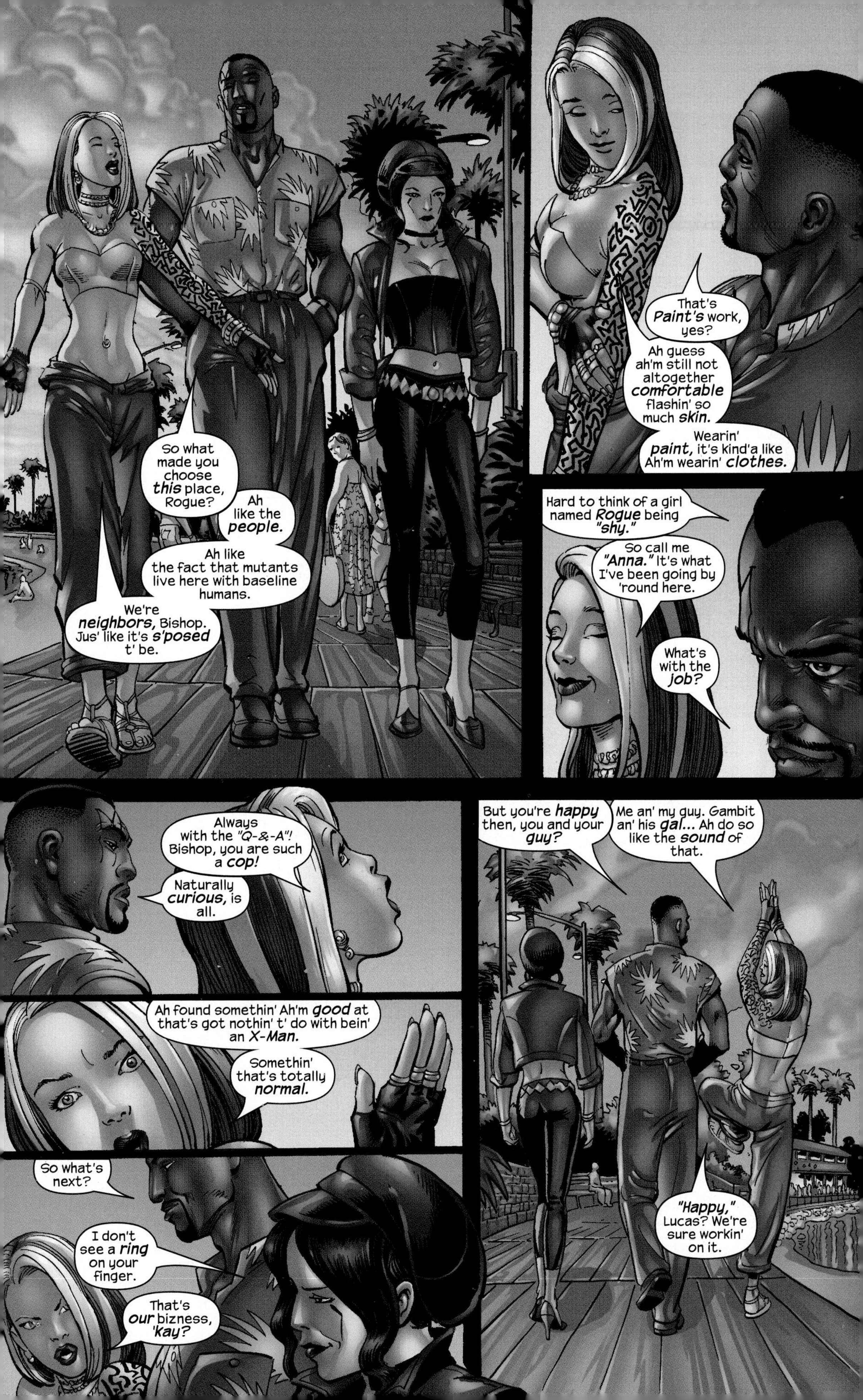
So what made you choose this place, Rogue?
Ah like the people.
Ah like the fact that mutants live here with baseline humans.
We're neighbors, Bishop. Jus' like it's s'posed t' be.
That's Paint's work, yes?
Ah guess ah'm still not altogether comfortable flashin' so much skin.
Wearin' paint, it's kind'a like Ah'm wearin' clothes.
Hard to think of a girl named Rogue being "shy."
So call me "Anna." It's what I've been going by 'round here.
What's with the job?
Always with the "Q-&-A"! Bishop, you are such a cop!
Naturally curious, is all.
Ah found somethin' Ah'm good at that's got nothin' t' do with bein' an X-Man.
Somethin' that's totally normal.
So what's next?
I don't see a ring on your finger.
That's our bizness, 'kay?
But you're happy then, you and your guy?
Me an' my guy. Gambit an' his gal... Ah do so like the sound of that.
"Happy," Lucas? We're sure workin' on it.

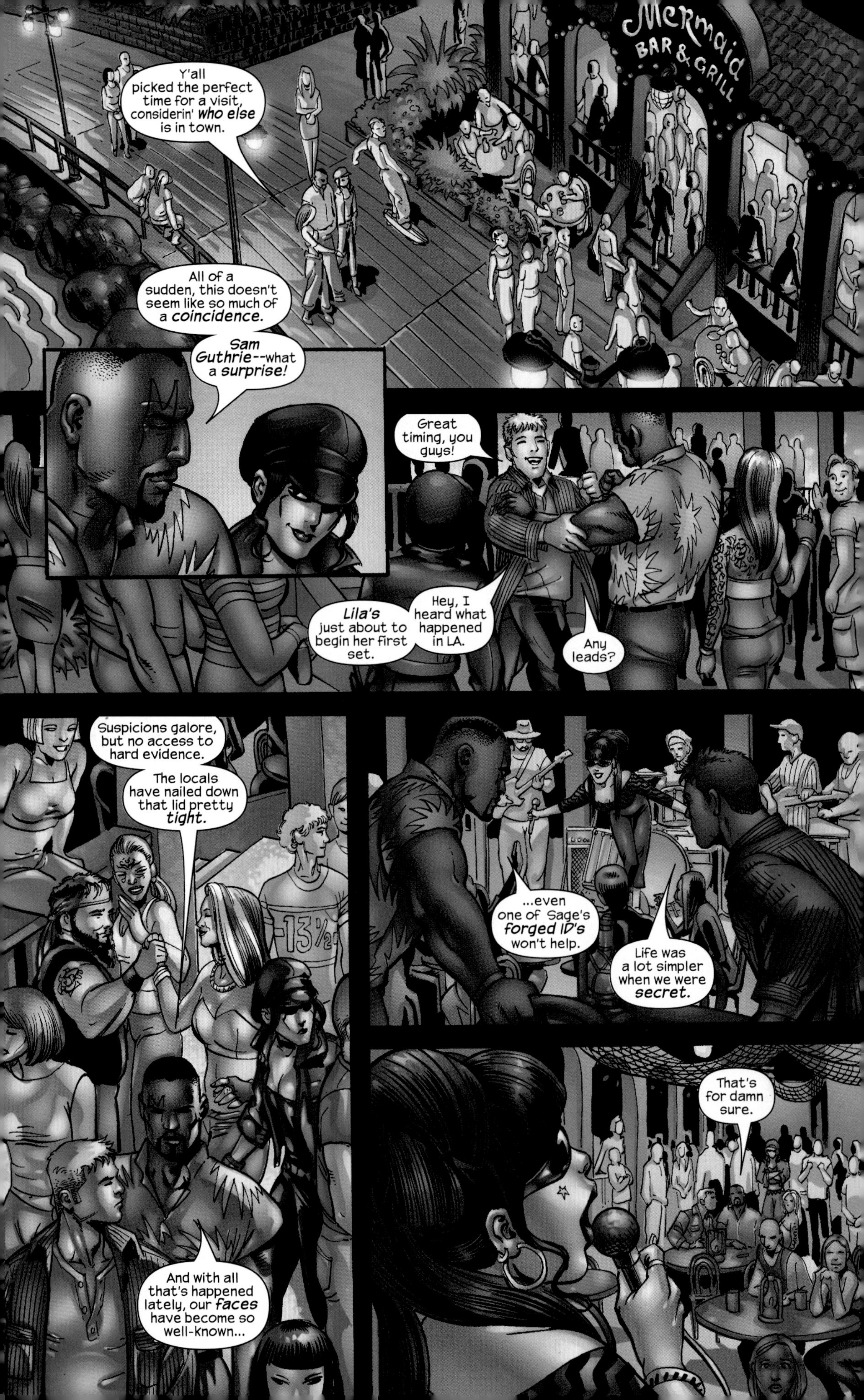

Mermaid
BAR & GRILL
Y'all picked the perfect time for a visit, considerin' who else is in town.
All of a sudden, this doesn't seem like so much of a coincidence.
Sam Guthrie--what a surprise!
Great timing, you guys!
Lila's just about to begin her first set.
Hey, I heard what happened in LA.
Any leads?
Suspicions galore, but no access to hard evidence.
The locals have nailed down that lid pretty tight.
And with all that's happened lately, our faces have become so well-known...
...even one of Sage's forged ID's won't help.
Life was a lot simpler when we were secret.
That's for damn sure.

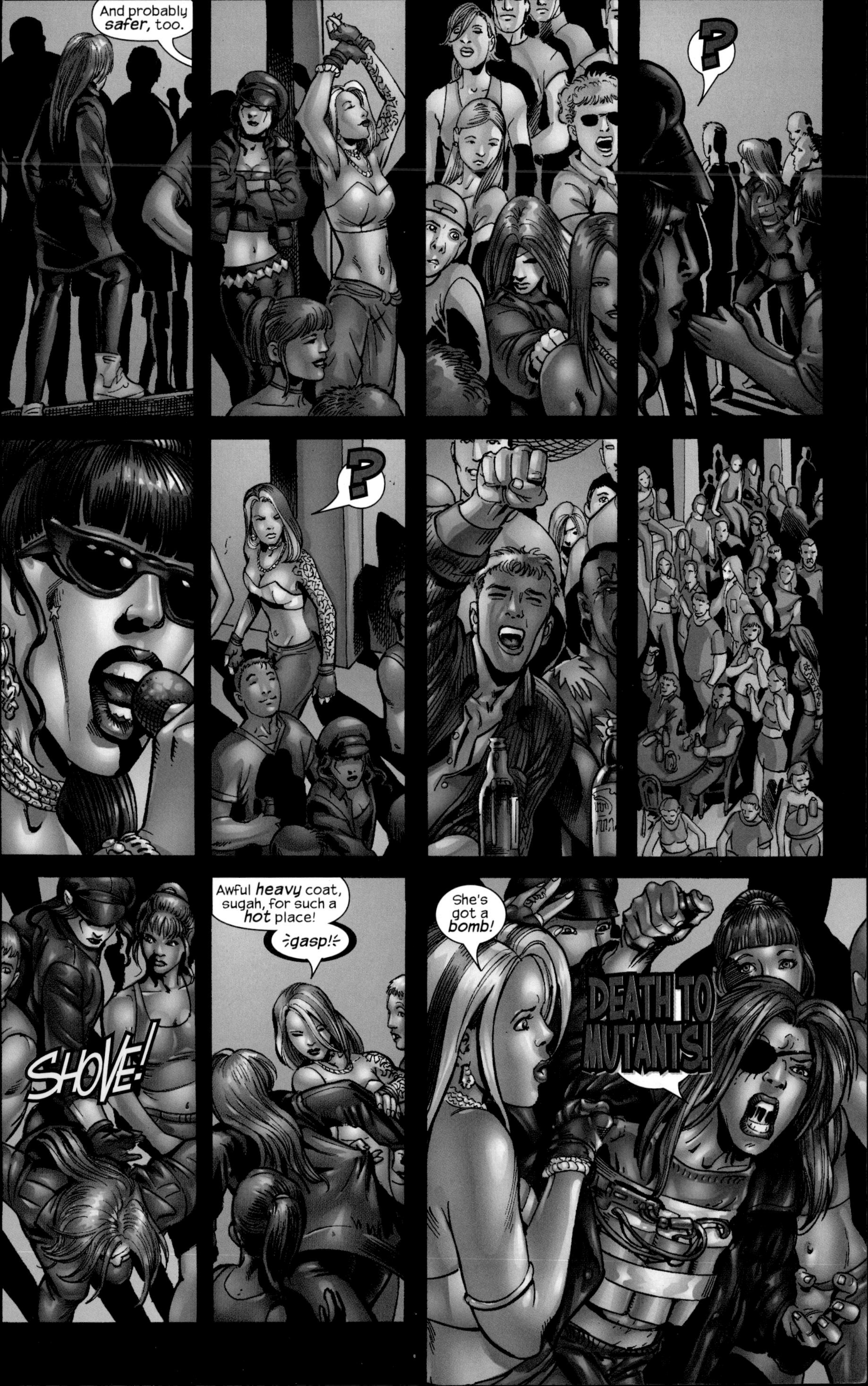
And probably safer, too.
?
?
SHOVE!
Awful heavy coat, sugah, for such a hot place!
gasp!
She's got a bomb!
DEATH TO MUTANTS!

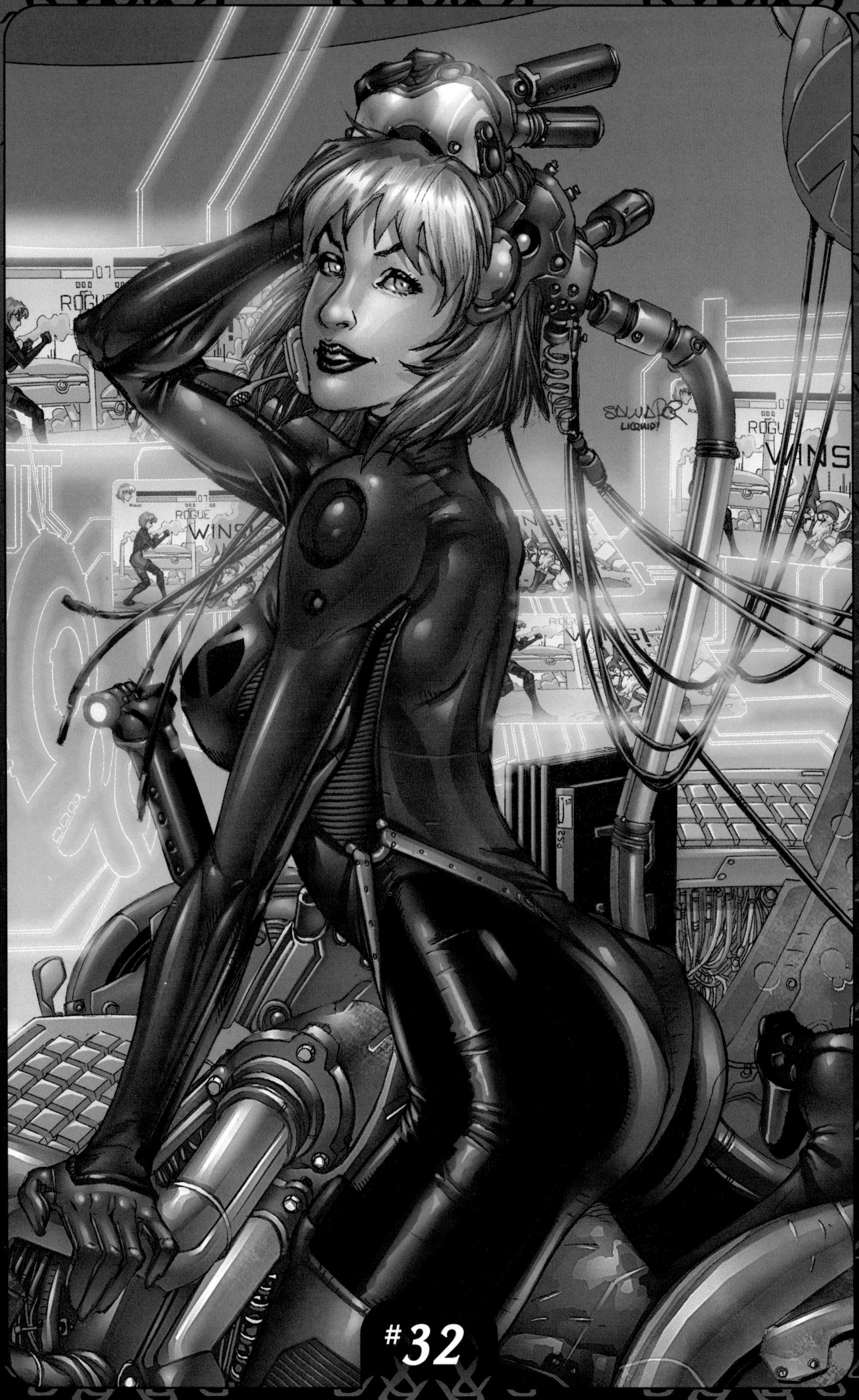
ROGUE
WINS!

#32

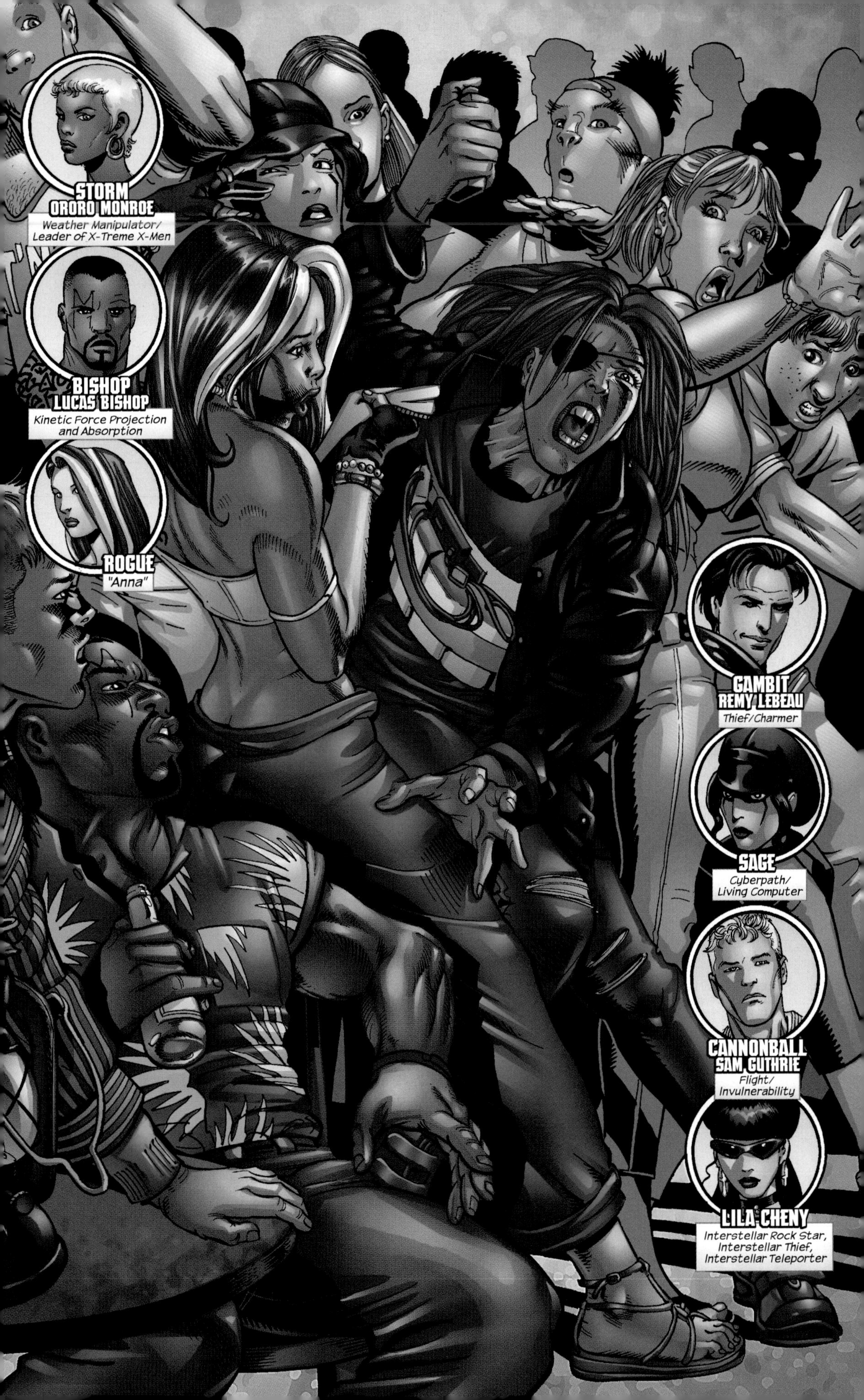

STORM
ORORO MONROE
Weather Manipulator/
Leader of X-Treme X-Men
BISHOP
LUCAS BISHOP
Kinetic Force Projection
and Absorption
ROGUE
"Anna"
GAMBIT
REMY LEBEAU
Thief/Charmer
SAGE
Cyberpath/
Living Computer
CANNONBALL
SAM GUTHRIE
Flight/
Invulnerability
LILA CHENY
Interstellar Rock Star,
Interstellar Thief,
Interstellar Teleporter

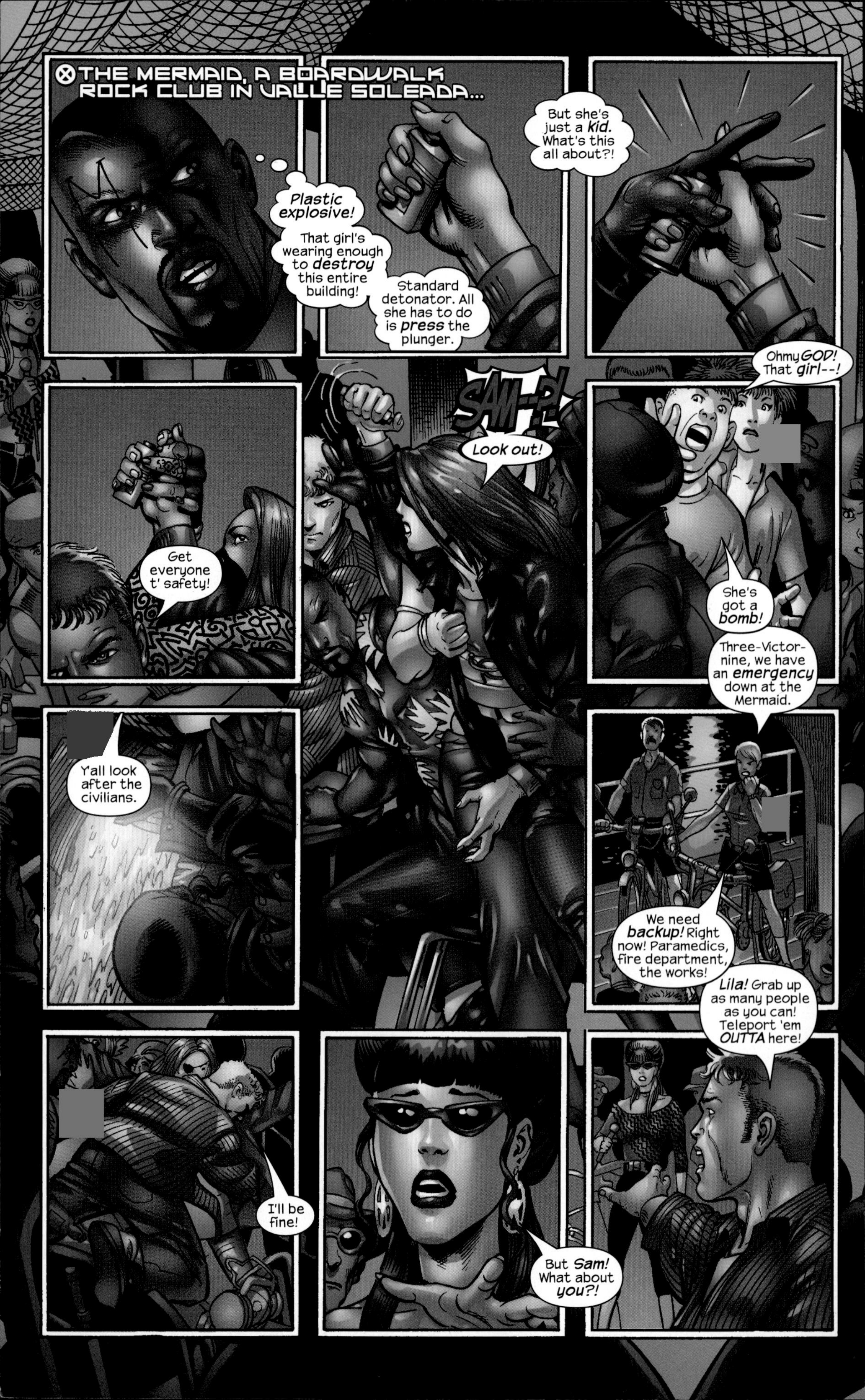
THE MERMAID, A BOARDWALK ROCK CLUB IN VALLE SOLEADA...
Plastic explosive!
That girl's wearing enough to destroy this entire building!
Standard detonator. All she has to do is press the plunger.
But she's just a kid. What's this all about?!
Get everyone t' safety!
SAM--?!
Look out!
Ohmy GOD! That girl--!
She's got a bomb!
Y'all look after the civilians.
Three-Victor-nine, we have an emergency down at the Mermaid.
We need backup! Right now! Paramedics, fire department, the works!
I'll be fine!
But Sam! What about you?!
Lila! Grab up as many people as you can! Teleport 'em OUTTA here!

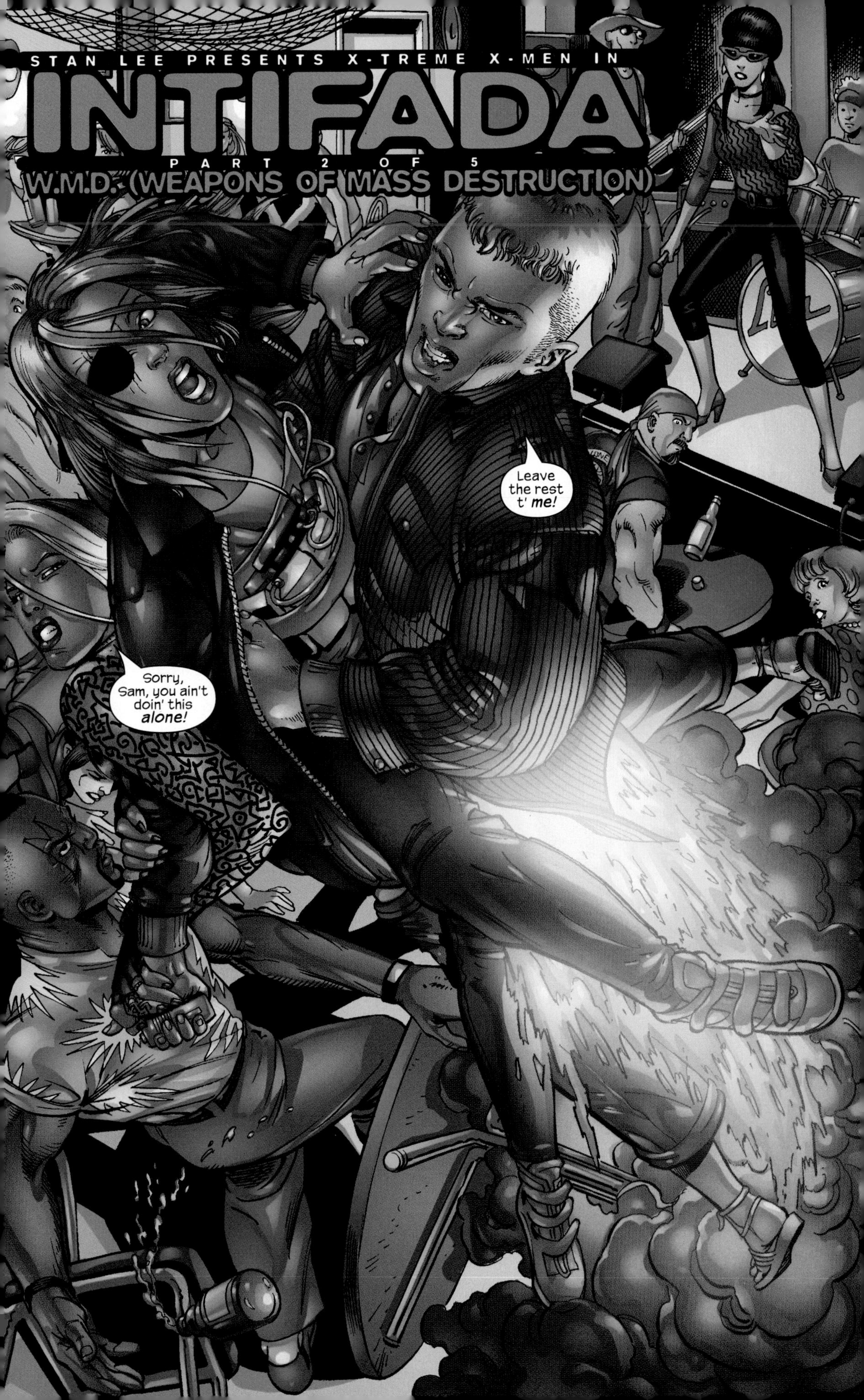
STAN LEE PRESENTS X-TREME X-MEN IN
INTIFADA
PART 2 OF 5
W.M.D. (WEAPONS OF MASS DESTRUCTION)
Leave the rest t' *me!*
Sorry, Sam, you ain't doin' this *alone!*

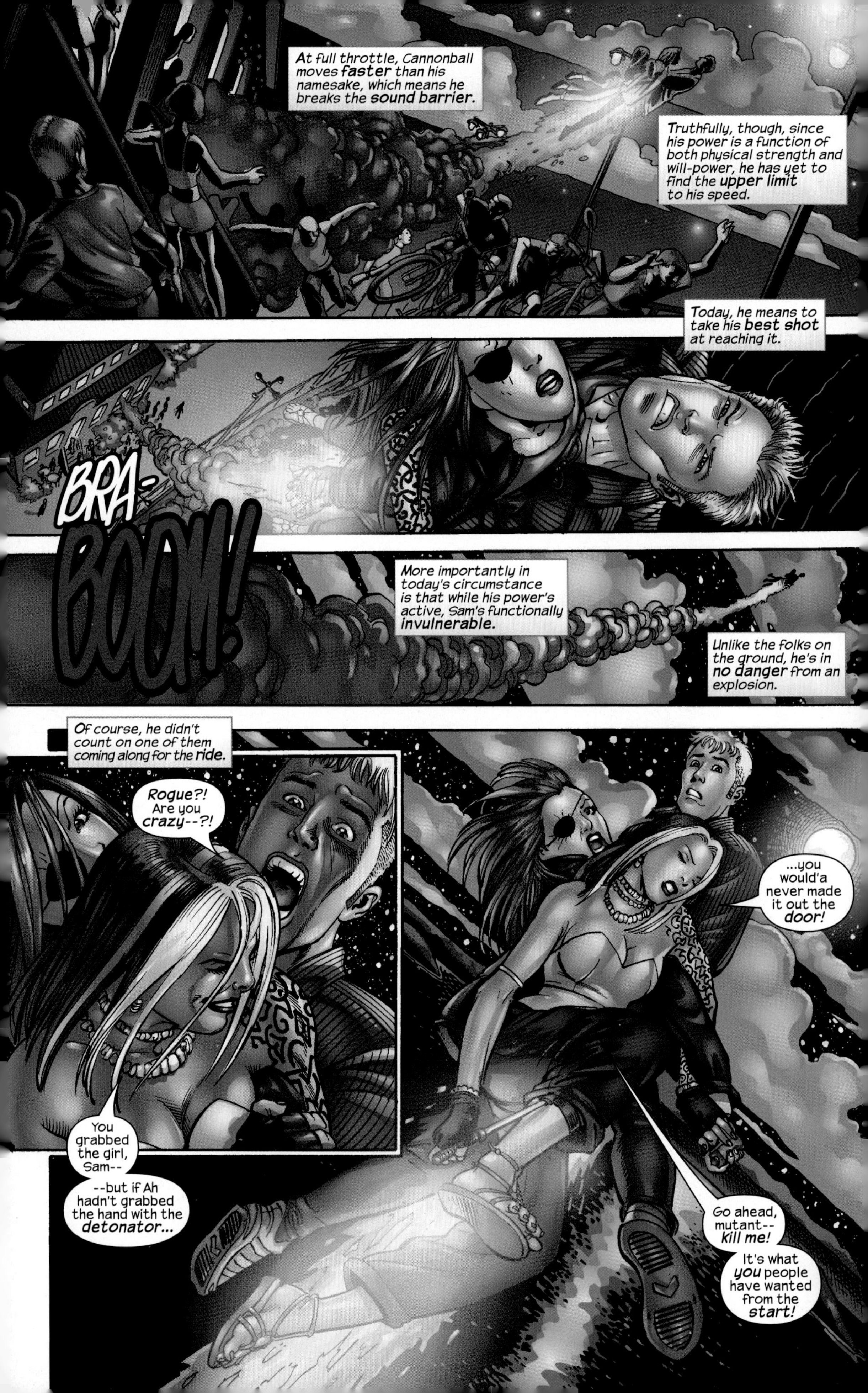

At full throttle, Cannonball moves faster than his namesake, which means he breaks the sound barrier.
Truthfully, though, since his power is a function of both physical strength and will-power, he has yet to find the upper limit to his speed.
Today, he means to take his best shot at reaching it.
BRA-
BOOM!
More importantly in today's circumstance is that while his power's active, Sam's functionally invulnerable.
Unlike the folks on the ground, he's in no danger from an explosion.
Of course, he didn't count on one of them coming along for the ride.
Rogue?! Are you crazy--?!
You grabbed the girl, Sam--
--but if Ah hadn't grabbed the hand with the detonator...
...you would'a never made it out the door!
Go ahead, mutant-- kill me!
It's what you people have wanted from the start!

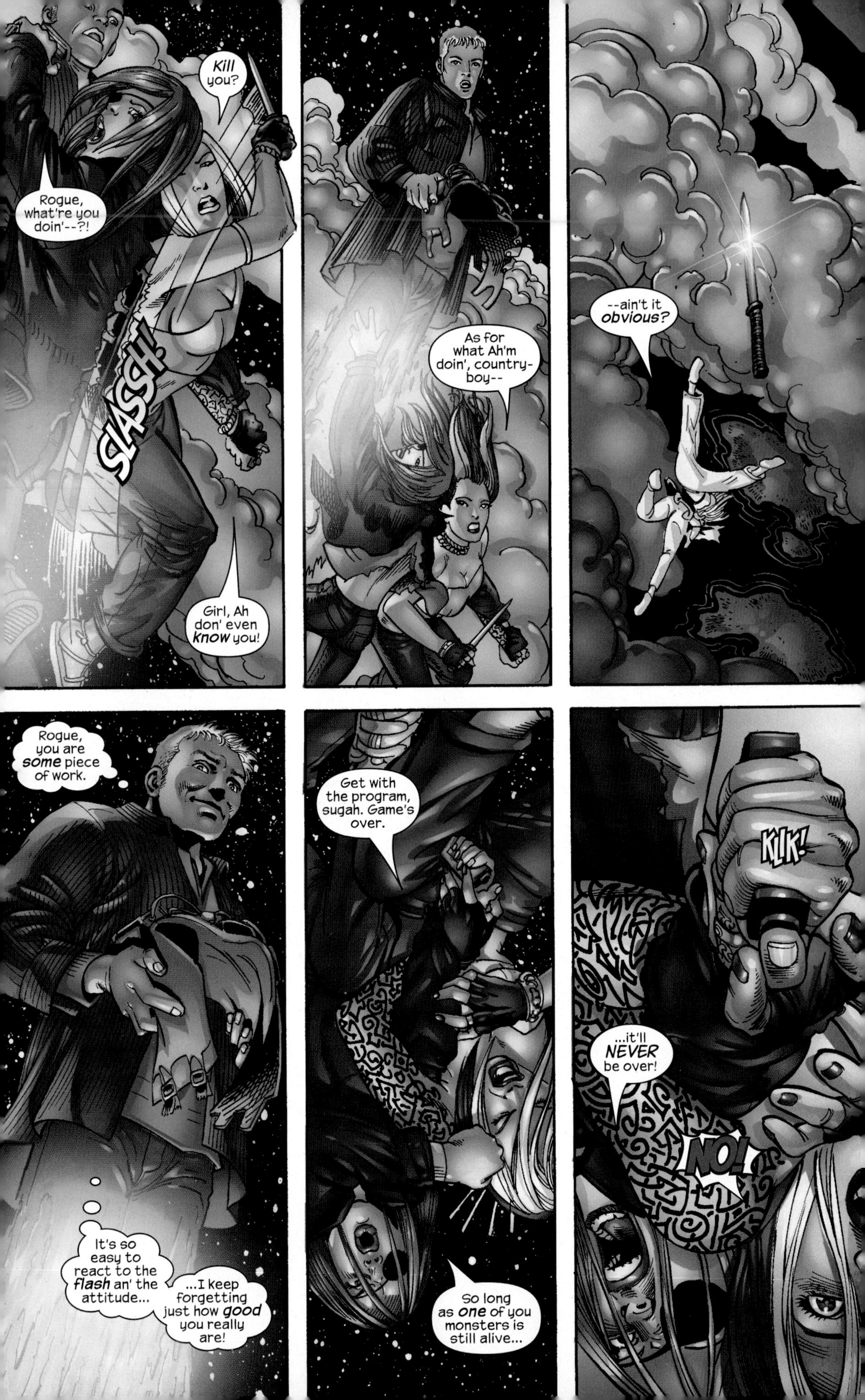
Kill you?
Rogue, what're you doin'--?!
SLASSH!
Girl, Ah don' even know you!
As for what Ah'm doin', country-boy--
--ain't it obvious?
Rogue, you are some piece of work.
It's so easy to react to the flash an' the attitude...
...I keep forgetting just how good you really are!
Get with the program, sugah. Game's over.
So long as one of you monsters is still alive...
KLIK!
...it'll NEVER be over!
NO!

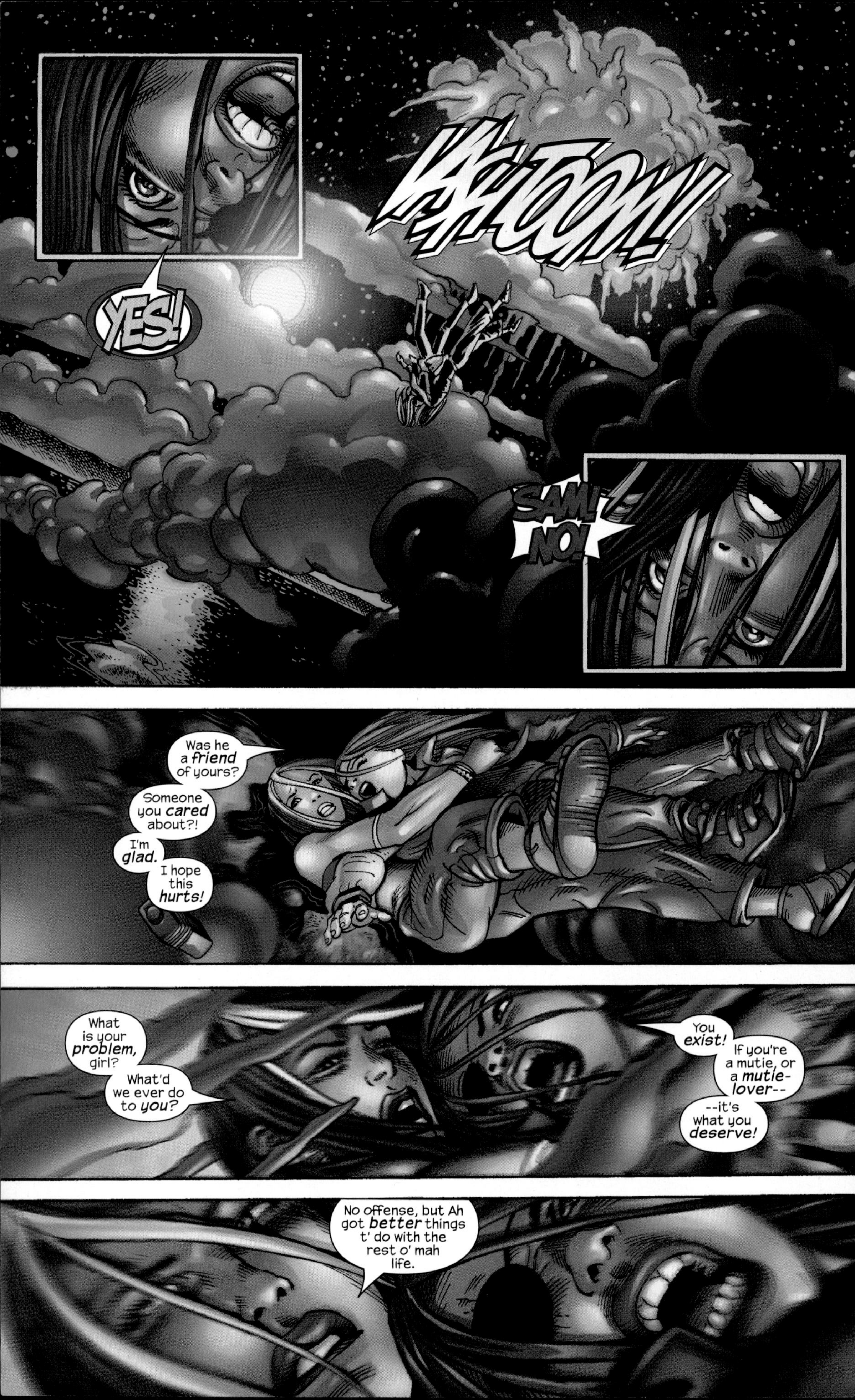
KA-TOOM!
YES!
SAM! NO!
Was he a friend of yours?
Someone you cared about?!
I'm glad.
I hope this hurts!
What is your problem, girl?
What'd we ever do to you?
You exist!
If you're a mutie, or a mutie-lover--
--it's what you deserve!
No offense, but Ah got better things t' do with the rest o' mah life.

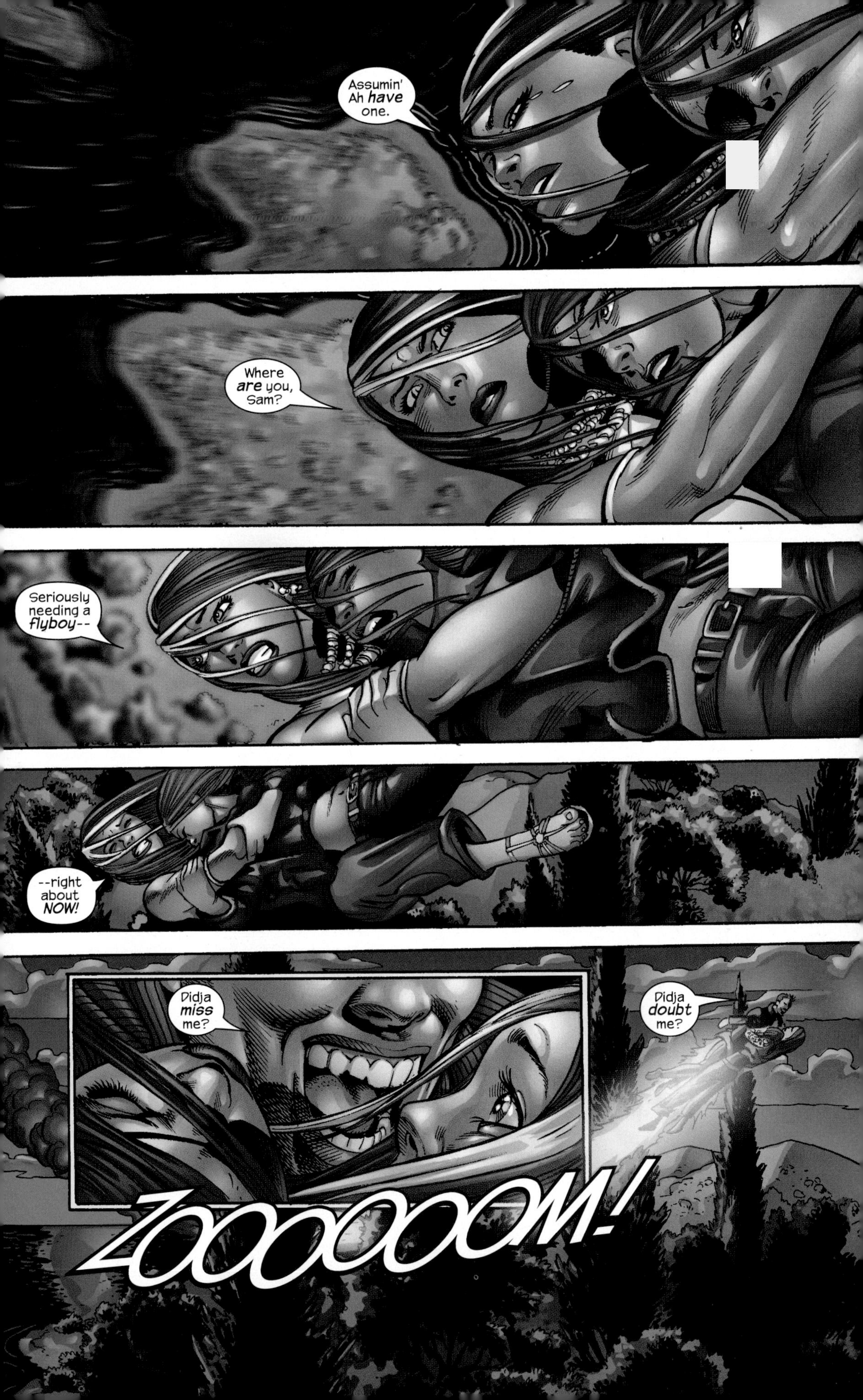
Assumin' Ah have one.
Where are you, Sam?
Seriously needing a flyboy--
--right about NOW!
Didja miss me?
Didja doubt me?
ZOOOOOOOM!

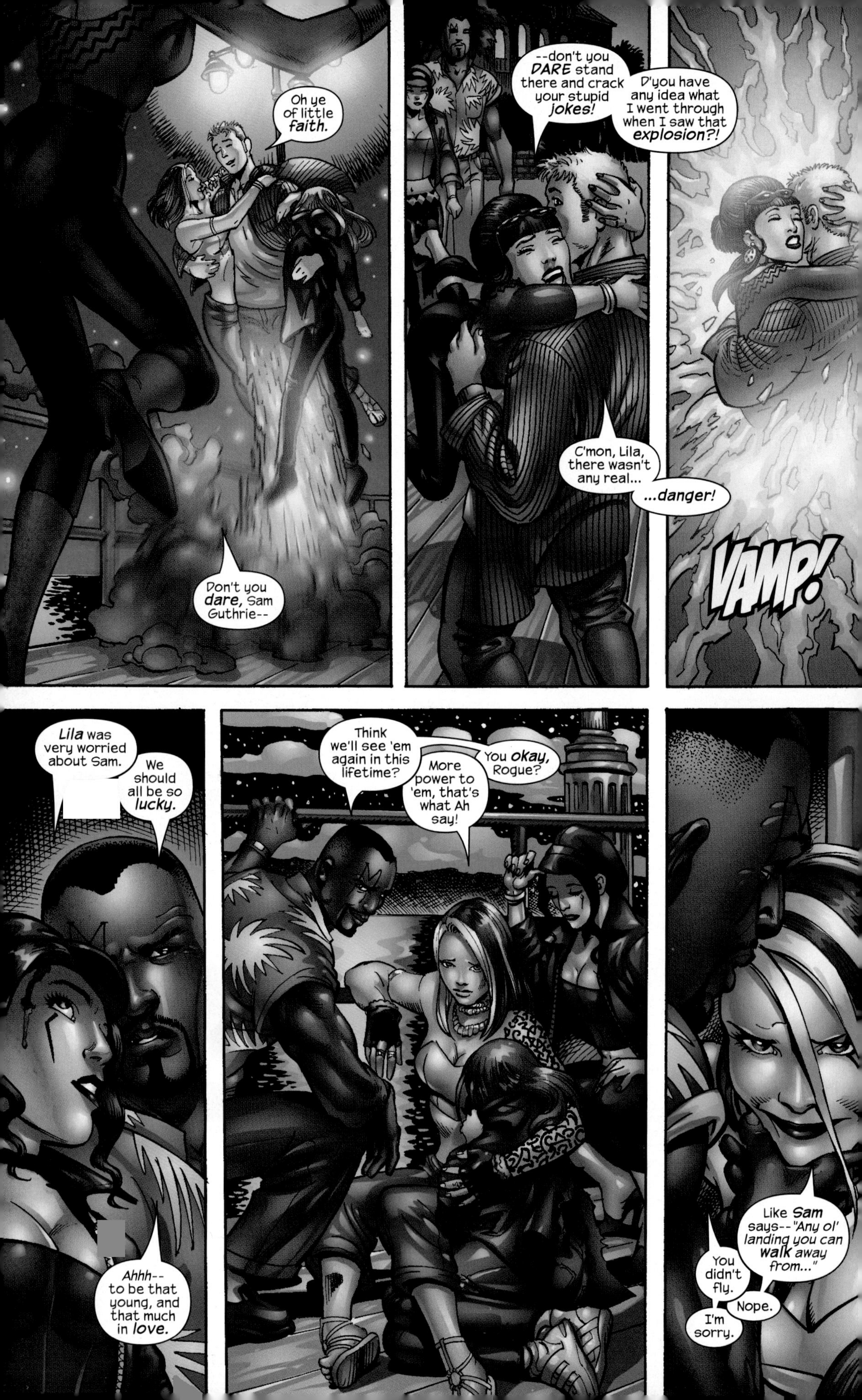
Oh ye of little faith.
Don't you dare, Sam Guthrie--
--don't you DARE stand there and crack your stupid jokes!
D'you have any idea what I went through when I saw that explosion?!
C'mon, Lila, there wasn't any real...
...danger!
VAMP!
Lila was very worried about Sam.
We should all be so lucky.
Ahhh-- to be that young, and that much in love.
Think we'll see 'em again in this lifetime?
More power to 'em, that's what Ah say!
You okay, Rogue?
Like Sam says--"Any ol' landing you can walk away from..."
You didn't fly.
Nope.
I'm sorry.

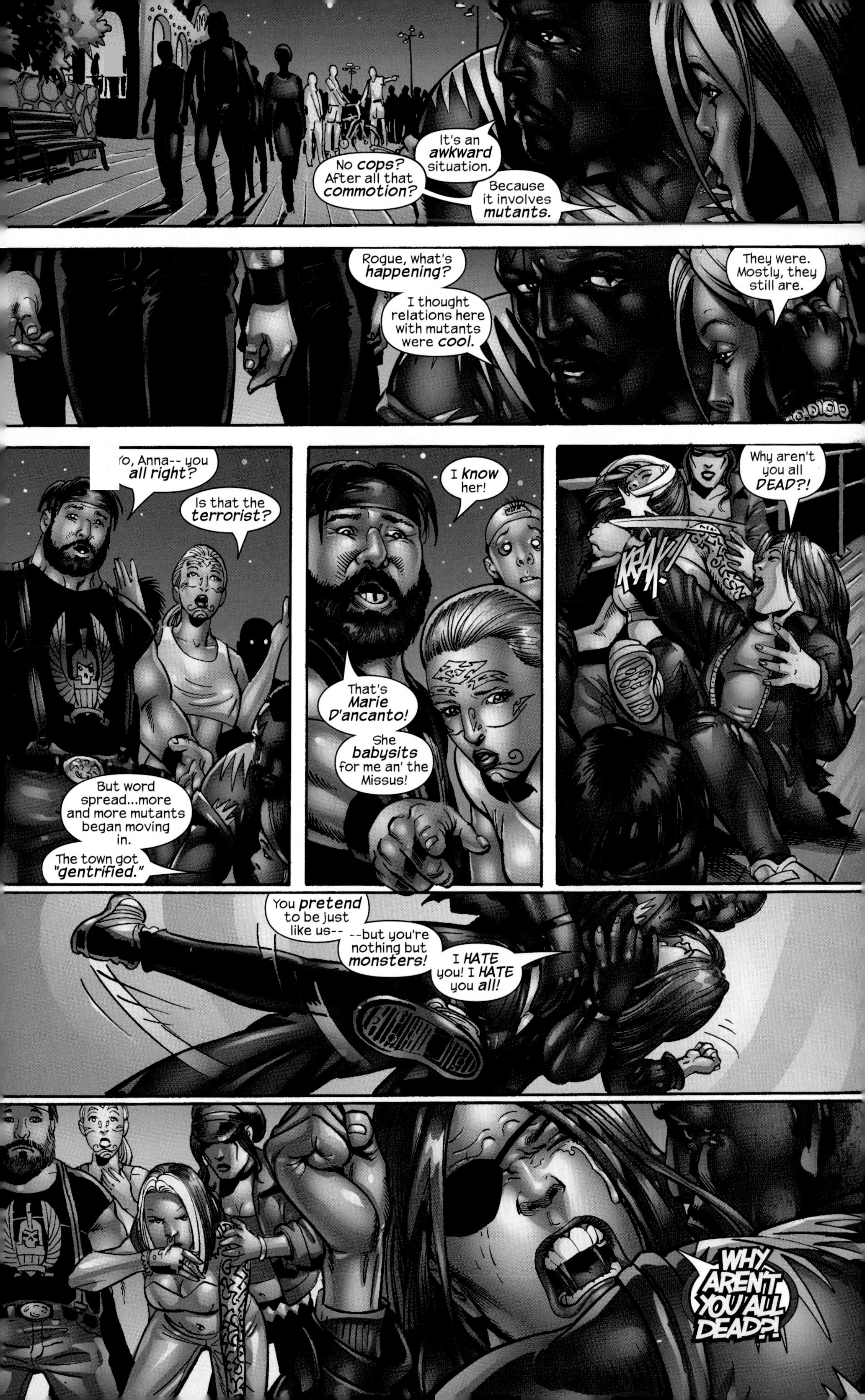

No cops? After all that commotion?
It's an awkward situation.
Because it involves mutants.
Rogue, what's happening?
I thought relations here with mutants were cool.
They were. Mostly, they still are.
o, Anna-- you all right?
Is that the terrorist?
But word spread...more and more mutants began moving in.
The town got "gentrified."
I know her!
That's Marie D'ancanto!
She babysits for me an' the Missus!
Why aren't you all DEAD?!
KRAK!
You pretend to be just like us--
--but you're nothing but monsters!
I HATE you! I HATE you all!
WHY AREN'T YOU ALL DEAD?!

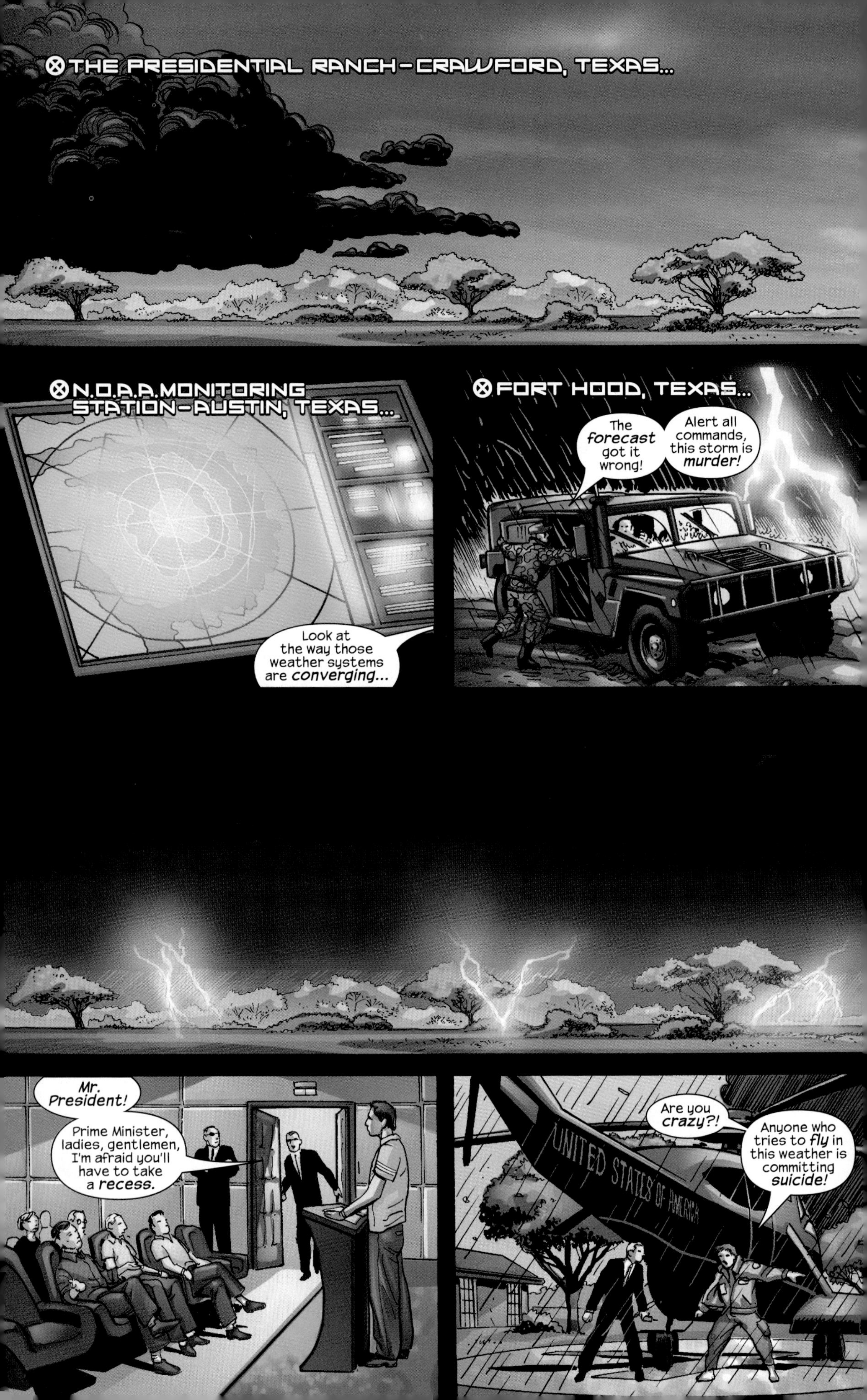
THE PRESIDENTIAL RANCH–CRAWFORD, TEXAS...
N.O.A.A. MONITORING STATION–AUSTIN, TEXAS...
Look at the way those weather systems are converging...
FORT HOOD, TEXAS...
The forecast got it wrong!
Alert all commands, this storm is murder!
Mr. President!
Prime Minister, ladies, gentlemen, I'm afraid you'll have to take a recess.
UNITED STATES OF AMERICA
Are you crazy?!
Anyone who tries to fly in this weather is committing suicide!

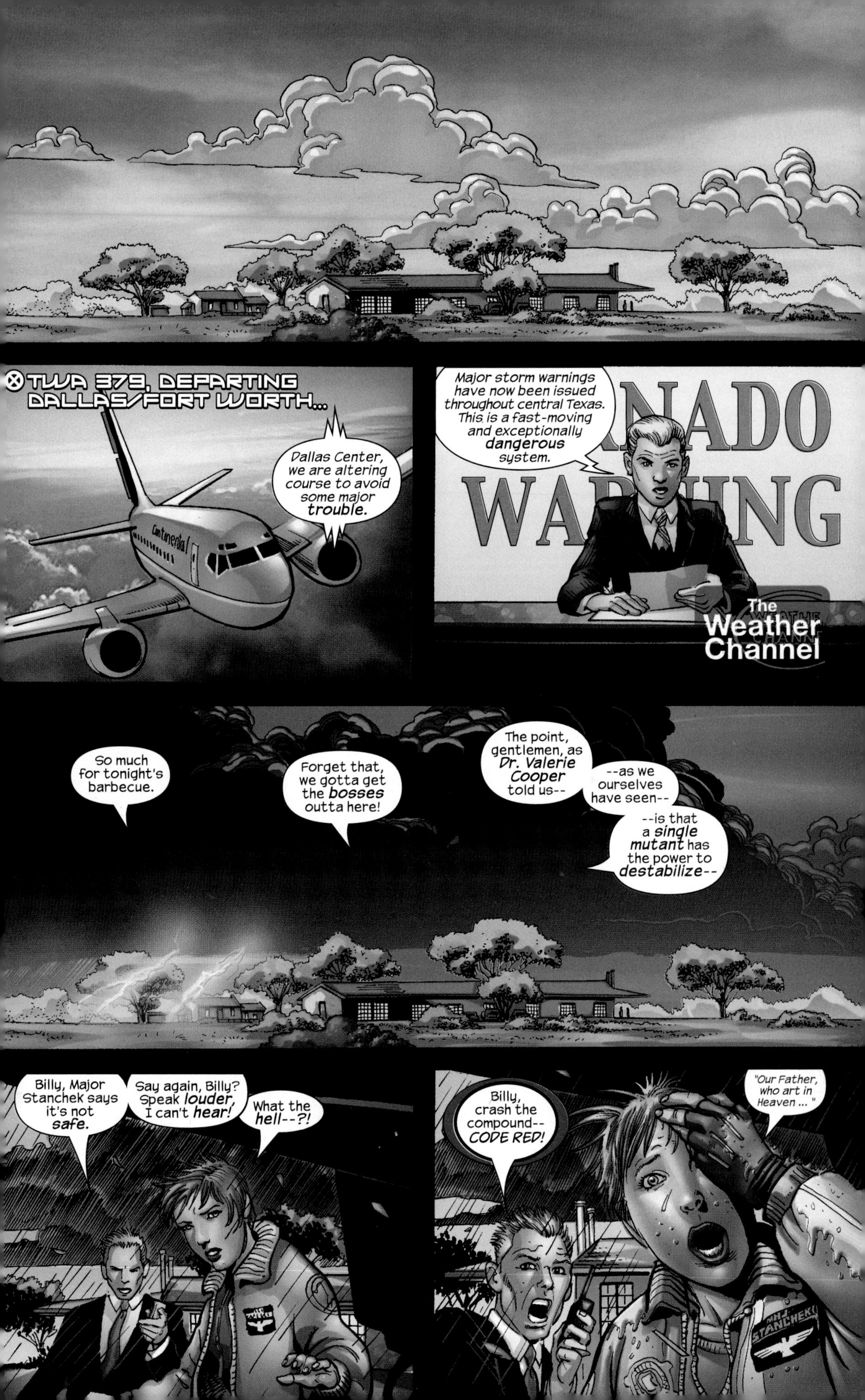

TWA 379, DEPARTING DALLAS/FORT WORTH...
Dallas Center, we are altering course to avoid some major trouble.
Continental
Major storm warnings have now been issued throughout central Texas. This is a fast-moving and exceptionally dangerous system.
NADO WAR NING
The Weather Channel
So much for tonight's barbecue.
Forget that, we gotta get the bosses outta here!
The point, gentlemen, as Dr. Valerie Cooper told us--
--as we ourselves have seen--
--is that a single mutant has the power to destabilize--
Billy, Major Stanchek says it's not safe.
Say again, Billy? Speak louder, I can't hear!
What the hell--?!
Billy, crash the compound-- CODE RED!
"Our Father, who art in Heaven ... "
STANCHEK

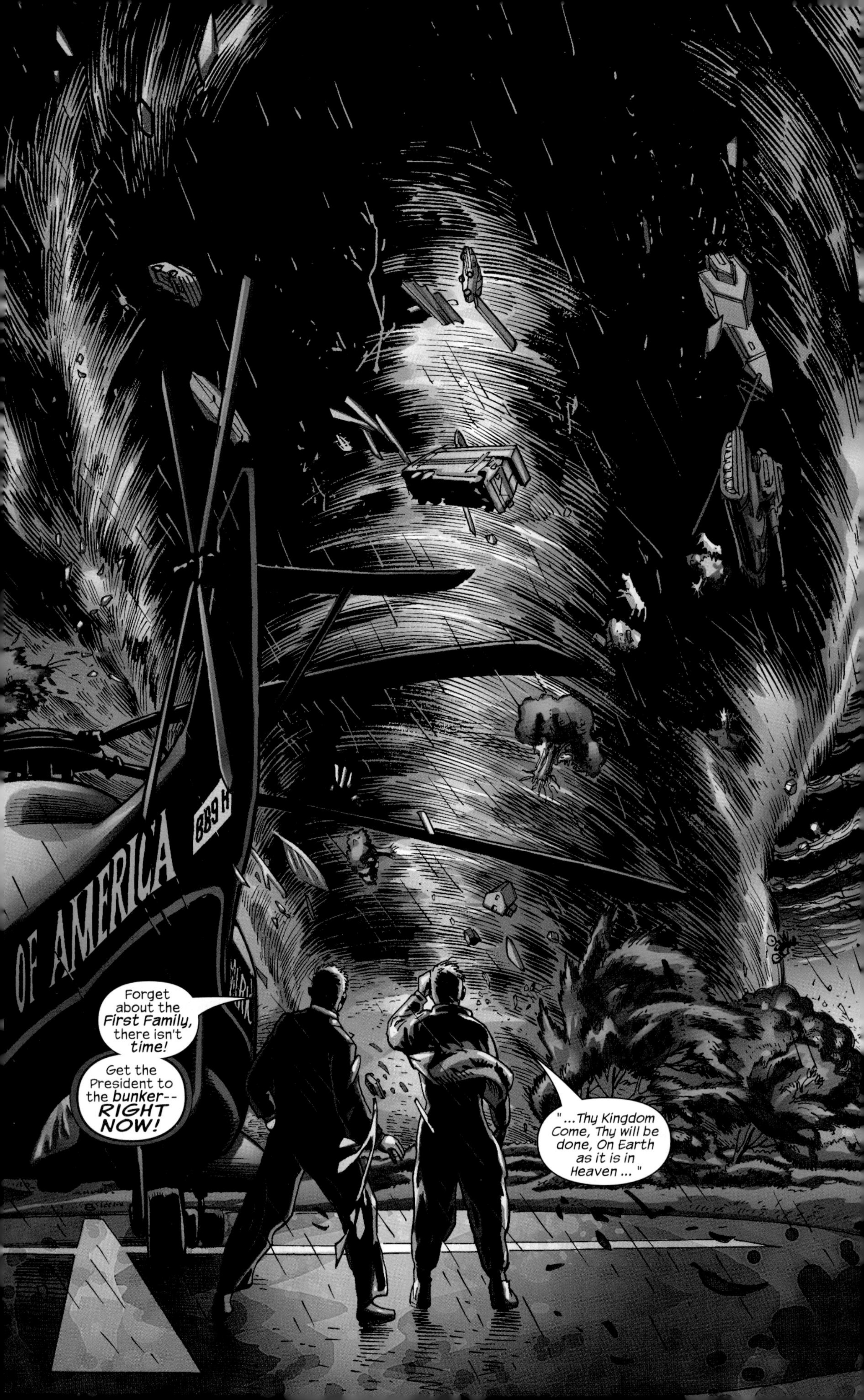
OF AMERICA
BB9 H
Forget about the *First Family,* there isn't *time!*
Get the President to the ***bunker--* RIGHT NOW!**
"...Thy Kingdom Come, Thy will be done, On Earth as it is in Heaven..."

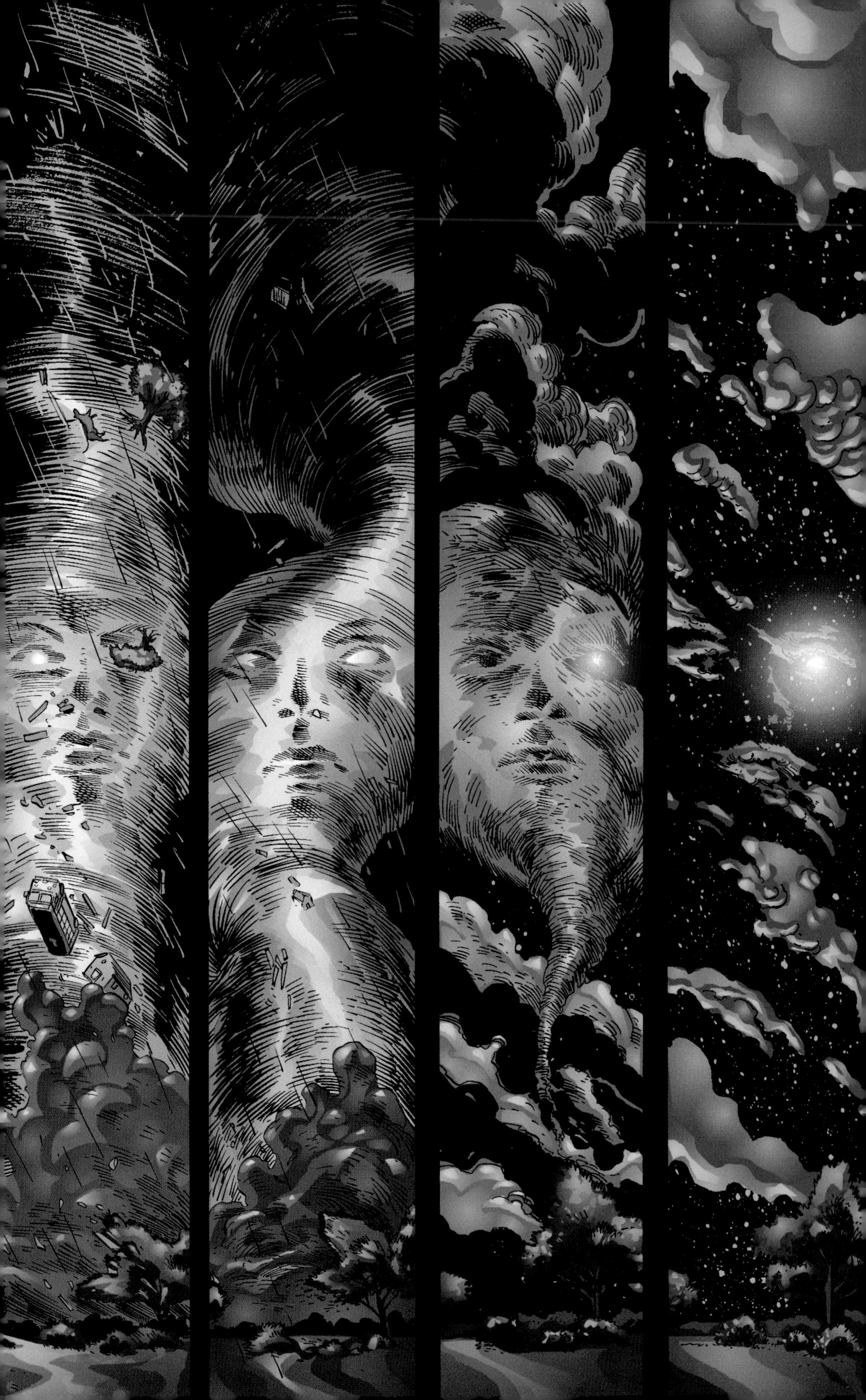

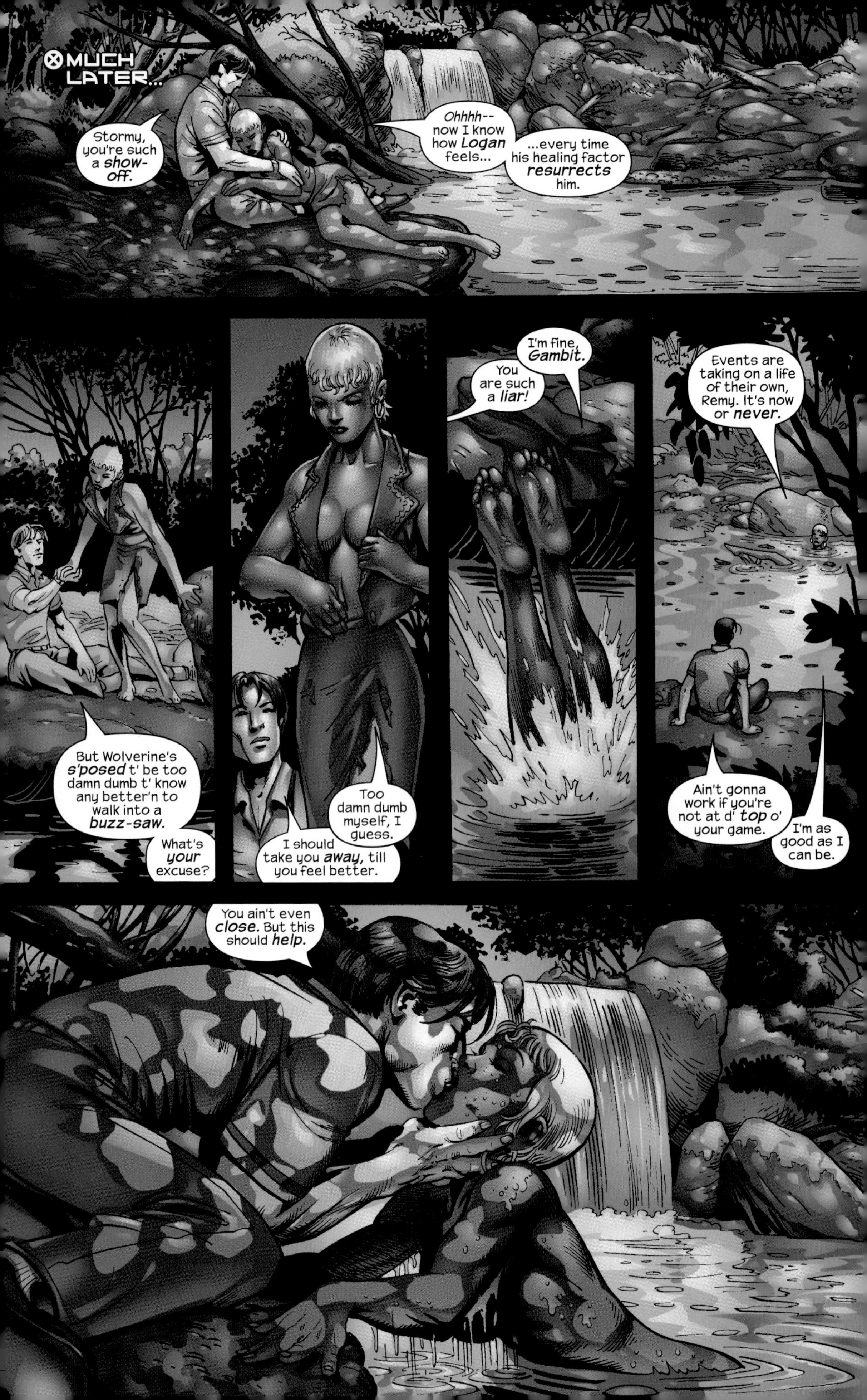
MUCH LATER...
Stormy, you're such a show-off.
Ohhhh-- now I know how Logan feels...
...every time his healing factor resurrects him.
But Wolverine's s'posed t' be too damn dumb t' know any better'n to walk into a buzz-saw.
What's your excuse?
Too damn dumb myself, I guess.
I should take you away, till you feel better.
I'm fine, Gambit.
You are such a liar!
Events are taking on a life of their own, Remy. It's now or never.
Ain't gonna work if you're not at d' top o' your game.
I'm as good as I can be.
You ain't even close. But this should help.

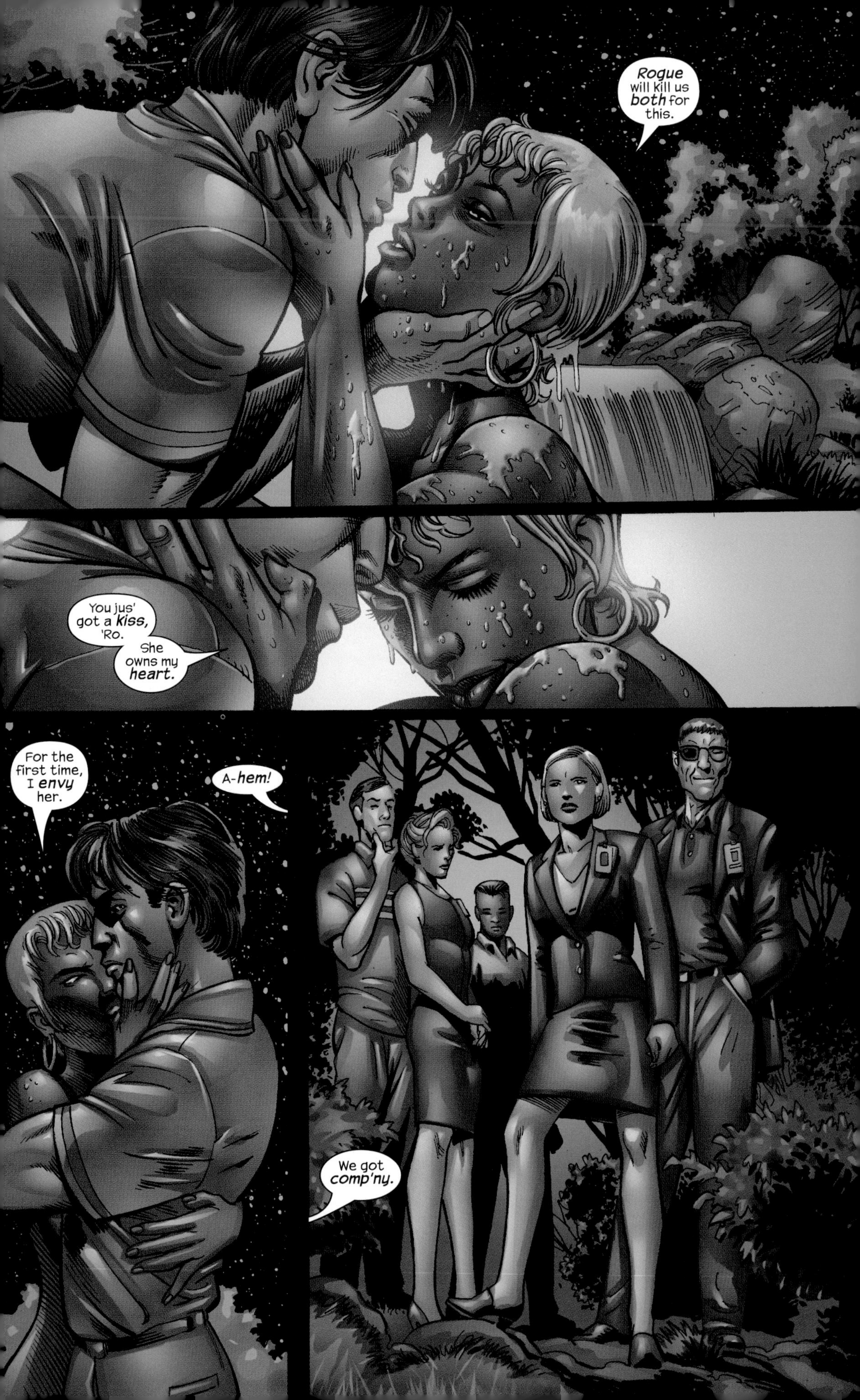
Rogue will kill us both for this.
You jus' got a kiss, 'Ro.
She owns my heart.
For the first time, I envy her.
A-hem!
We got comp'ny.

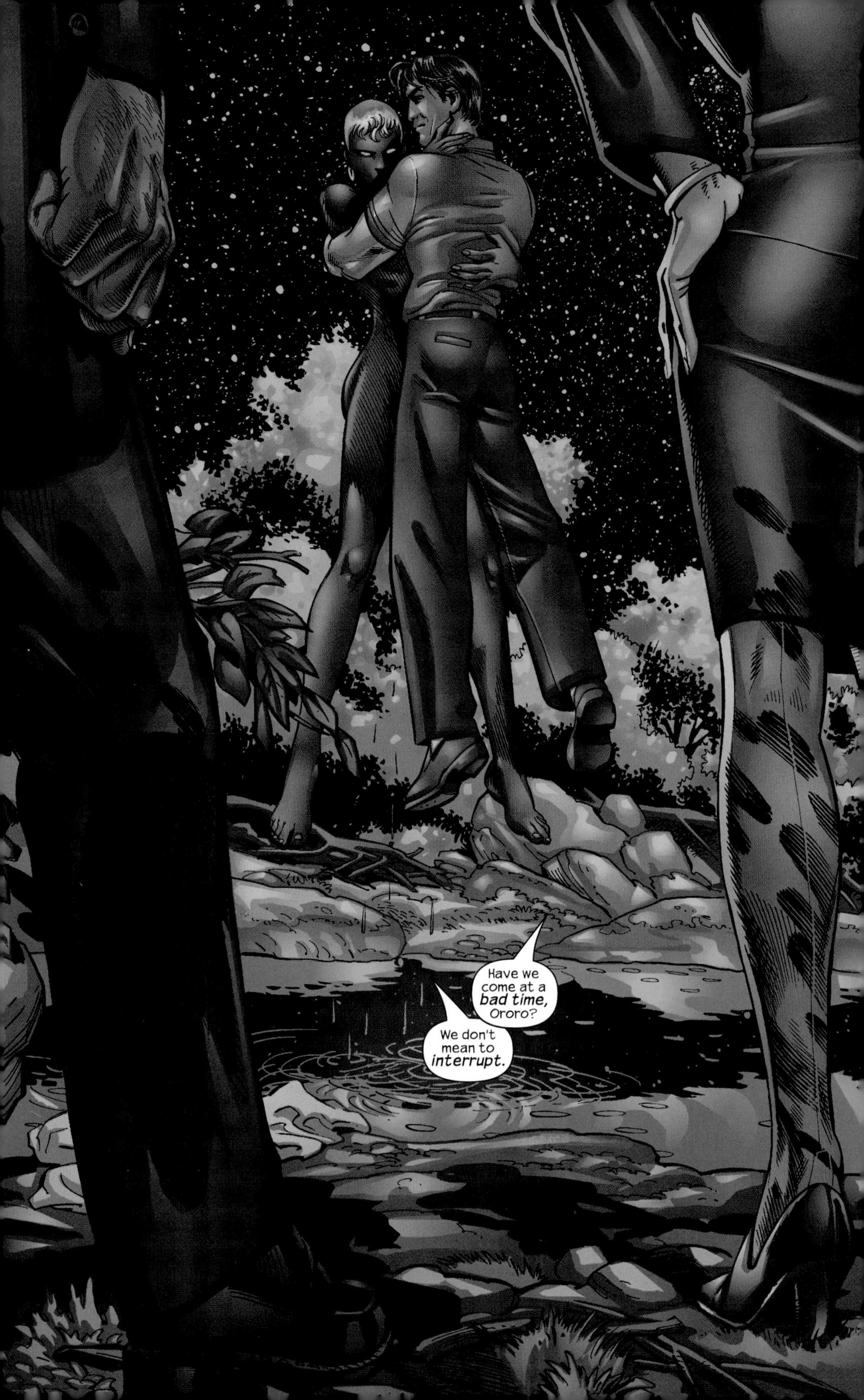
Have we come at a bad time, Ororo?
We don't mean to interrupt.

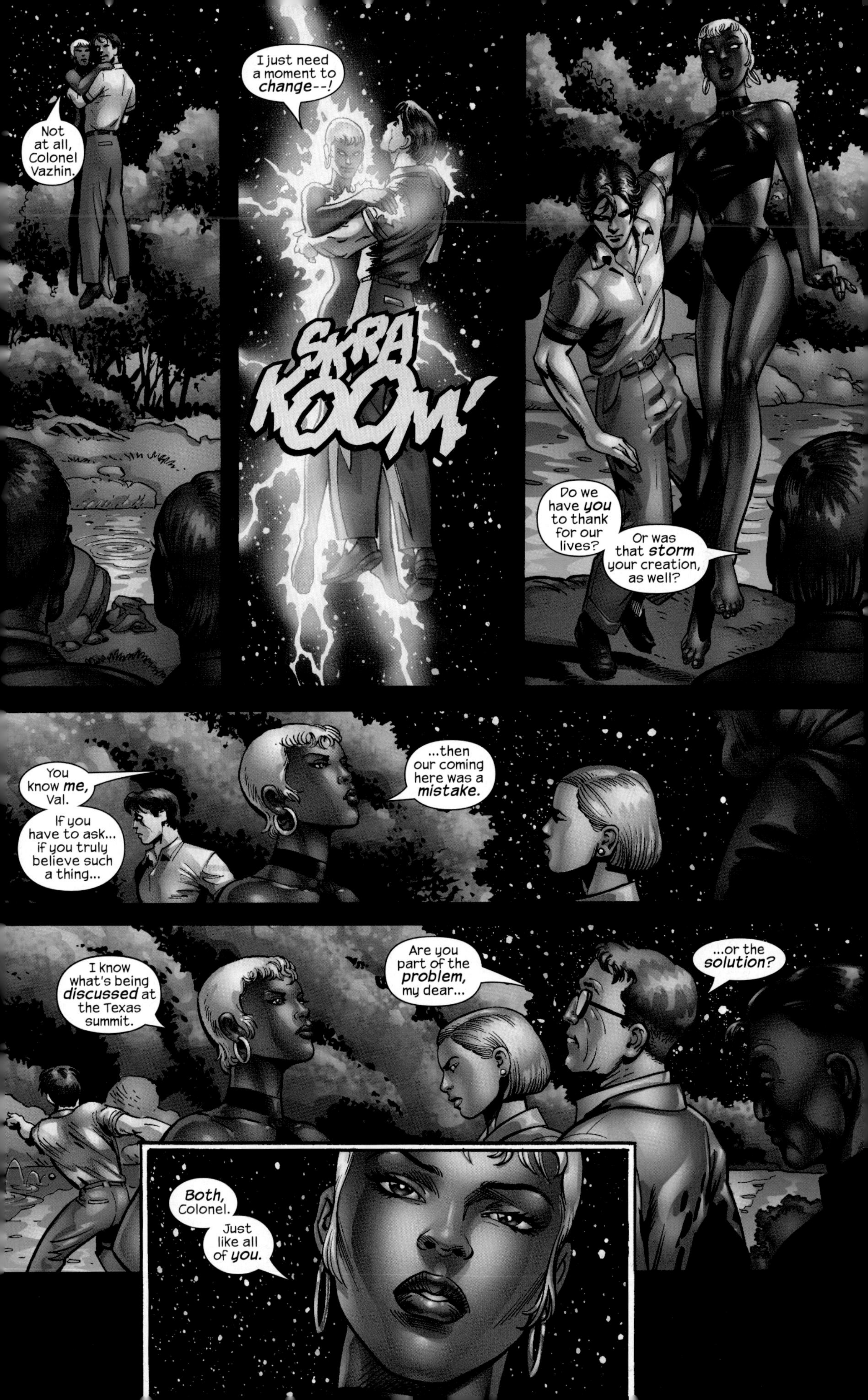
Not at all, Colonel Vazhin.
I just need a moment to change--!
SKRA KOOM!
Do we have you to thank for our lives?
Or was that storm your creation, as well?
You know me, Val.
If you have to ask... if you truly believe such a thing...
...then our coming here was a mistake.
I know what's being discussed at the Texas summit.
Are you part of the problem, my dear...
...or the solution?
Both, Colonel.
Just like all of you.

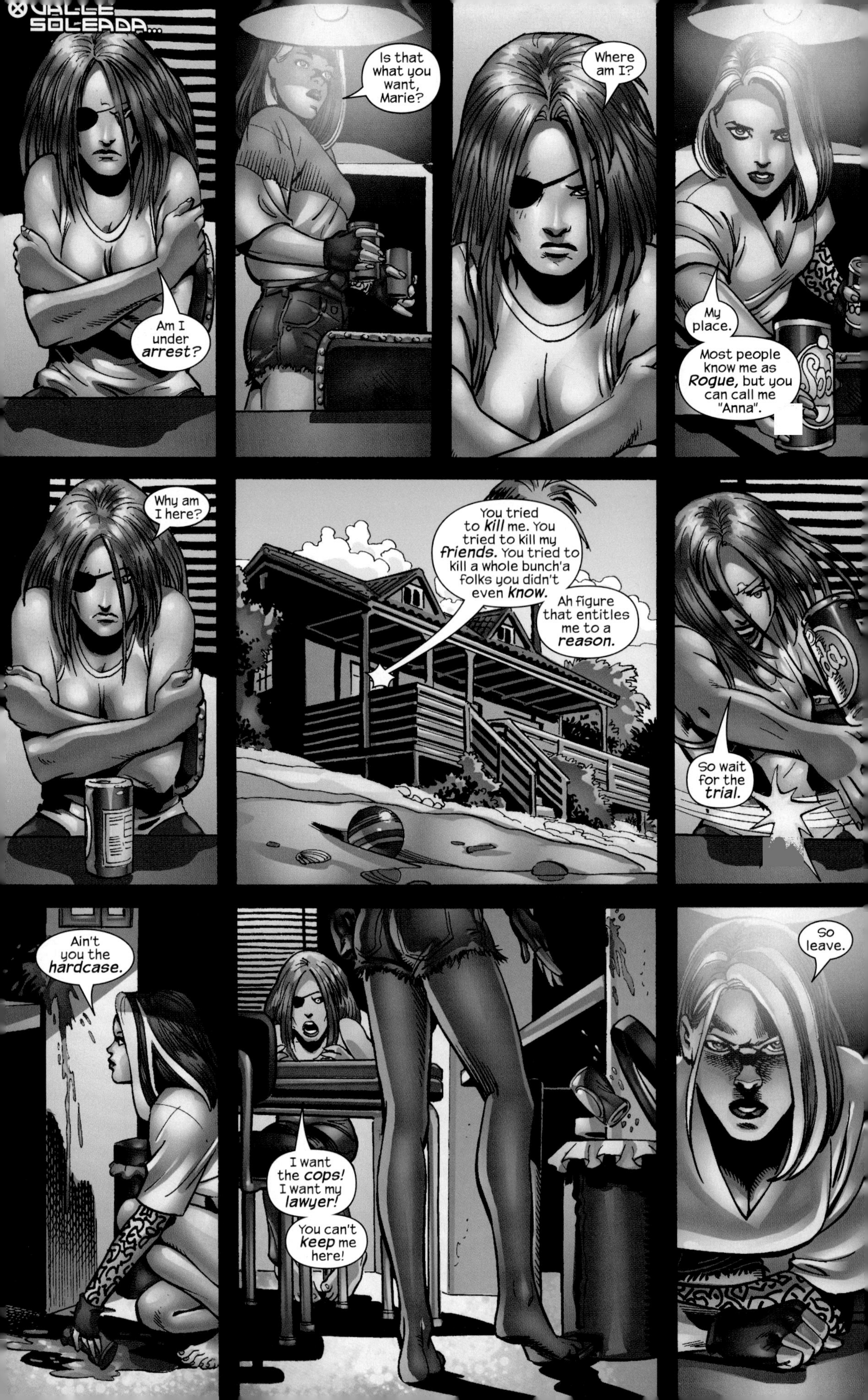

VALLE SOLEADA...
Am I under *arrest?*
Is that what you want, Marie?
Where am I?
My place.
Most people know me as *Rogue,* but you can call me "Anna".
Why am I here?
You tried to *kill* me. You tried to kill my *friends.* You tried to kill a whole bunch'a folks you didn't even *know.*
Ah figure that entitles me to a *reason.*
So wait for the *trial.*
Ain't you the *hardcase.*
I want the *cops!* I want my *lawyer!*
You can't *keep* me here!
So leave.

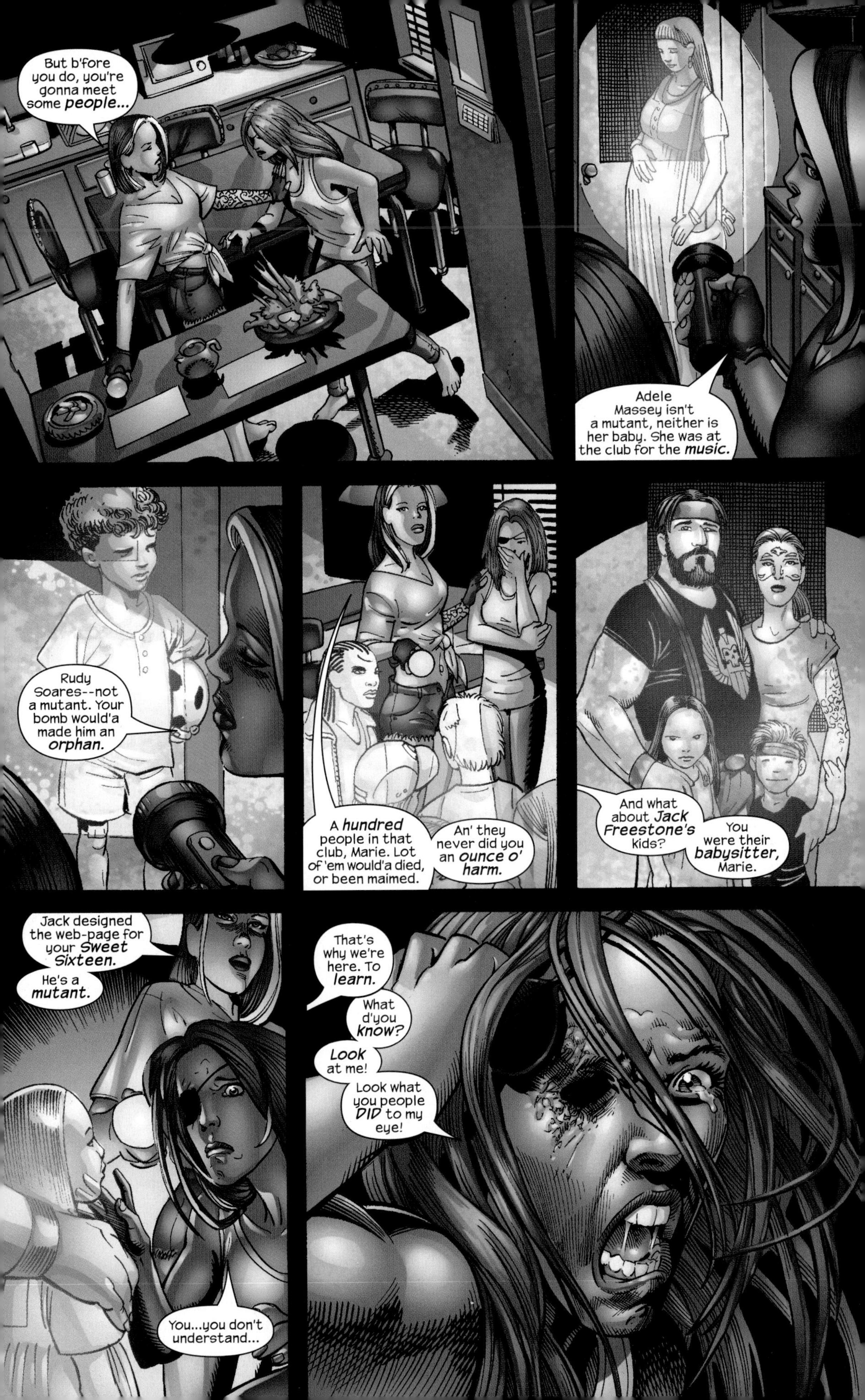
But b'fore you do, you're gonna meet some *people*...
Adele Massey isn't a mutant, neither is her baby. She was at the club for the *music*.
Rudy Soares--not a mutant. Your bomb would'a made him an *orphan*.
A *hundred* people in that club, Marie. Lot of 'em would'a died, or been maimed.
An' they never did you an *ounce o' harm*.
And what about *Jack Freestone's* kids?
You were their *babysitter*, Marie.
Jack designed the web-page for your *Sweet Sixteen*.
He's a *mutant*.
You...you don't understand...
That's why we're here. To *learn*.
What d'you *know*?
Look at me!
Look what you people *DID* to my eye!

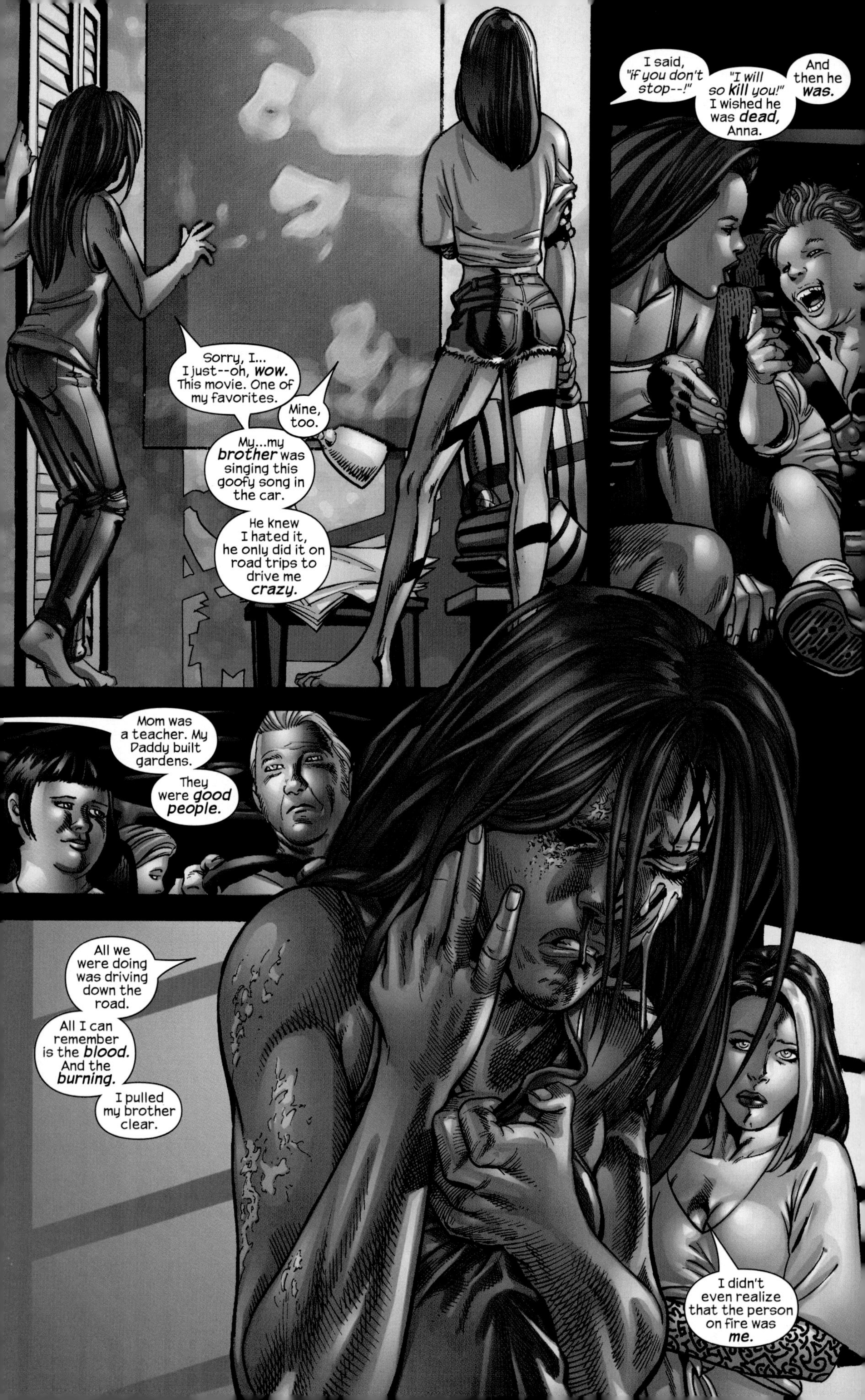
Sorry, I... I just--oh, WOW. This movie. One of my favorites.
Mine, too.
My...my brother was singing this goofy song in the car.
He knew I hated it, he only did it on road trips to drive me crazy.
I said, "if you don't stop--!"
"I will so kill you!" I wished he was dead, Anna.
And then he was.
Mom was a teacher. My Daddy built gardens.
They were good people.
All we were doing was driving down the road.
All I can remember is the blood. And the burning.
I pulled my brother clear.
I didn't even realize that the person on fire was me.

Afterwards, the police did *nothing*.

They said they had no case, but that was a *lie*.

They were *scared*, is what it was. Of *you*. Of *mutants*.

My uncle, bless him, wouldn't quit.

He kept pestering the cops, the papers, the TV...

...then he got a visit from some *suits*.

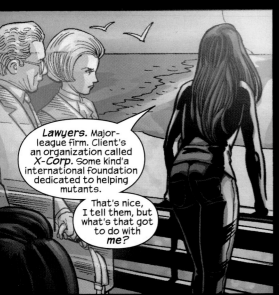

Lawyers. Major-league firm. Client's an organization called *X-Corp.* Some kind'a international foundation dedicated to helping mutants.

That's nice, I tell them, but what's that got to do with *me*?

Turns out what we're doing can be construed as *species harassment*, maybe even a *hate crime.*

I was so *tired*. I just wanted things to *end*.

No, that's not right...

...I just wanted them *back* the way they were.

I never even got my driver's license... and now I *never will.*

I can't even wear a one-piece bathing suit for all the burn scars, much less a *bikini.*

But that was just the *beginning.*

From there on, things got *worse.*

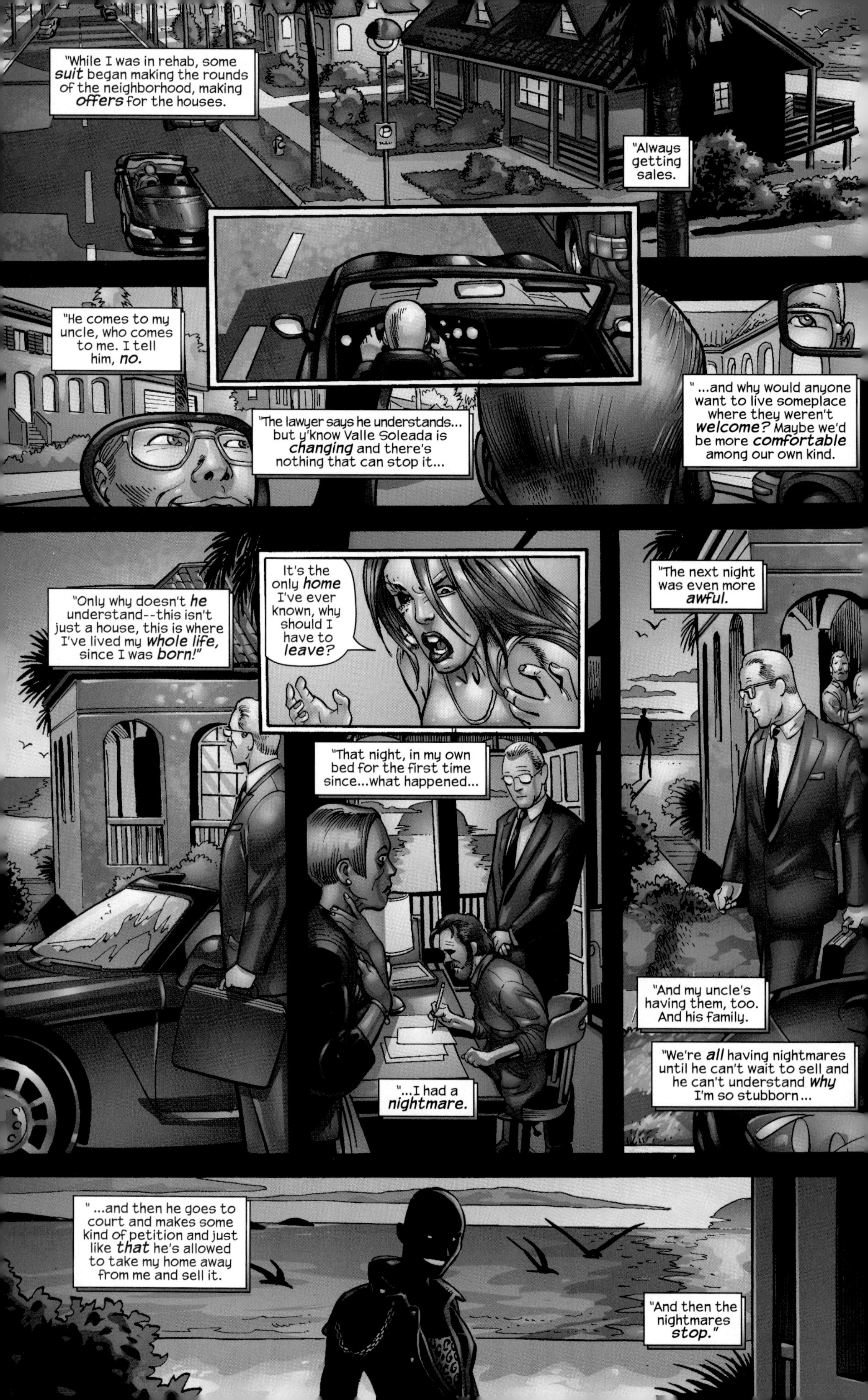
"While I was in rehab, some suit began making the rounds of the neighborhood, making offers for the houses.
"Always getting sales.
"He comes to my uncle, who comes to me. I tell him, no.
"The lawyer says he understands... but y'know Valle Soleada is changing and there's nothing that can stop it...
"...and why would anyone want to live someplace where they weren't welcome? Maybe we'd be more comfortable among our own kind.
"Only why doesn't he understand--this isn't just a house, this is where I've lived my whole life, since I was born!"
It's the only home I've ever known, why should I have to leave?
"That night, in my own bed for the first time since...what happened...
"...I had a nightmare.
"The next night was even more awful.
"And my uncle's having them, too. And his family.
"We're all having nightmares until he can't wait to sell and he can't understand why I'm so stubborn...
"...and then he goes to court and makes some kind of petition and just like that he's allowed to take my home away from me and sell it.
"And then the nightmares stop."

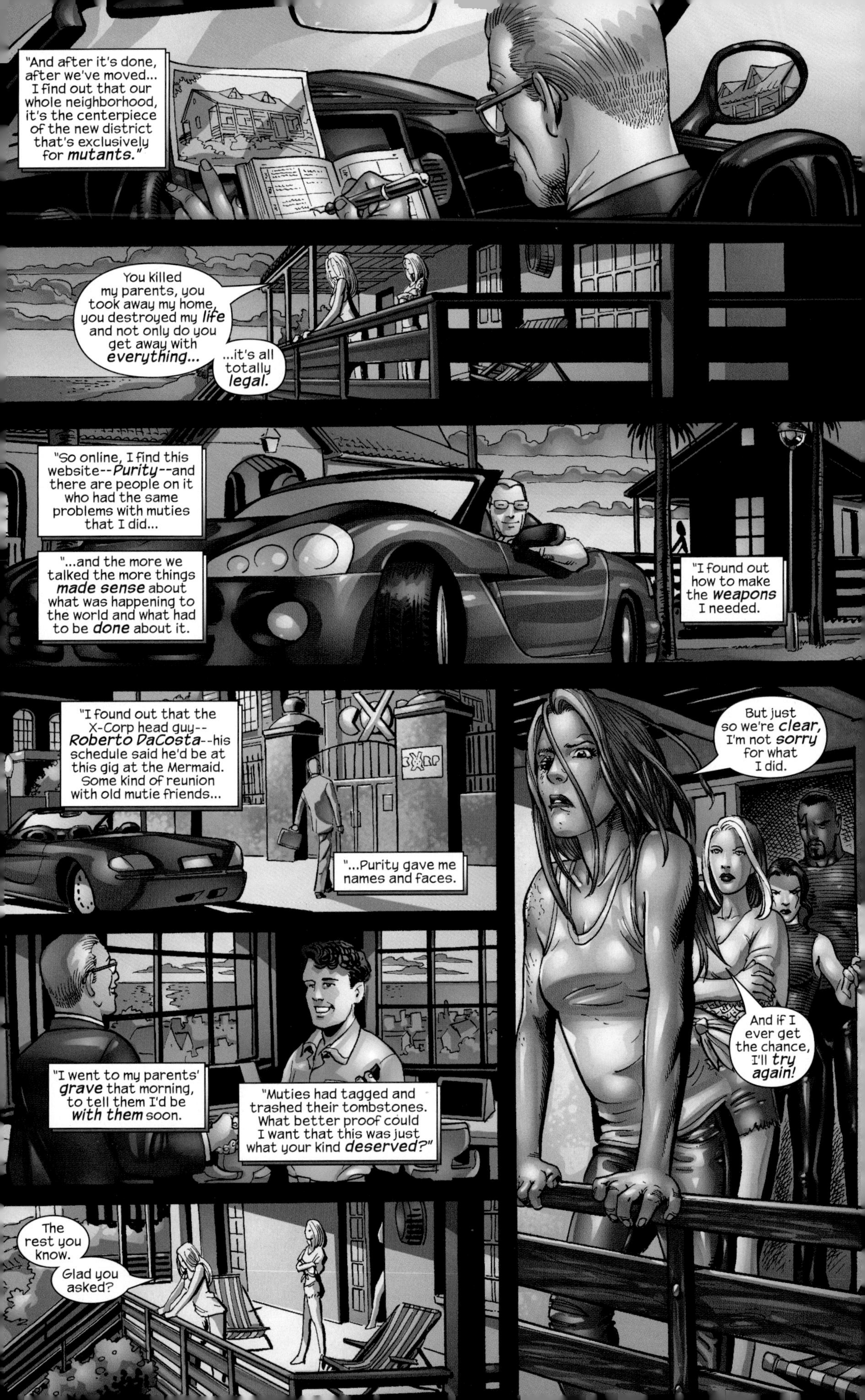
"And after it's done, after we've moved... I find out that our whole neighborhood, it's the centerpiece of the new district that's exclusively for mutants."
You killed my parents, you took away my home, you destroyed my life and not only do you get away with everything...
...it's all totally legal.
"So online, I find this website--Purity--and there are people on it who had the same problems with muties that I did...
"...and the more we talked the more things made sense about what was happening to the world and what had to be done about it.
"I found out how to make the weapons I needed.
"I found out that the X-Corp head guy--Roberto DaCosta--his schedule said he'd be at this gig at the Mermaid. Some kind of reunion with old mutie friends...
"...Purity gave me names and faces.
"I went to my parents' grave that morning, to tell them I'd be with them soon.
"Muties had tagged and trashed their tombstones. What better proof could I want that this was just what your kind deserved?"
The rest you know.
Glad you asked?
But just so we're clear, I'm not sorry for what I did.
And if I ever get the chance, I'll try again!

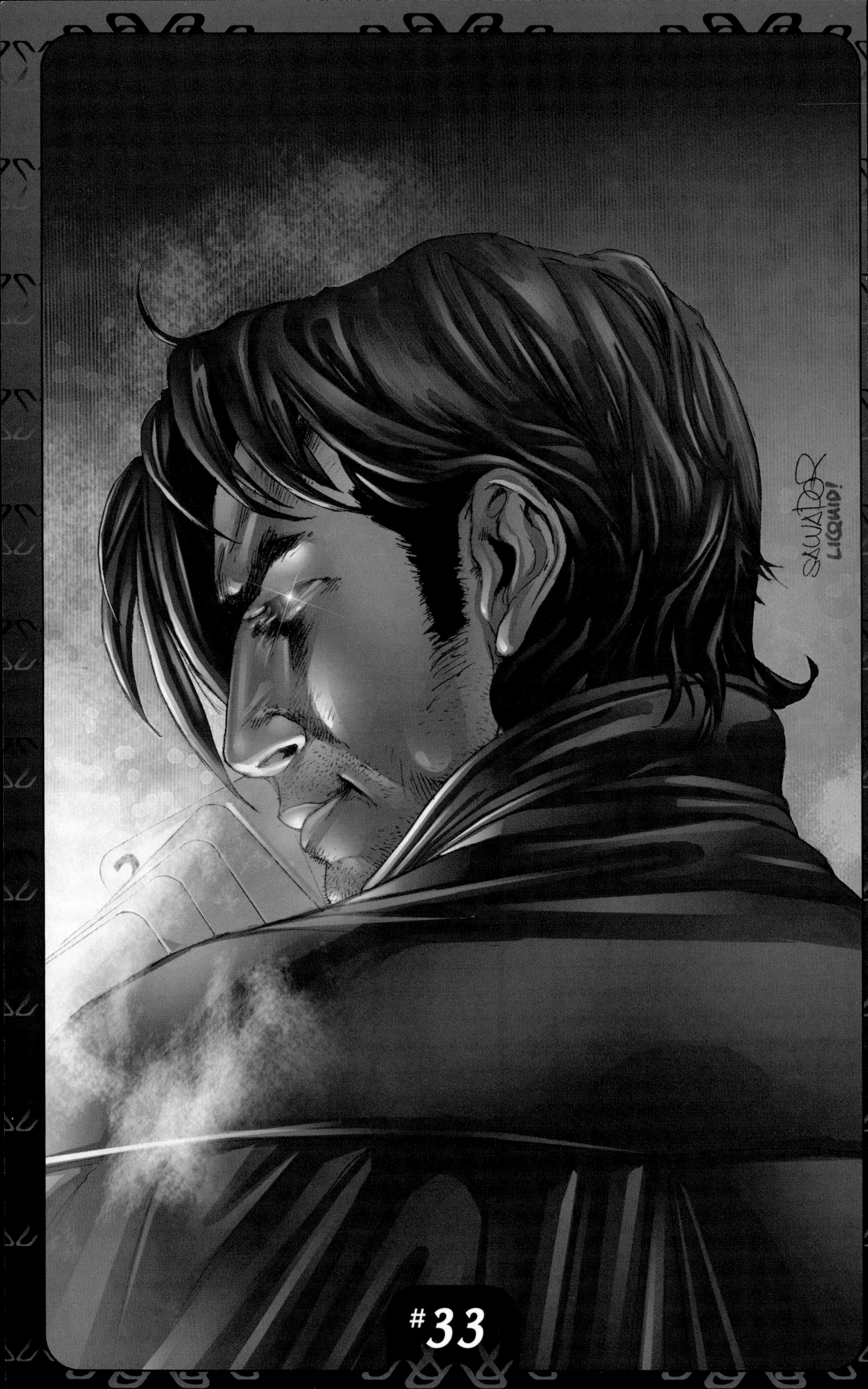
SALVADOR
LIQUID!
#33

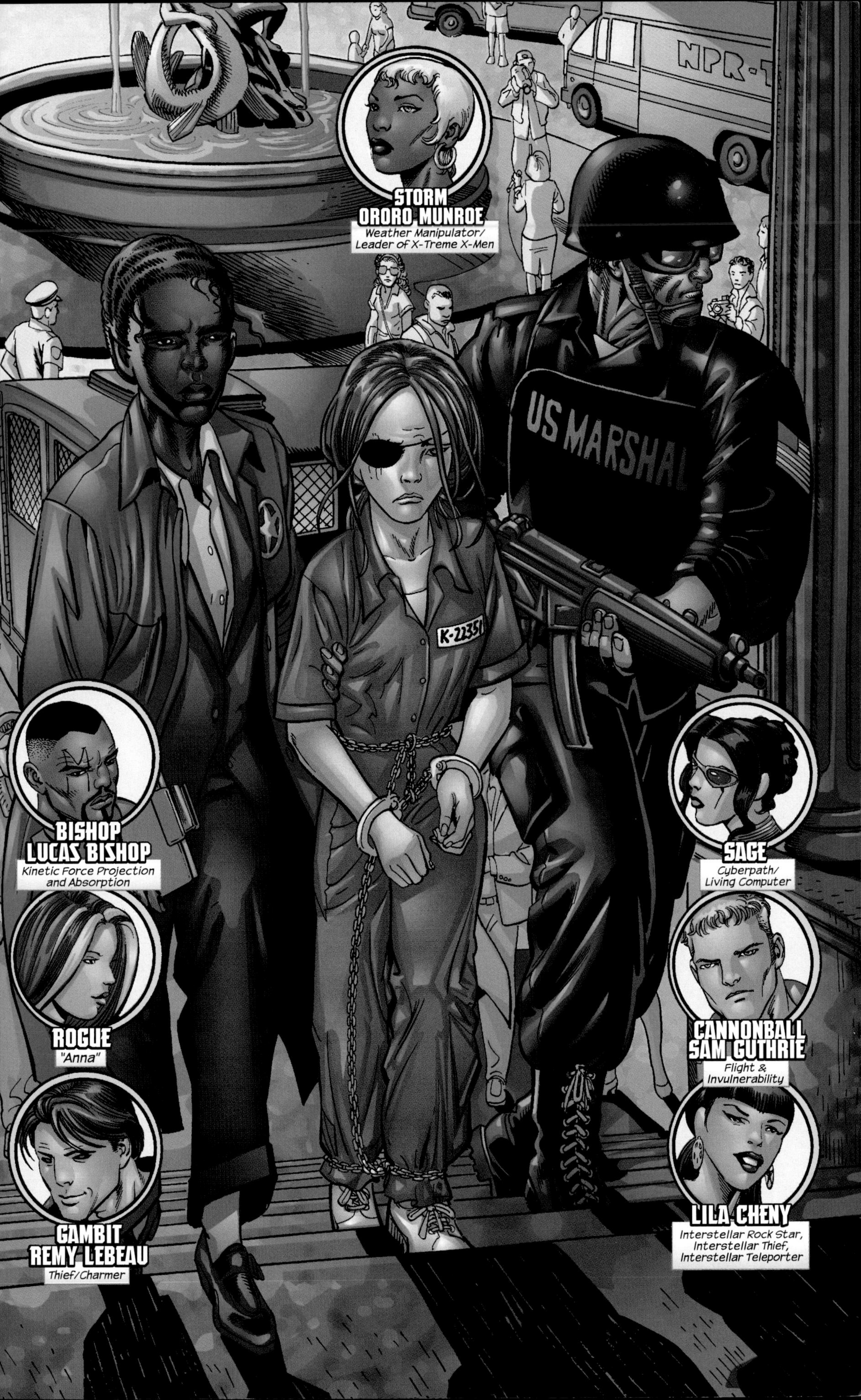

NPR-T
STORM
ORORO MUNROE
Weather Manipulator/
Leader of X-Treme X-Men
US MARSHAL
K-2235
BISHOP
LUCAS BISHOP
Kinetic Force Projection
and Absorption
SAGE
Cyberpath/
Living Computer
ROGUE
"Anna"
CANNONBALL
SAM GUTHRIE
Flight &
Invulnerability
GAMBIT
REMY LEBEAU
Thief/Charmer
LILA CHENY
Interstellar Rock Star,
Interstellar Thief,
Interstellar Teleporter

Once upon a time, a man named **Charles Xavier** had a dream...

Before Marie

...of a world where two competing subsets of the same **species**...

...one labeled **baseline humanity** and the other, **mutants**...

Mitzie's DINER

OPEN

...might find a way to **live together.**

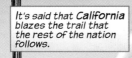

WELCOME TO **Valle Soleada**

It's said that *California* blazes the trail that the rest of the nation follows.

If so, then **Valle Soleada**, on the northern coastal outskirts of **Los Angeles**...

4TH OF JULY

...may well be the prototype of that dream **come true.**

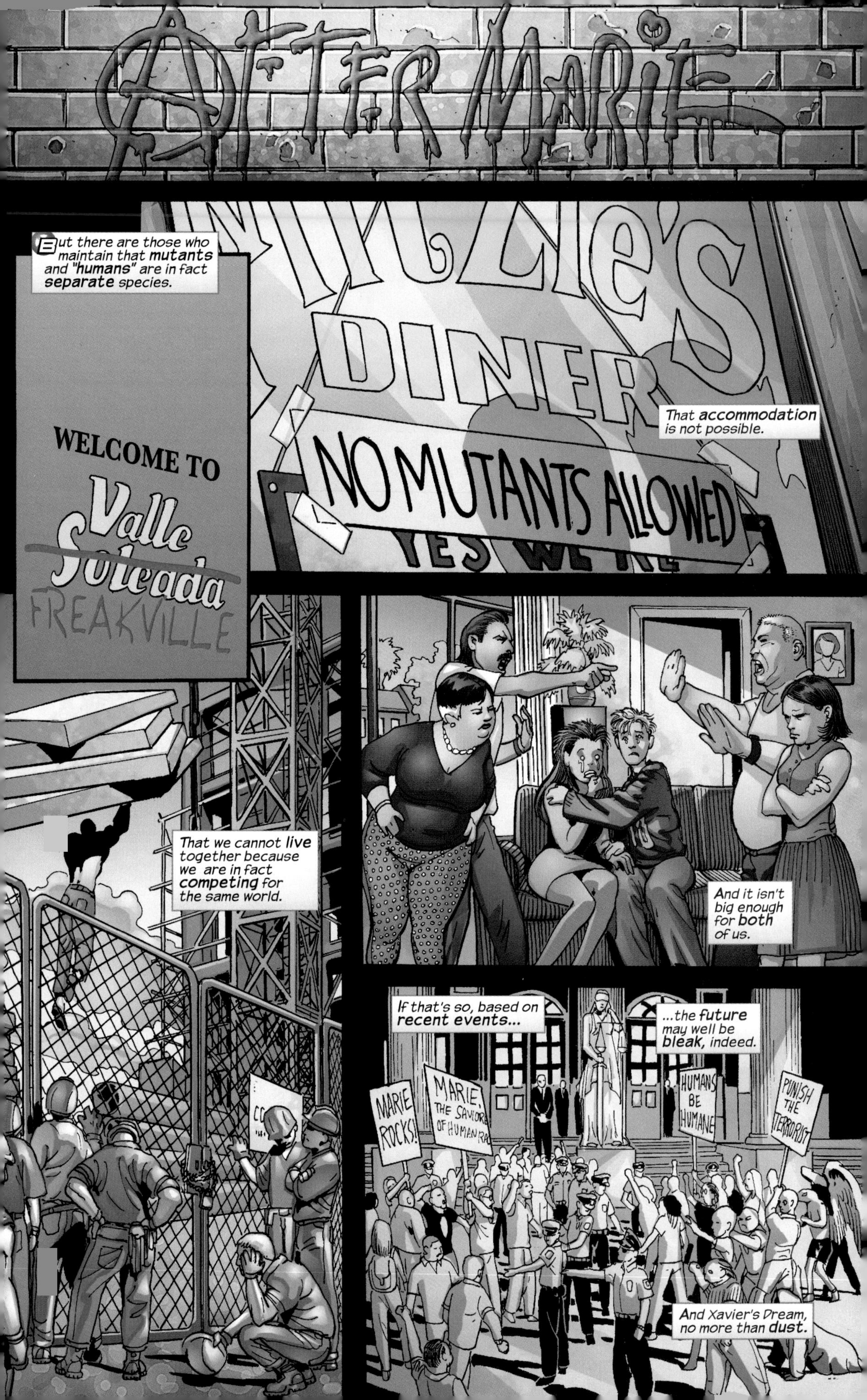
AFTER MARIE
But there are those who maintain that **mutants** and "**humans**" are in fact **separate** species.
DINER
NO MUTANTS ALLOWED
That **accommodation** is not possible.
WELCOME TO
Valle
Soleada
FREAKVILLE
That we cannot **live** together because we are in fact **competing** for the same world.
And it isn't big enough for **both** of us.
If that's so, based on **recent events...**
...the **future** may well be **bleak,** indeed.
MARIE ROCKS!
HUMANS BE HUMANE
PUNISH THE TERRORIST
And Xavier's Dream, no more than **dust.**

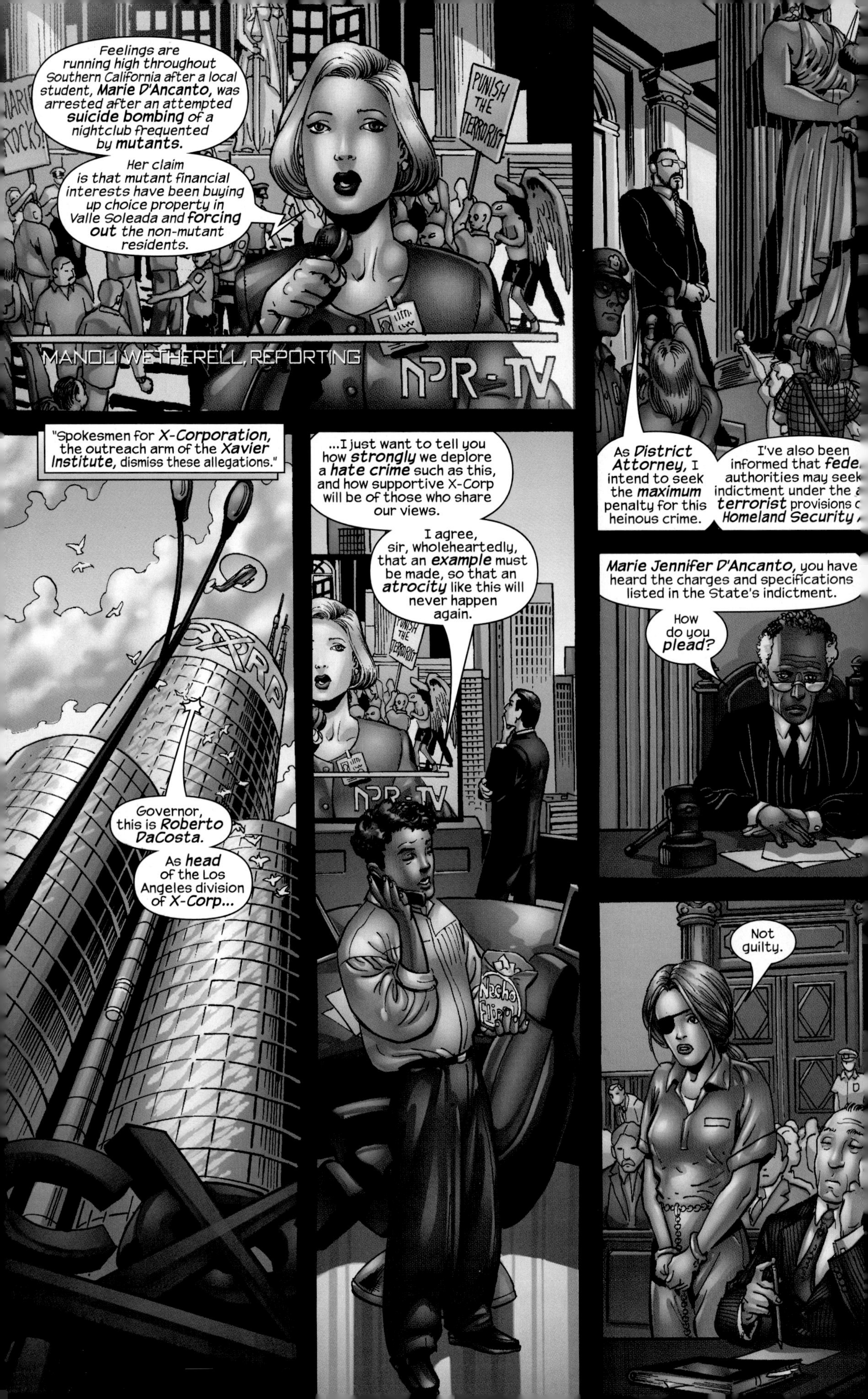

Feelings are running high throughout Southern California after a local student, Marie D'Ancanto, was arrested after an attempted suicide bombing of a nightclub frequented by mutants.
Her claim is that mutant financial interests have been buying up choice property in Valle Soleada and forcing out the non-mutant residents.
PUNISH THE TERRORIST
MANOLI WETHERELL, REPORTING
NPR-TV
As District Attorney, I intend to seek the maximum penalty for this heinous crime.
I've also been informed that fede authorities may seek indictment under the a terrorist provisions o Homeland Security
"Spokesmen for X-Corporation, the outreach arm of the Xavier Institute, dismiss these allegations."
Governor, this is Roberto DaCosta.
As head of the Los Angeles division of X-Corp...
...I just want to tell you how strongly we deplore a hate crime such as this, and how supportive X-Corp will be of those who share our views.
I agree, sir, wholeheartedly, that an example must be made, so that an atrocity like this will never happen again.
NPR-TV
Nacho Flips
Marie Jennifer D'Ancanto, you have heard the charges and specifications listed in the State's indictment.
How do you plead?
Not guilty.

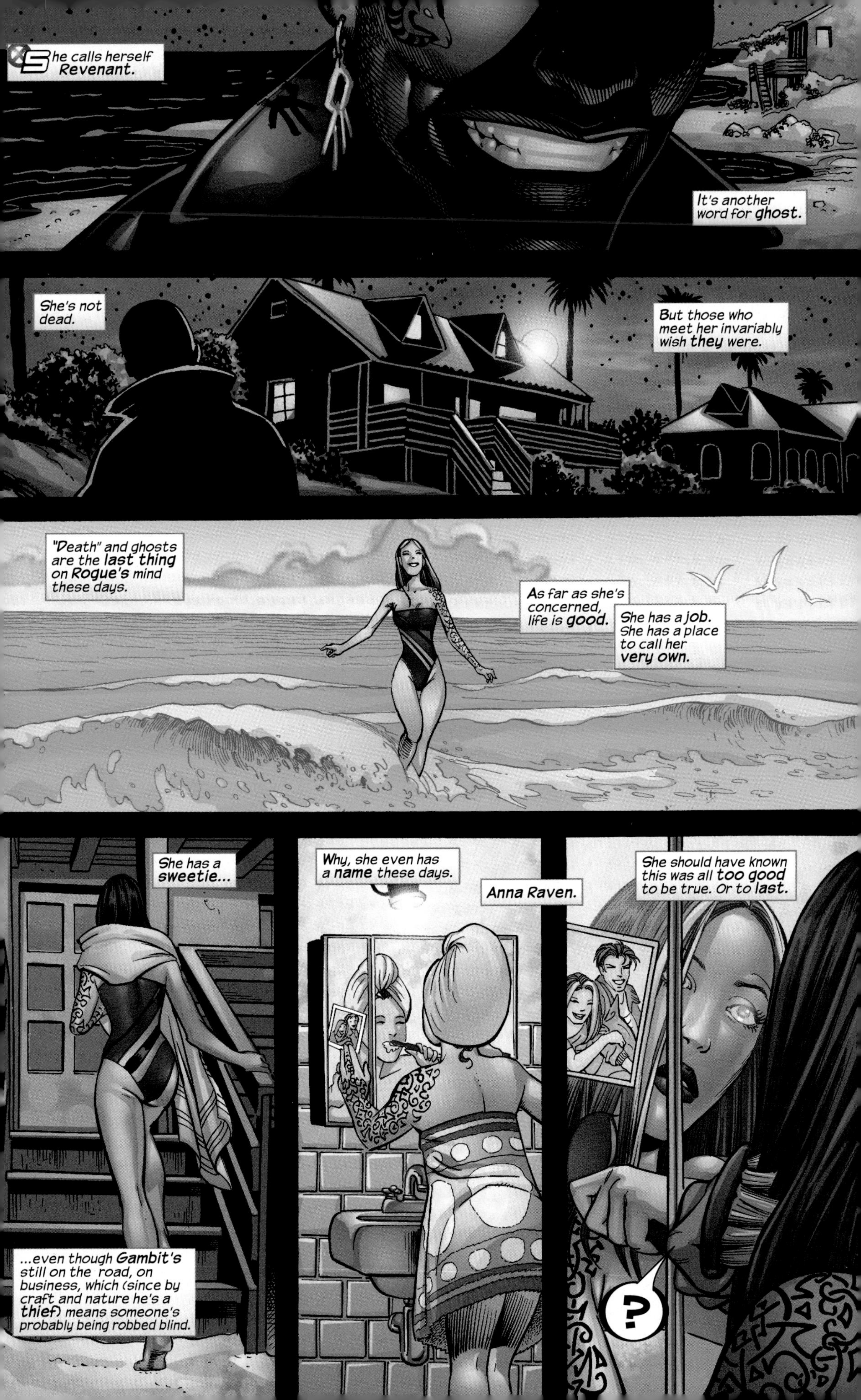
She calls herself Revenant.
It's another word for ghost.
She's not dead.
But those who meet her invariably wish they were.
"Death" and ghosts are the last thing on Rogue's mind these days.
As far as she's concerned, life is good.
She has a job. She has a place to call her very own.
She has a sweetie...
...even though Gambit's still on the road, on business, which (since by craft and nature he's a thief) means someone's probably being robbed blind.
Why, she even has a name these days.
Anna Raven.
She should have known this was all too good to be true. Or to last.
?

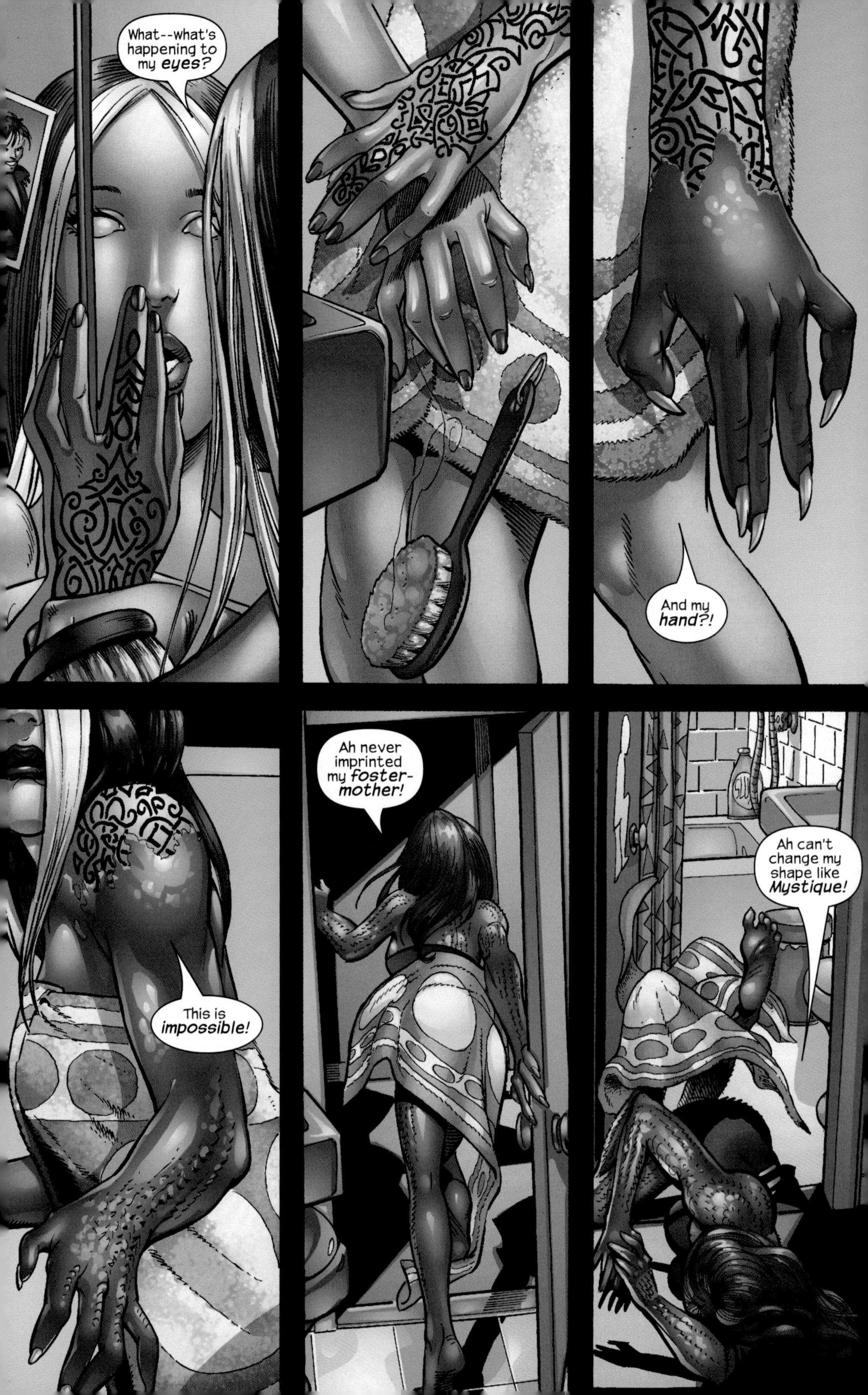

What--what's happening to my *eyes?*
And my *hand?!*
This is *impossible!*
Ah never imprinted my *foster-mother!*
Ah can't change my shape like *Mystique!*

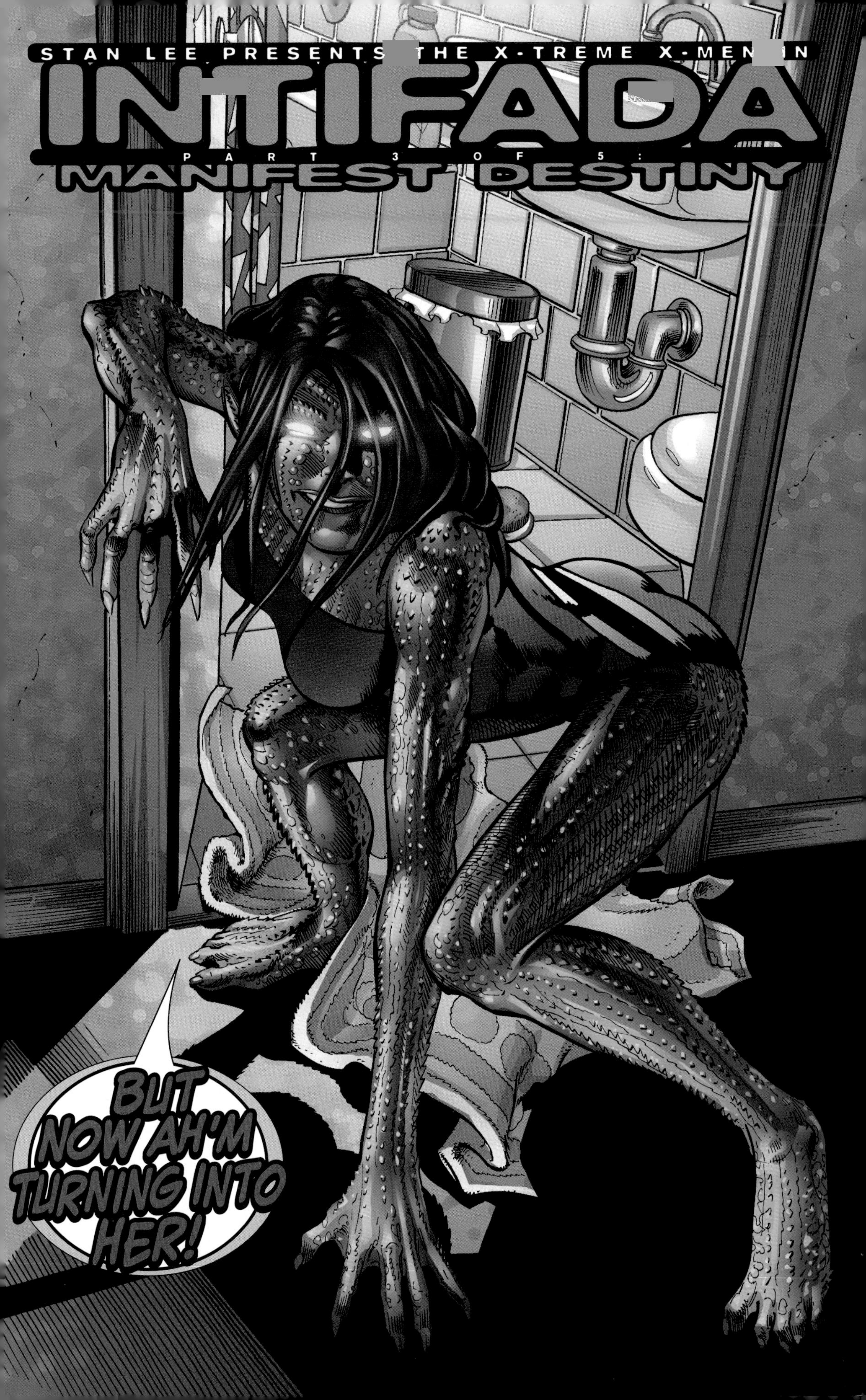
STAN LEE PRESENTS THE X-TREME X-MEN IN
INTIFADA
PART 3 OF 5:
MANIFEST DESTINY
BUT NOW AH'M TURNING INTO HER!

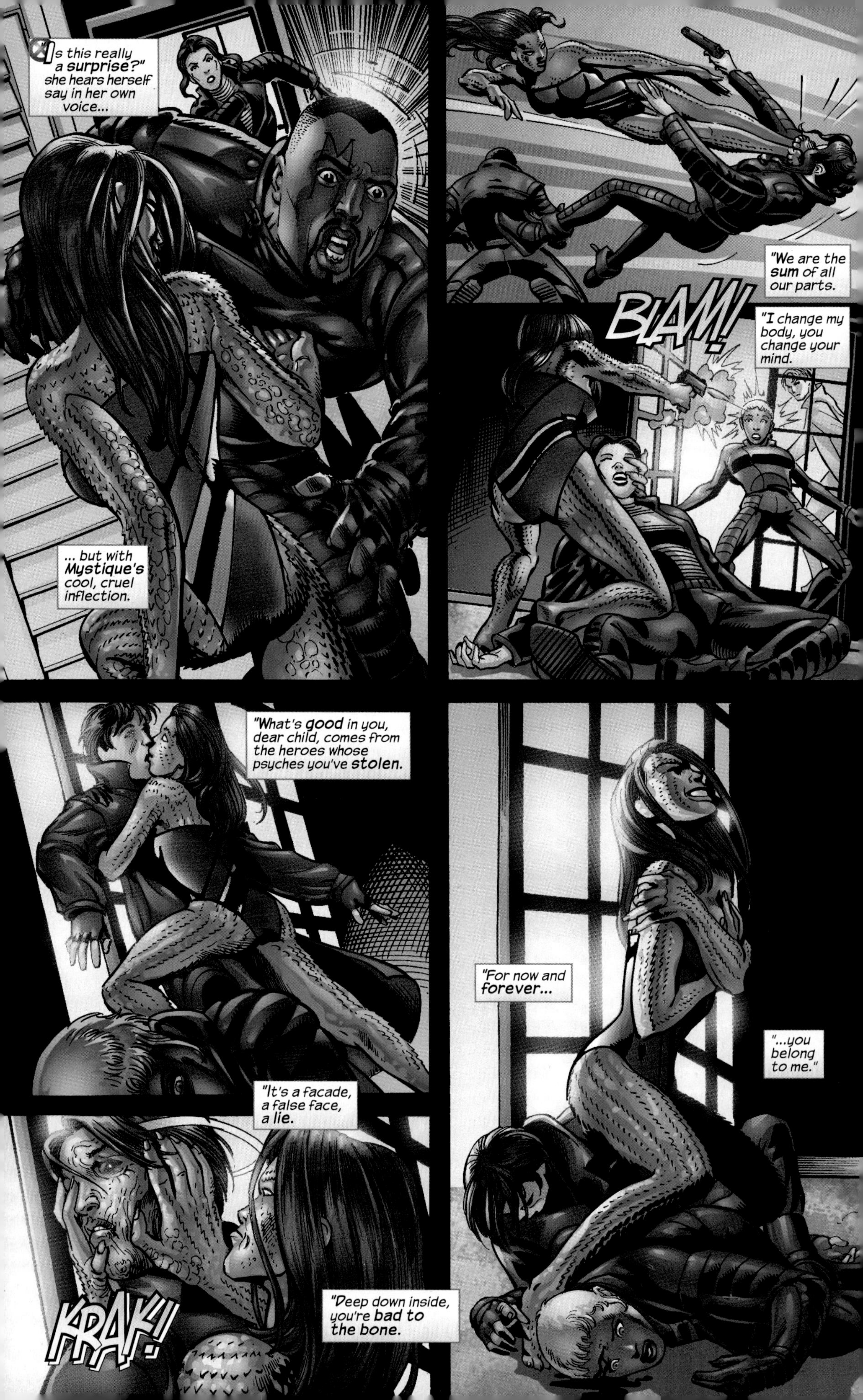
"Is this really a surprise?" she hears herself say in her own voice...
... but with Mystique's cool, cruel inflection.
"We are the sum of all our parts.
BLAM!
"I change my body, you change your mind.
"What's good in you, dear child, comes from the heroes whose psyches you've stolen.
"It's a facade, a false face, a lie.
"Deep down inside, you're bad to the bone.
KRAK!!
"For now and forever...
"...you belong to me."

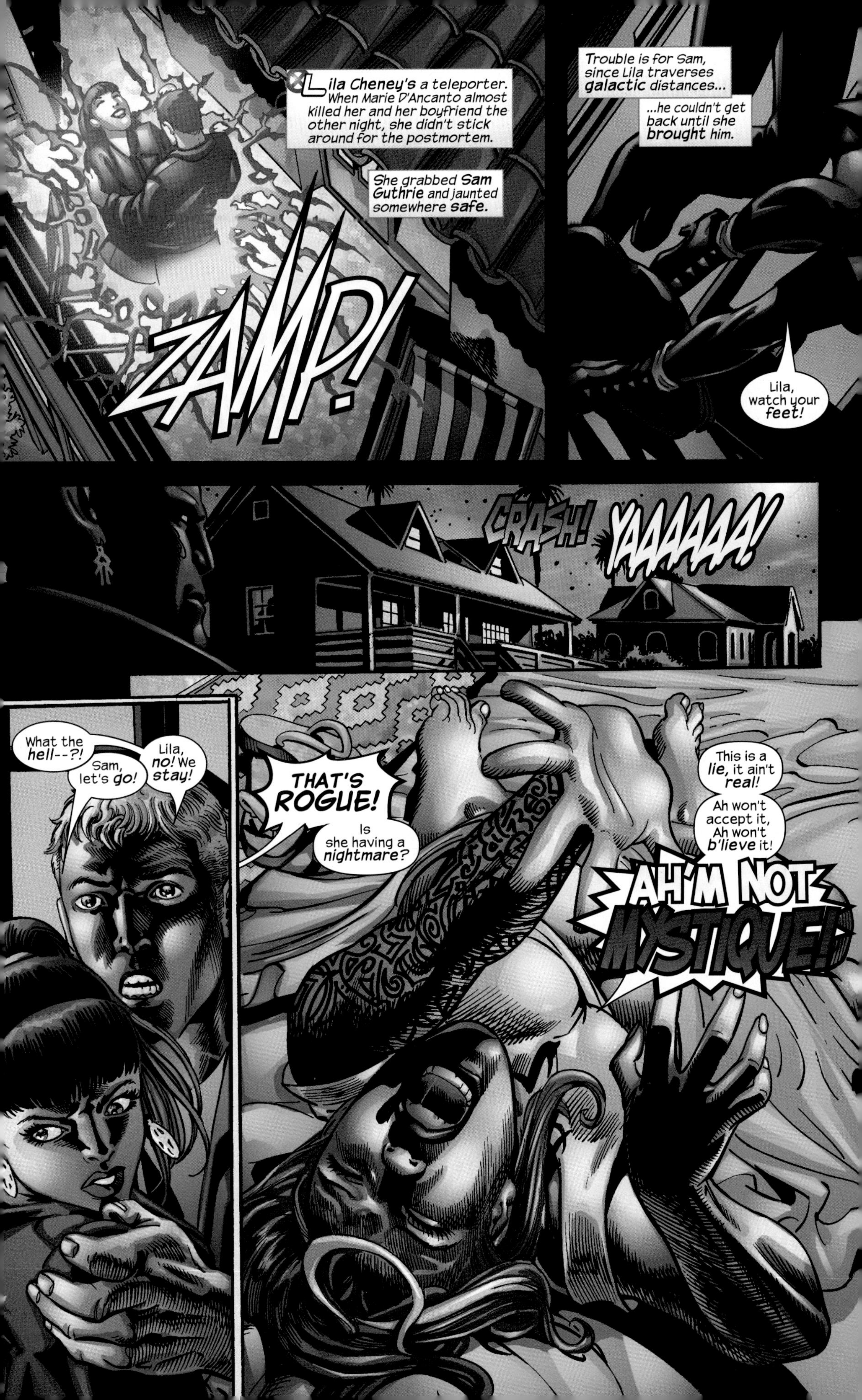
Lila Cheney's a teleporter. When Marie D'Ancanto almost killed her and her boyfriend the other night, she didn't stick around for the postmortem.
She grabbed Sam Guthrie and jaunted somewhere safe.
ZAMP!
Trouble is for Sam, since Lila traverses galactic distances...
...he couldn't get back until she brought him.
Lila, watch your feet!
CRASH!
YAAAAAA!
What the hell--?!
Sam, let's go!
Lila, no! We stay!
THAT'S ROGUE!
Is she having a nightmare?
This is a lie, it ain't real!
Ah won't accept it, Ah won't b'lieve it!
AH'M NOT MYSTIQUE!

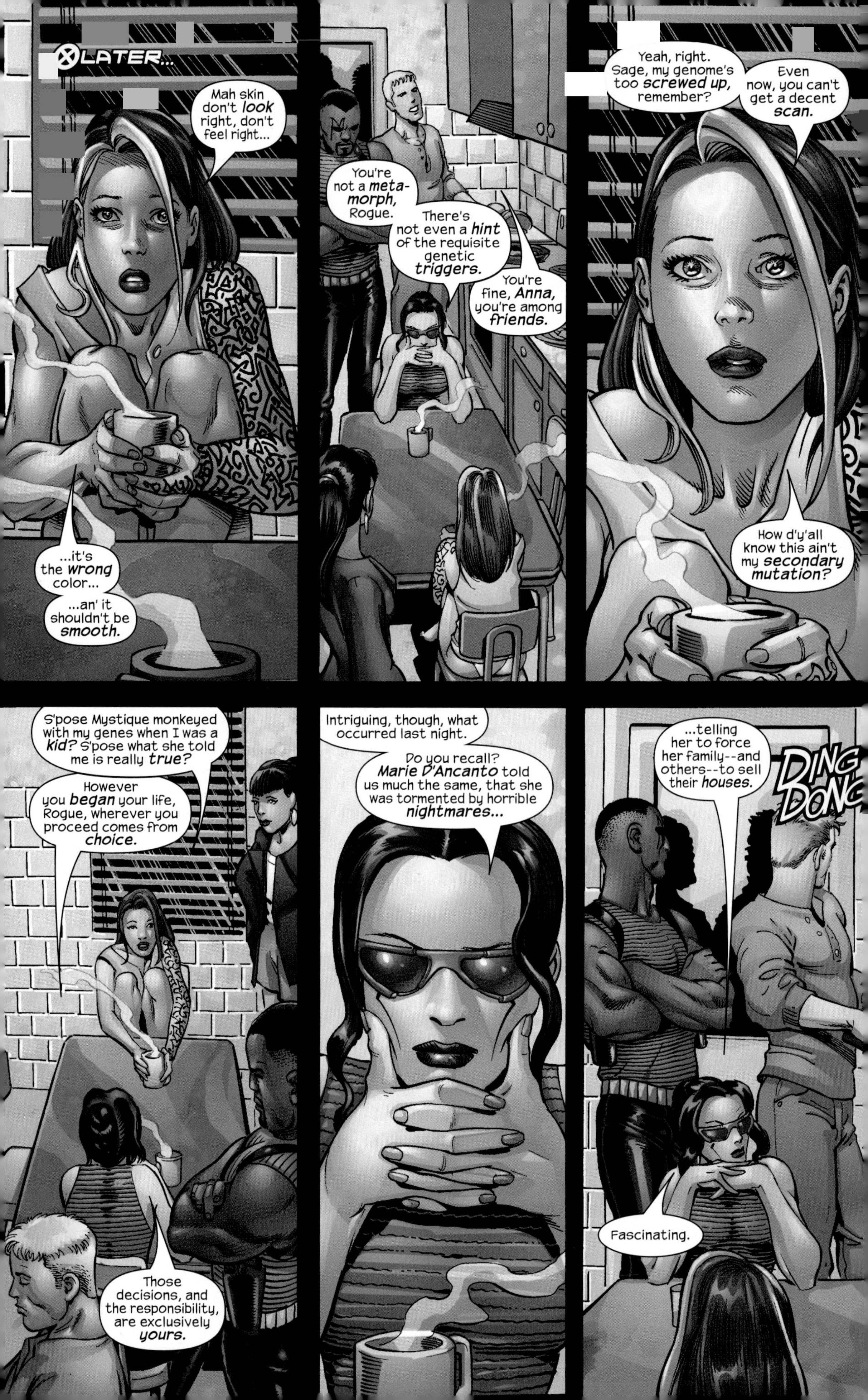
LATER...
Mah skin don't look right, don't feel right...
...it's the wrong color...
...an' it shouldn't be smooth.
You're not a meta-morph, Rogue.
There's not even a hint of the requisite genetic triggers.
You're fine, Anna, you're among friends.
Yeah, right. Sage, my genome's too screwed up, remember?
Even now, you can't get a decent scan.
How d'y'all know this ain't my secondary mutation?
S'pose Mystique monkeyed with my genes when I was a kid? S'pose what she told me is really true?
However you began your life, Rogue, wherever you proceed comes from choice.
Those decisions, and the responsibility, are exclusively yours.
Intriguing, though, what occurred last night.
Do you recall? Marie D'Ancanto told us much the same, that she was tormented by horrible nightmares...
...telling her to force her family--and others--to sell their houses.
DING DONG
Fascinating.

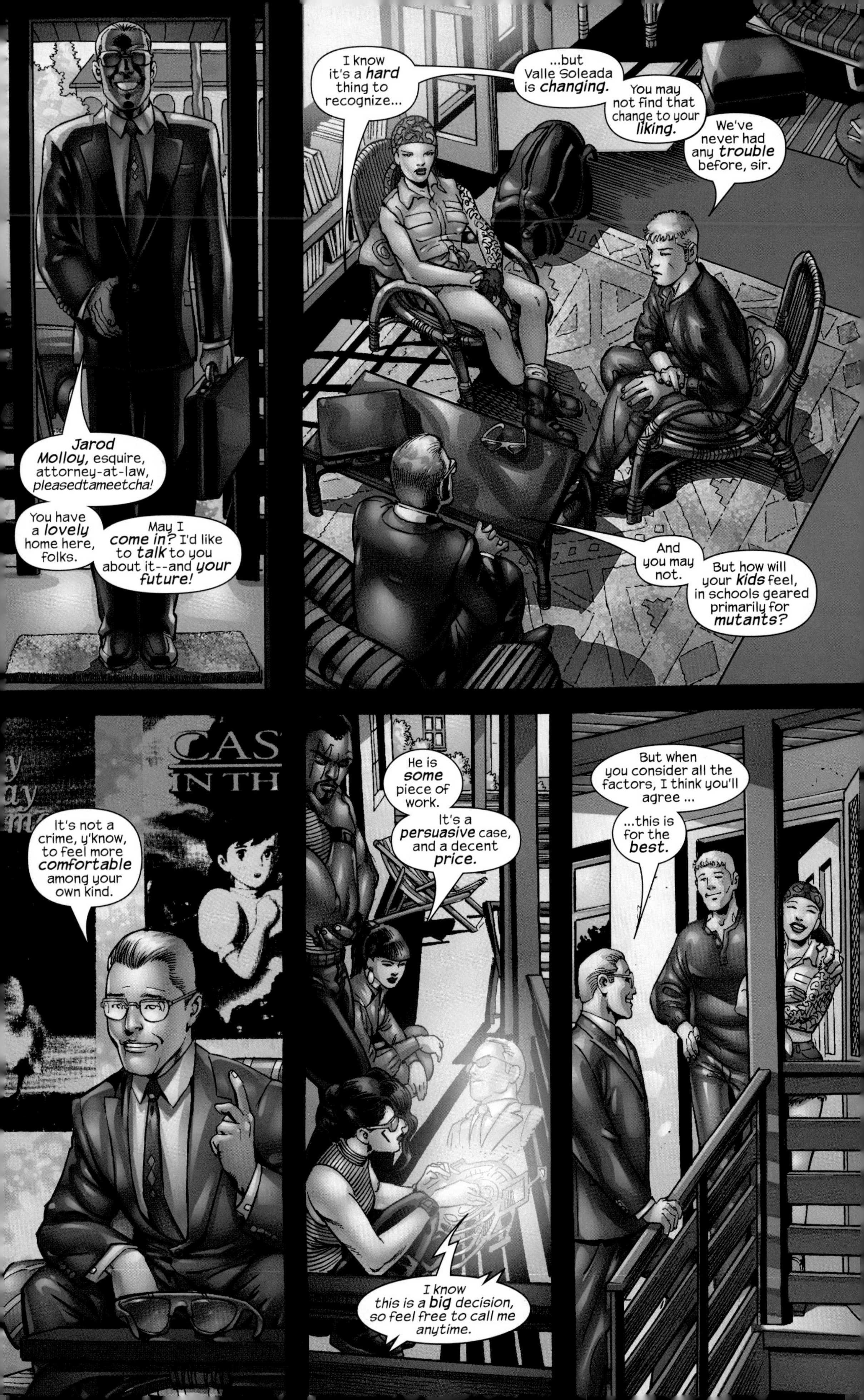

Jarod Molloy, esquire, attorney-at-law, pleasedtameetcha!
You have a lovely home here, folks.
May I come in? I'd like to talk to you about it--and your future!
I know it's a hard thing to recognize...
...but Valle Soleada is changing.
You may not find that change to your liking.
We've never had any trouble before, sir.
And you may not.
But how will your kids feel, in schools geared primarily for mutants?
It's not a crime, y'know, to feel more comfortable among your own kind.
He is some piece of work.
It's a persuasive case, and a decent price.
I know this is a big decision, so feel free to call me anytime.
But when you consider all the factors, I think you'll agree ...
...this is for the best.

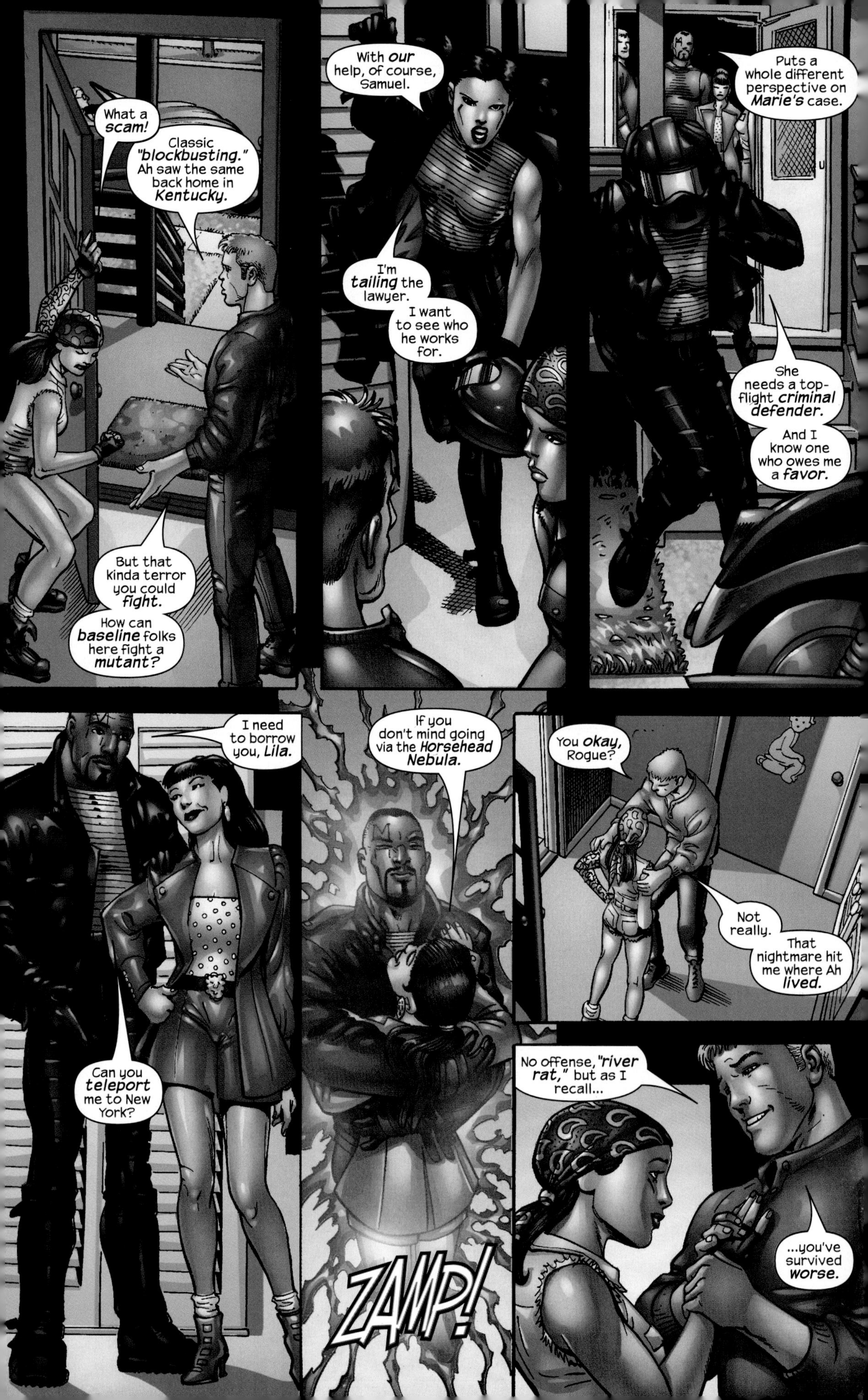
What a scam!
Classic "blockbusting." Ah saw the same back home in Kentucky.
But that kinda terror you could fight.
How can baseline folks here fight a mutant?
With our help, of course, Samuel.
I'm tailing the lawyer.
I want to see who he works for.
Puts a whole different perspective on Marie's case.
She needs a top-flight criminal defender.
And I know one who owes me a favor.
I need to borrow you, Lila.
Can you teleport me to New York?
If you don't mind going via the Horsehead Nebula.
ZAMP!
You okay, Rogue?
Not really.
That nightmare hit me where Ah lived.
No offense, "river rat," but as I recall...
...you've survived worse.

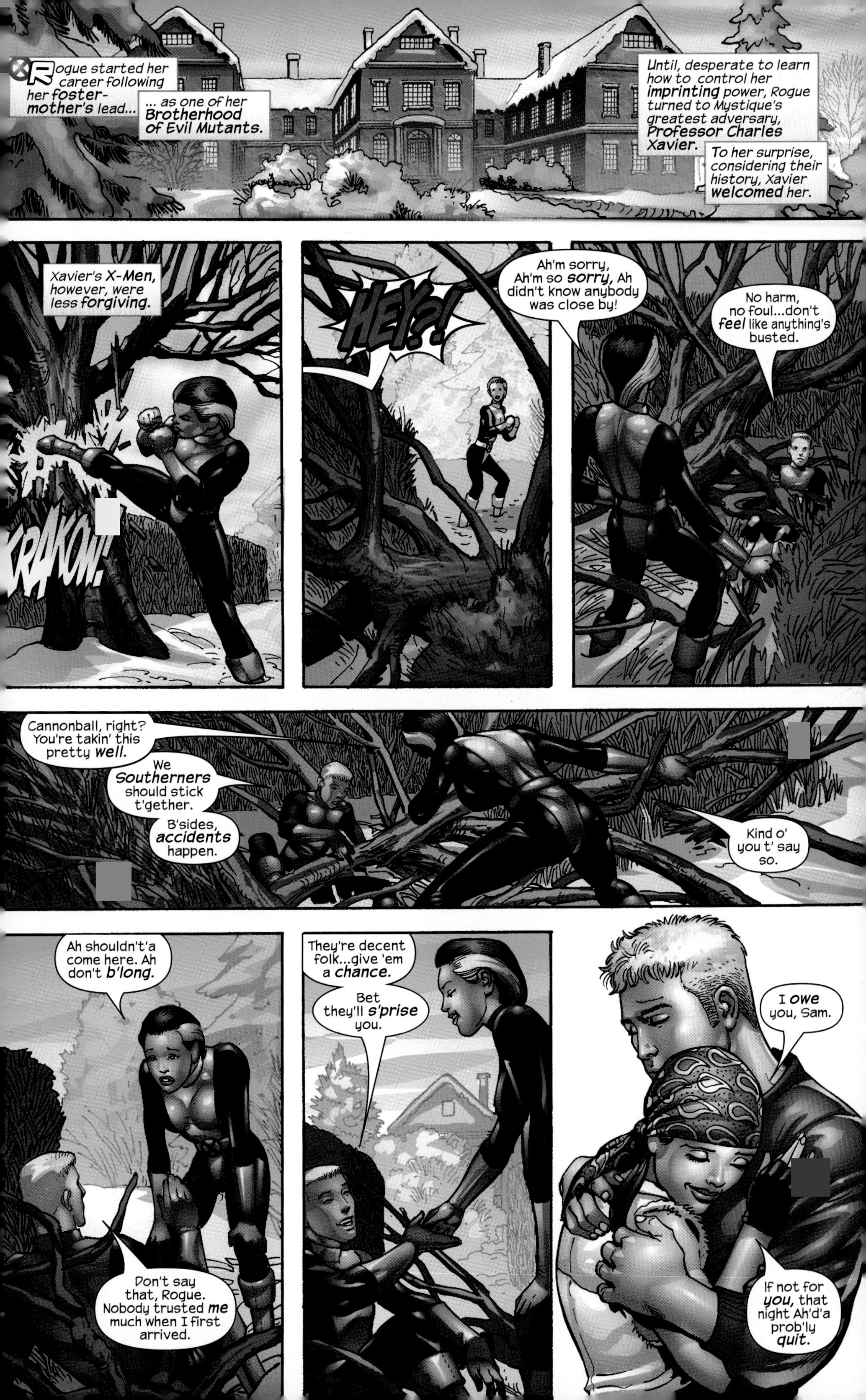

Rogue started her career following her foster-mother's lead...
... as one of her Brotherhood of Evil Mutants.
Until, desperate to learn how to control her imprinting power, Rogue turned to Mystique's greatest adversary, Professor Charles Xavier.
To her surprise, considering their history, Xavier welcomed her.
Xavier's X-Men, however, were less forgiving.
KRAKOW!
HEY?!
Ah'm sorry, Ah'm so sorry, Ah didn't know anybody was close by!
No harm, no foul...don't feel like anything's busted.
Cannonball, right? You're takin' this pretty well.
We Southerners should stick t'gether.
B'sides, accidents happen.
Kind o' you t' say so.
Ah shouldn't'a come here. Ah don't b'long.
Don't say that, Rogue. Nobody trusted me much when I first arrived.
They're decent folk...give 'em a chance.
Bet they'll s'prise you.
I owe you, Sam.
If not for you, that night Ah'd'a prob'ly quit.

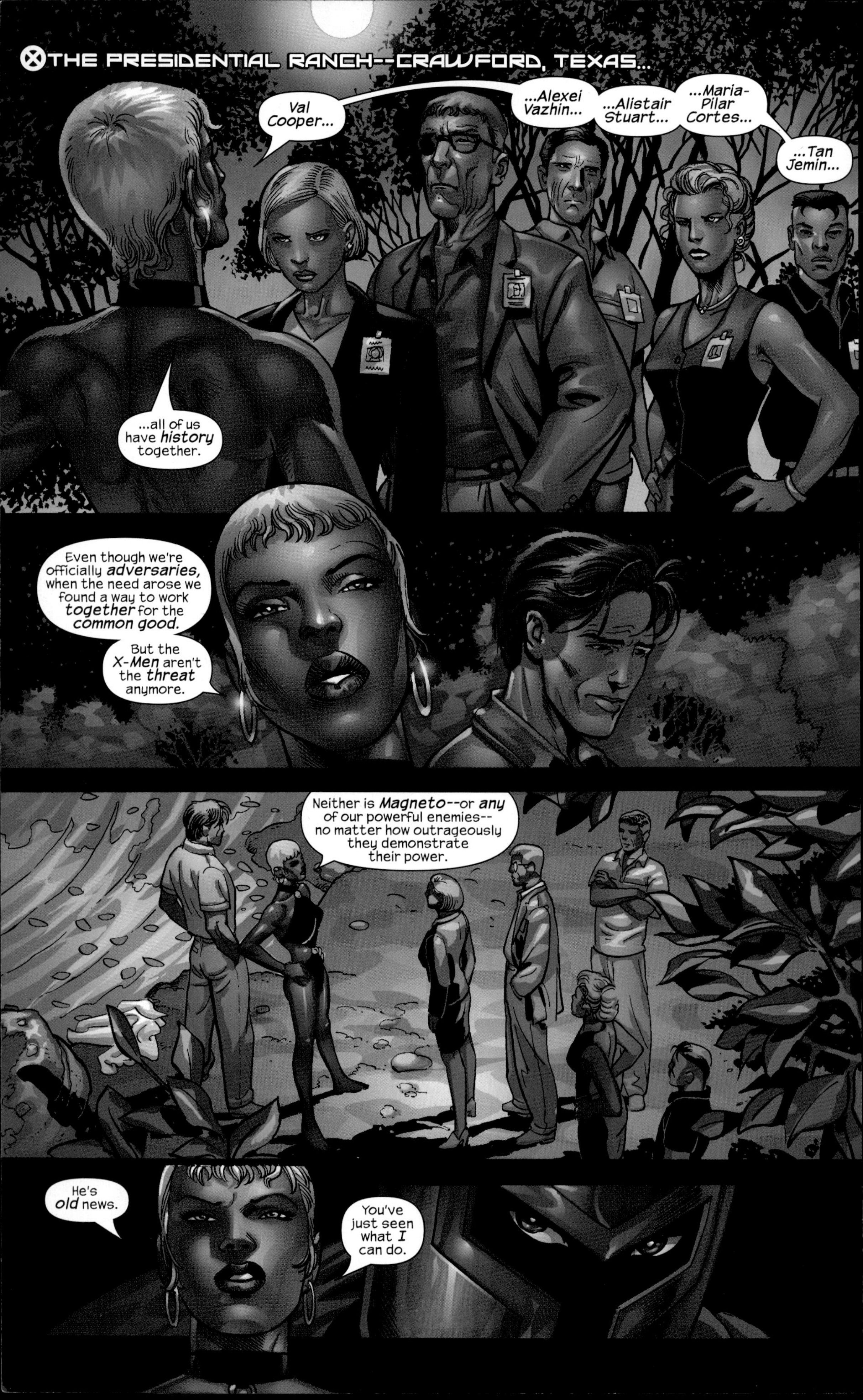
THE PRESIDENTIAL RANCH--CRAWFORD, TEXAS...
Val Cooper...
...Alexei Vazhin...
...Alistair Stuart...
...Maria-Pilar Cortes...
...Tan Jemin...
...all of us have *history* together.
Even though we're officially *adversaries,* when the need arose we found a way to work *together* for the *common good.*
But the *X-Men* aren't the *threat* anymore.
Neither is *Magneto*--or *any* of our powerful enemies--no matter how outrageously they demonstrate their power.
He's *old* news.
You've just seen what *I* can do.

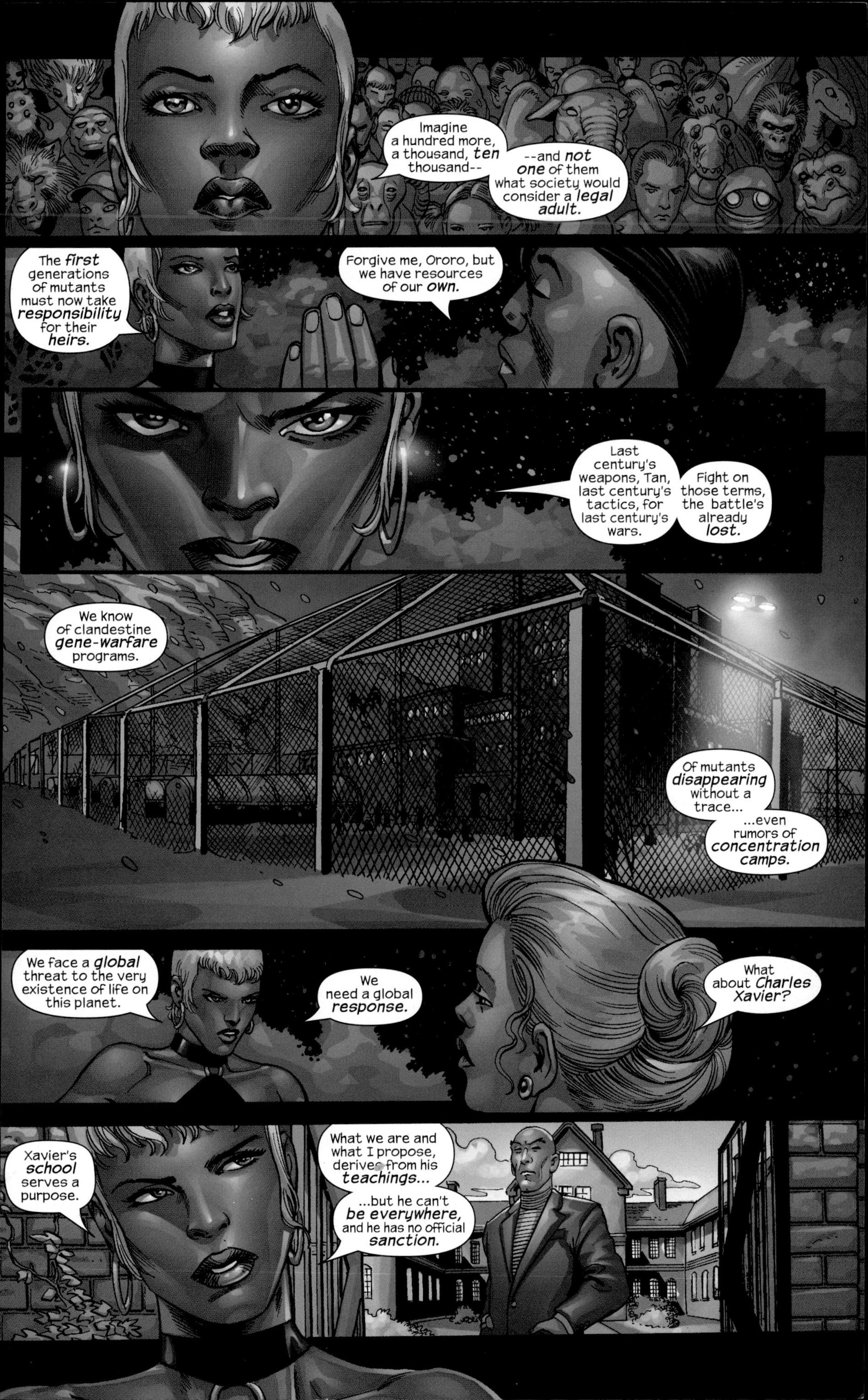
Imagine a hundred more, a thousand, ten thousand--
--and not one of them what society would consider a legal adult.
The first generations of mutants must now take responsibility for their heirs.
Forgive me, Ororo, but we have resources of our own.
Last century's weapons, Tan, last century's tactics, for last century's wars.
Fight on those terms, the battle's already lost.
We know of clandestine gene-warfare programs.
Of mutants disappearing without a trace...
...even rumors of concentration camps.
We face a global threat to the very existence of life on this planet.
We need a global response.
What about Charles Xavier?
Xavier's school serves a purpose.
What we are and what I propose, derives from his teachings...
...but he can't be everywhere, and he has no official sanction.

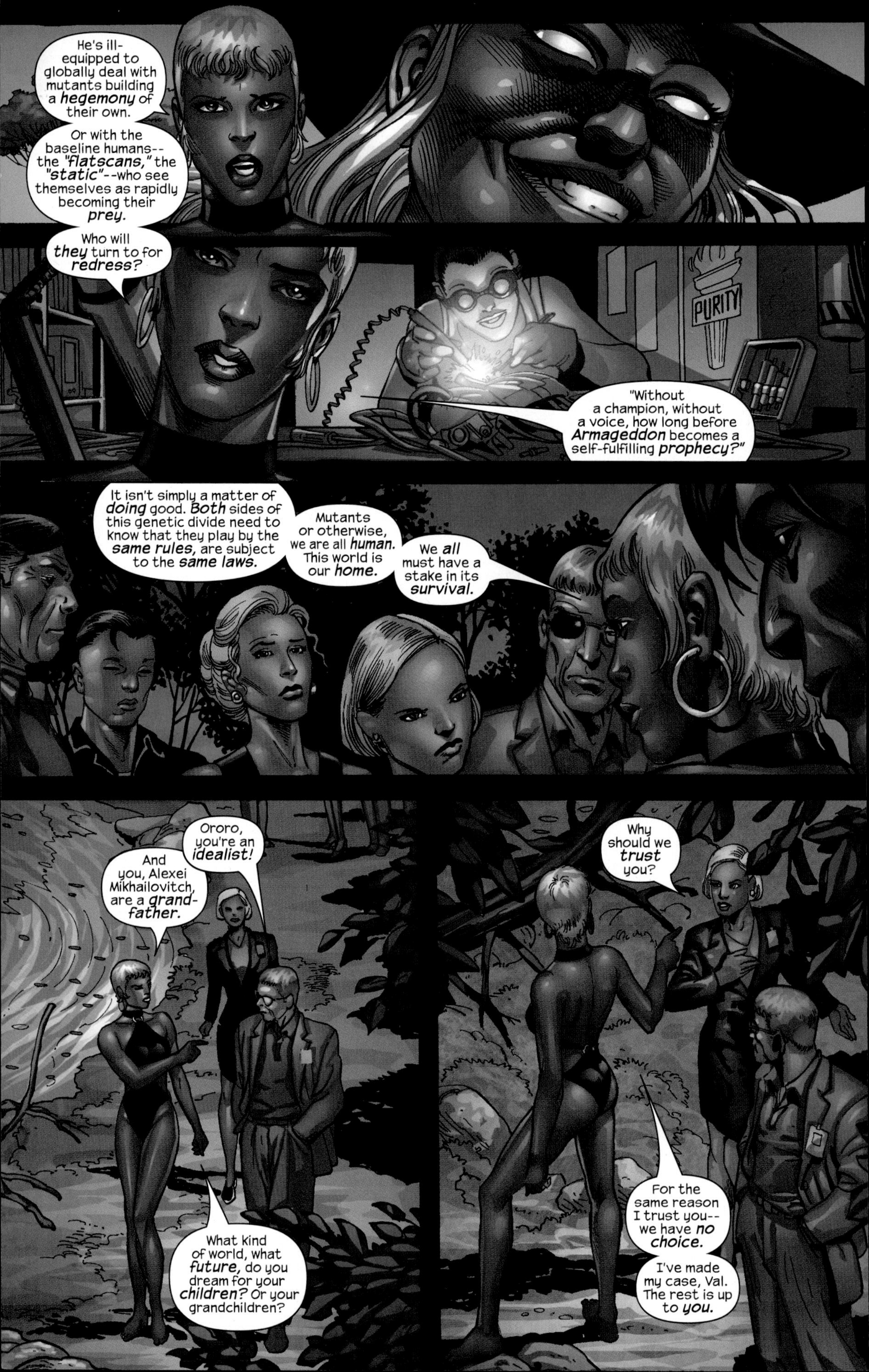

He's ill-equipped to globally deal with mutants building a hegemony of their own.
Or with the baseline humans--the "flatscans," the "static"--who see themselves as rapidly becoming their prey.
Who will they turn to for redress?
"Without a champion, without a voice, how long before Armageddon becomes a self-fulfilling prophecy?"
PURITY
It isn't simply a matter of doing good. Both sides of this genetic divide need to know that they play by the same rules, are subject to the same laws.
Mutants or otherwise, we are all human. This world is our home.
We all must have a stake in its survival.
Ororo, you're an idealist!
And you, Alexei Mikhailovitch, are a grand-father.
What kind of world, what future, do you dream for your children? Or your grandchildren?
Why should we trust you?
For the same reason I trust you--we have no choice.
I've made my case, Val. The rest is up to you.

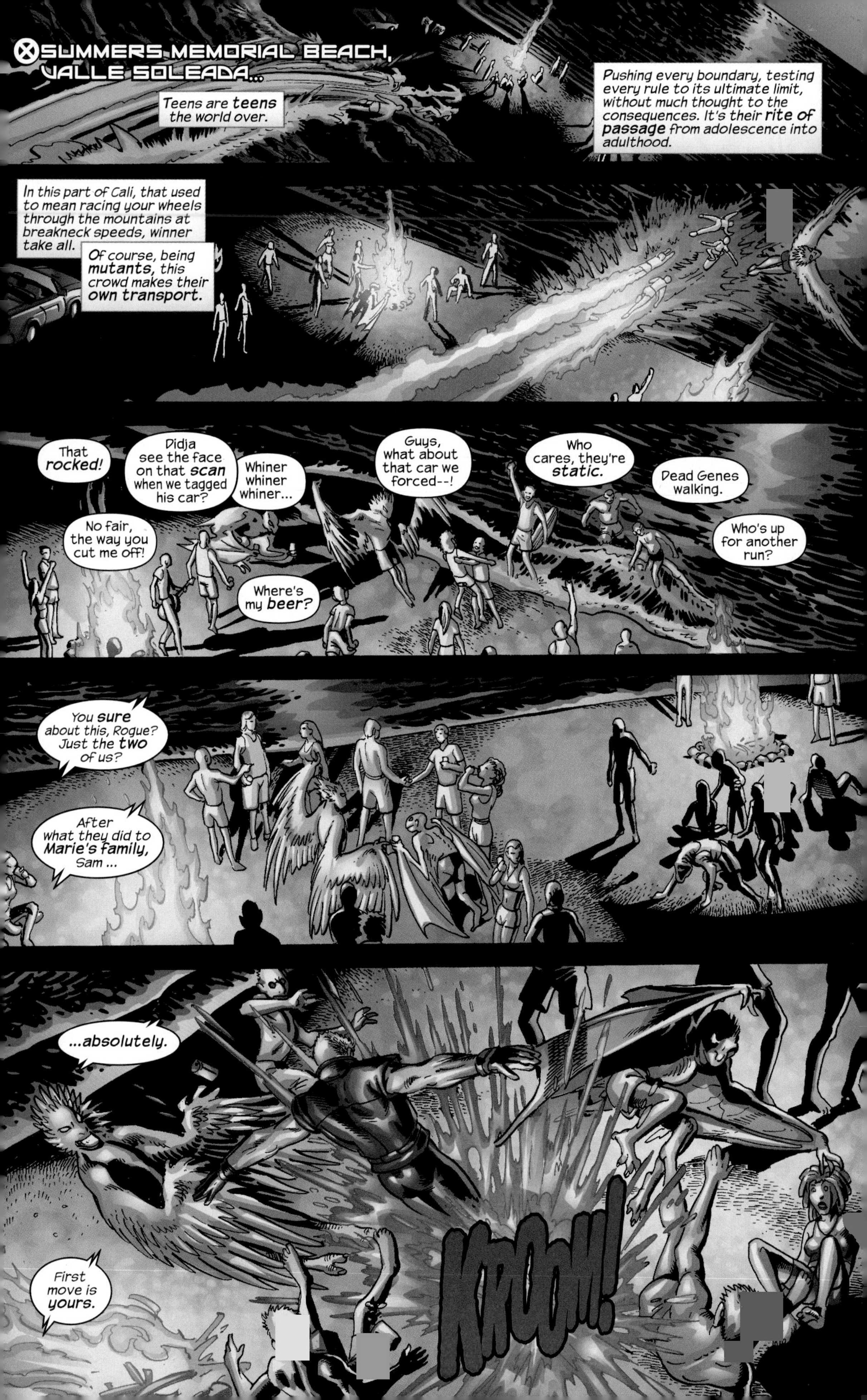

SUMMERS MEMORIAL BEACH, VALLE SOLEADA...
Teens are teens the world over.
Pushing every boundary, testing every rule to its ultimate limit, without much thought to the consequences. It's their rite of passage from adolescence into adulthood.
In this part of Cali, that used to mean racing your wheels through the mountains at breakneck speeds, winner take all.
Of course, being mutants, this crowd makes their own transport.
That rocked!
Didja see the face on that scan when we tagged his car?
Whiner whiner whiner...
Guys, what about that car we forced--!
Who cares, they're static.
Dead Genes walking.
No fair, the way you cut me off!
Where's my beer?
Who's up for another run?
You sure about this, Rogue? Just the two of us?
After what they did to Marie's family, Sam ...
...absolutely.
First move is yours.
KRAOOM!

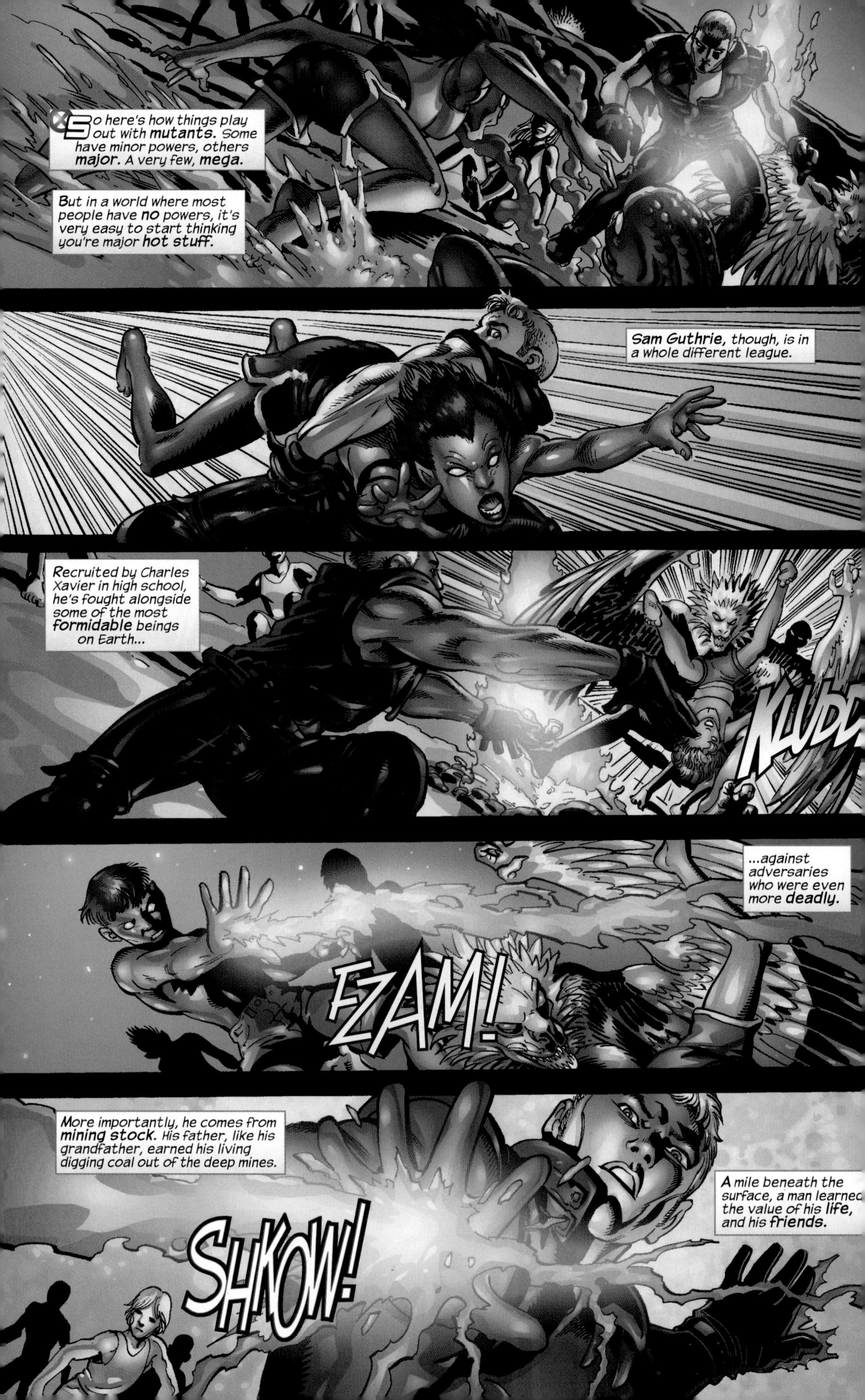

So here's how things play out with **mutants**. Some have minor powers, others **major**. A very few, **mega**.
But in a world where most people have **no** powers, it's very easy to start thinking you're major **hot stuff**.
Sam Guthrie, though, is in a whole different league.
Recruited by Charles Xavier in high school, he's fought alongside some of the most **formidable** beings on Earth...
...against adversaries who were even more **deadly**.
FZAM!
More importantly, he comes from **mining stock**. His father, like his grandfather, earned his living digging coal out of the deep mines.
A mile beneath the surface, a man learned the value of his **life**, and his **friends**.
SHKOW!

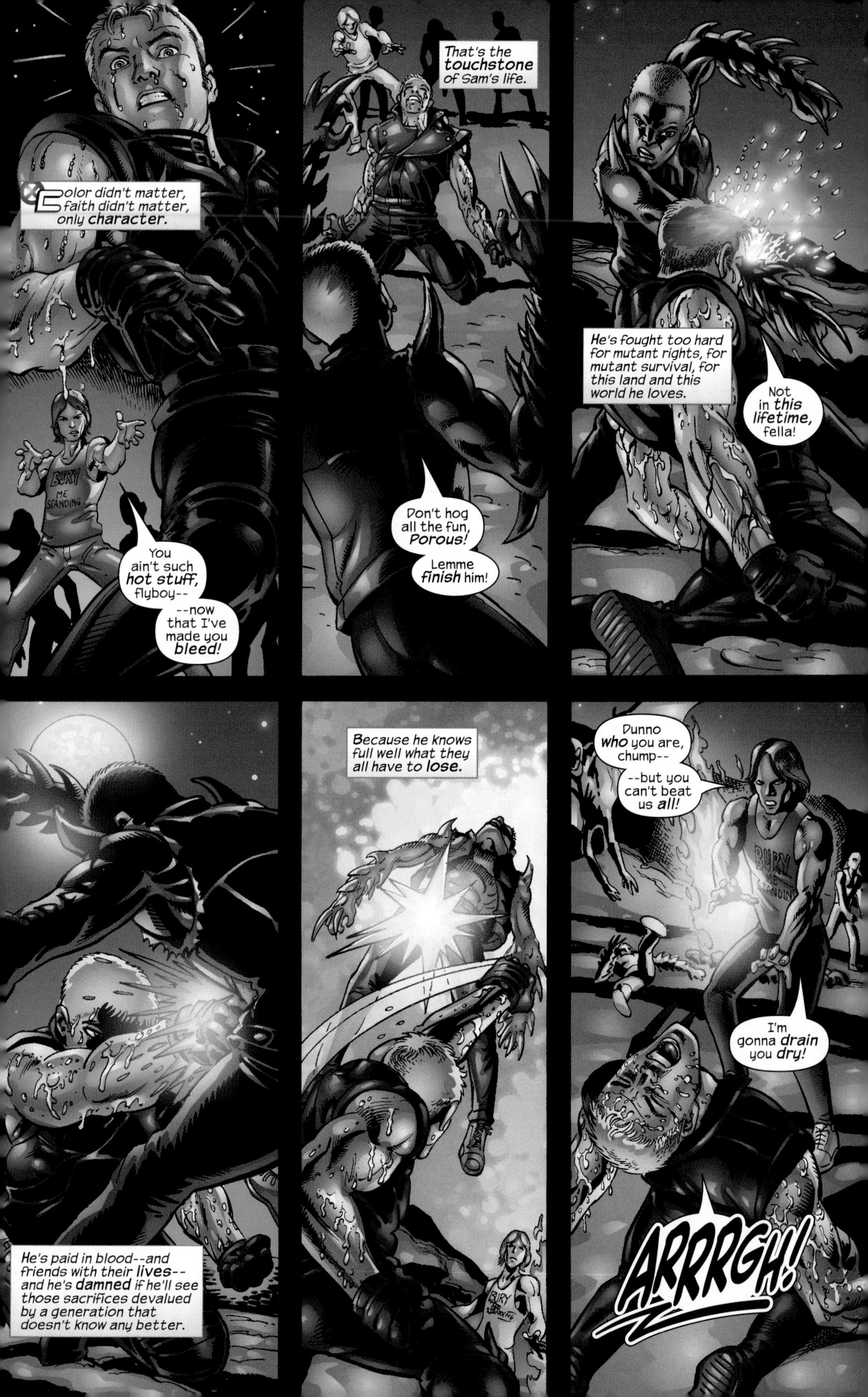
Color didn't matter, faith didn't matter, only character.
You ain't such hot stuff, flyboy--
--now that I've made you bleed!
BURY ME STANDING
That's the touchstone of Sam's life.
Don't hog all the fun, Porous!
Lemme finish him!
He's fought too hard for mutant rights, for mutant survival, for this land and this world he loves.
Not in this lifetime, fella!
He's paid in blood--and friends with their lives--and he's damned if he'll see those sacrifices devalued by a generation that doesn't know any better.
Because he knows full well what they all have to lose.
Dunno who you are, chump--
--but you can't beat us all!
I'm gonna drain you dry!
ARRRGH!

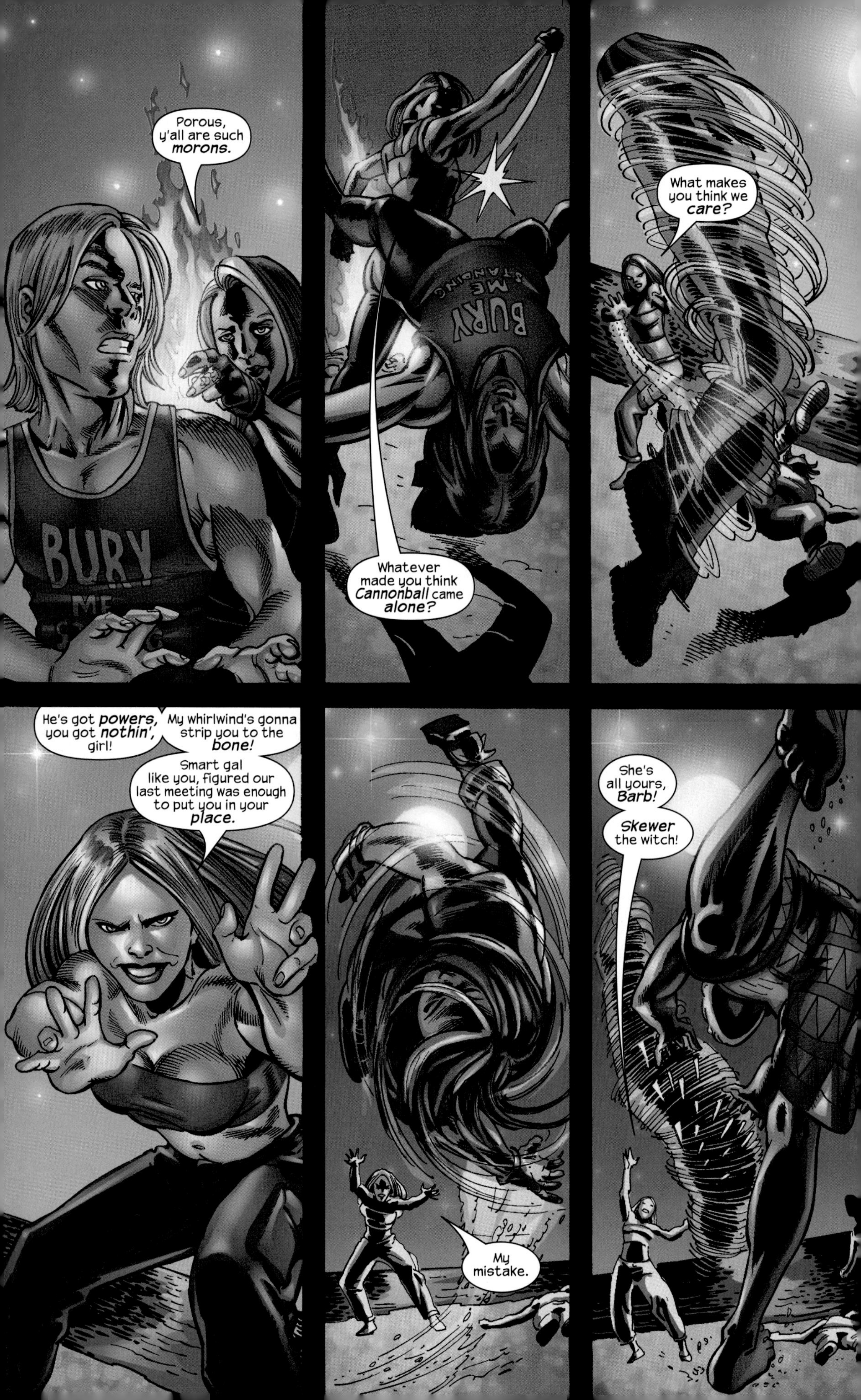

Porous, y'all are such *morons.*
Whatever made you think *Cannonball* came *alone?*
What makes you think we *care?*
He's got *powers,* you got *nothin',* girl!
My whirlwind's gonna strip you to the *bone!*
Smart gal like you, figured our last meeting was enough to put you in your *place.*
My mistake.
She's all yours, *Barb!*
Skewer the witch!

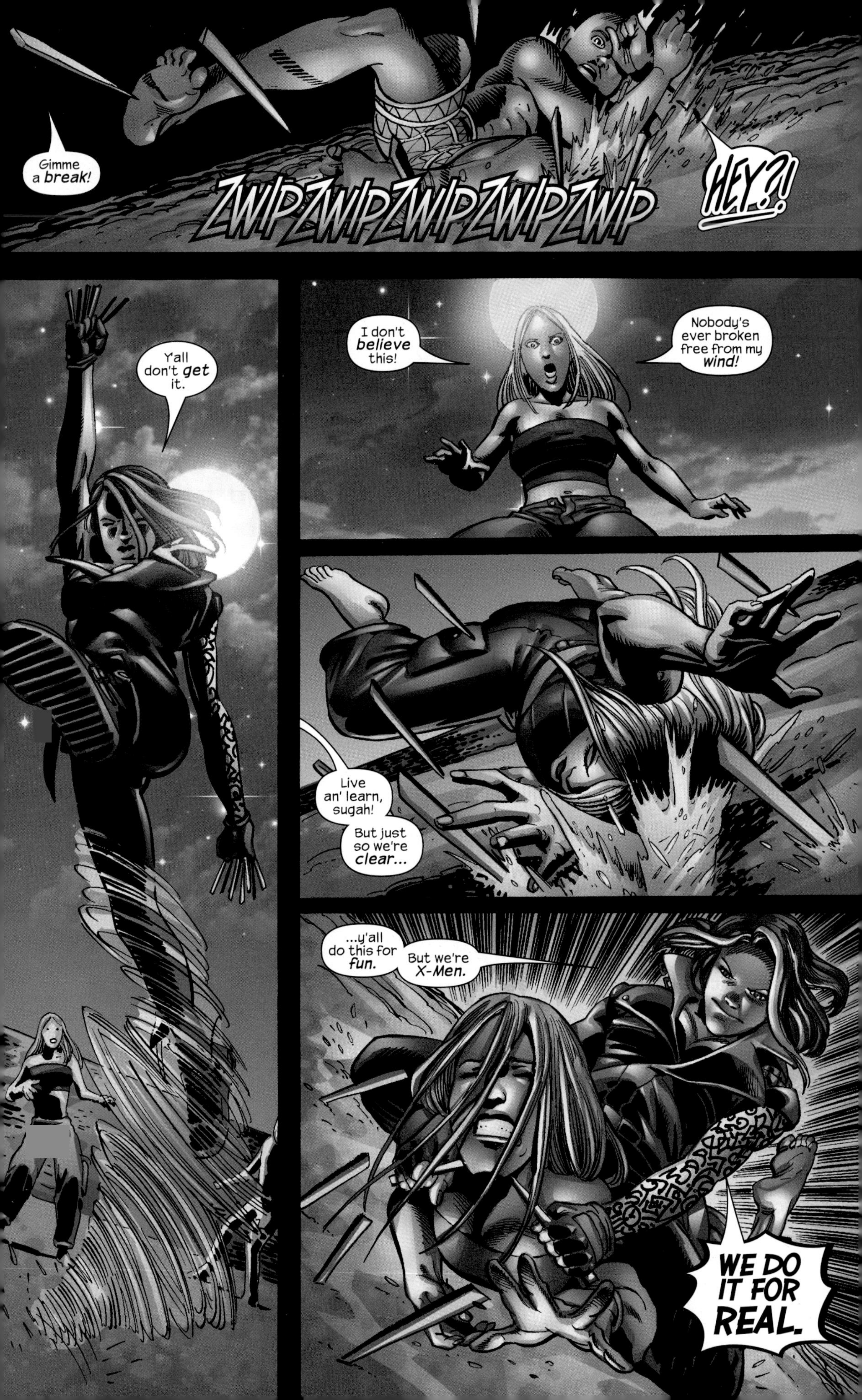
Gimme a break!
ZWIP ZWIP ZWIP ZWIP ZWIP
HEY?!
Y'all don't get it.
I don't believe this!
Nobody's ever broken free from my wind!
Live an' learn, sugah!
But just so we're clear...
...y'all do this for fun.
But we're X-Men.
WE DO IT FOR REAL.

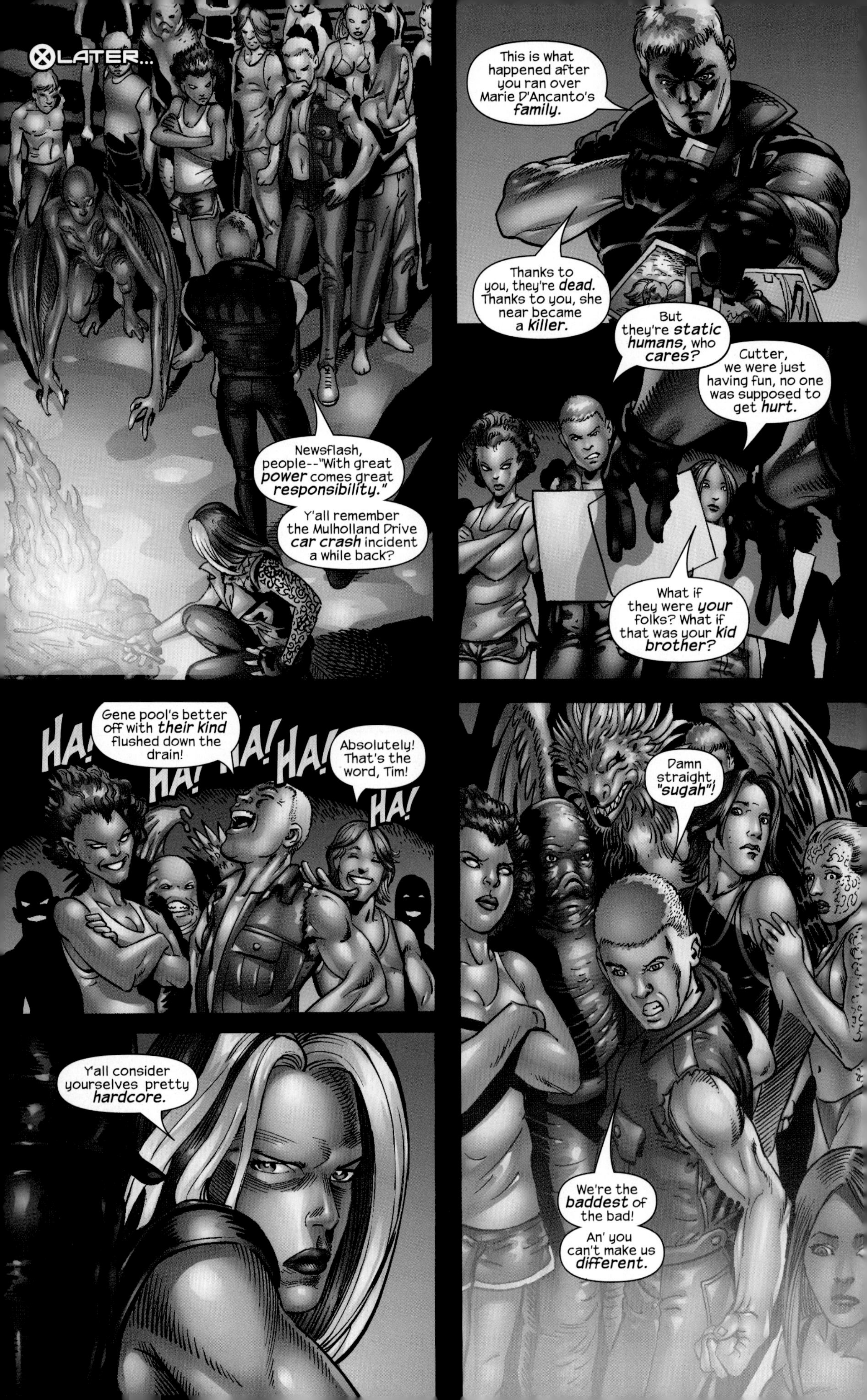
LATER...
Newsflash, people--"With great power comes great responsibility."
Y'all remember the Mulholland Drive car crash incident a while back?
This is what happened after you ran over Marie D'Ancanto's family.
Thanks to you, they're dead. Thanks to you, she near became a killer.
But they're static humans, who cares?
Cutter, we were just having fun, no one was supposed to get hurt.
What if they were your folks? What if that was your kid brother?
HA!
Gene pool's better off with their kind flushed down the drain!
HA! HA! HA!
Absolutely! That's the word, Tim!
HA!
Y'all consider yourselves pretty hardcore.
Damn straight, "sugah"!
We're the baddest of the bad!
An' you can't make us different.

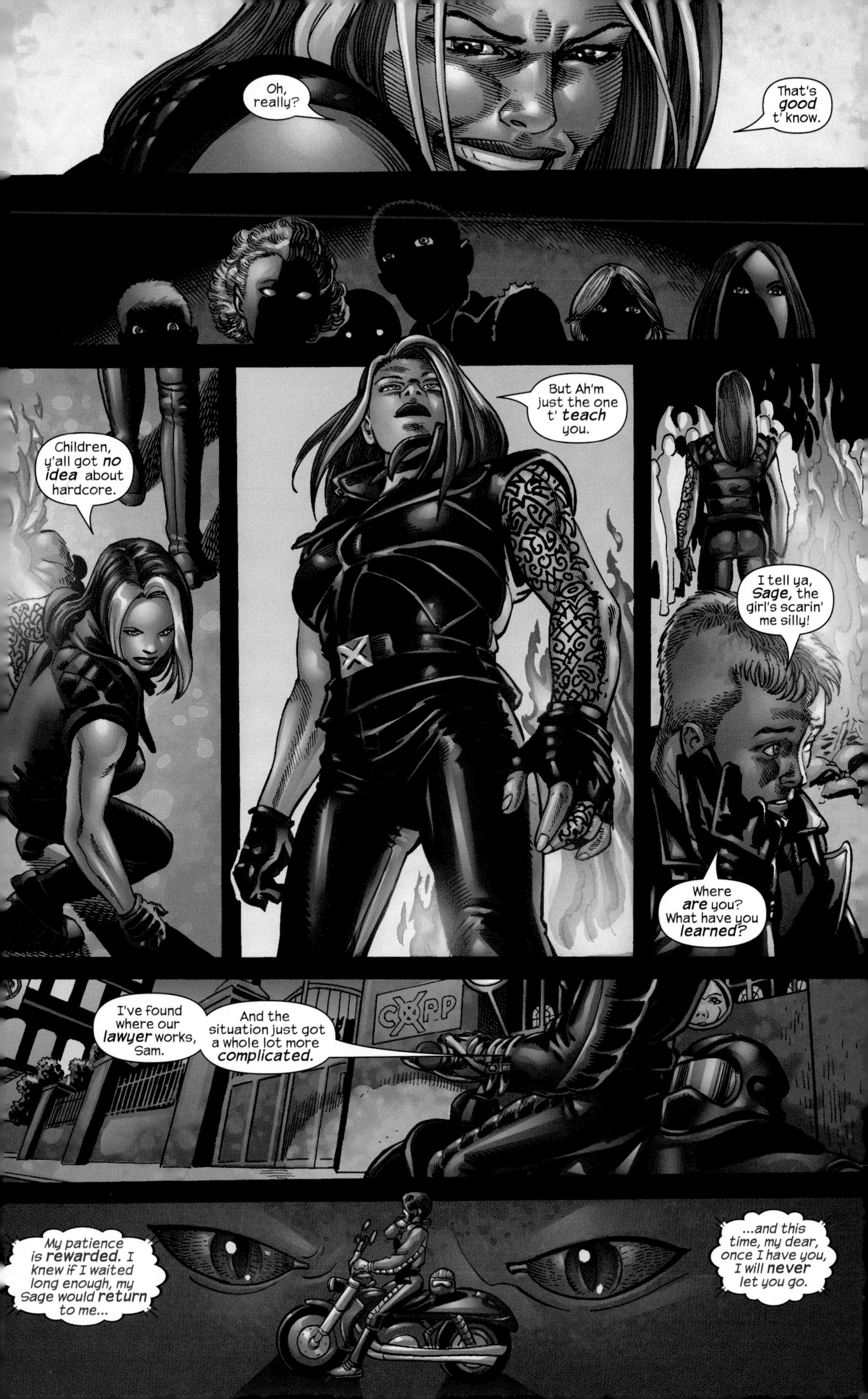

Oh, really?
That's good t' know.
Children, y'all got no idea about hardcore.
But Ah'm just the one t' teach you.
I tell ya, Sage, the girl's scarin' me silly!
Where are you? What have you learned?
I've found where our lawyer works, Sam.
And the situation just got a whole lot more complicated.
CXPP
My patience is rewarded. I knew if I waited long enough, my Sage would return to me...
...and this time, my dear, once I have you, I will never let you go.

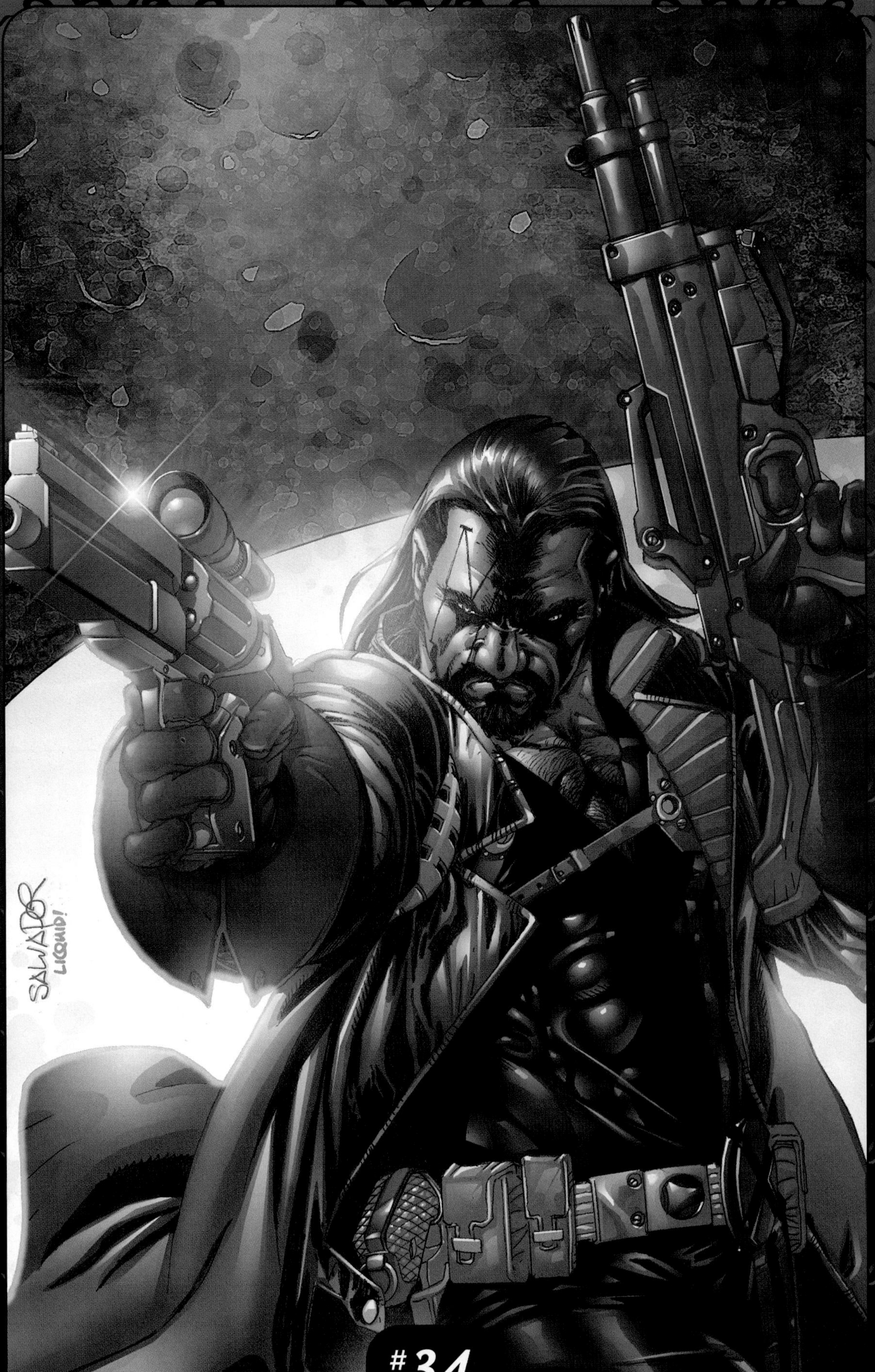
SALVADOR
LIQUID!

#34

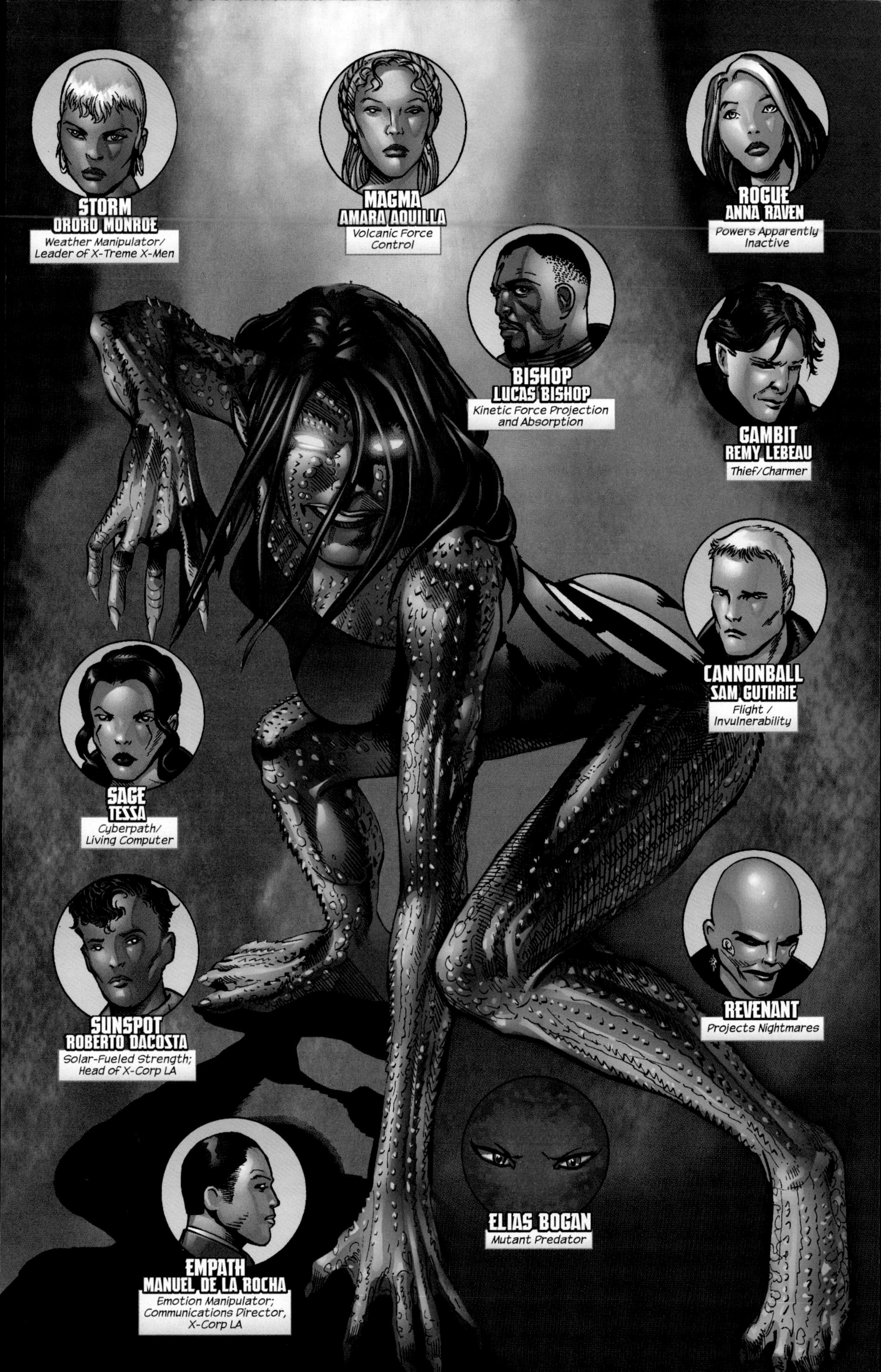

STORM
ORORO MONROE
Weather Manipulator/ Leader of X-Treme X-Men
MAGMA
AMARA AQUILLA
Volcanic Force Control
ROGUE
ANNA RAVEN
Powers Apparently Inactive
BISHOP
LUCAS BISHOP
Kinetic Force Projection and Absorption
GAMBIT
REMY LEBEAU
Thief/Charmer
CANNONBALL
SAM GUTHRIE
Flight / Invulnerability
SAGE
TESSA
Cyberpath/ Living Computer
SUNSPOT
ROBERTO DACOSTA
Solar-Fueled Strength; Head of X-Corp LA
REVENANT
Projects Nightmares
ELIAS BOGAN
Mutant Predator
EMPATH
MANUEL DE LA ROCHA
Emotion Manipulator; Communications Director, X-Corp LA

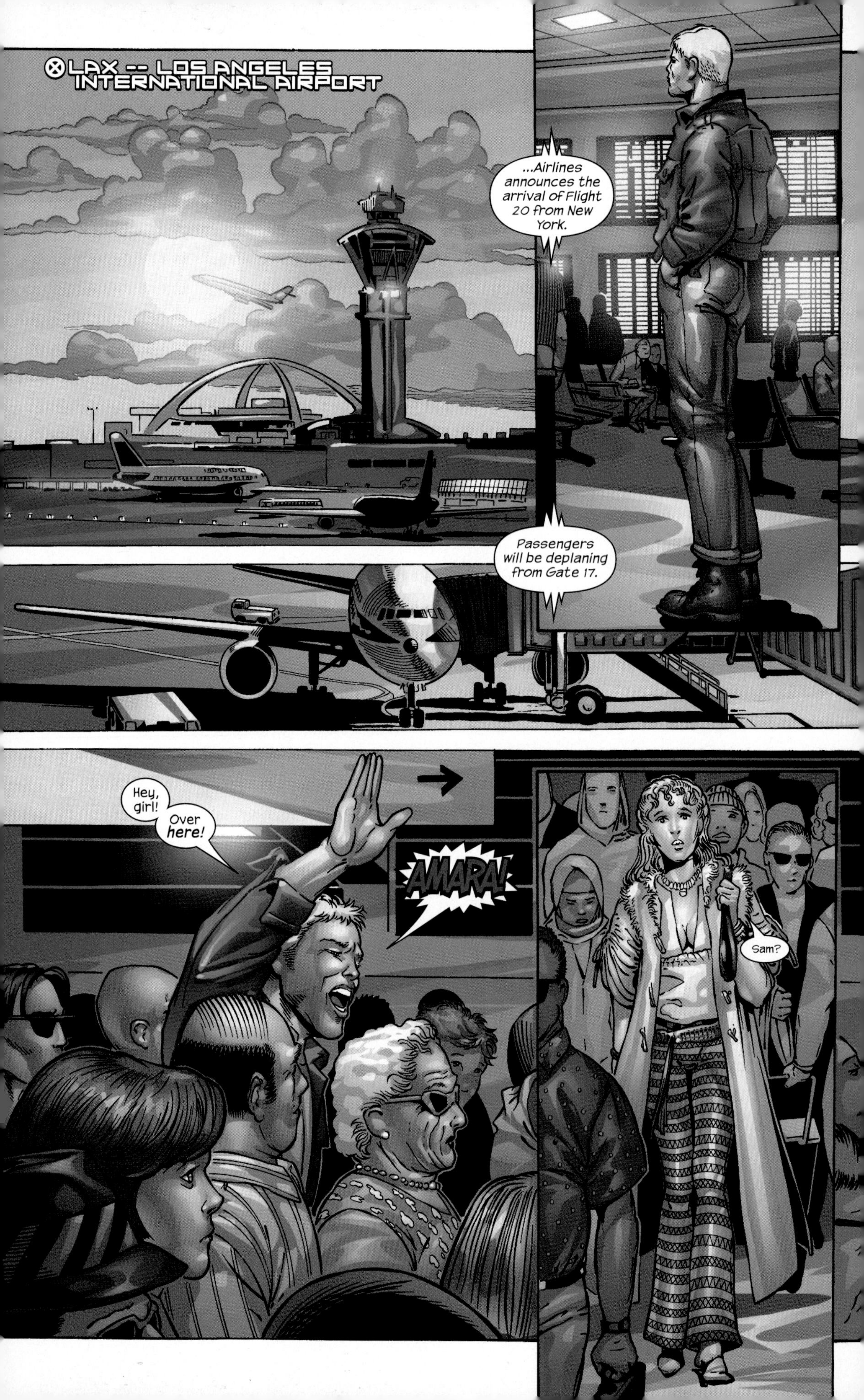
LAX -- LOS ANGELES INTERNATIONAL AIRPORT
...Airlines announces the arrival of Flight 20 from New York.
Passengers will be deplaning from Gate 17.
Hey, girl!
Over here!
AMARA!
Sam?

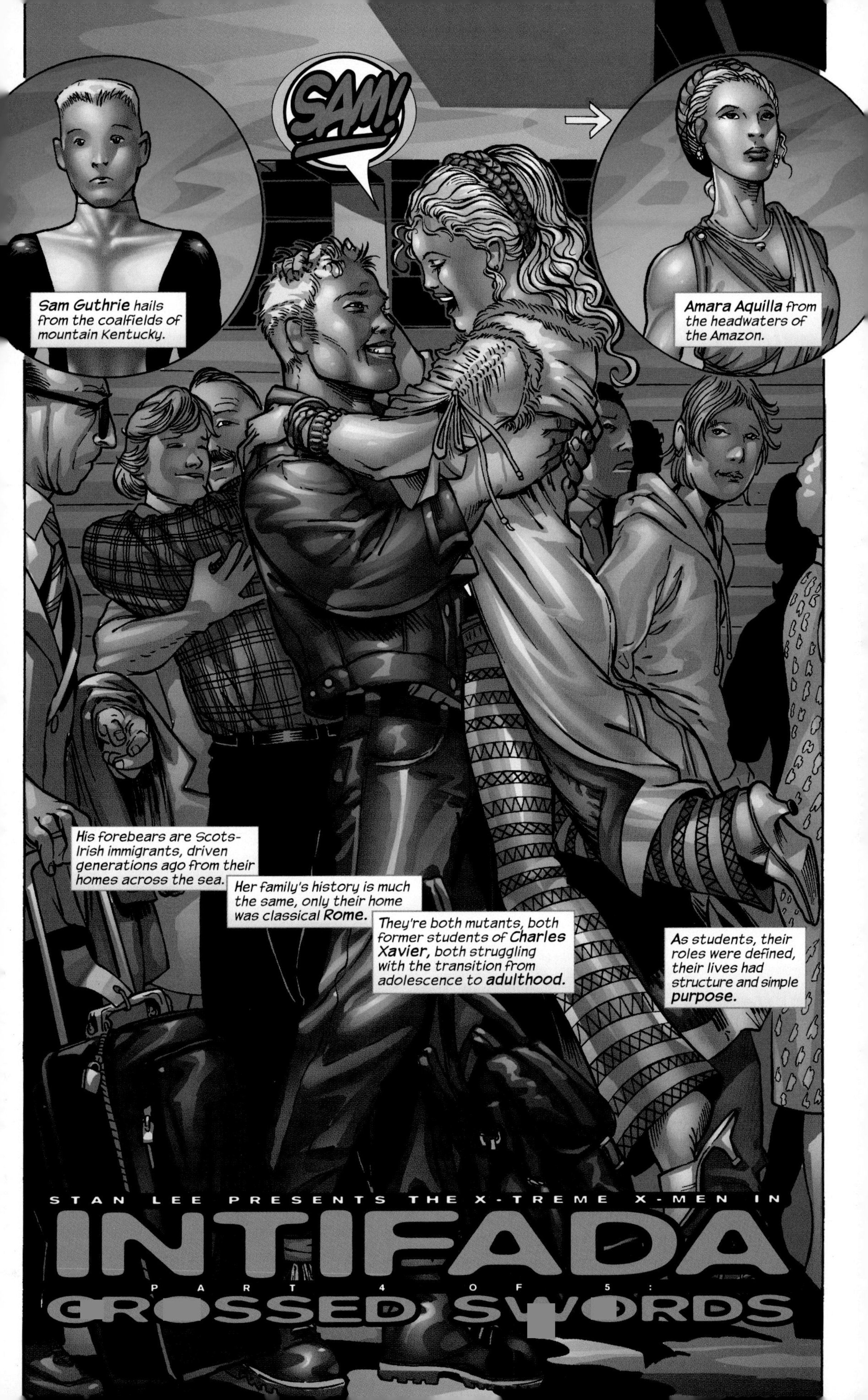

SAM!
Sam Guthrie hails from the coalfields of mountain Kentucky.
Amara Aquilla from the headwaters of the Amazon.
His forebears are Scots-Irish immigrants, driven generations ago from their homes across the sea.
Her family's history is much the same, only their home was classical Rome.
They're both mutants, both former students of Charles Xavier, both struggling with the transition from adolescence to adulthood.
As students, their roles were defined, their lives had structure and simple purpose.
STAN LEE PRESENTS THE X-TREME X-MEN IN
INTIFADA
PART 4 OF 5:
CROSSED SWORDS

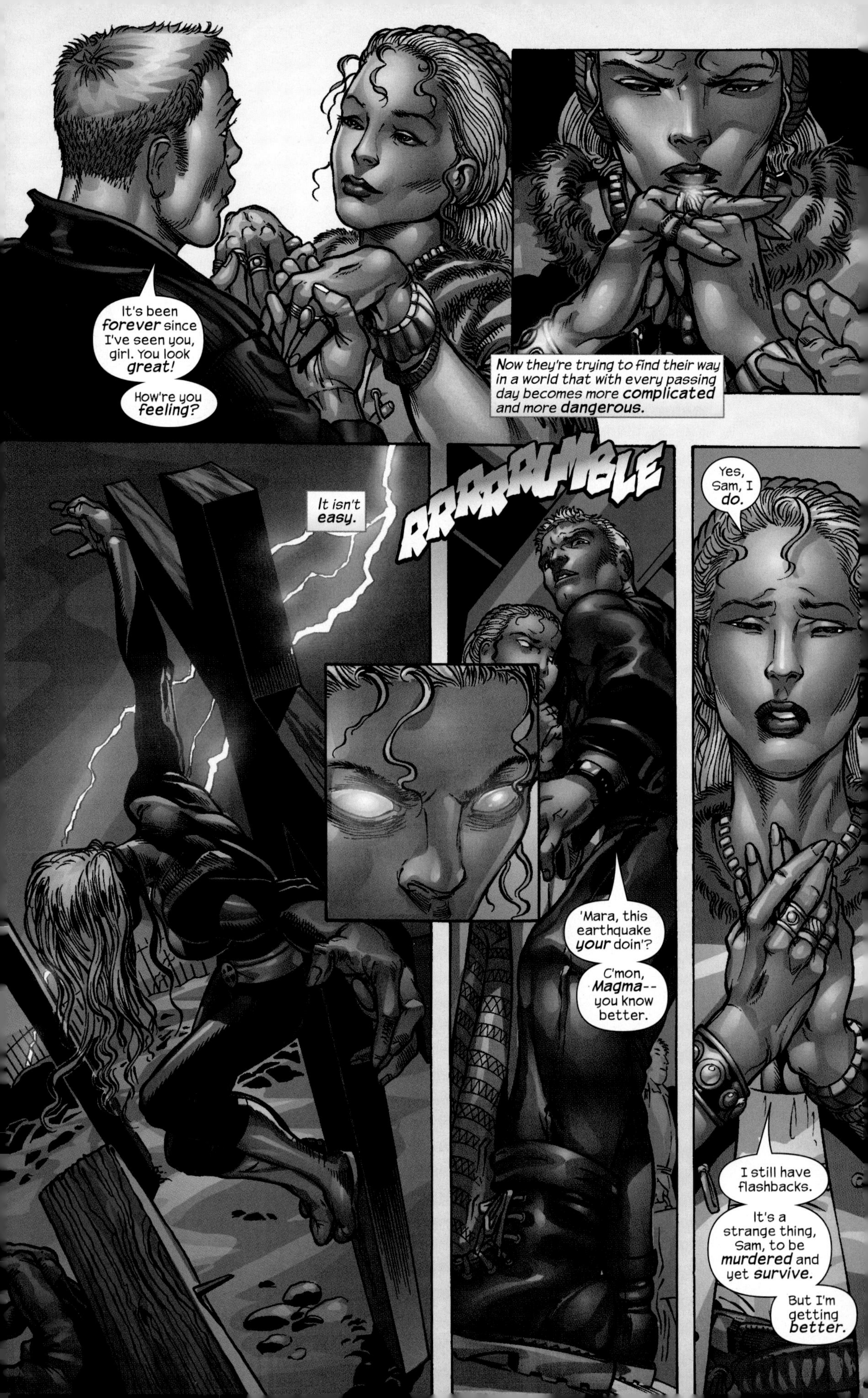

It's been *forever* since I've seen you, girl. You look *great!*
How're you *feeling?*
Now they're trying to find their way in a world that with every passing day becomes more **complicated** and more **dangerous.**
It isn't *easy.*
RRRRRUMBLE
'Mara, this earthquake *your* doin'?
C'mon, *Magma*-- you know better.
Yes, Sam, I *do.*
I still have flashbacks.
It's a strange thing, Sam, to be *murdered* and yet *survive.*
But I'm getting *better.*

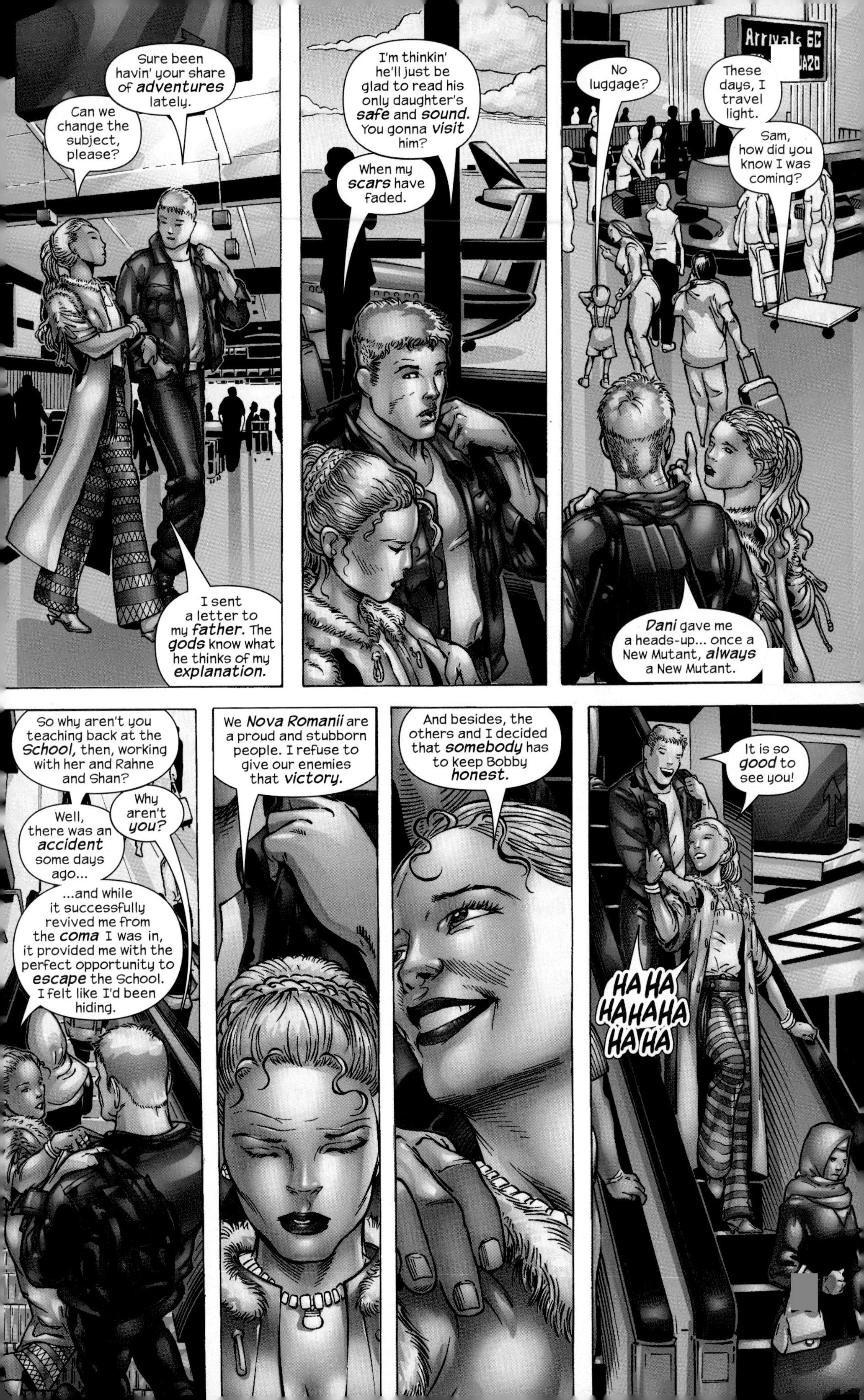

Sure been havin' your share of adventures lately.
Can we change the subject, please?
I sent a letter to my father. The gods know what he thinks of my explanation.
I'm thinkin' he'll just be glad to read his only daughter's safe and sound. You gonna visit him?
When my scars have faded.
Arrivals 6C
No luggage?
These days, I travel light.
Sam, how did you know I was coming?
Dani gave me a heads-up... once a New Mutant, always a New Mutant.
So why aren't you teaching back at the School, then, working with her and Rahne and Shan?
Why aren't you?
Well, there was an accident some days ago...
...and while it successfully revived me from the coma I was in, it provided me with the perfect opportunity to escape the School. I felt like I'd been hiding.
We Nova Romanii are a proud and stubborn people. I refuse to give our enemies that victory.
And besides, the others and I decided that somebody has to keep Bobby honest.
It is so good to see you!
HA HA HAHAHA HA HA

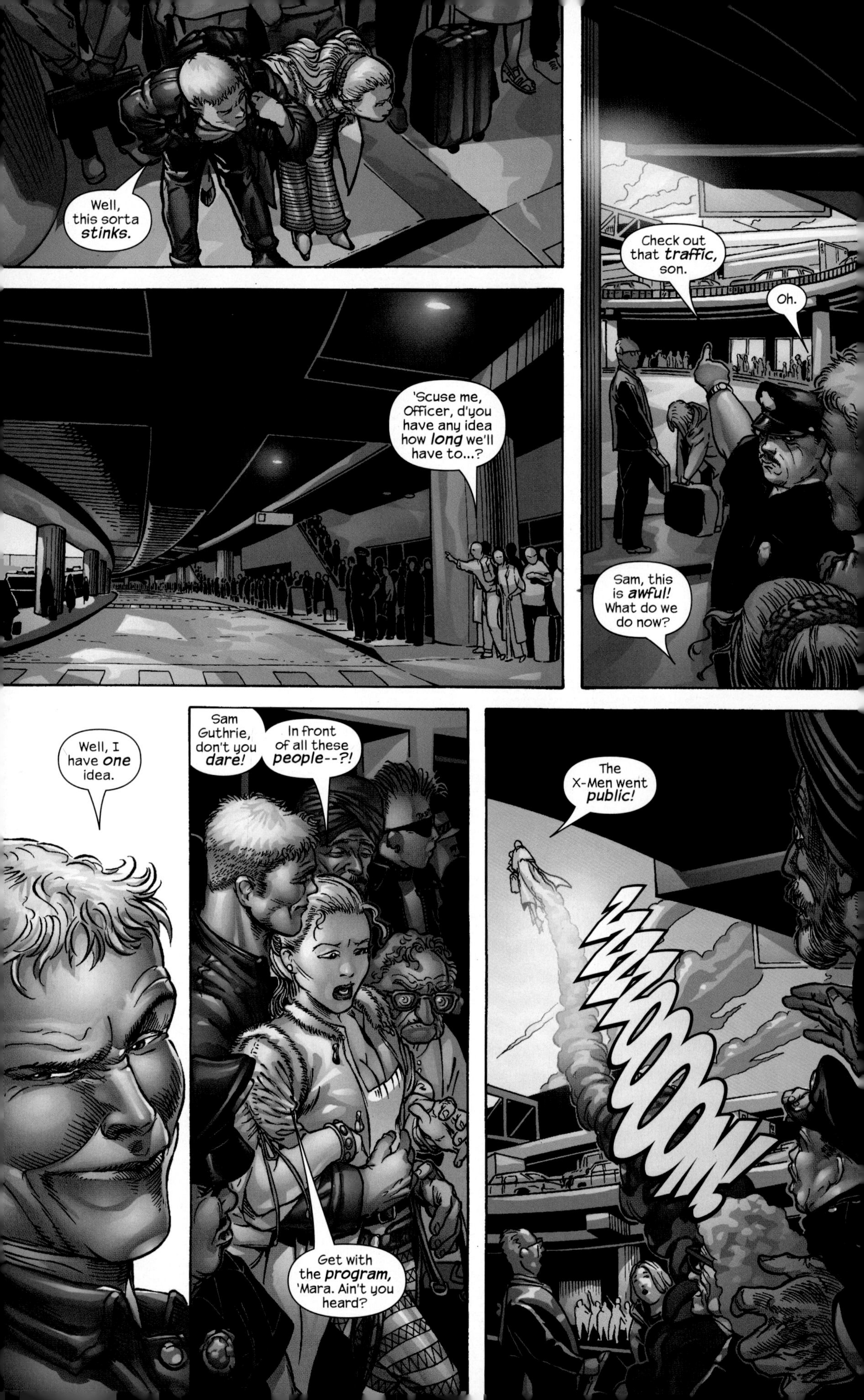
Well, this sorta *stinks.*
'Scuse me, Officer, d'you have any idea how *long* we'll have to...?
Check out that *traffic,* son.
Oh.
Sam, this is *awful!* What do we do now?
Well, I have *one* idea.
Sam Guthrie, don't you *dare!*
In front of all these *people--?!*
Get with the *program,* 'Mara. Ain't you heard?
The X-Men went *public!*
ZZZOOOOOM

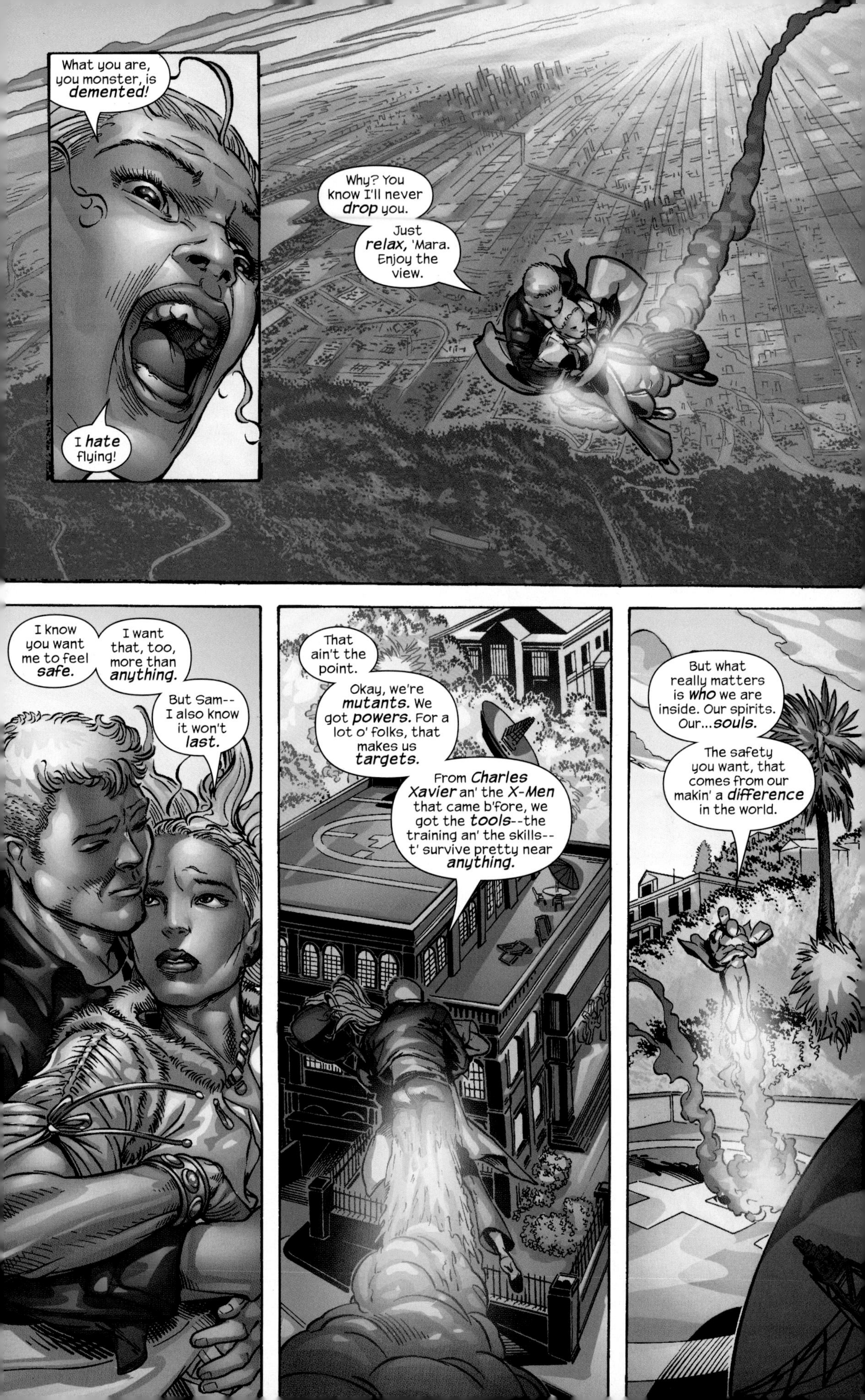
What you are, you monster, is *demented!*
I *hate* flying!
Why? You know I'll never *drop* you.
Just *relax,* 'Mara. Enjoy the view.
I know you want me to feel *safe.*
I want that, too, more than *anything.*
But Sam-- I also know it won't *last.*
That ain't the point.
Okay, we're *mutants.* We got *powers.* For a lot o' folks, that makes us *targets.*
From *Charles Xavier* an' the *X-Men* that came b'fore, we got the *tools*--the training an' the skills-- t' survive pretty near *anything.*
But what really matters is *who* we are inside. Our spirits. Our...*souls.*
The safety you want, that comes from our makin' a *difference* in the world.

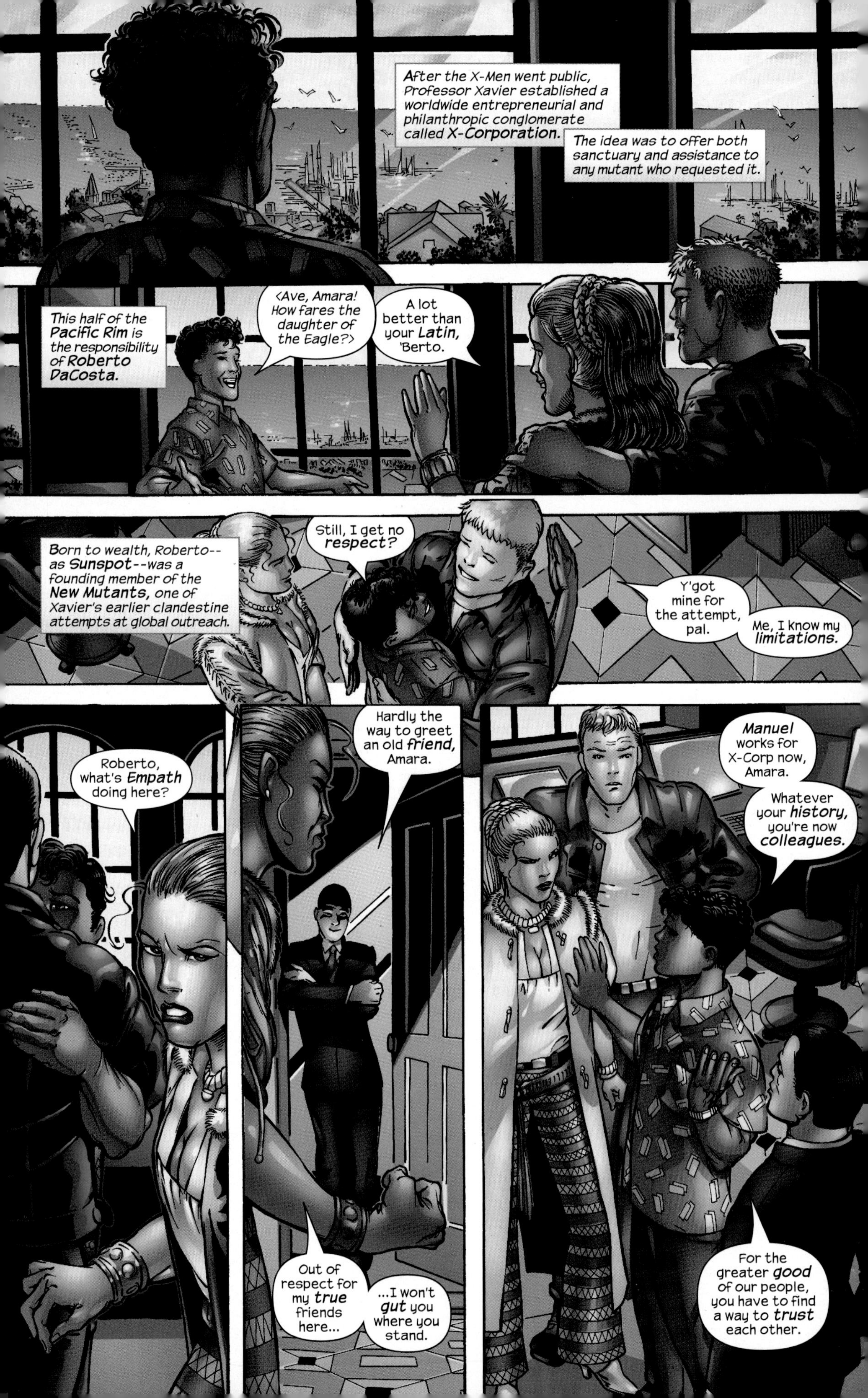

After the X-Men went public, Professor Xavier established a worldwide entrepreneurial and philanthropic conglomerate called X-Corporation.
The idea was to offer both sanctuary and assistance to any mutant who requested it.
This half of the Pacific Rim is the responsibility of Roberto DaCosta.
<Ave, Amara! How fares the daughter of the Eagle?>
A lot better than your Latin, 'Berto.
Born to wealth, Roberto--as Sunspot--was a founding member of the New Mutants, one of Xavier's earlier clandestine attempts at global outreach.
Still, I get no respect?
Y'got mine for the attempt, pal.
Me, I know my limitations.
Roberto, what's Empath doing here?
Hardly the way to greet an old friend, Amara.
Out of respect for my true friends here...
...I won't gut you where you stand.
Manuel works for X-Corp now, Amara.
Whatever your history, you're now colleagues.
For the greater good of our people, you have to find a way to trust each other.

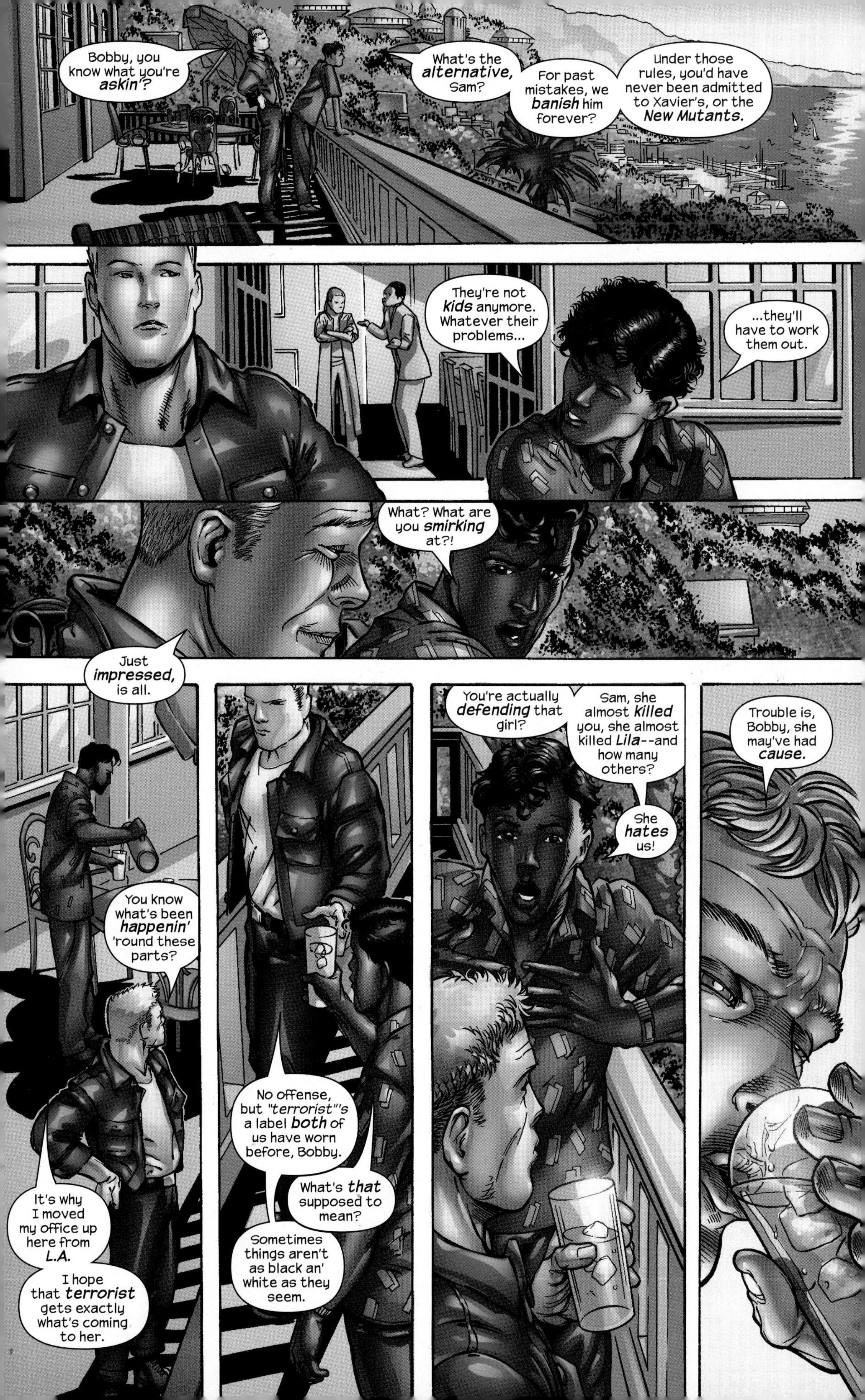
Bobby, you know what you're askin'?
What's the alternative, Sam?
For past mistakes, we banish him forever?
Under those rules, you'd have never been admitted to Xavier's, or the New Mutants.
They're not kids anymore. Whatever their problems...
...they'll have to work them out.
What? What are you smirking at?!
Just impressed, is all.
You know what's been happenin' 'round these parts?
It's why I moved my office up here from L.A.
I hope that terrorist gets exactly what's coming to her.
No offense, but "terrorist"'s a label both of us have worn before, Bobby.
What's that supposed to mean?
Sometimes things aren't as black an' white as they seem.
You're actually defending that girl?
Sam, she almost killed you, she almost killed Lila--and how many others?
She hates us!
Trouble is, Bobby, she may've had cause.

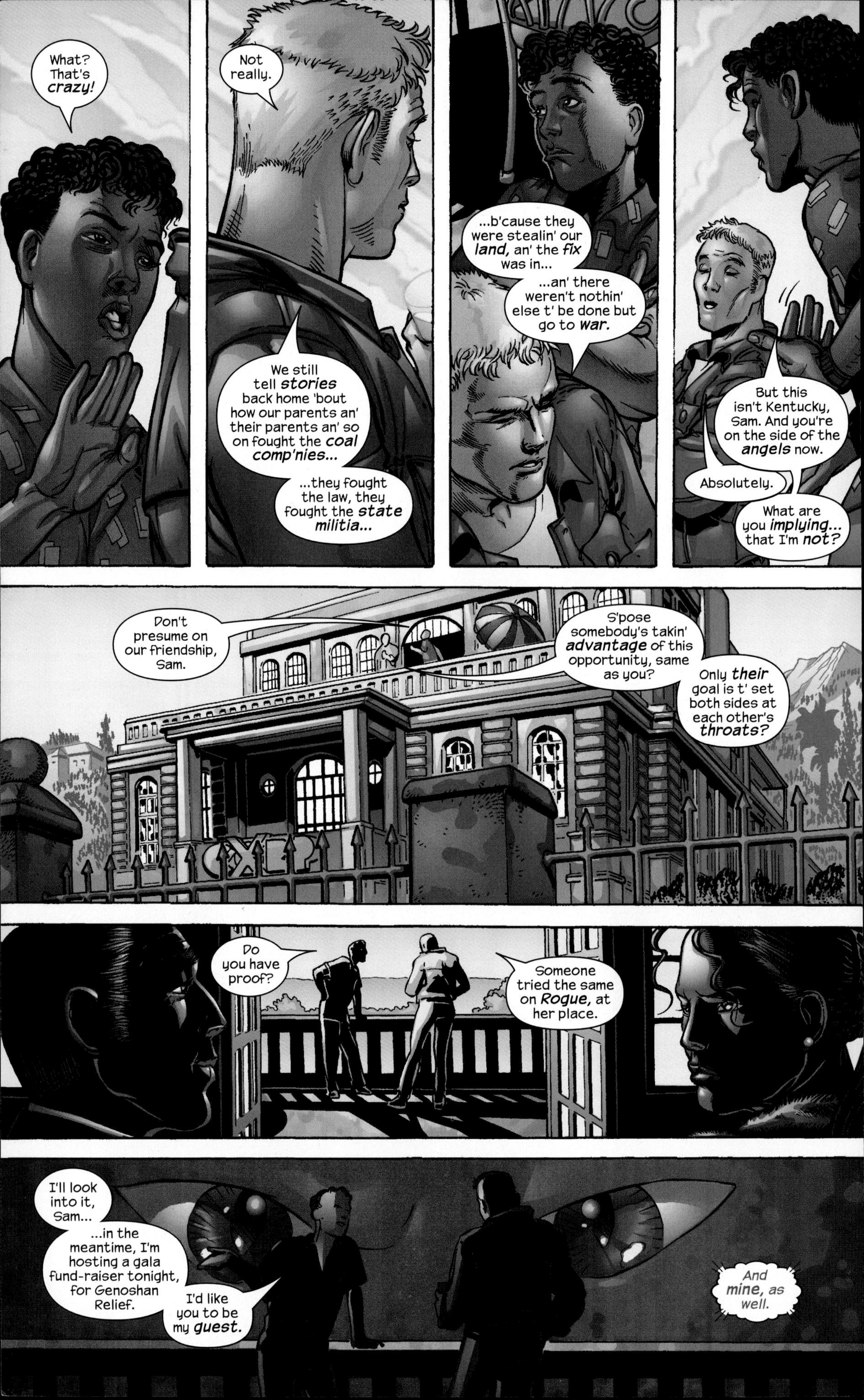
What? That's *crazy!*
Not really.
We still tell *stories* back home 'bout how our parents an' their parents an' so on fought the *coal comp'nies...*
...they fought the law, they fought the *state militia...*
...b'cause they were stealin' our *land,* an' the *fix* was in...
...an' there weren't nothin' else t' be done but go to *war.*
But this isn't Kentucky, Sam. And you're on the side of the *angels* now.
Absolutely.
What are you *implying...* that I'm *not?*
Don't presume on our friendship, Sam.
S'pose somebody's takin' *advantage* of this opportunity, same as you?
Only *their* goal is t' set both sides at each other's *throats?*
Do you have proof?
Someone tried the same on *Rogue,* at her place.
I'll look into it, Sam...
...in the meantime, I'm hosting a gala fund-raiser tonight, for Genoshan Relief.
I'd like you to be my *guest.*
And ***mine,*** *as well.*

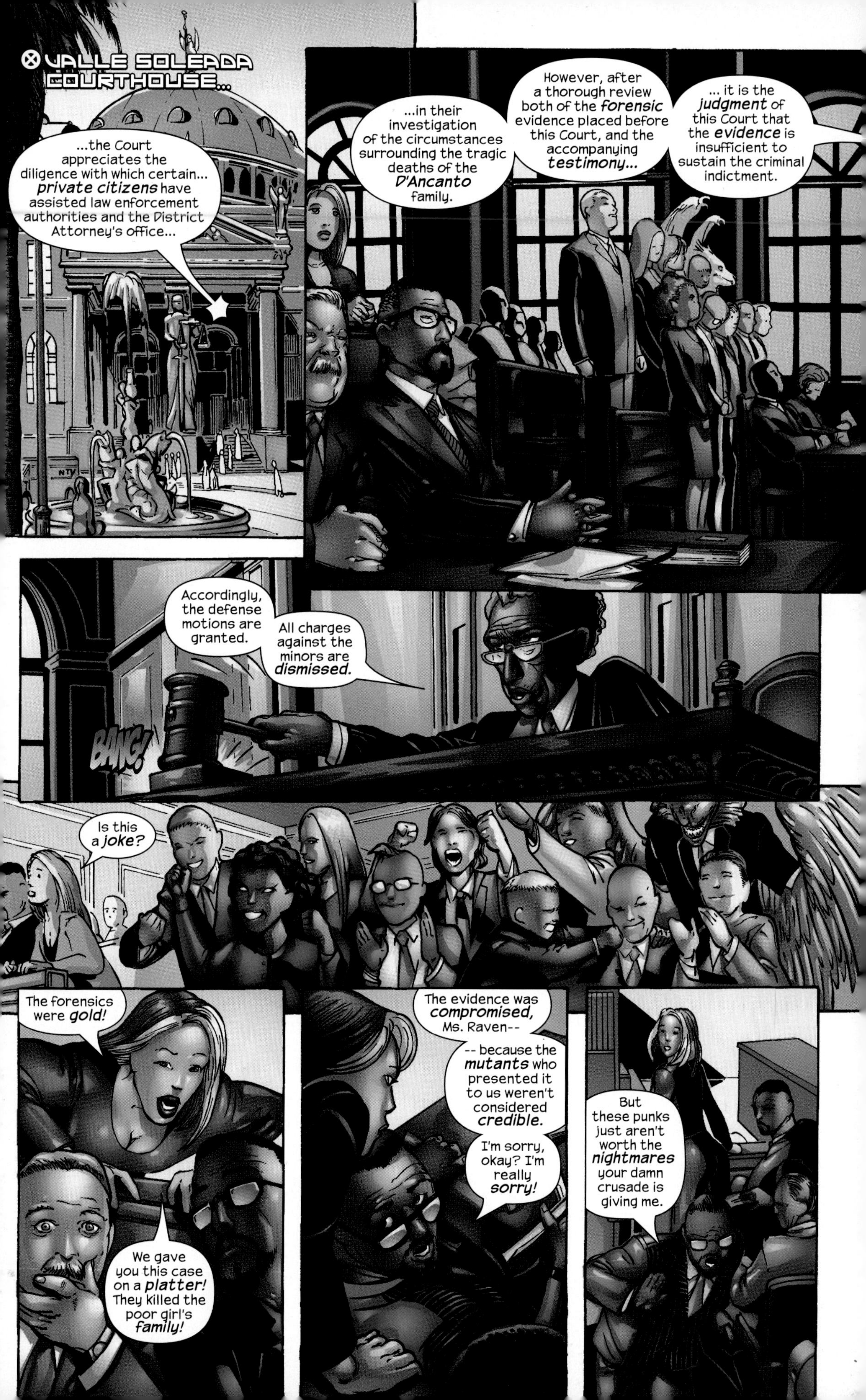
VALLE SOLEADA COURTHOUSE...
...the Court appreciates the diligence with which certain... private citizens have assisted law enforcement authorities and the District Attorney's office...
...in their investigation of the circumstances surrounding the tragic deaths of the D'Ancanto family.
However, after a thorough review both of the forensic evidence placed before this Court, and the accompanying testimony...
... it is the judgment of this Court that the evidence is insufficient to sustain the criminal indictment.
Accordingly, the defense motions are granted.
All charges against the minors are dismissed.
BANG!
Is this a joke?
The forensics were gold!
We gave you this case on a platter! They killed the poor girl's family!
The evidence was compromised, Ms. Raven--
-- because the mutants who presented it to us weren't considered credible.
I'm sorry, okay? I'm really sorry!
But these punks just aren't worth the nightmares your damn crusade is giving me.

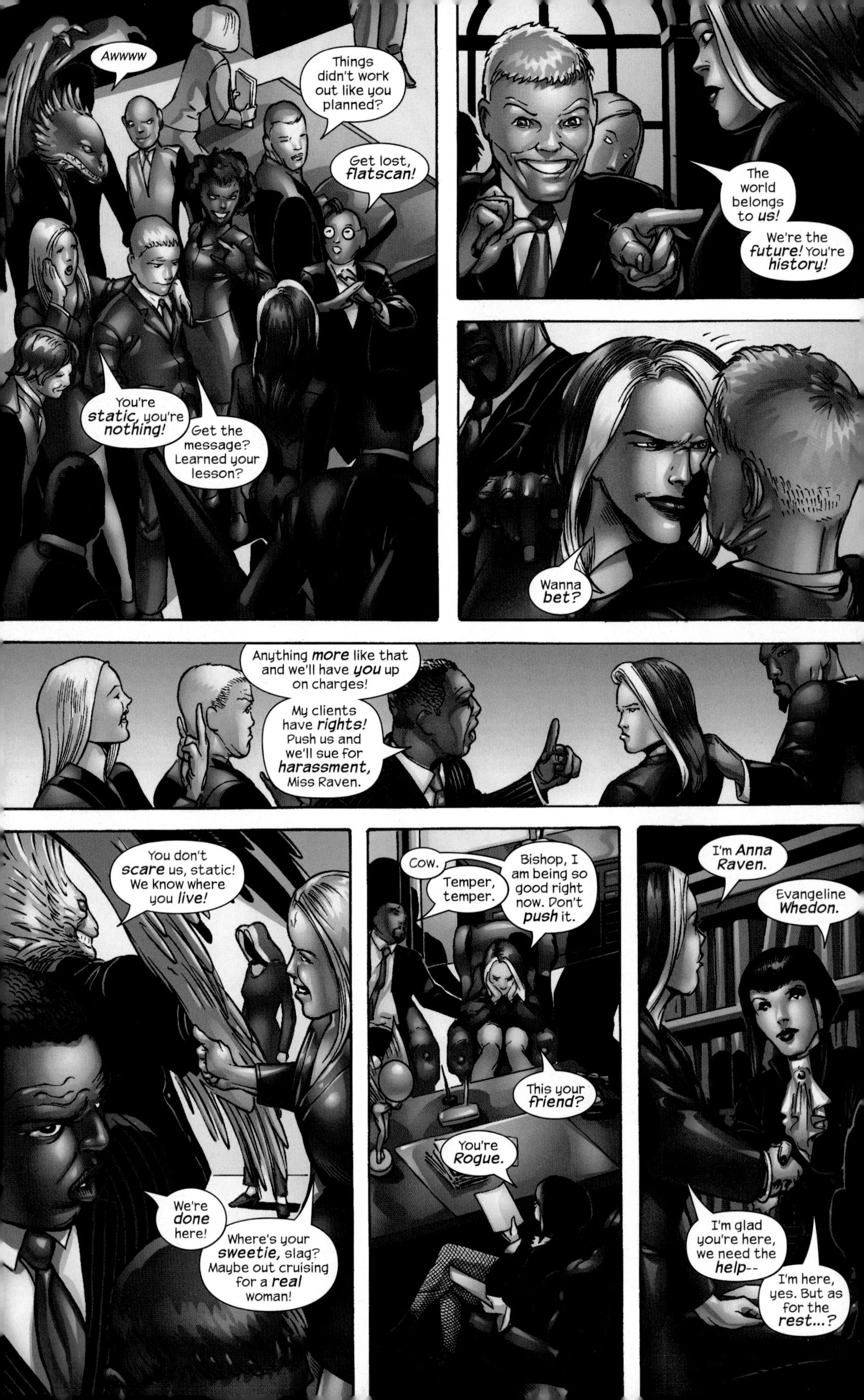
Awwww
Things didn't work out like you planned?
Get lost, flatscan!
You're static, you're nothing!
Get the message? Learned your lesson?
The world belongs to us!
We're the future! You're history!
Wanna bet?
Anything more like that and we'll have you up on charges!
My clients have rights! Push us and we'll sue for harassment, Miss Raven.
You don't scare us, static! We know where you live!
We're done here!
Where's your sweetie, slag? Maybe out cruising for a real woman!
Cow.
Temper, temper.
Bishop, I am being so good right now. Don't push it.
This your friend?
You're Rogue.
I'm Anna Raven.
Evangeline Whedon.
I'm glad you're here, we need the help--
I'm here, yes. But as for the rest...?

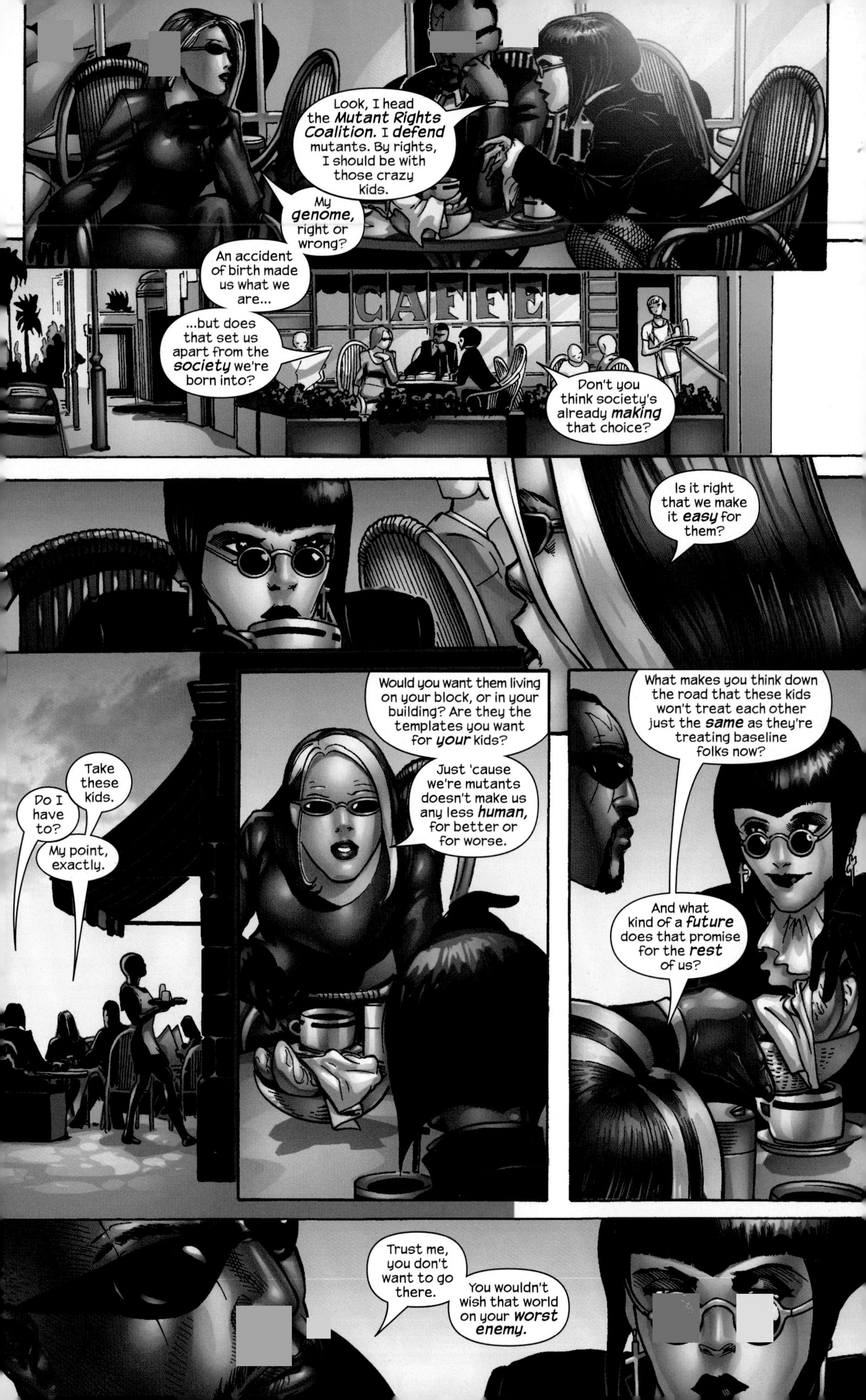

Look, I head the *Mutant Rights Coalition.* I *defend* mutants. By rights, I should be with those crazy kids.
My *genome,* right or wrong?
An accident of birth made us what we are...
...but does that set us apart from the *society* we're born into?
Don't you think society's already *making* that choice?
Is it right that we make it *easy* for them?
Take these kids.
Do I have to?
My point, exactly.
Would you want them living on your block, or in your building? Are they the templates you want for *your* kids?
Just 'cause we're mutants doesn't make us any less *human,* for better or for worse.
What makes you think down the road that these kids won't treat each other just the *same* as they're treating baseline folks now?
And what kind of a *future* does that promise for the *rest* of us?
Trust me, you don't want to go there.
You wouldn't wish that world on your *worst enemy.*

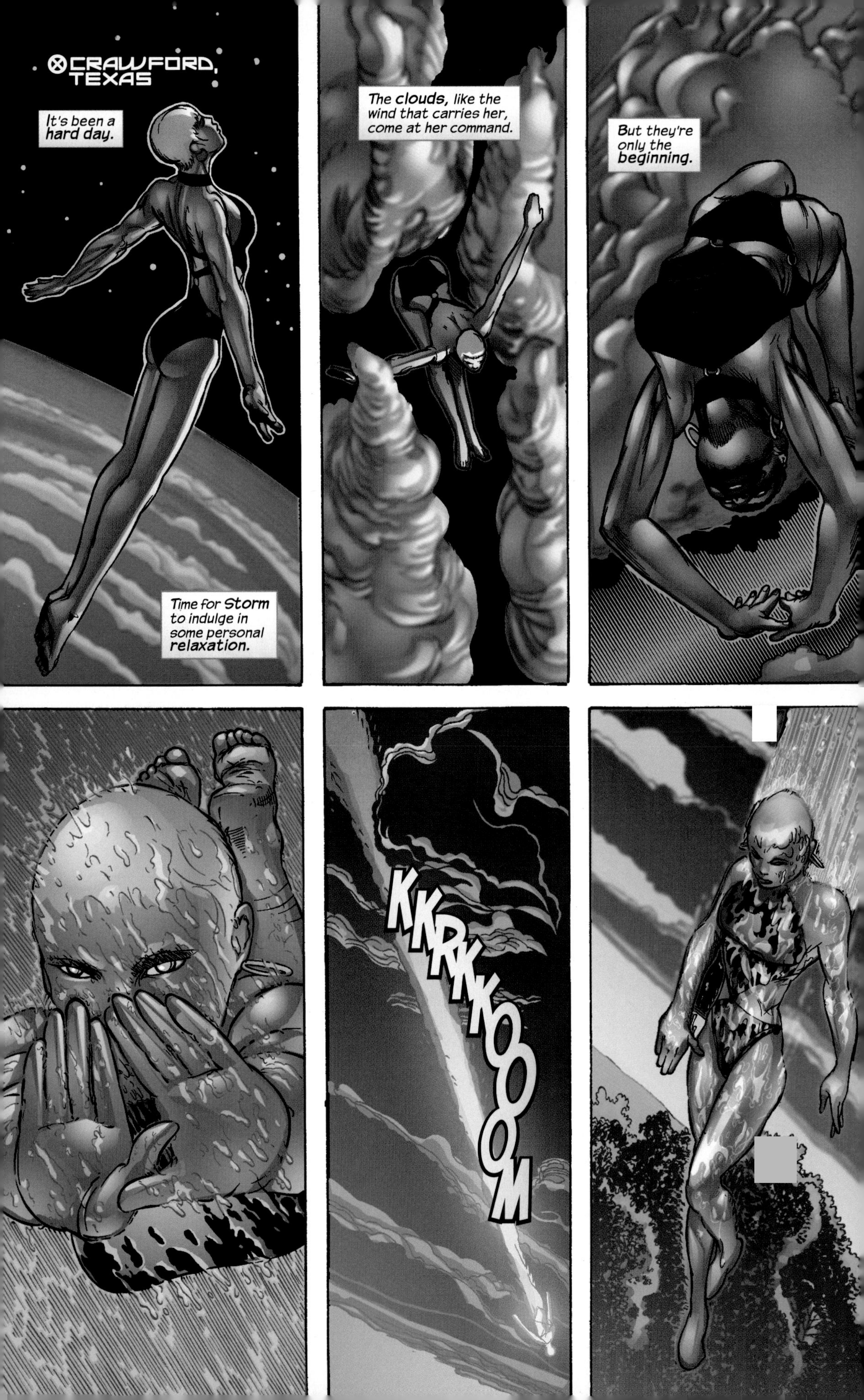
CRAWFORD, TEXAS
It's been a hard day.
Time for Storm to indulge in some personal relaxation.
The clouds, like the wind that carries her, come at her command.
But they're only the beginning.
KKRKKOOOOM

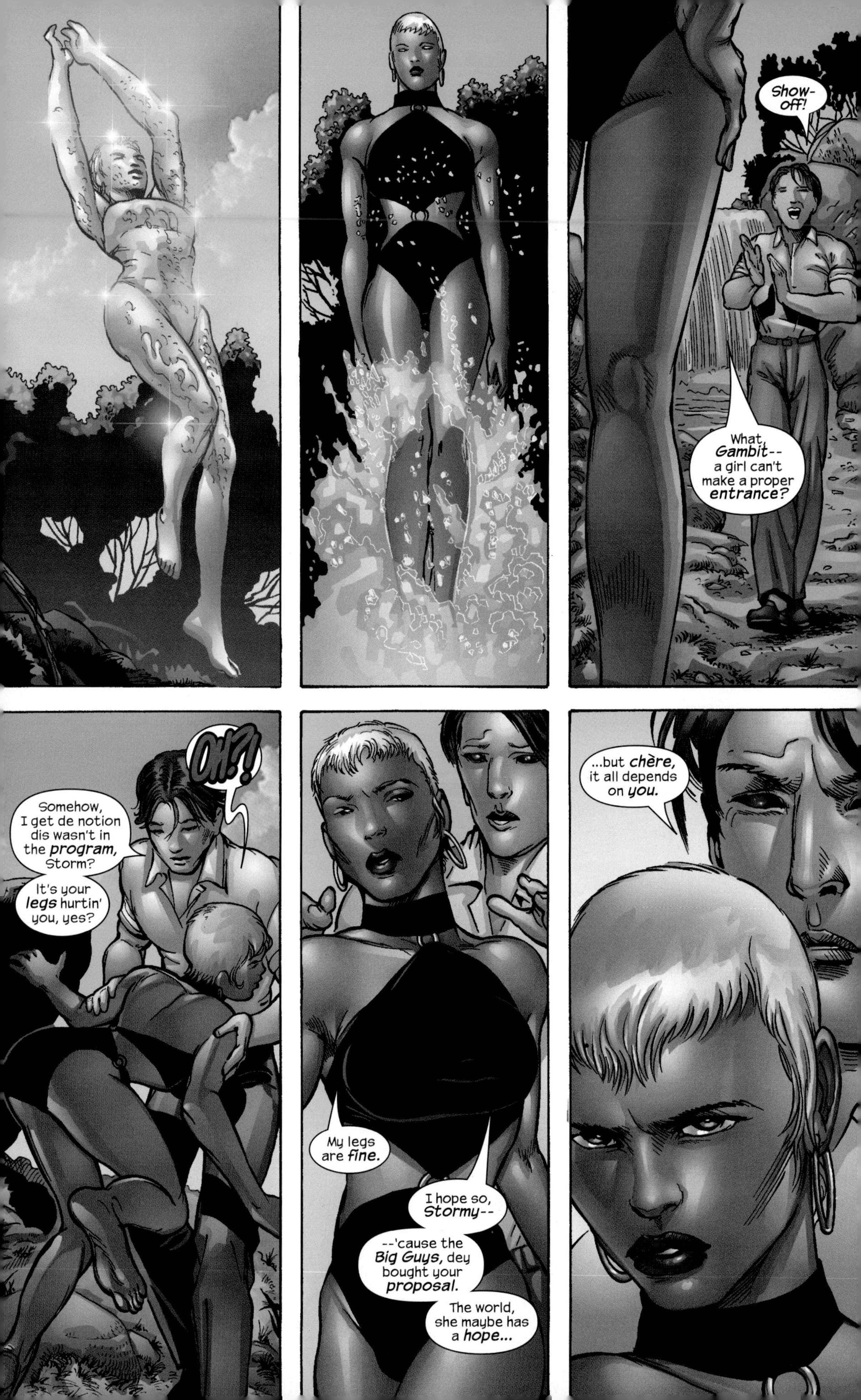
Show-off!
What, Gambit-- a girl can't make a proper entrance?
OH?!
Somehow, I get de notion dis wasn't in the program, Storm?
It's your legs hurtin' you, yes?
My legs are fine.
I hope so, Stormy--
--'cause the Big Guys, dey bought your proposal.
The world, she maybe has a hope...
...but chère, it all depends on you.

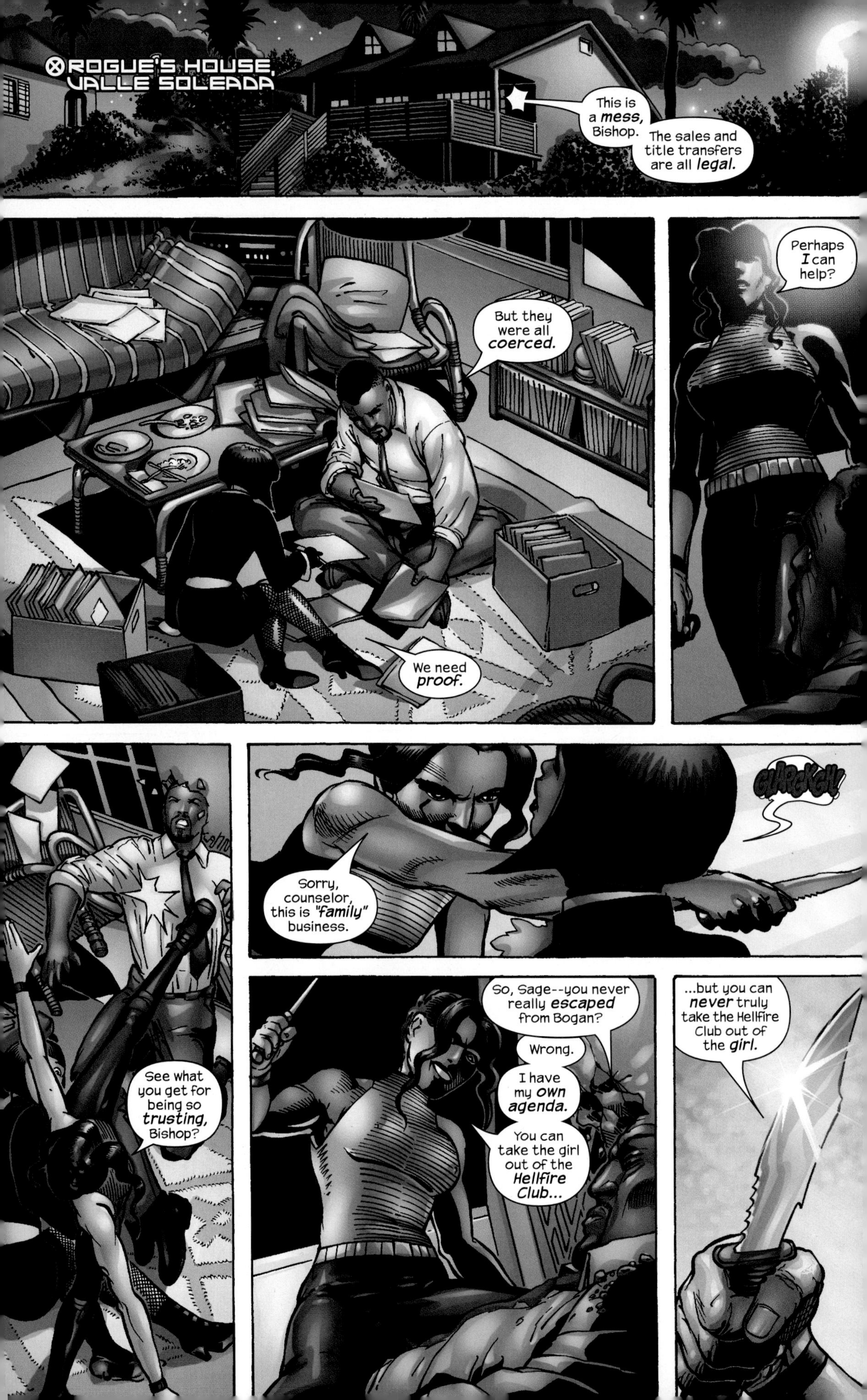
ROGUE'S HOUSE, VALLE SOLEADA
This is a mess, Bishop.
The sales and title transfers are all legal.
But they were all coerced.
We need proof.
Perhaps I can help?
Sorry, counselor, this is "family" business.
GLARCKGH!
See what you get for being so trusting, Bishop?
So, Sage--you never really escaped from Bogan?
Wrong.
I have my own agenda.
You can take the girl out of the Hellfire Club...
...but you can never truly take the Hellfire Club out of the girl.

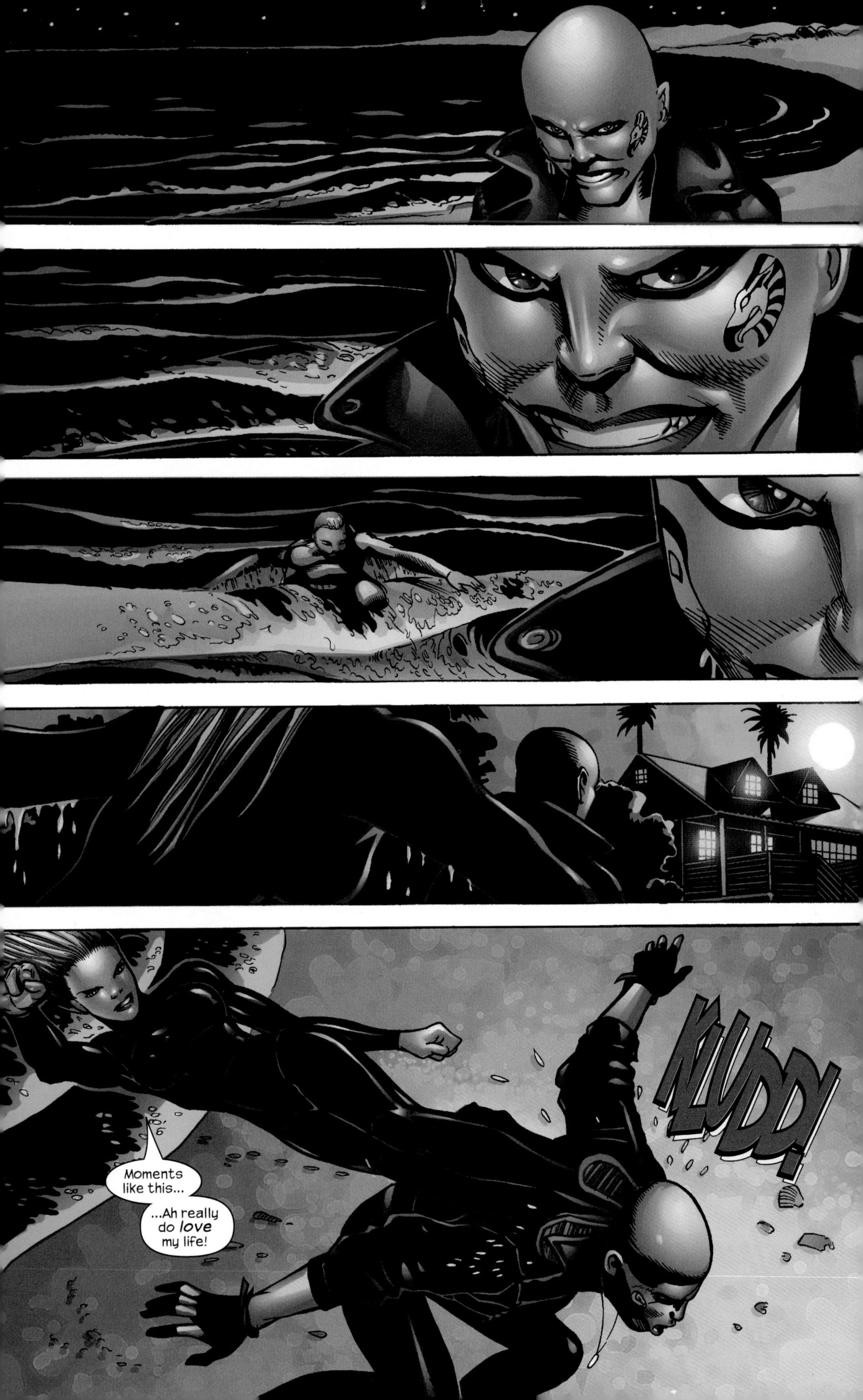

KLUDD!
Moments like this...
...Ah really do *love* my life!

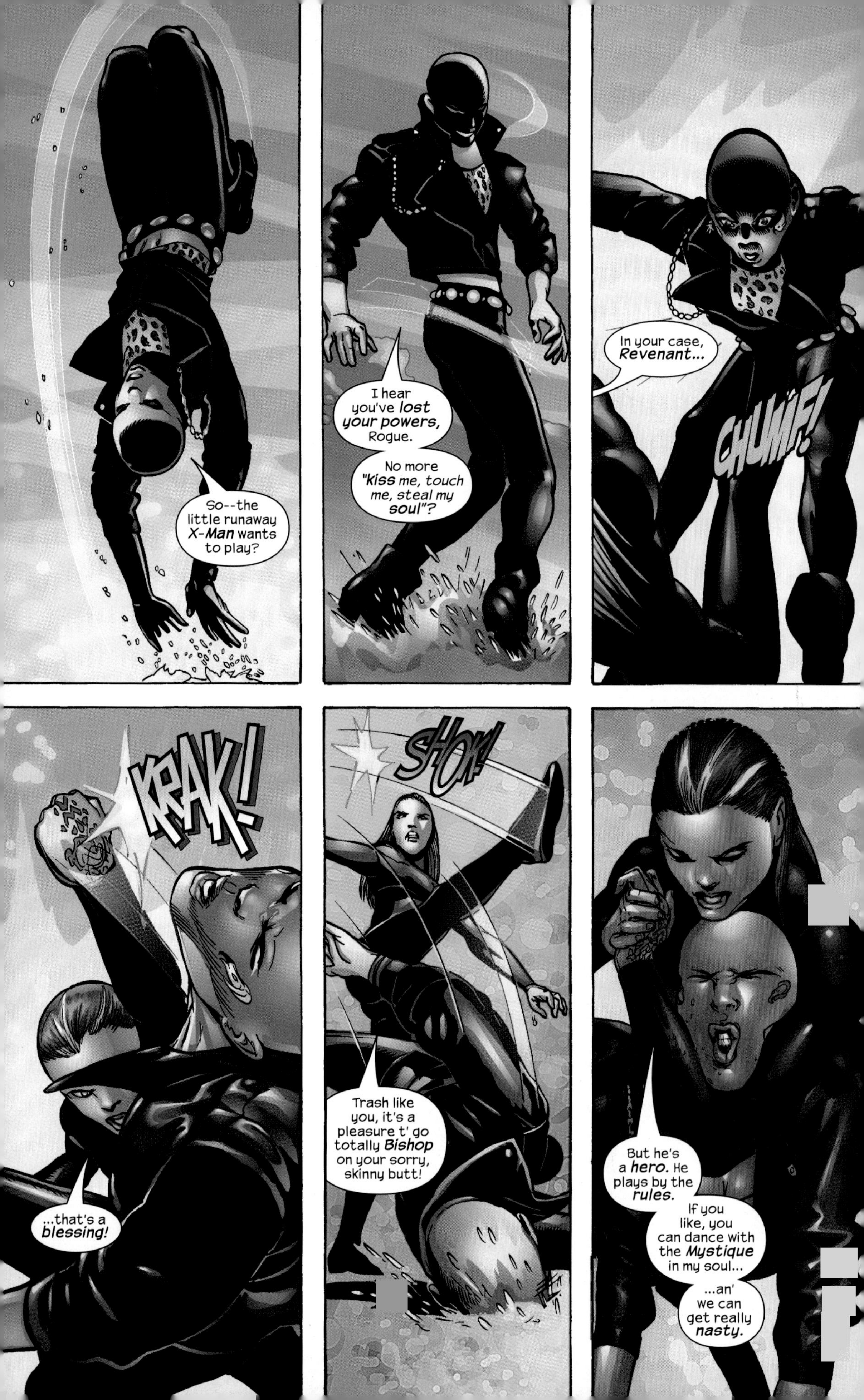
So--the little runaway X-Man wants to play?
I hear you've lost your powers, Rogue.
No more "kiss me, touch me, steal my soul"?
In your case, Revenant...
CHUMF!
KRAK!
...that's a blessing!
SHOK!
Trash like you, it's a pleasure t' go totally Bishop on your sorry, skinny butt!
But he's a hero. He plays by the rules.
If you like, you can dance with the Mystique in my soul...
...an' we can get really nasty.

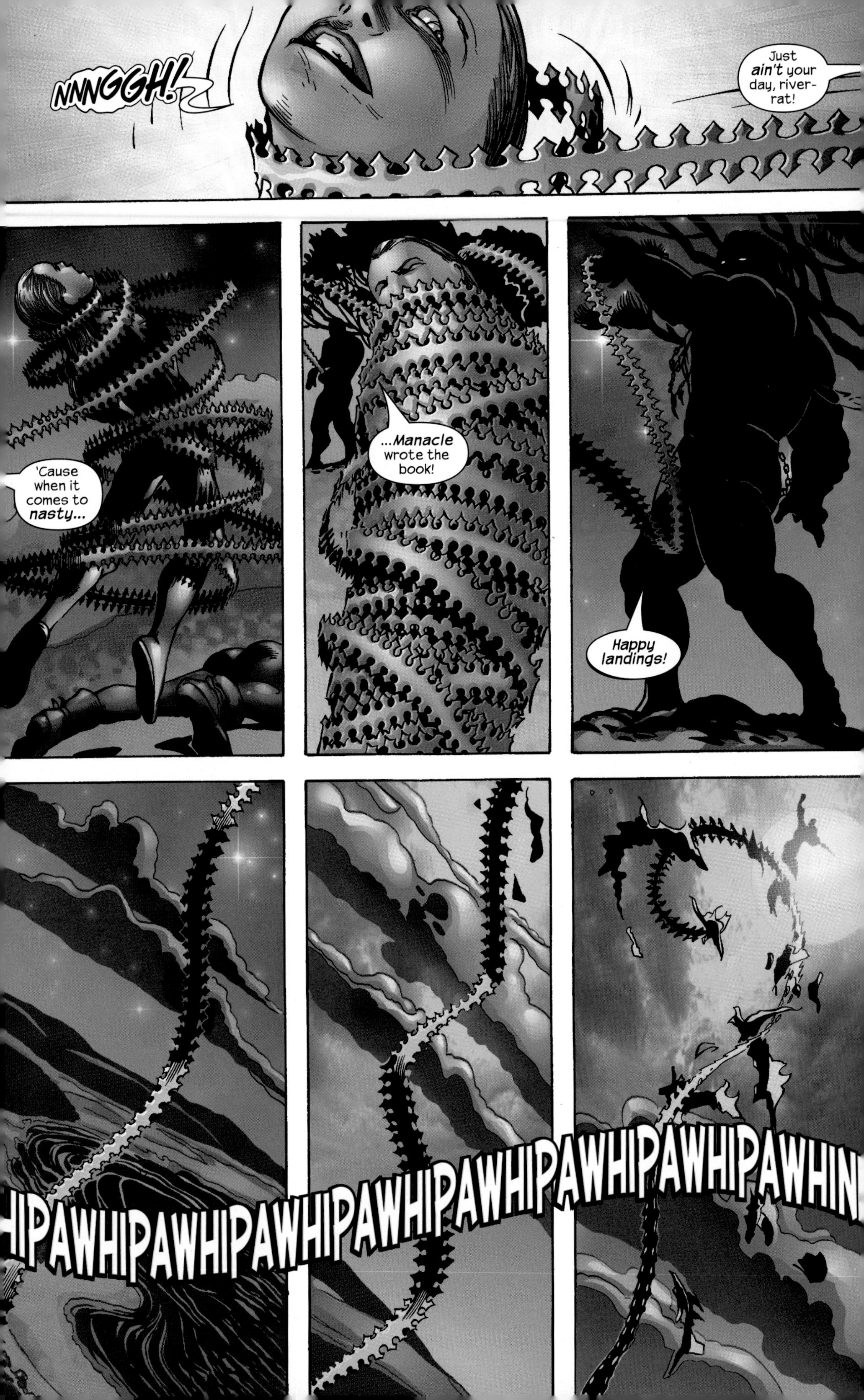

NNNGGH!
Just *ain't* your day, river-rat!
'Cause when it comes to *nasty*...
...*Manacle* wrote the book!
Happy landings!
HIPAWHIPAWHIPAWHIPAWHIPAWHIPAWHIPAWHI

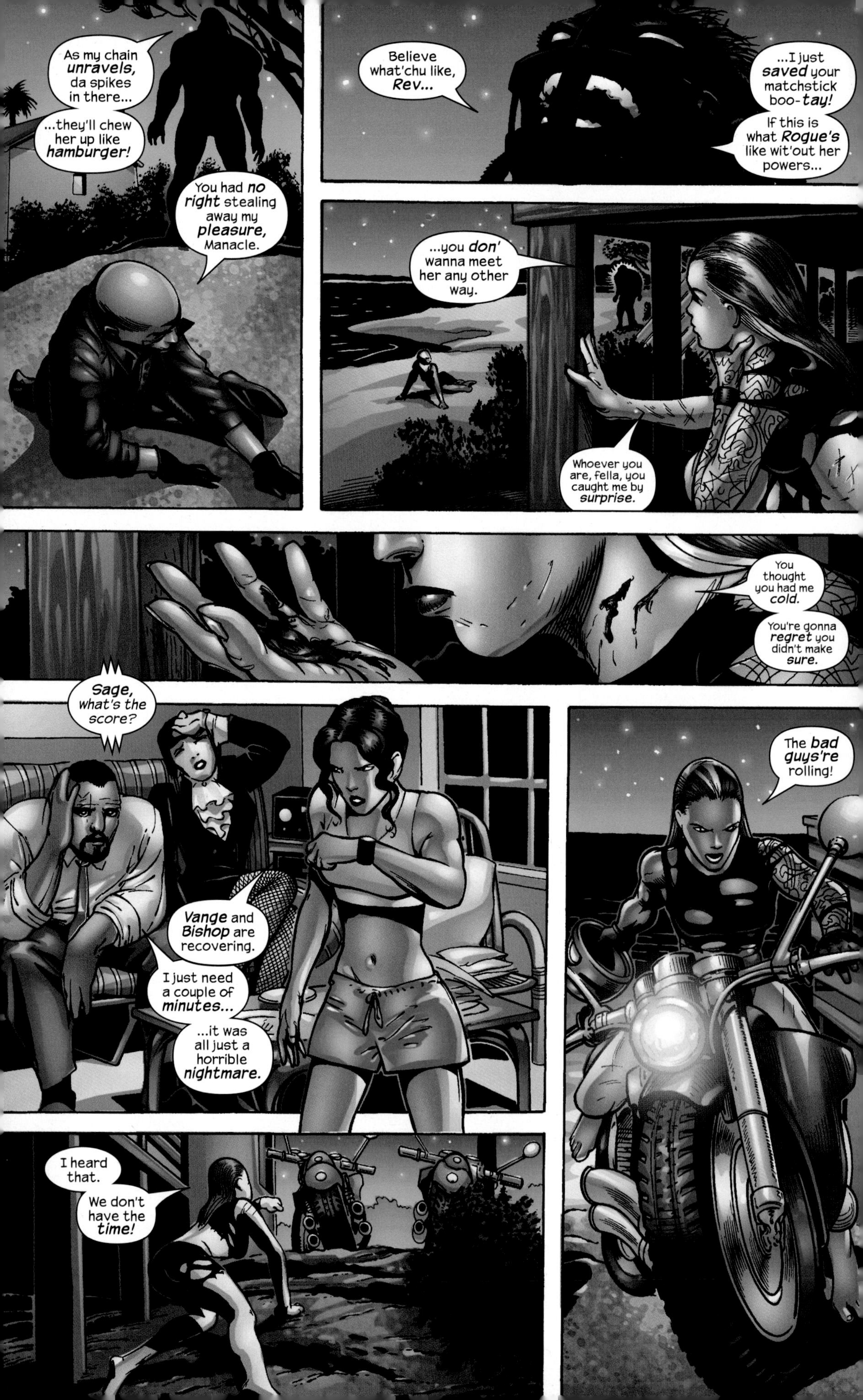
As my chain unravels, da spikes in there...
...they'll chew her up like hamburger!
You had no right stealing away my pleasure, Manacle.
Believe what'chu like, Rev...
...I just saved your matchstick boo-tay!
If this is what Rogue's like wit'out her powers...
...you don' wanna meet her any other way.
Whoever you are, fella, you caught me by surprise.
You thought you had me cold.
You're gonna regret you didn't make sure.
Sage, what's the score?
Vange and Bishop are recovering.
I just need a couple of minutes...
...it was all just a horrible nightmare.
The bad guys're rolling!
I heard that.
We don't have the time!

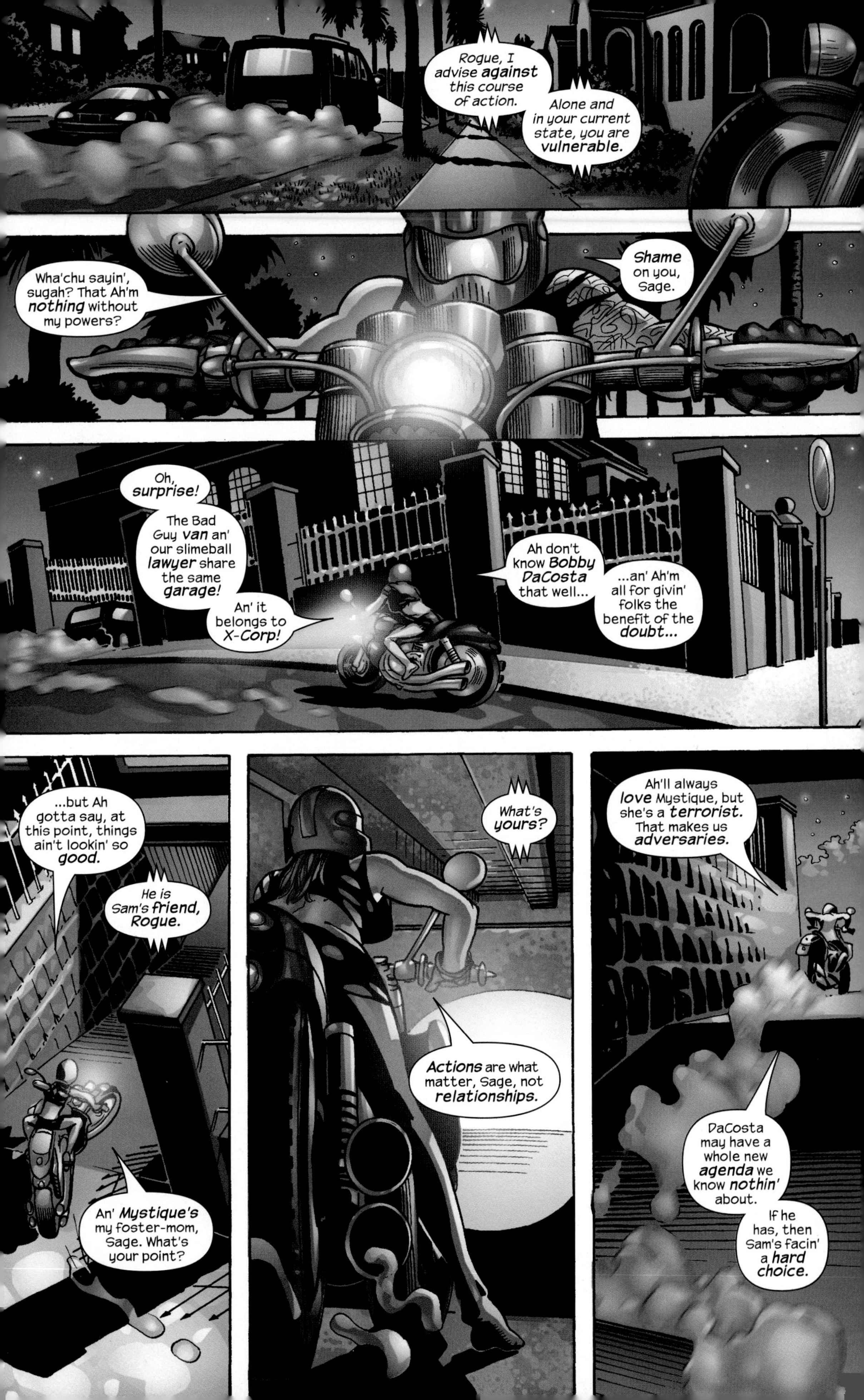

Rogue, I advise against this course of action.
Alone and in your current state, you are vulnerable.
Wha'chu sayin', sugah? That Ah'm nothing without my powers?
Shame on you, Sage.
Oh, surprise!
The Bad Guy van an' our slimeball lawyer share the same garage!
An' it belongs to X-Corp!
Ah don't know Bobby DaCosta that well...
...an' Ah'm all for givin' folks the benefit of the doubt...
...but Ah gotta say, at this point, things ain't lookin' so good.
He is Sam's friend, Rogue.
An' Mystique's my foster-mom, Sage. What's your point?
What's yours?
Actions are what matter, Sage, not relationships.
Ah'll always love Mystique, but she's a terrorist. That makes us adversaries.
DaCosta may have a whole new agenda we know nothin' about.
If he has, then Sam's facin' a hard choice.

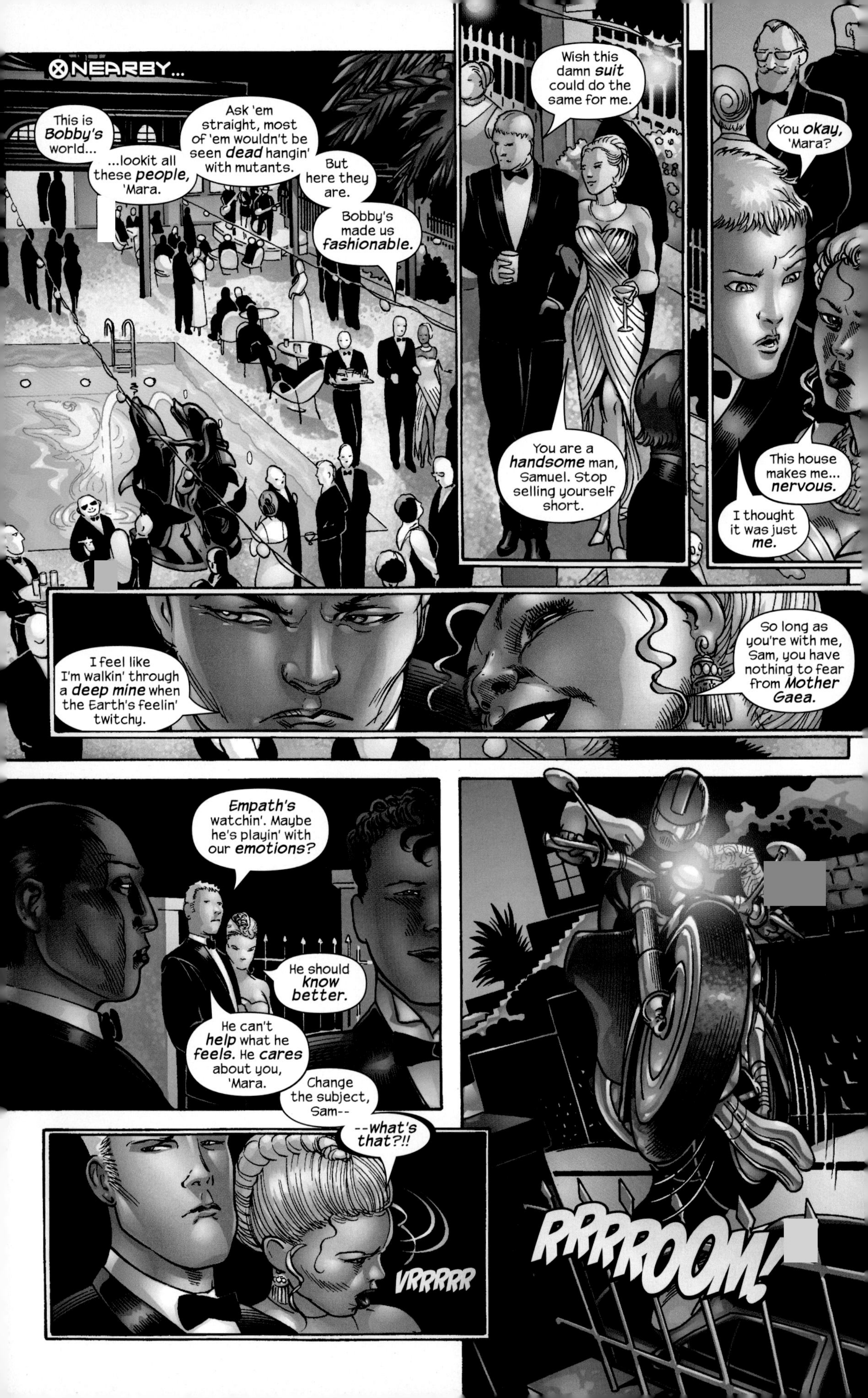
NEARBY...
This is Bobby's world...
...lookit all these people, 'Mara.
Ask 'em straight, most of 'em wouldn't be seen dead hangin' with mutants.
But here they are.
Bobby's made us fashionable.
Wish this damn suit could do the same for me.
You are a handsome man, Samuel. Stop selling yourself short.
You okay, 'Mara?
This house makes me... nervous.
I thought it was just me.
I feel like I'm walkin' through a deep mine when the Earth's feelin' twitchy.
So long as you're with me, Sam, you have nothing to fear from Mother Gaea.
Empath's watchin'. Maybe he's playin' with our emotions?
He should know better.
He can't help what he feels. He cares about you, 'Mara.
Change the subject, Sam--
--what's that?!!
VRRRRR
RRRROOM!

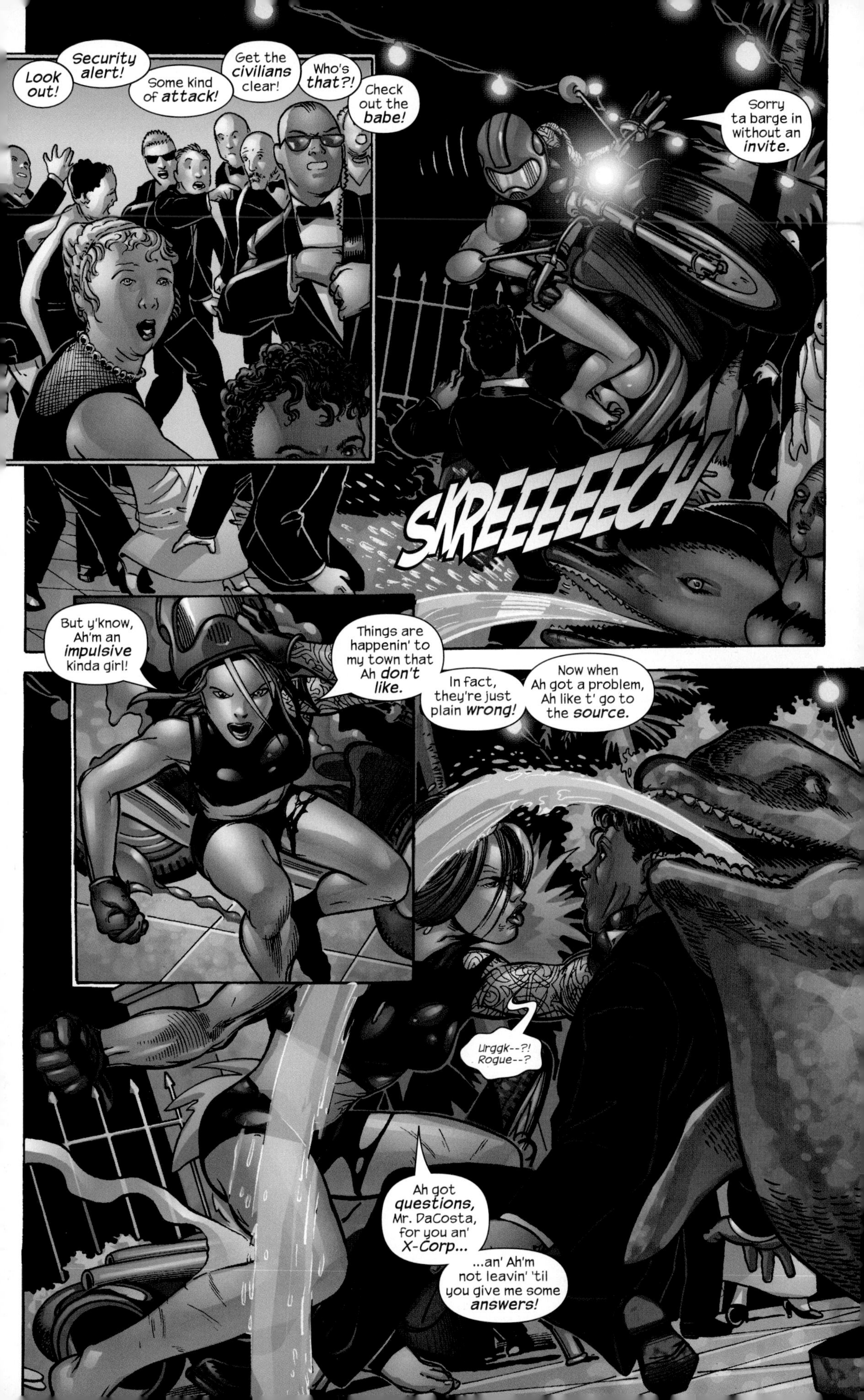

Look out!
Security alert!
Some kind of attack!
Get the civilians clear!
Who's that?!
Check out the babe!
Sorry ta barge in without an invite.
SKREEEEEECH
But y'know, Ah'm an impulsive kinda girl!
Things are happenin' to my town that Ah don't like.
In fact, they're just plain wrong!
Now when Ah got a problem, Ah like t' go to the source.
Urggk--?! Rogue--?
Ah got questions, Mr. DaCosta, for you an' X-Corp...
...an' Ah'm not leavin' 'til you give me some answers!

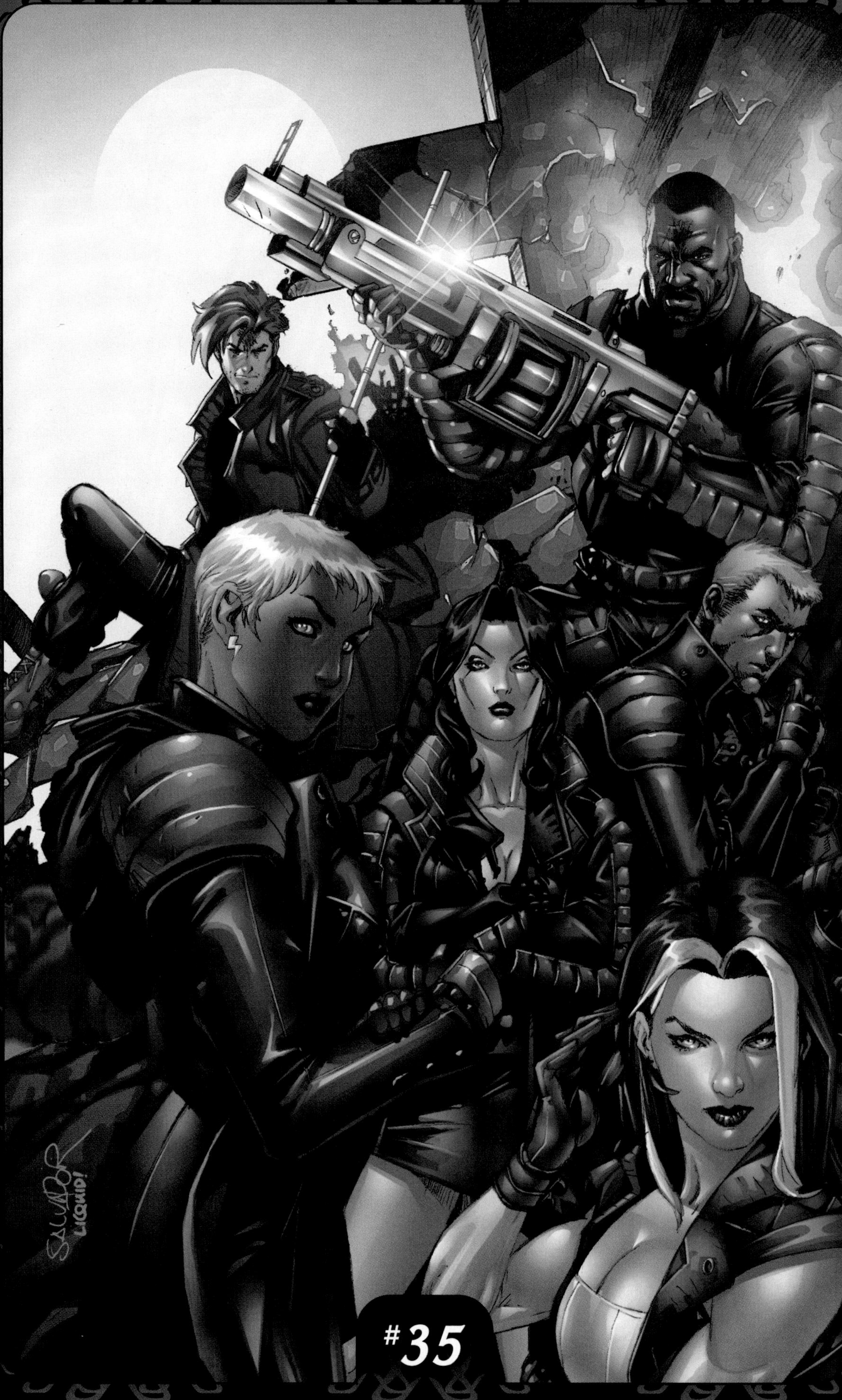
SALVADOR
LIQUID!

#35

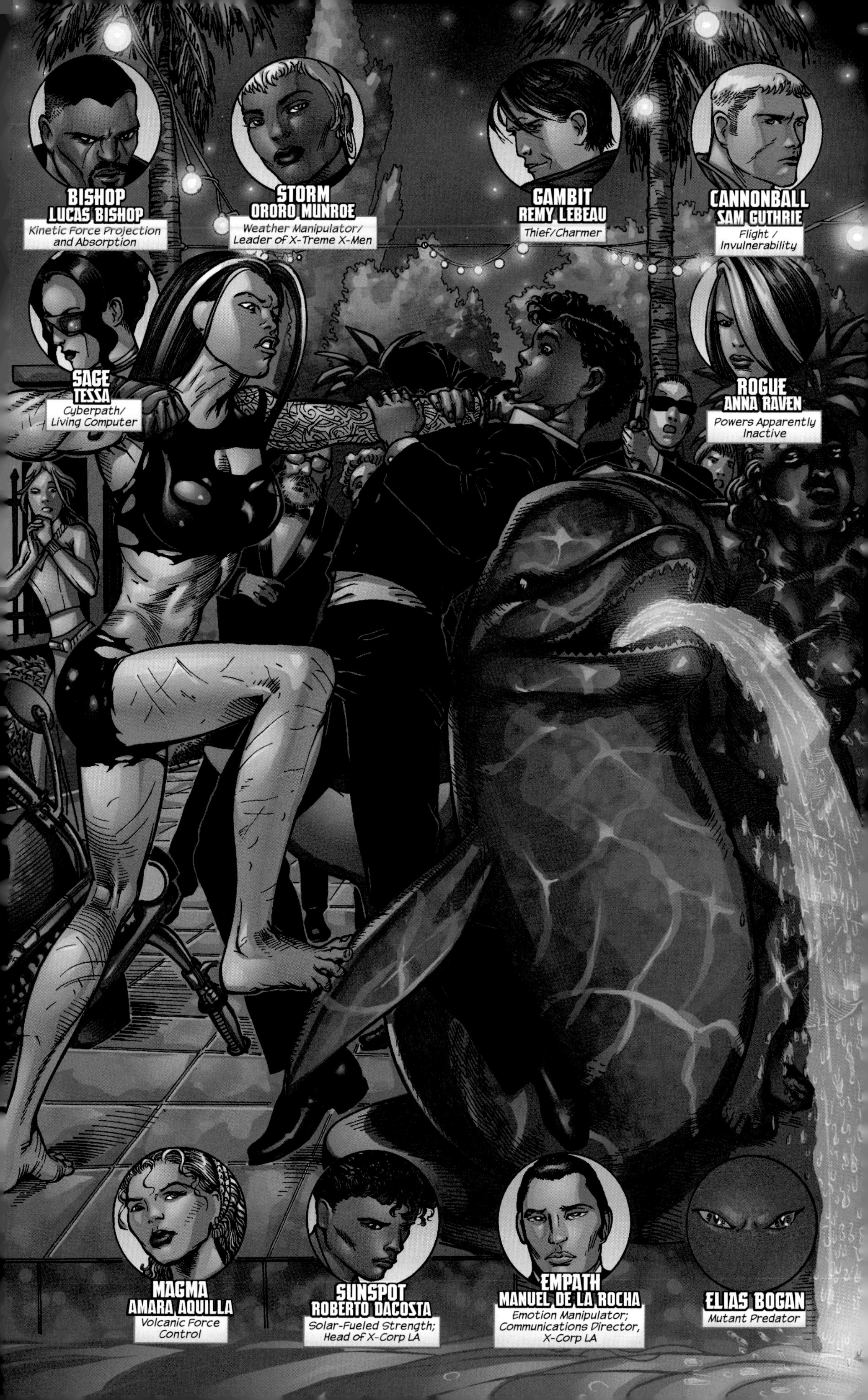

BISHOP
LUCAS BISHOP
Kinetic Force Projection and Absorption
STORM
ORORO MUNROE
Weather Manipulator/ Leader of X-Treme X-Men
GAMBIT
REMY LEBEAU
Thief/Charmer
CANNONBALL
SAM GUTHRIE
Flight / Invulnerability
SAGE
TESSA
Cyberpath/ Living Computer
ROGUE
ANNA RAVEN
Powers Apparently Inactive
MAGMA
AMARA AQUILLA
Volcanic Force Control
SUNSPOT
ROBERTO DACOSTA
Solar-Fueled Strength; Head of X-Corp LA
EMPATH
MANUEL DE LA ROCHA
Emotion Manipulator; Communications Director, X-Corp LA
ELIAS BOGAN
Mutant Predator

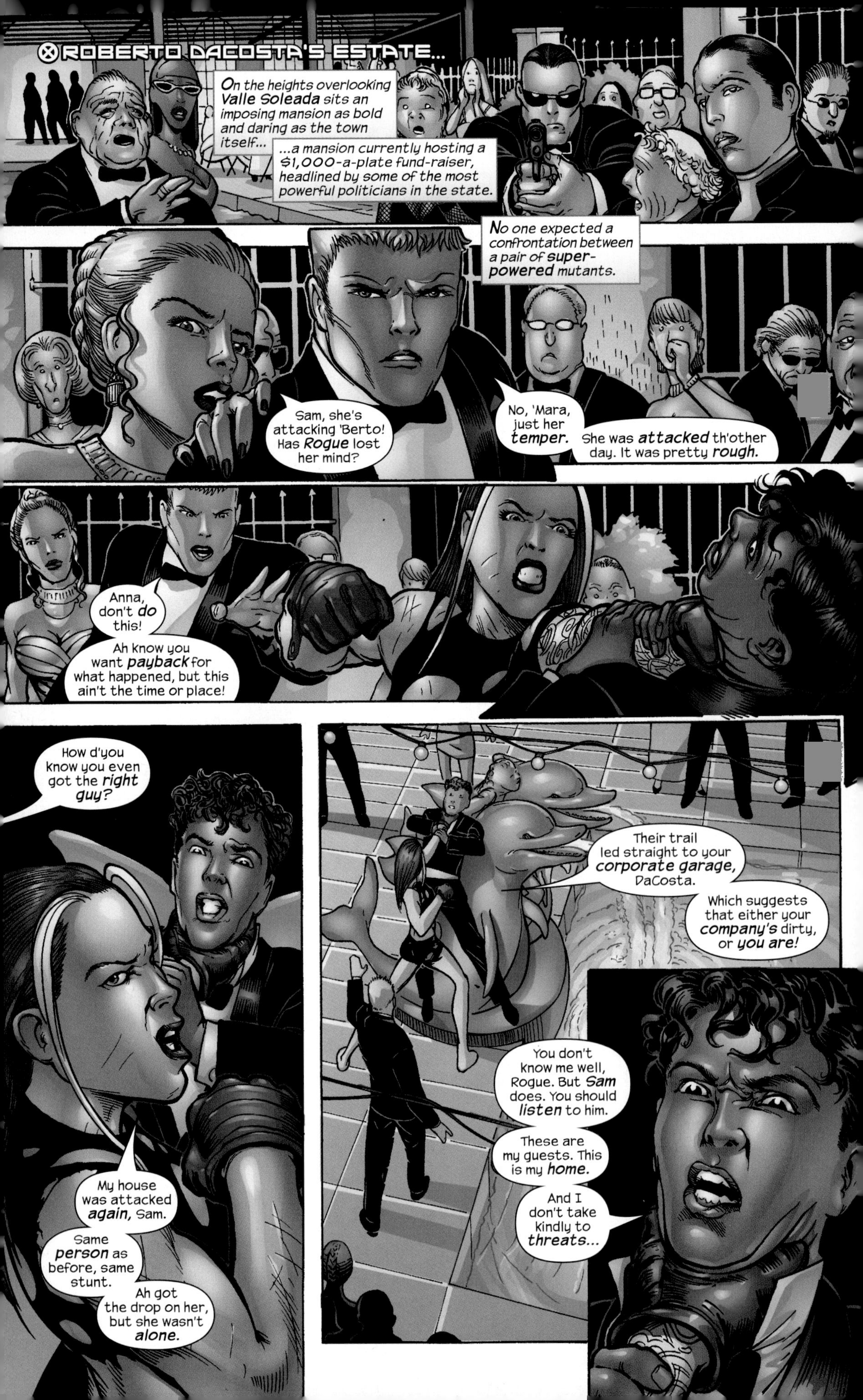
ROBERTO DACOSTA'S ESTATE...
On the heights overlooking Valle Soleada sits an imposing mansion as bold and daring as the town itself...
...a mansion currently hosting a $1,000-a-plate fund-raiser, headlined by some of the most powerful politicians in the state.
No one expected a confrontation between a pair of super-powered mutants.
Sam, she's attacking 'Berto! Has Rogue lost her mind?
No, 'Mara, just her temper.
She was attacked th'other day. It was pretty rough.
Anna, don't do this!
Ah know you want payback for what happened, but this ain't the time or place!
How d'you know you even got the right guy?
My house was attacked again, Sam.
Same person as before, same stunt.
Ah got the drop on her, but she wasn't alone.
Their trail led straight to your corporate garage, DaCosta.
Which suggests that either your company's dirty, or you are!
You don't know me well, Rogue. But Sam does. You should listen to him.
These are my guests. This is my home.
And I don't take kindly to threats...

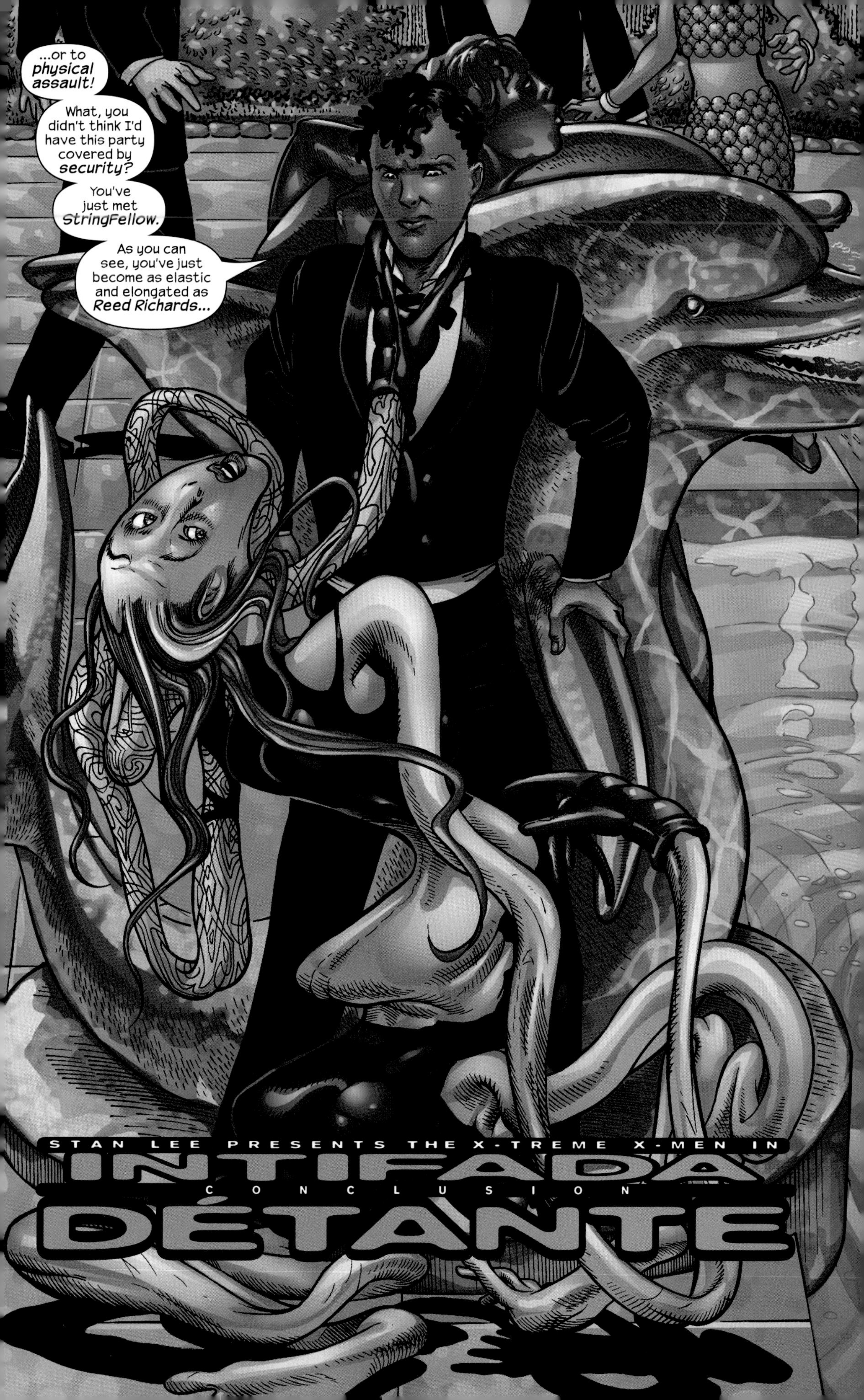
...or to *physical assault!*
What, you didn't think I'd have this party covered by *security?*
You've just met *StringFellow.*
As you can see, you've just become as elastic and elongated as *Reed Richards...*
STAN LEE PRESENTS THE X-TREME X-MEN IN
INTIFADA
CONCLUSION
DÉTANTE

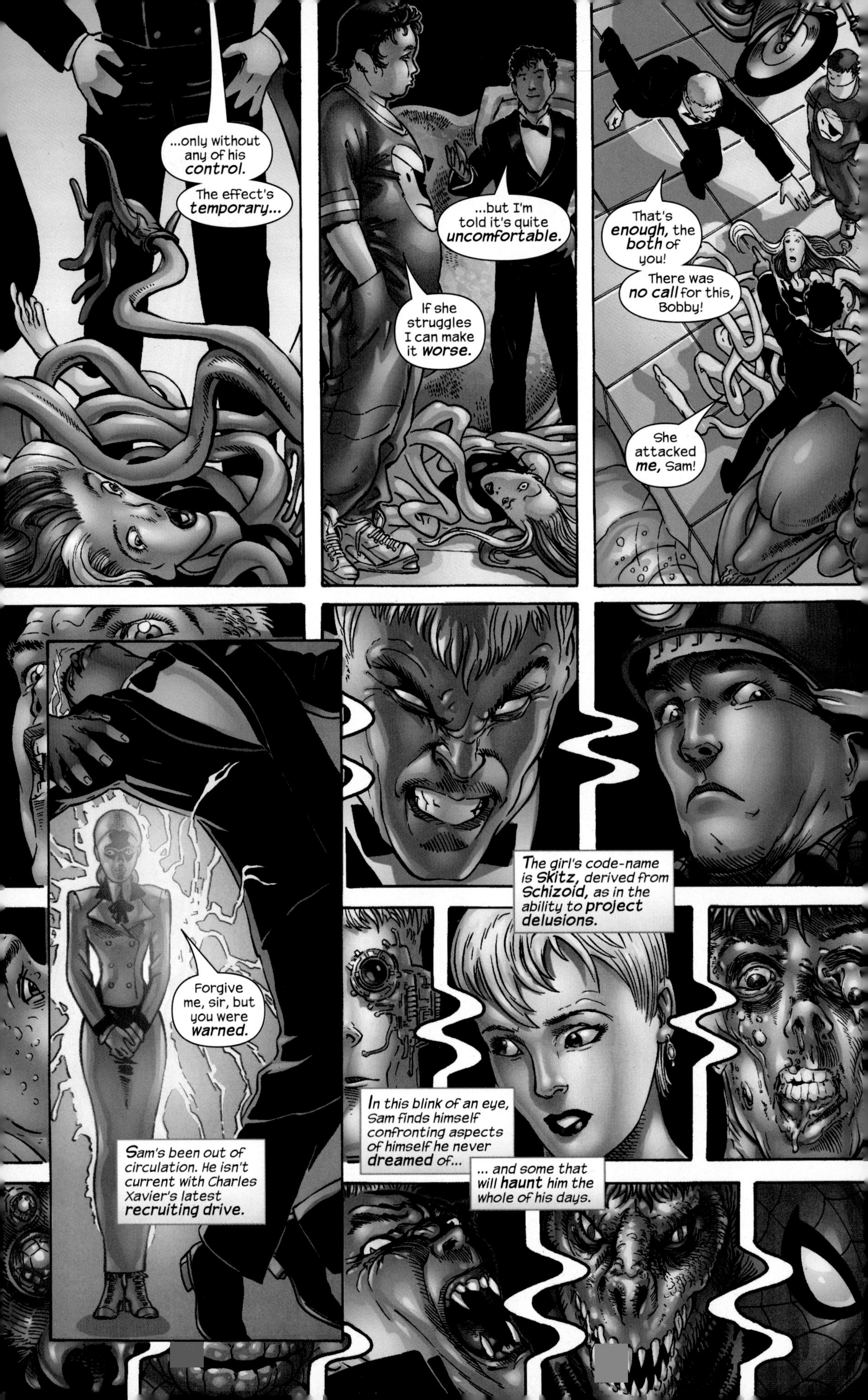
...only without any of his control.
The effect's temporary...
...but I'm told it's quite uncomfortable.
If she struggles I can make it worse.
That's enough, the both of you!
There was no call for this, Bobby!
She attacked me, Sam!
Forgive me, sir, but you were warned.
Sam's been out of circulation. He isn't current with Charles Xavier's latest recruiting drive.
The girl's code-name is Skitz, derived from Schizoid, as in the ability to project delusions.
In this blink of an eye, Sam finds himself confronting aspects of himself he never dreamed of...
... and some that will haunt him the whole of his days.

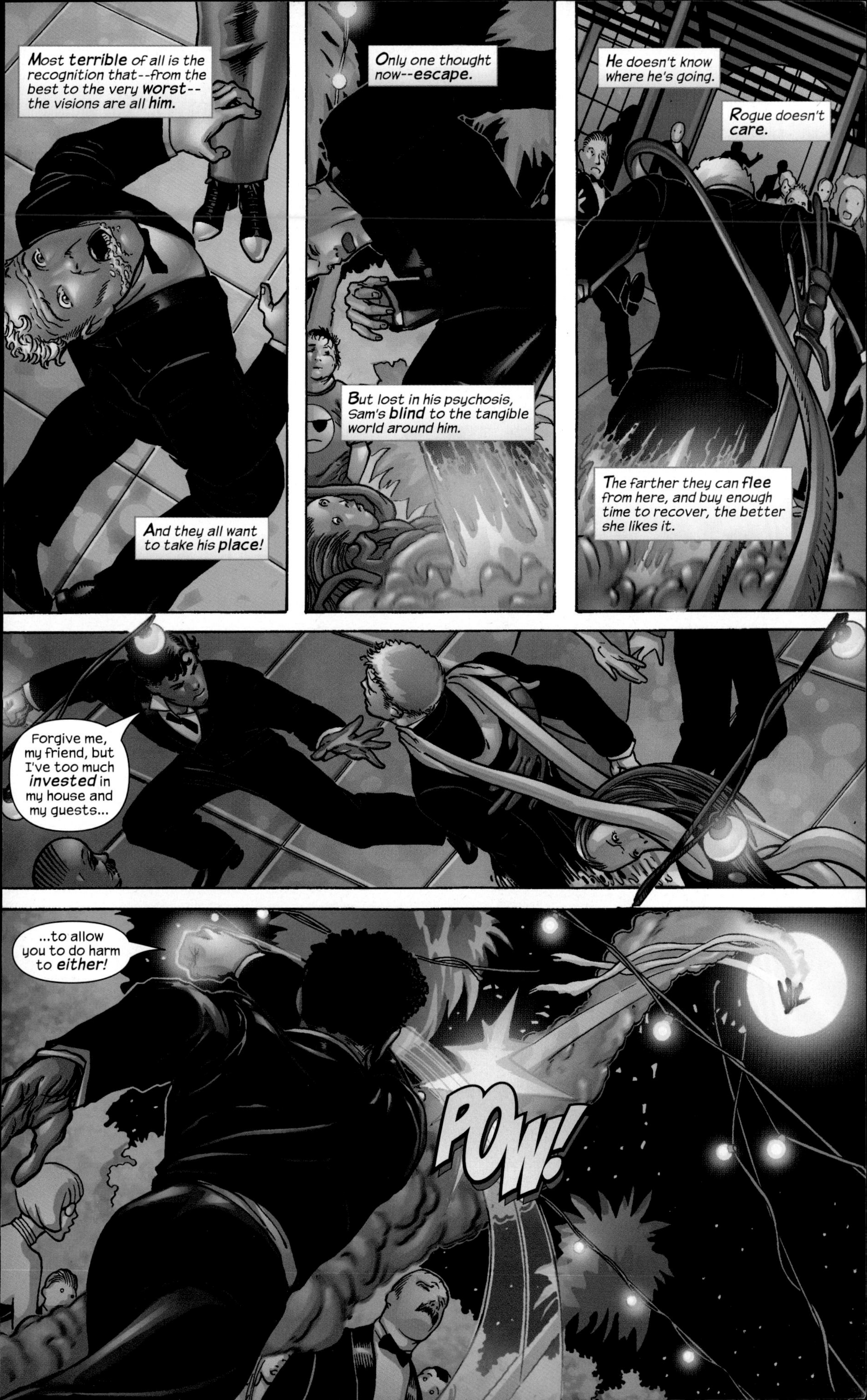
Most terrible of all is the recognition that--from the best to the very worst--the visions are all him.
And they all want to take his place!
Only one thought now--escape.
But lost in his psychosis, Sam's blind to the tangible world around him.
He doesn't know where he's going.
Rogue doesn't care.
The farther they can flee from here, and buy enough time to recover, the better she likes it.
Forgive me, my friend, but I've too much invested in my house and my guests...
...to allow you to do harm to either!
POW!

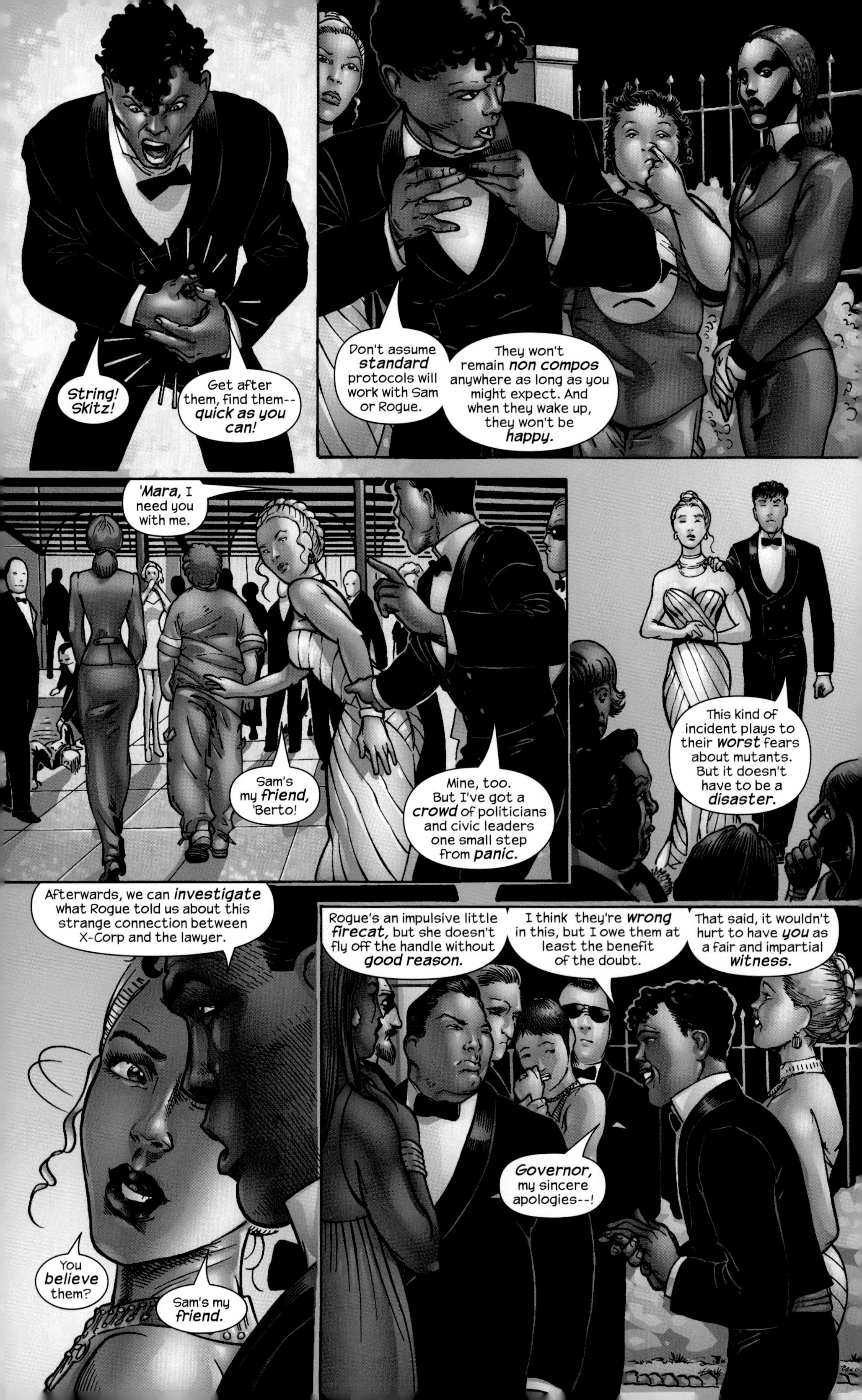
String! Skitz!
Get after them, find them-- *quick as you can!*
Don't assume *standard* protocols will work with Sam or Rogue.
They won't remain *non compos* anywhere as long as you might expect. And when they wake up, they won't be *happy.*
'*Mara,* I need you with me.
Sam's my *friend,* 'Berto!
Mine, too. But I've got a *crowd* of politicians and civic leaders one small step from *panic.*
This kind of incident plays to their *worst* fears about mutants. But it doesn't have to be a *disaster.*
Afterwards, we can *investigate* what Rogue told us about this strange connection between X-Corp and the lawyer.
You *believe* them?
Sam's my *friend.*
Rogue's an impulsive little *firecat,* but she doesn't fly off the handle without *good reason.*
I think they're *wrong* in this, but I owe them at least the benefit of the doubt.
That said, it wouldn't hurt to have *you* as a fair and impartial *witness.*
Governor, my sincere apologies--!

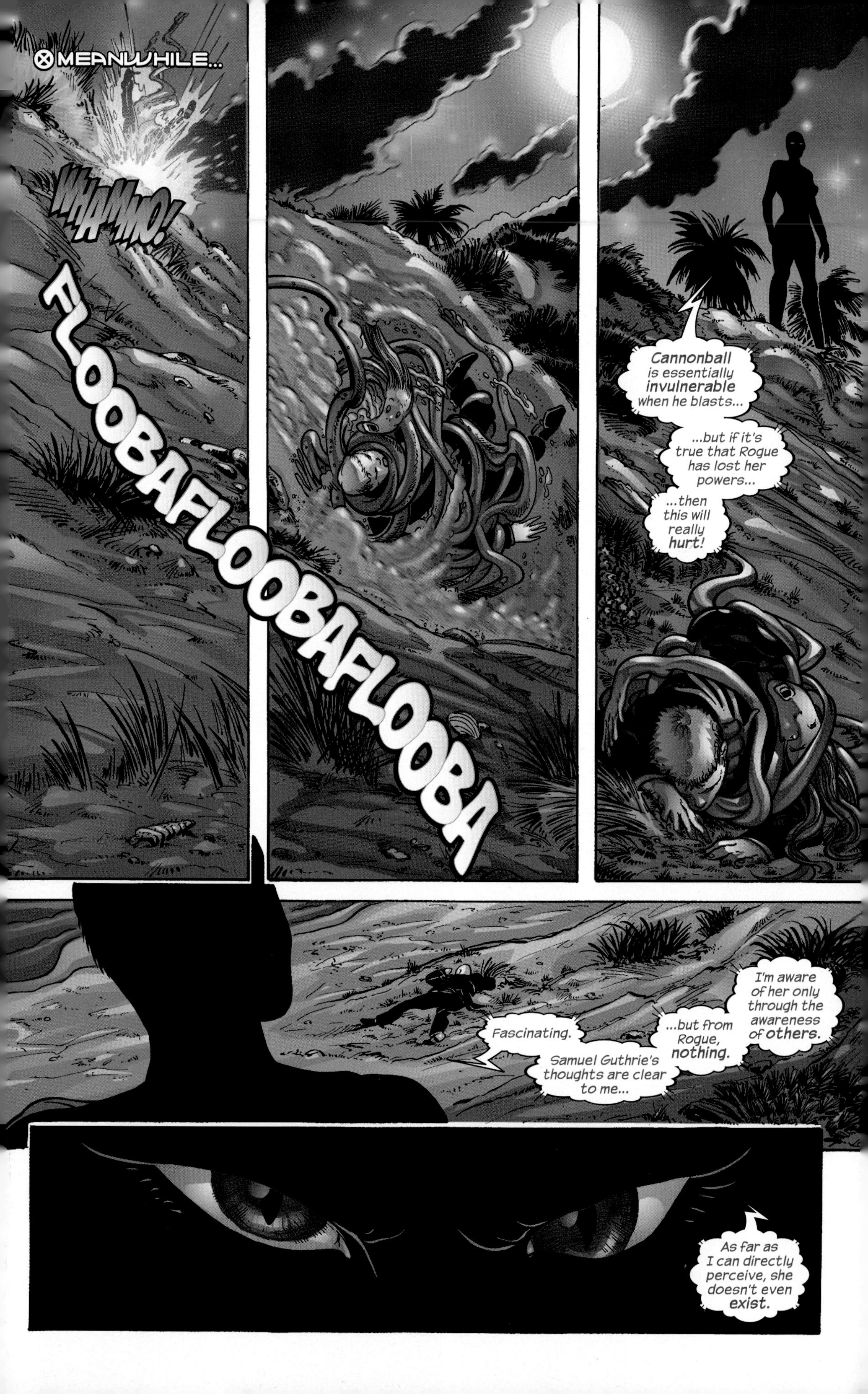
MEANWHILE...
WHAMMO!
FLOOBAFLOOBAFLOOBA
Cannonball is essentially invulnerable when he blasts...
...but if it's true that Rogue has lost her powers...
...then this will really hurt!
Fascinating.
Samuel Guthrie's thoughts are clear to me...
...but from Rogue, nothing.
I'm aware of her only through the awareness of others.
As far as I can directly perceive, she doesn't even exist.

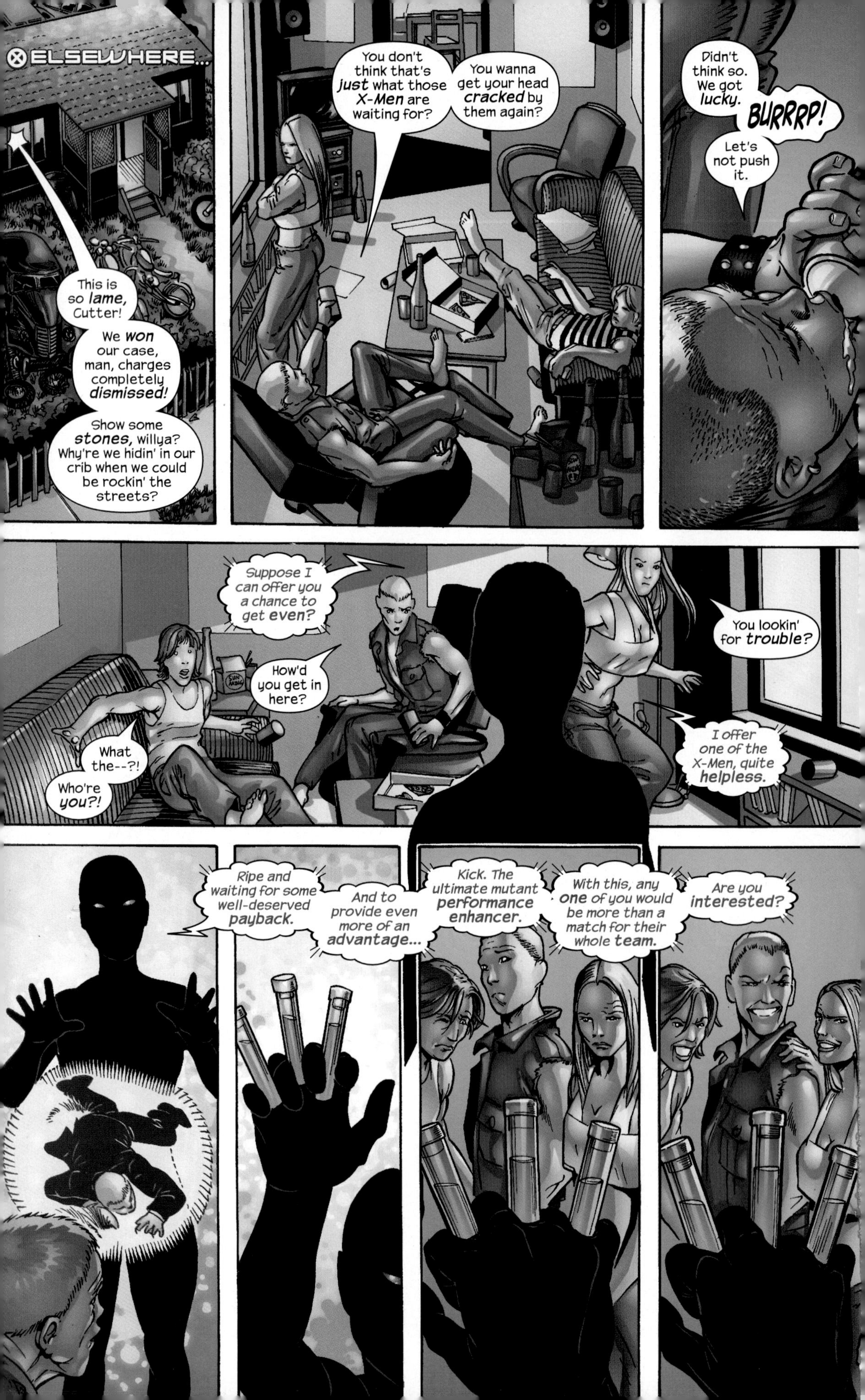
ELSEWHERE...
This is so lame, Cutter!
We won our case, man, charges completely dismissed!
Show some stones, willya? Why're we hidin' in our crib when we could be rockin' the streets?
You don't think that's just what those X-Men are waiting for?
You wanna get your head cracked by them again?
Didn't think so. We got lucky.
BURRRP!
Let's not push it.
Suppose I can offer you a chance to get even?
How'd you get in here?
What the--?!
Who're you?!
You lookin' for trouble?
I offer one of the X-Men, quite helpless.
Ripe and waiting for some well-deserved payback.
And to provide even more of an advantage...
Kick. The ultimate mutant performance enhancer.
With this, any one of you would be more than a match for their whole team.
Are you interested?

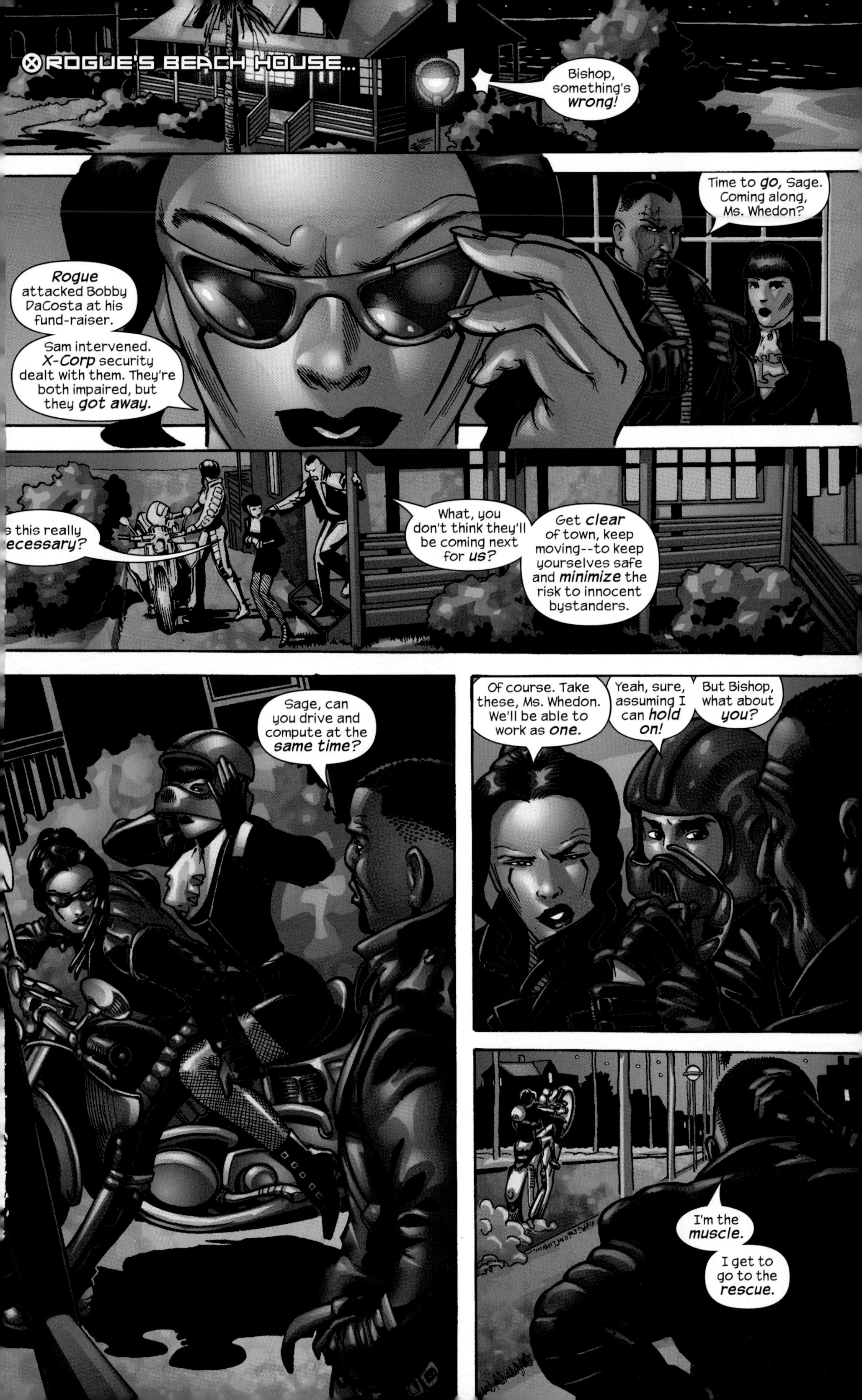

ROGUE'S BEACH HOUSE...
Bishop, something's *wrong!*
Rogue attacked Bobby DaCosta at his fund-raiser.
Sam intervened. *X-Corp* security dealt with them. They're both impaired, but they *got away.*
Time to *go,* Sage. Coming along, Ms. Whedon?
s this really ecessary?
What, you don't think they'll be coming next for *us?*
Get *clear* of town, keep moving--to keep yourselves safe and *minimize* the risk to innocent bystanders.
Sage, can you drive and compute at the *same time?*
Of course. Take these, Ms. Whedon. We'll be able to work as *one.*
Yeah, sure, assuming I can *hold on!*
But Bishop, what about *you?*
I'm the *muscle.*
I get to go to the *rescue.*

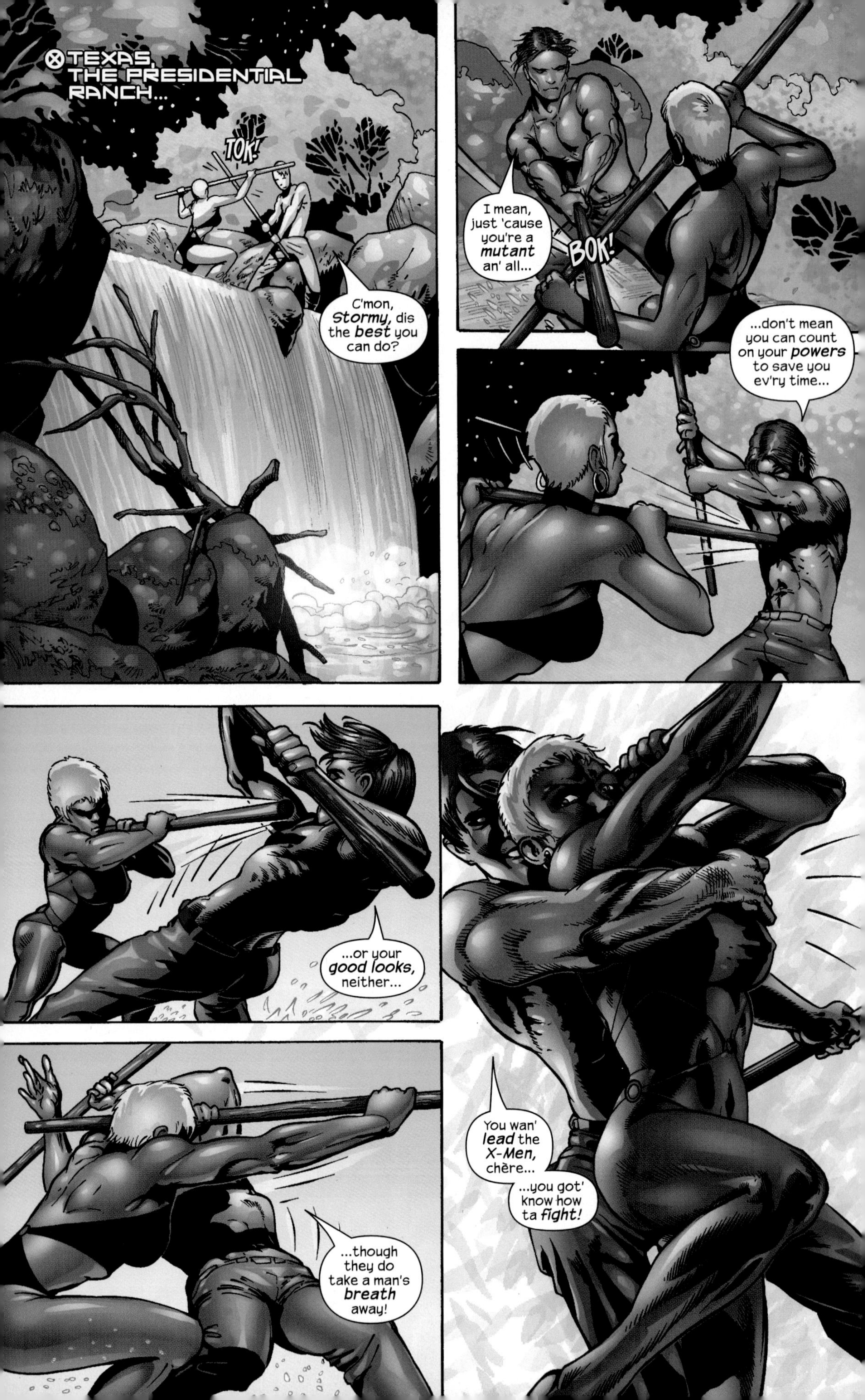
TEXAS, THE PRESIDENTIAL RANCH...
TOK!
C'mon, Stormy, dis the best you can do?
I mean, just 'cause you're a mutant an' all...
BOK!
...don't mean you can count on your powers to save you ev'ry time...
...or your good looks, neither...
...though they do take a man's breath away!
You wan' lead the X-Men, chère...
...you got' know how ta fight!

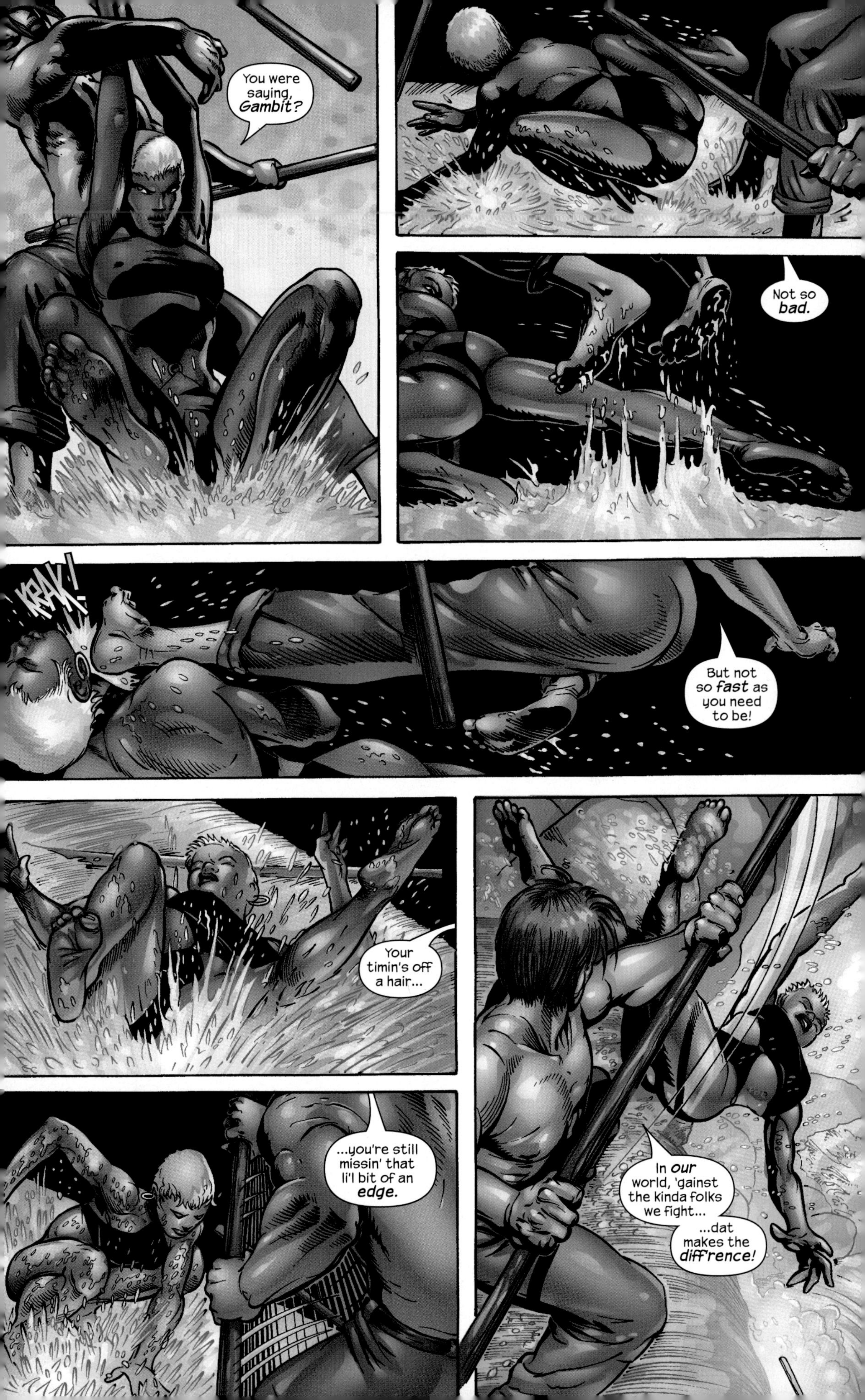
You were saying, Gambit?
Not so bad.
KRAK!
But not so fast as you need to be!
Your timin's off a hair...
...you're still missin' that li'l bit of an edge.
In our world, 'gainst the kinda folks we fight...
...dat makes the diff'rence!

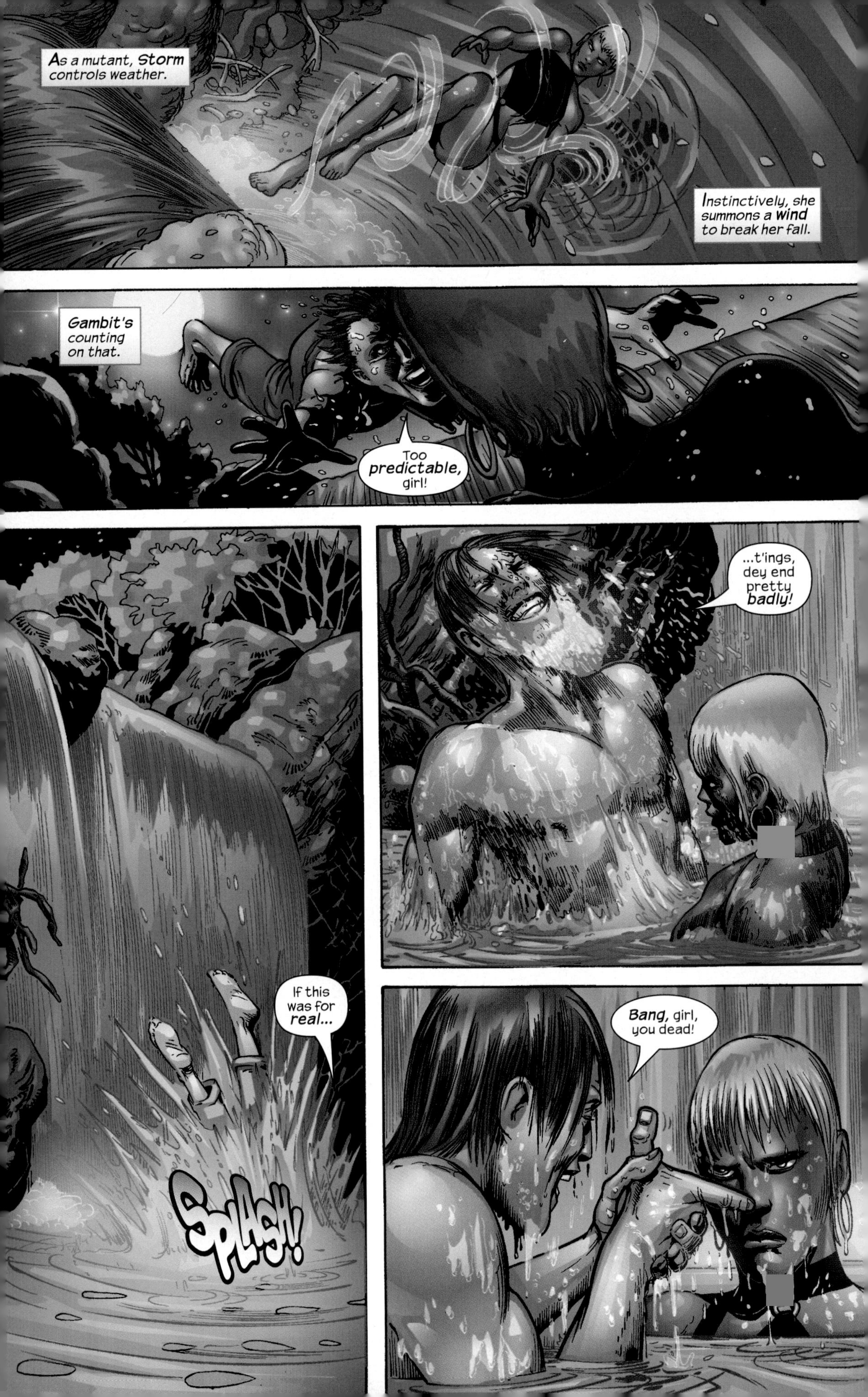
As a mutant, Storm controls weather.
Instinctively, she summons a wind to break her fall.
Gambit's counting on that.
Too predictable, girl!
SPLASH!
If this was for real...
...t'ings, dey end pretty badly!
Bang, girl, you dead!

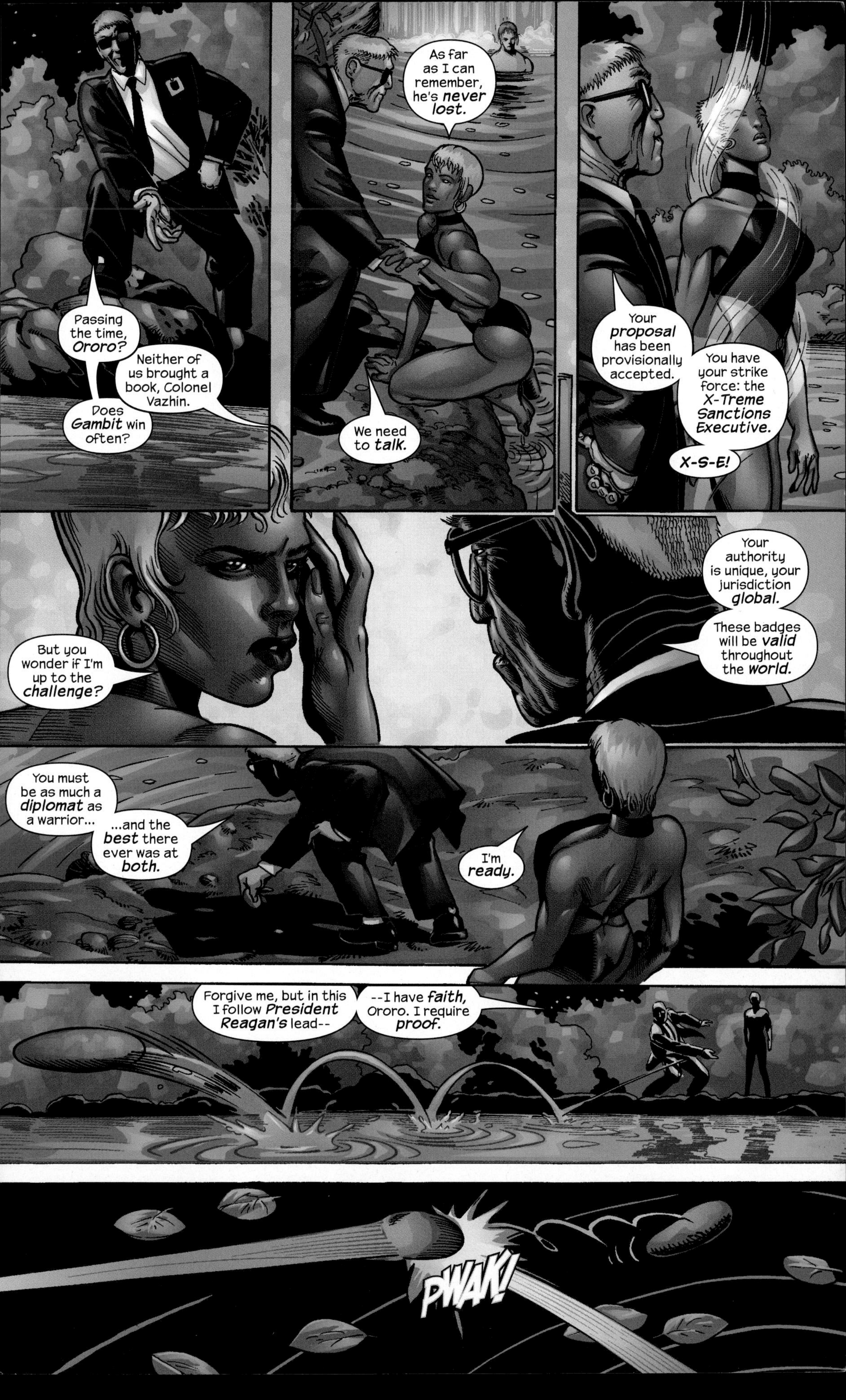

Passing the time, Ororo?
Neither of us brought a book, Colonel Vazhin.
Does Gambit win often?
As far as I can remember, he's never lost.
We need to talk.
Your proposal has been provisionally accepted.
You have your strike force: the X-Treme Sanctions Executive.
X-S-E!
Your authority is unique, your jurisdiction global.
These badges will be valid throughout the world.
But you wonder if I'm up to the challenge?
You must be as much a diplomat as a warrior...
...and the best there ever was at both.
I'm ready.
Forgive me, but in this I follow President Reagan's lead--
--I have faith, Ororo. I require proof.
PWAK!

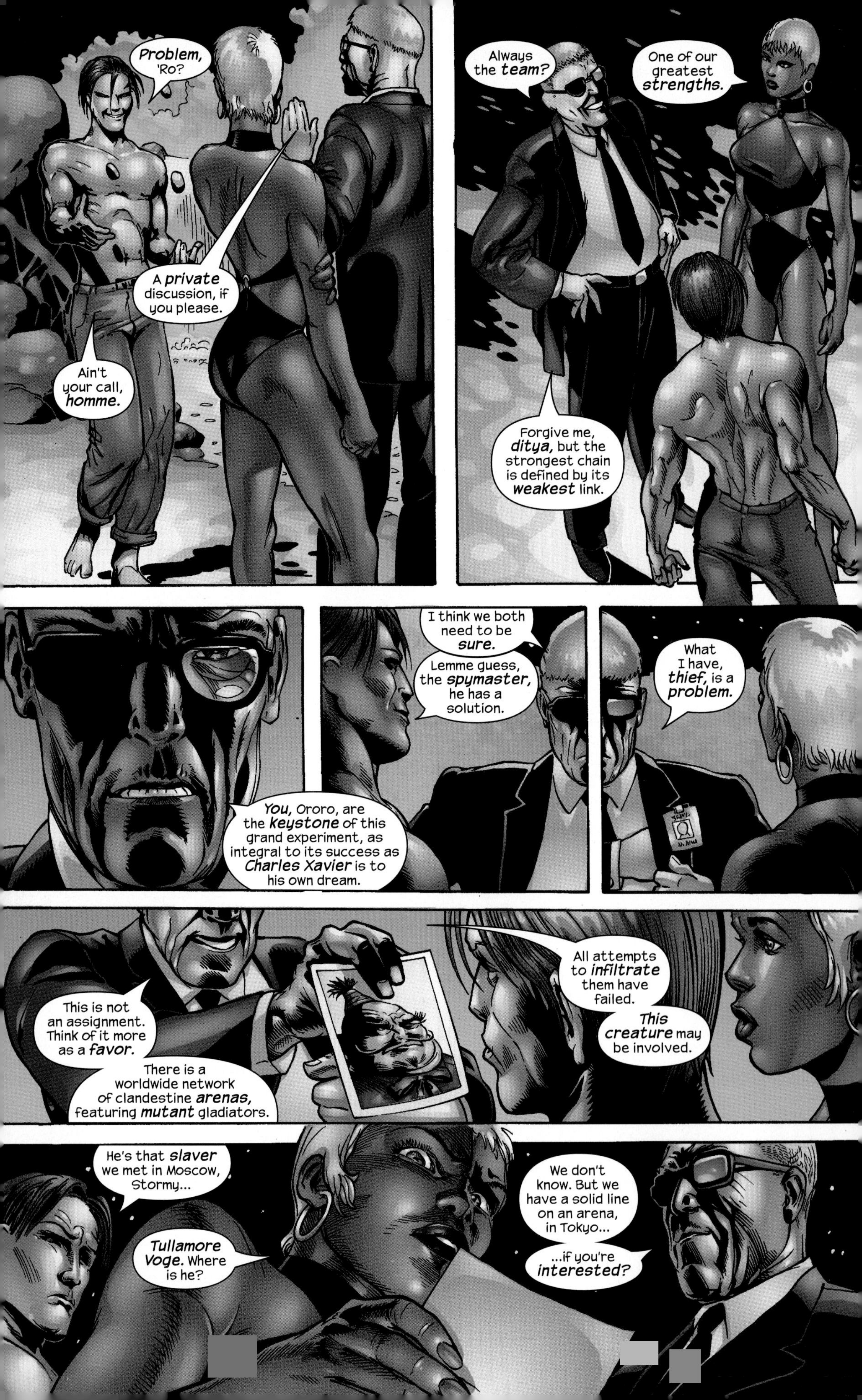

Problem, 'Ro?
A private discussion, if you please.
Ain't your call, homme.
Always the team?
One of our greatest strengths.
Forgive me, ditya, but the strongest chain is defined by its weakest link.
You, Ororo, are the keystone of this grand experiment, as integral to its success as Charles Xavier is to his own dream.
I think we both need to be sure.
Lemme guess, the spymaster, he has a solution.
What I have, thief, is a problem.
This is not an assignment. Think of it more as a favor.
There is a worldwide network of clandestine arenas, featuring mutant gladiators.
All attempts to infiltrate them have failed.
This creature may be involved.
He's that slaver we met in Moscow, Stormy...
Tullamore Voge. Where is he?
We don't know. But we have a solid line on an arena, in Tokyo...
...if you're interested?

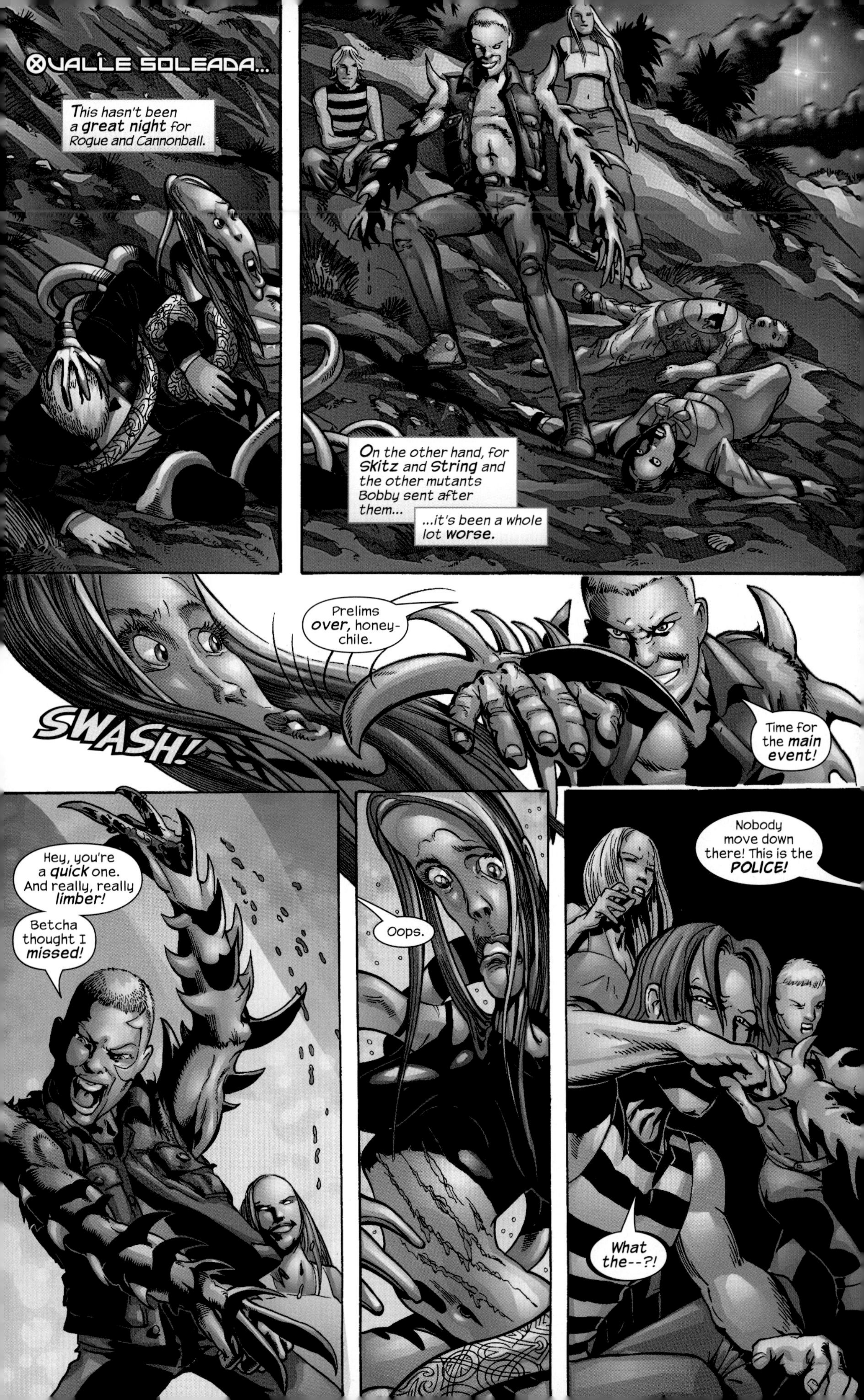
VALLE SOLEADA...
This hasn't been a great night for Rogue and Cannonball.
On the other hand, for Skitz and String and the other mutants Bobby sent after them...
...it's been a whole lot worse.
Prelims over, honey-chile.
SWASH!
Time for the main event!
Hey, you're a quick one. And really, really limber!
Betcha thought I missed!
Oops.
Nobody move down there! This is the POLICE!
What the--?!

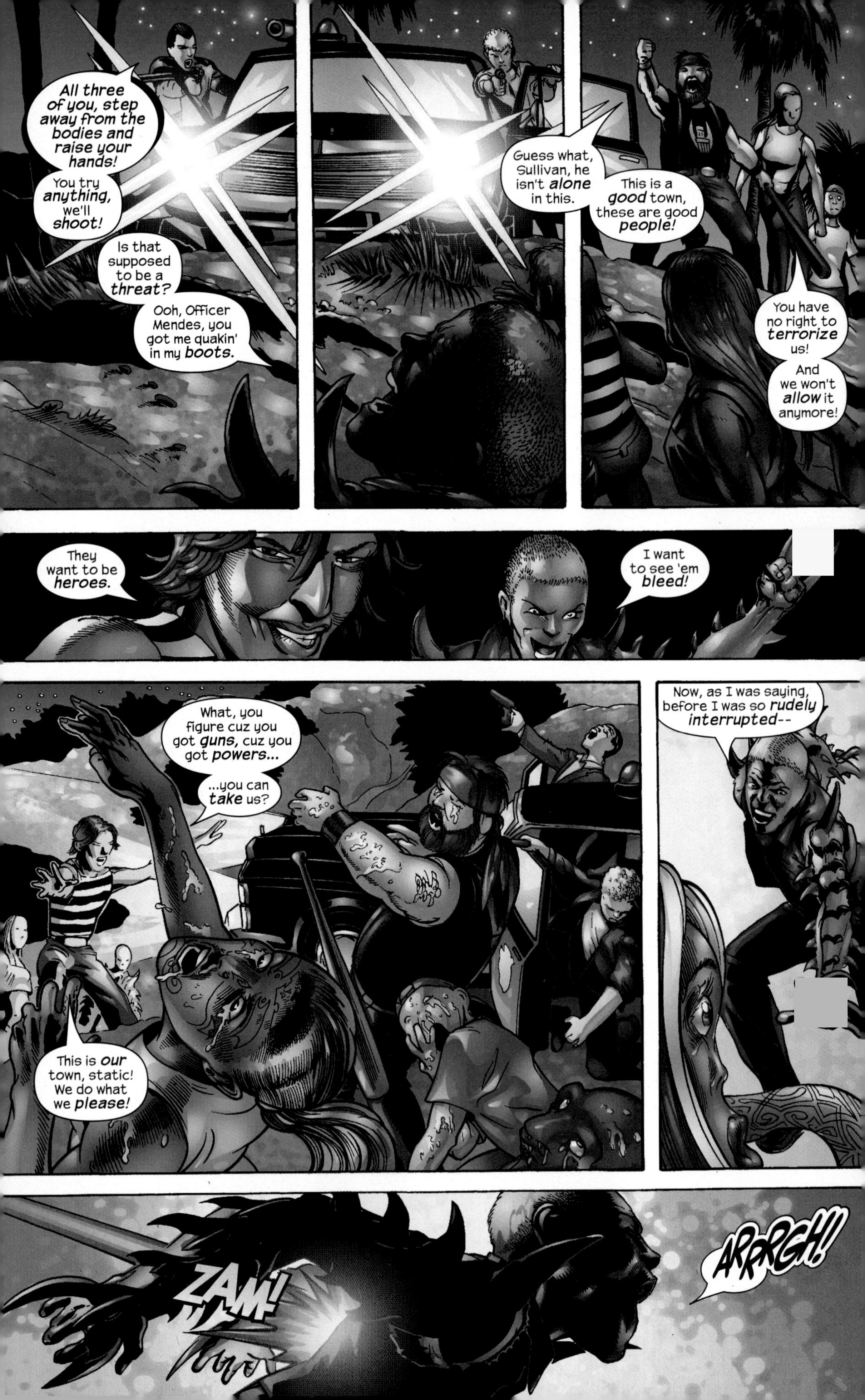

All three of you, step away from the bodies and raise your hands!
You try anything, we'll shoot!
Is that supposed to be a threat?
Ooh, Officer Mendes, you got me quakin' in my boots.
Guess what, Sullivan, he isn't alone in this.
This is a good town, these are good people!
You have no right to terrorize us!
And we won't allow it anymore!
They want to be heroes.
I want to see 'em bleed!
What, you figure cuz you got guns, cuz you got powers...
...you can take us?
This is our town, static! We do what we please!
Now, as I was saying, before I was so rudely interrupted--
ZAM!
ARRRGH!!

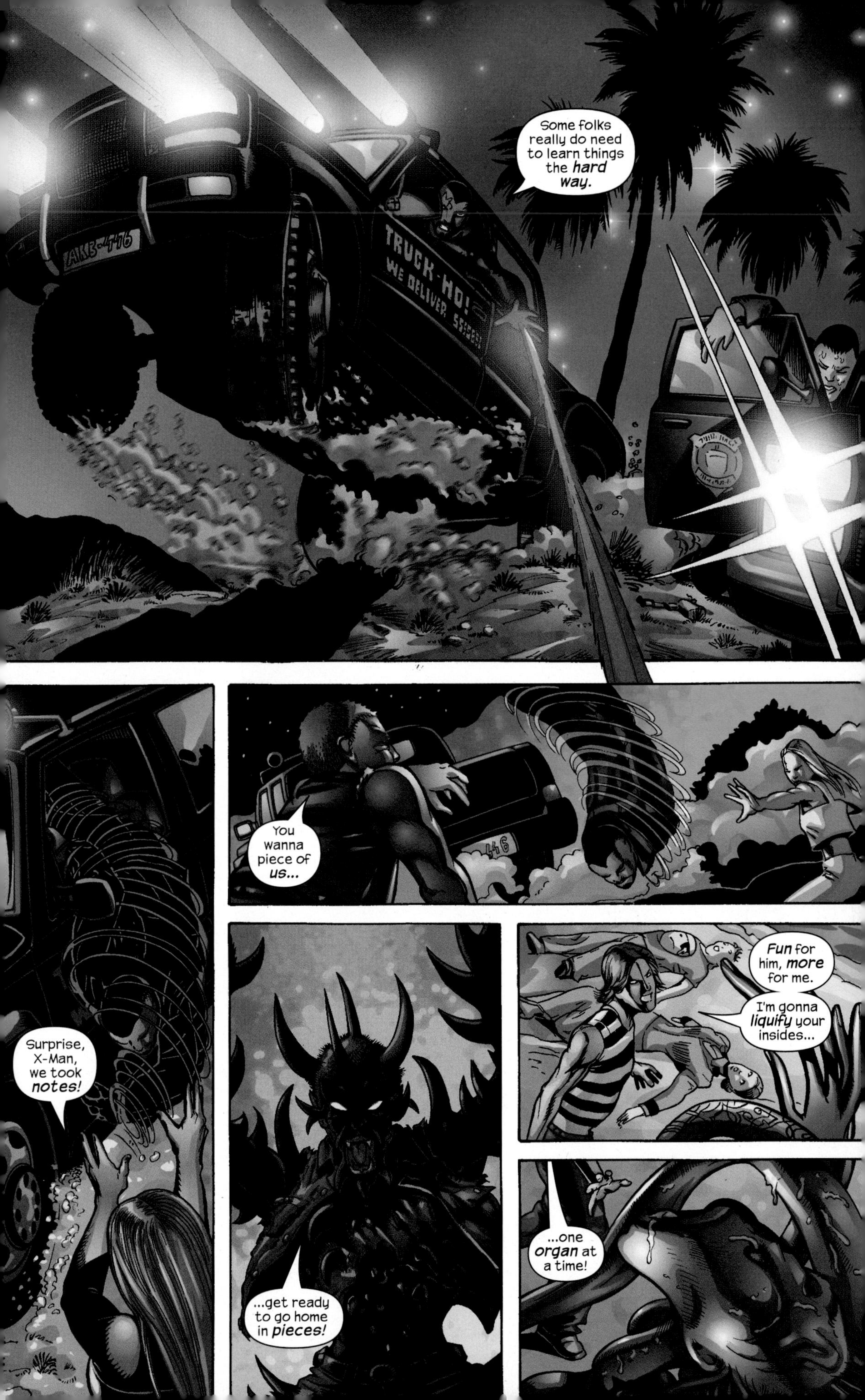
Some folks really do need to learn things the *hard* *way.*
TRUCK-HO!
WE DELIVER
You wanna piece of *us...*
Surprise, X-Man, we took *notes!*
...get ready to go home in *pieces!*
Fun for him, *more* for me.
I'm gonna *liquify* your insides...
...one *organ* at a time!

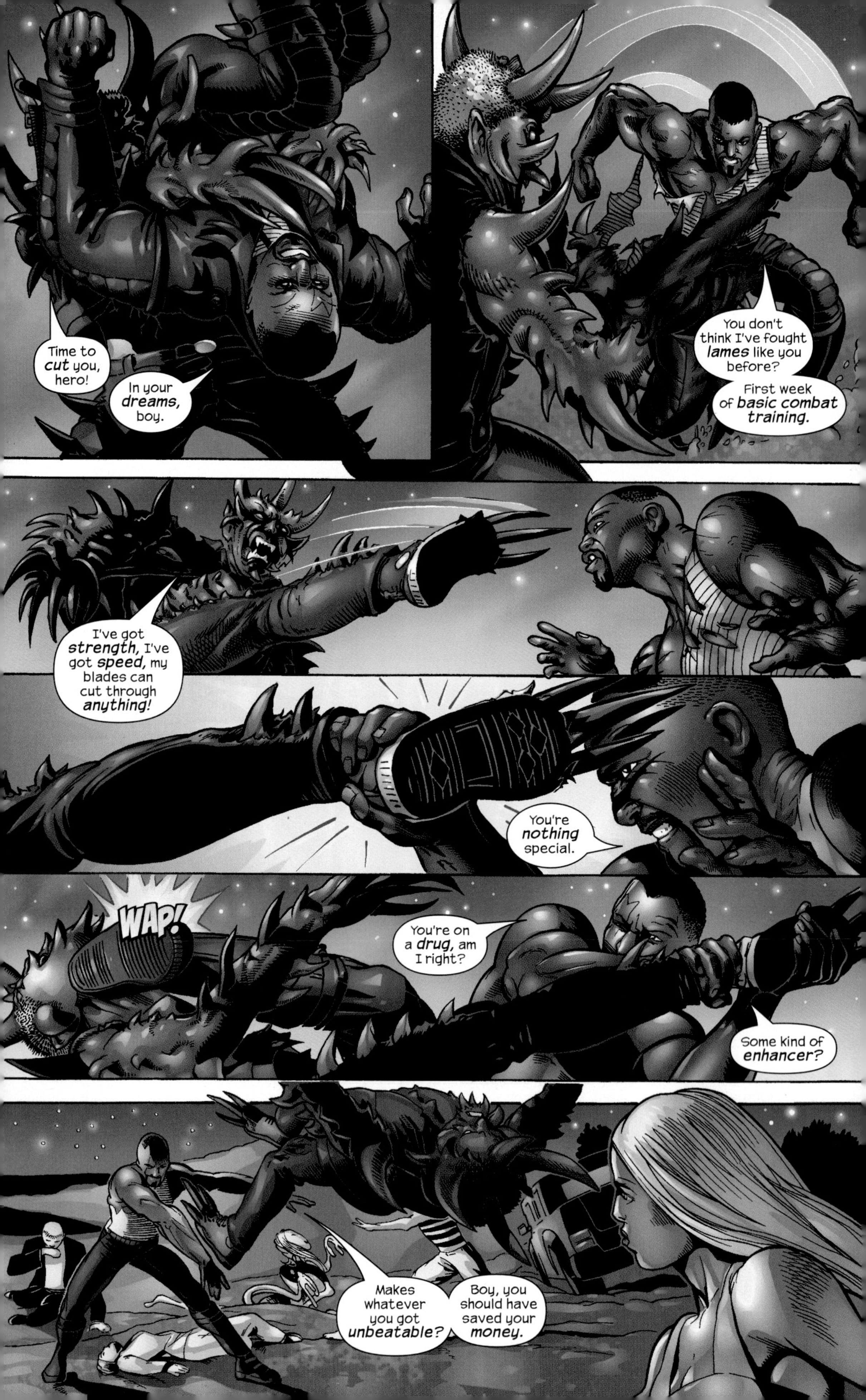

Time to *cut* you, hero!
In your *dreams,* boy.
You don't think I've fought *lames* like you before?
First week of ***basic combat training.***
I've got *strength,* I've got *speed,* my blades can cut through *anything!*
You're *nothing* special.
WAP!
You're on a *drug,* am I right?
Some kind of *enhancer?*
Makes whatever you got *unbeatable?*
Boy, you should have saved your *money.*

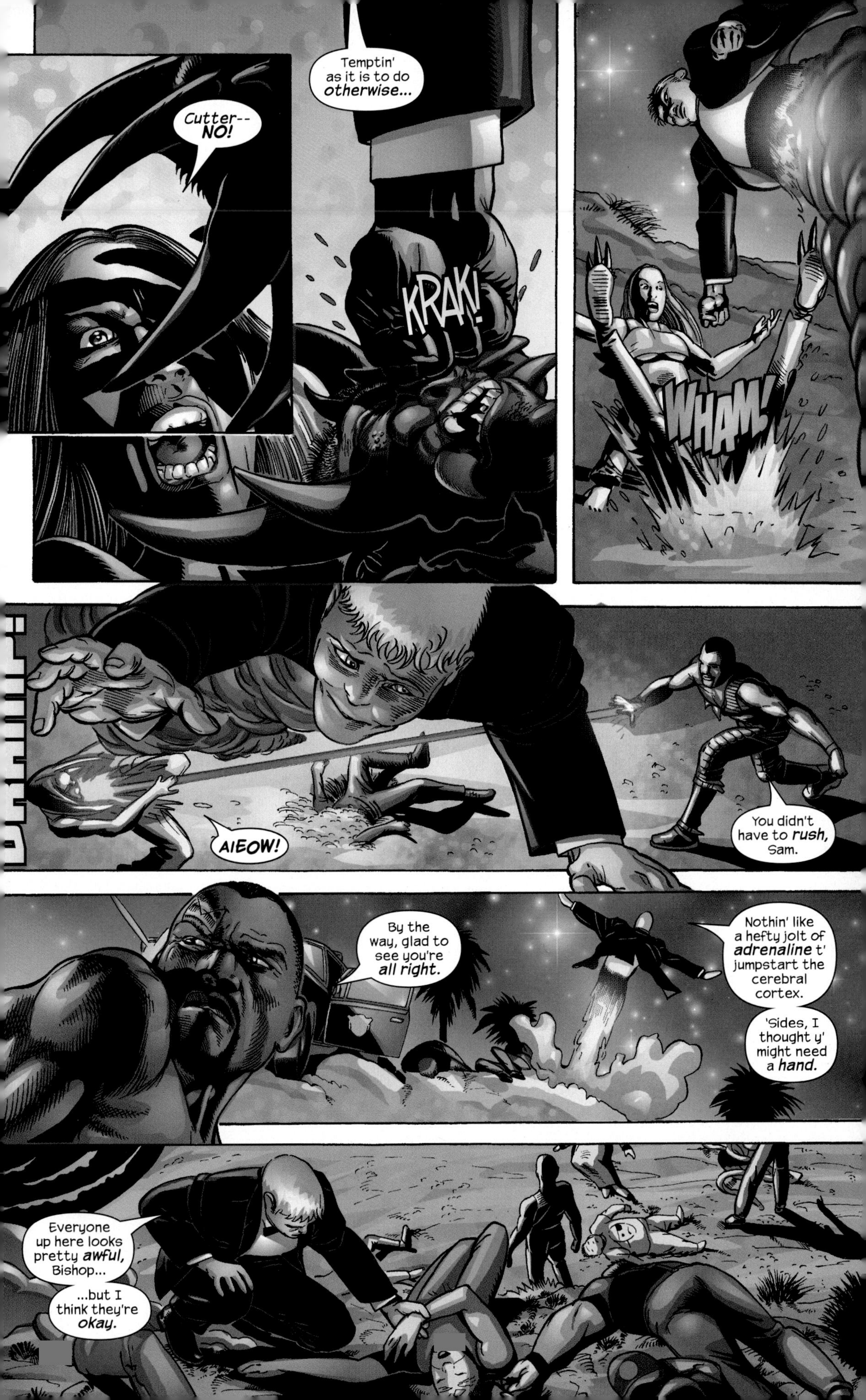
Cutter--
NO!
Temptin' as it is to do otherwise...
KRAK!
WHAM!
AIEOW!
You didn't have to rush, Sam.
By the way, glad to see you're all right.
Nothin' like a hefty jolt of adrenaline t' jumpstart the cerebral cortex.
'Sides, I thought y' might need a hand.
Everyone up here looks pretty awful, Bishop...
...but I think they're okay.

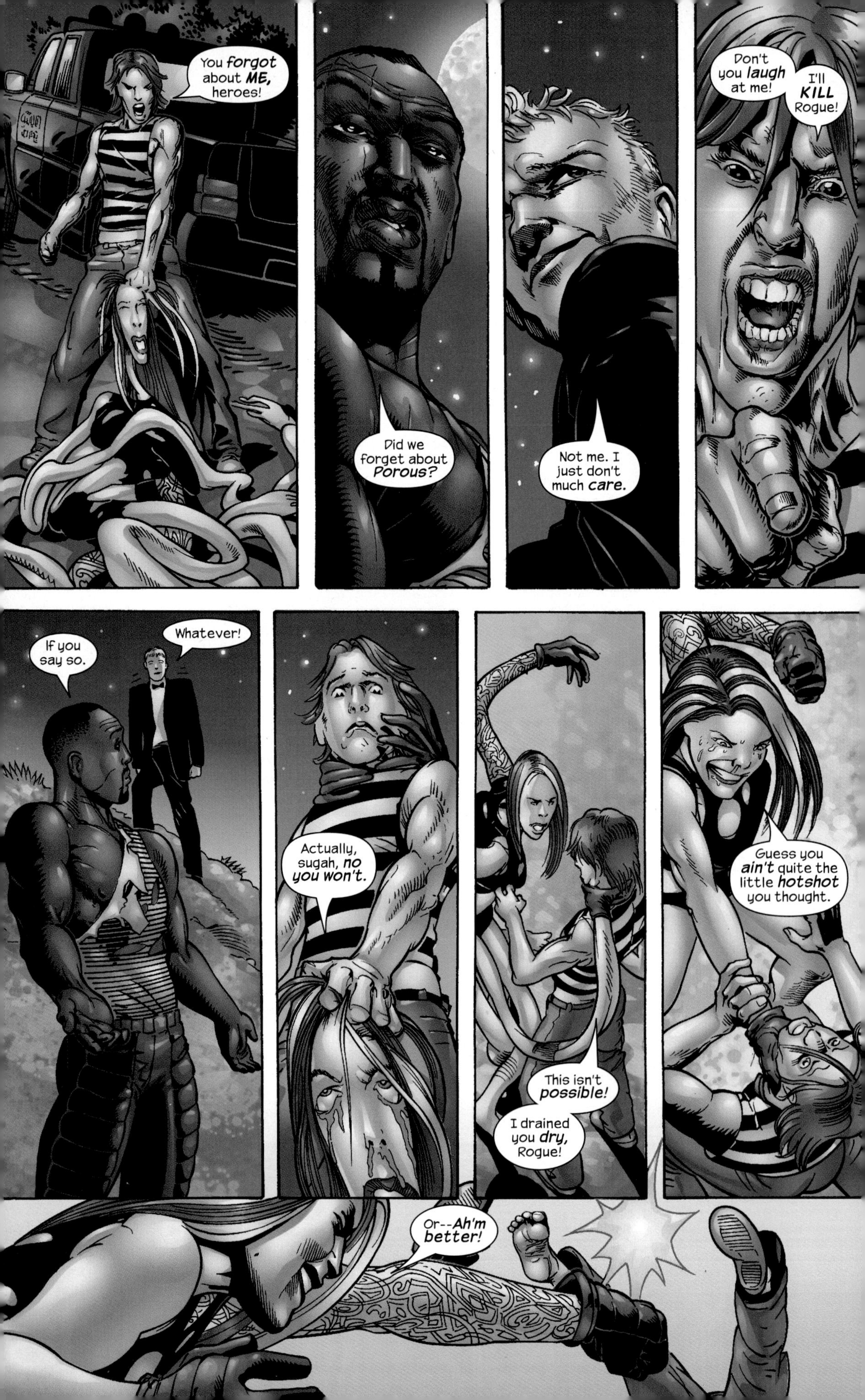
You forgot about ME, heroes!
Did we forget about Porous?
Not me. I just don't much care.
Don't you laugh at me!
I'll KILL Rogue!
If you say so.
Whatever!
Actually, sugah, no you won't.
This isn't possible!
I drained you dry, Rogue!
Guess you ain't quite the little hotshot you thought.
Or--Ah'm better!

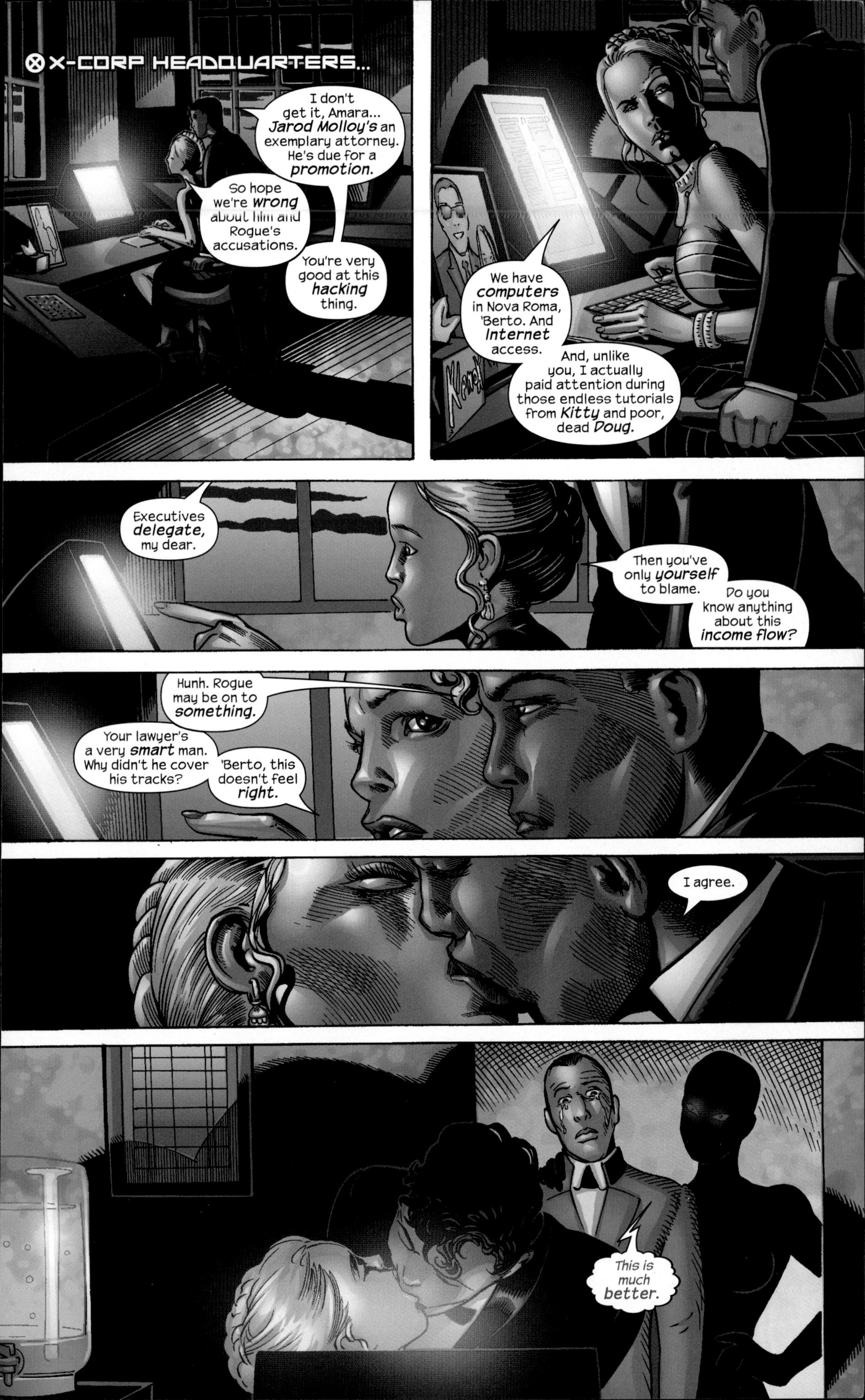
X-CORP HEADQUARTERS...
I don't get it, Amara... Jarod Molloy's an exemplary attorney. He's due for a promotion.
So hope we're wrong about him and Rogue's accusations.
You're very good at this hacking thing.
We have computers in Nova Roma, 'Berto. And Internet access.
And, unlike you, I actually paid attention during those endless tutorials from Kitty and poor, dead Doug.
Executives delegate, my dear.
Then you've only yourself to blame.
Do you know anything about this income flow?
Hunh. Rogue may be on to something.
Your lawyer's a very smart man. Why didn't he cover his tracks?
'Berto, this doesn't feel right.
I agree.
This is much better.

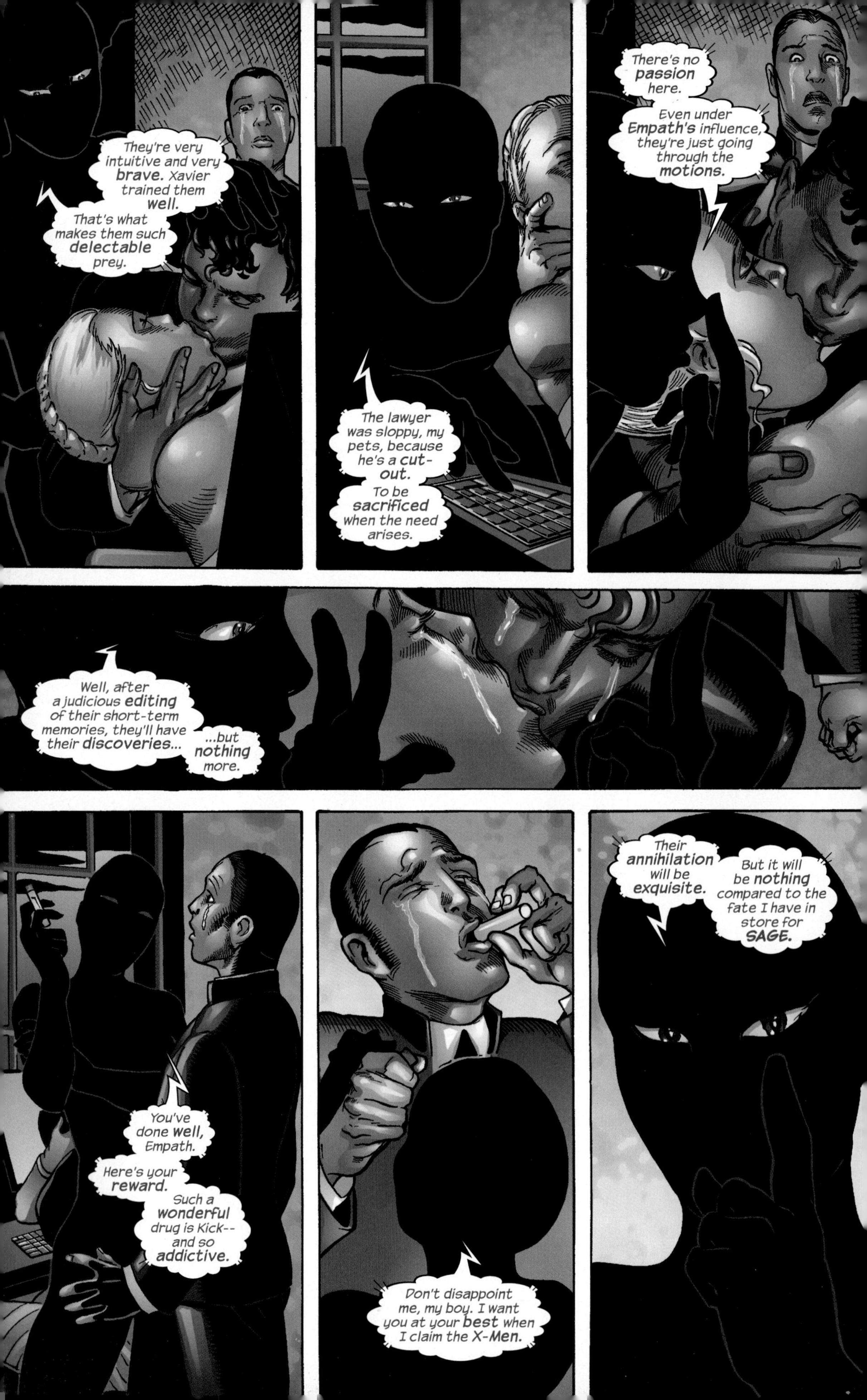
They're very intuitive and very brave. Xavier trained them well.
That's what makes them such delectable prey.
The lawyer was sloppy, my pets, because he's a cut-out.
To be sacrificed when the need arises.
There's no passion here.
Even under Empath's influence, they're just going through the motions.
Well, after a judicious editing of their short-term memories, they'll have their discoveries...
...but nothing more.
You've done well, Empath.
Here's your reward.
Such a wonderful drug is Kick-- and so addictive.
Don't disappoint me, my boy. I want you at your best when I claim the X-Men.
Their annihilation will be exquisite.
But it will be nothing compared to the fate I have in store for SAGE.

X-Corp is taking immediate steps to *rectify* this regrettable situation.

We are not about *exclusion.*

Valle Soleada is Charles Xavier's dream brought to life.

We seek to help *mutants* because with mutants there is a great and growing *need.*

The *goal* of that help is to build a society much like this community, where all the branches of humanity live in peace *together.*

We'll see.

It's not *over,* Lucas.

This is just the *beginning.*

SUBJECT: ELIAS BOGAN
THING...SEARCHING... SEARCHING...

Mommy... Daddy... I'm so *sorry.*

What happened to you was wrong. What I did was just as *bad.*

But sometimes there are *miracles.*

I got a *second chance.*

I'm gonna use it to make you *proud.*

PURITY

OSE WITH NOTHING TO HIDE
AVE NOTHING TO FEAR!

The goal of that help is to build a society much like this community...

...where all the branches of humanity live in peace *together.*

That was *Roberto DaCosta,* head of the mutant advocacy initiative X-Corp, speaking at today's news conference.

In other news...

KLAK!

X NEXT:
STORM: THE ARENA!

Costume Sketches

by Igor Kordey

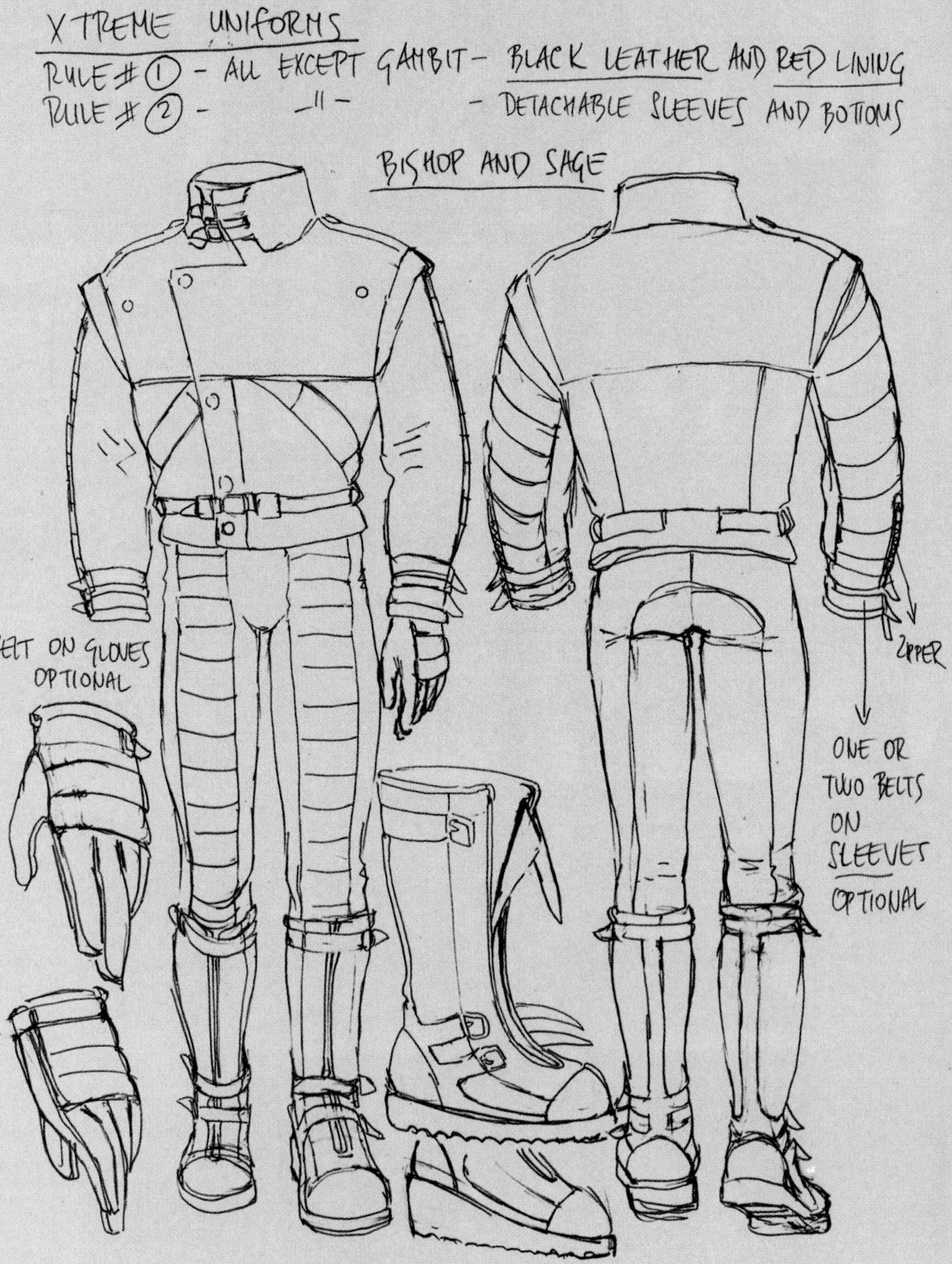

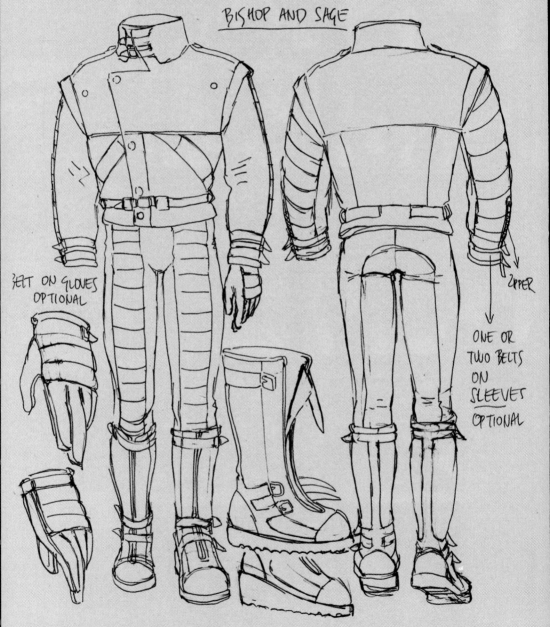

XTREME UNIFORMS
RULE #1 - ALL EXCEPT GAMBIT - BLACK LEATHER AND RED LINING
RULE #2 - -"- - DETACHABLE SLEEVES AND BOTTOMS
BISHOP AND SAGE
BELT ON GLOVES OPTIONAL
ZIPPER
ONE OR TWO BELTS ON SLEEVES OPTIONAL

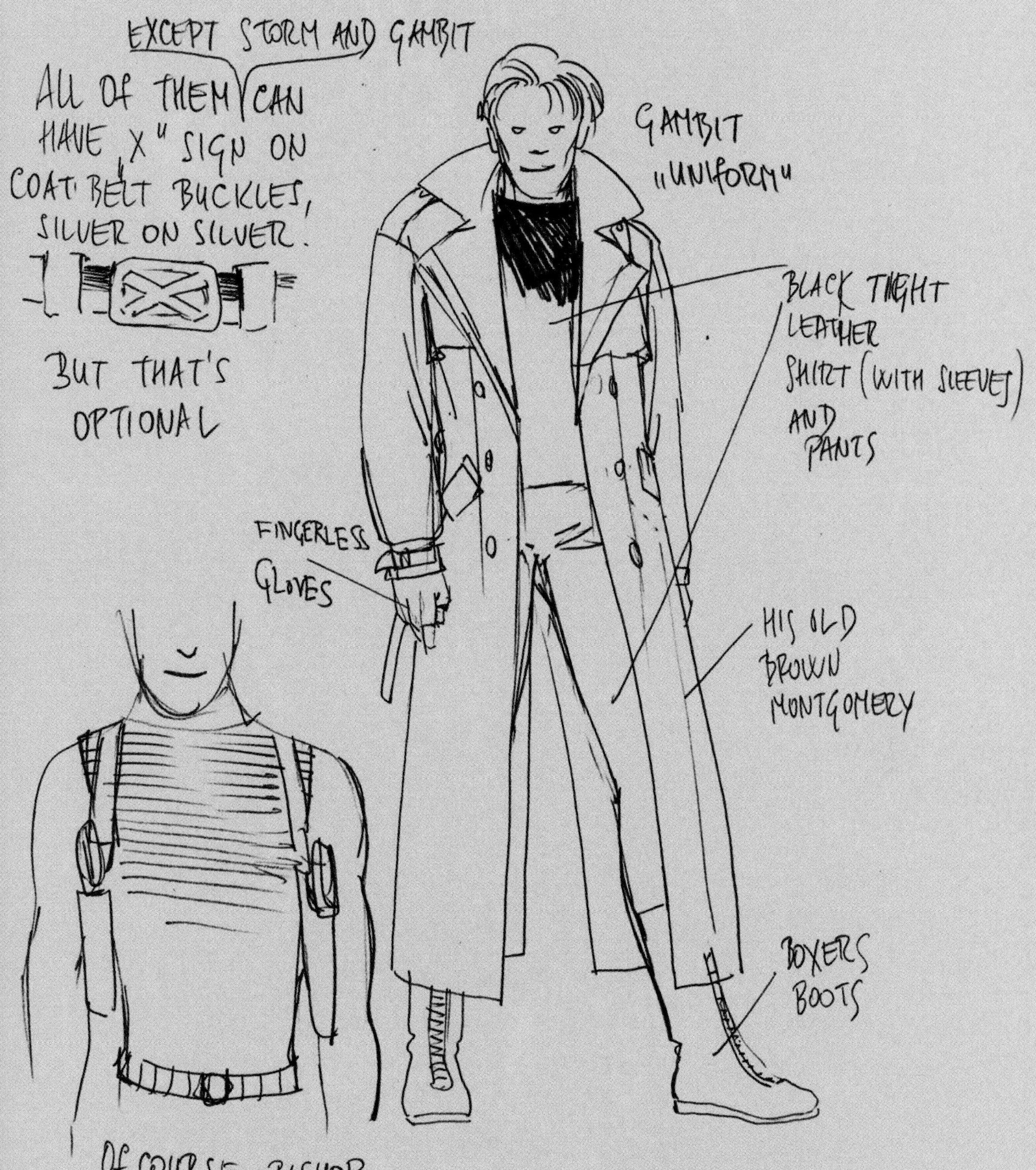
EXCEPT STORM AND GAMBIT
ALL OF THEM CAN HAVE „X" SIGN ON COAT BELT BUCKLES, SILVER ON SILVER.
BUT THAT'S OPTIONAL
GAMBIT „UNIFORM"
BLACK TIGHT LEATHER SHIRT (WITH SLEEVES) AND PANTS
FINGERLESS GLOVES
HIS OLD BROWN MONTGOMERY
BOXERS BOOTS
OF COURSE, BISHOP AND SAGE WEAR GUNS

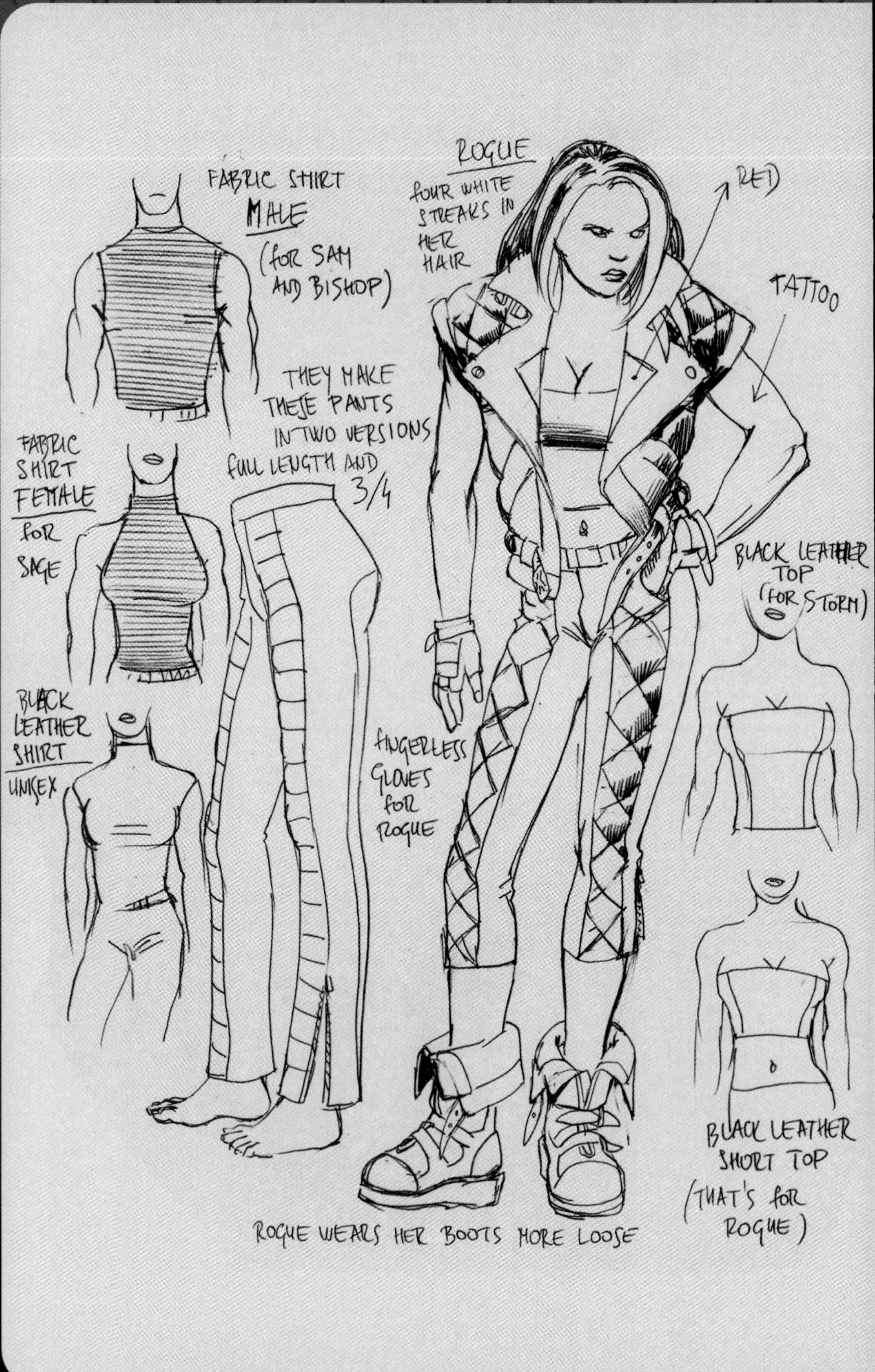
FABRIC SHIRT
MALE
(FOR SAM AND BISHOP)
ROGUE
FOUR WHITE STREAKS IN HER HAIR
RED
TATTOO
THEY MAKE THESE PANTS IN TWO VERSIONS FULL LENGTH AND 3/4
FABRIC SHIRT FEMALE
FOR SAGE
BLACK LEATHER SHIRT
UNISEX
BLACK LEATHER TOP (FOR STORM)
FINGERLESS GLOVES FOR ROGUE
BLACK LEATHER SHORT TOP
(THAT'S FOR ROGUE)
ROGUE WEARS HER BOOTS MORE LOOSE

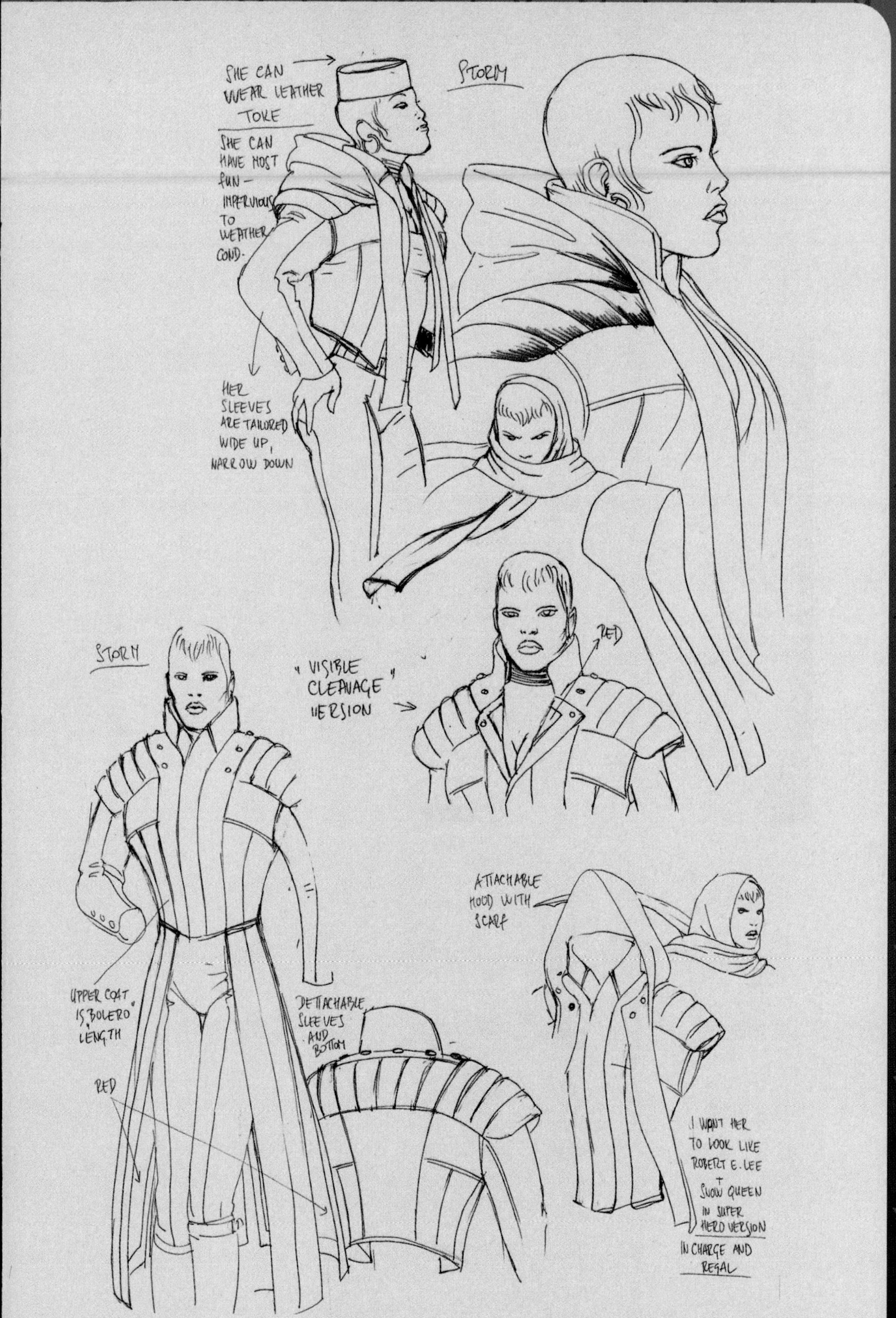
SHE CAN WEAR LEATHER TOKE
STORM
SHE CAN HAVE MOST FUN — IMPERVIOUS TO WEATHER COND.
HER SLEEVES ARE TAILORED WIDE UP, NARROW DOWN
STORM
"VISIBLE CLEAVAGE" VERSION
RED
ATTACHABLE HOOD WITH SCARF
UPPER COAT IS "BOLERO" LENGTH
DETTACHABLE SLEEVES AND BOTTOM
RED
I WANT HER TO LOOK LIKE ROBERT E. LEE + SNOW QUEEN IN SUPER HERO VERSION
IN CHARGE AND REGAL

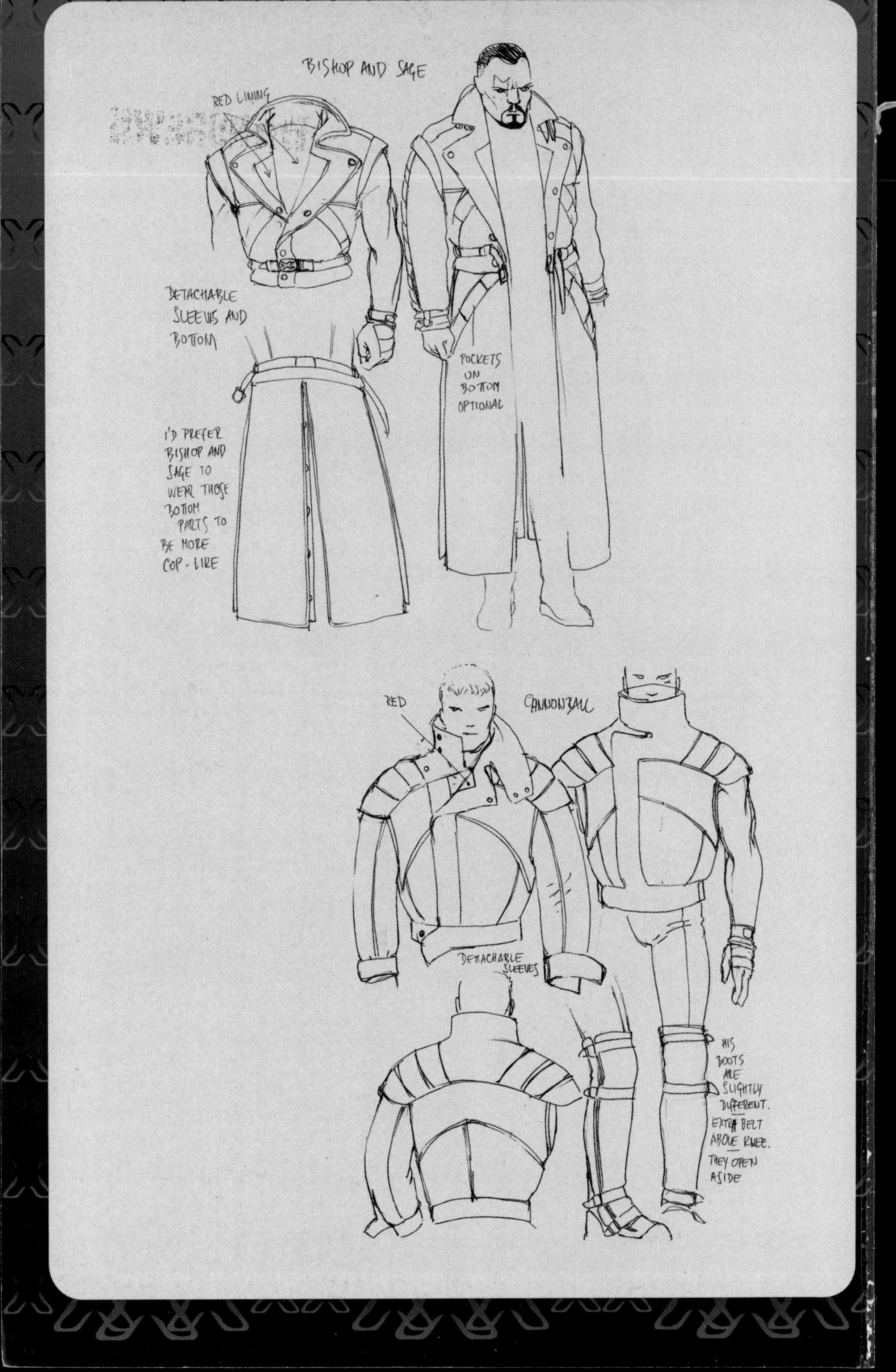
BISHOP AND SAGE
RED LINING
DETACHABLE SLEEVES AND BOTTOM
POCKETS ON BOTTOM OPTIONAL
I'D PREFER BISHOP AND SAGE TO WEAR THOSE BOTTOM PARTS TO BE MORE COP-LIKE
RED
CANNONBALL
DETACHABLE SLEEVES
HIS BOOTS ARE SLIGHTLY DIFFERENT. EXTRA BELT ABOVE KNEE. THEY OPEN ASIDE